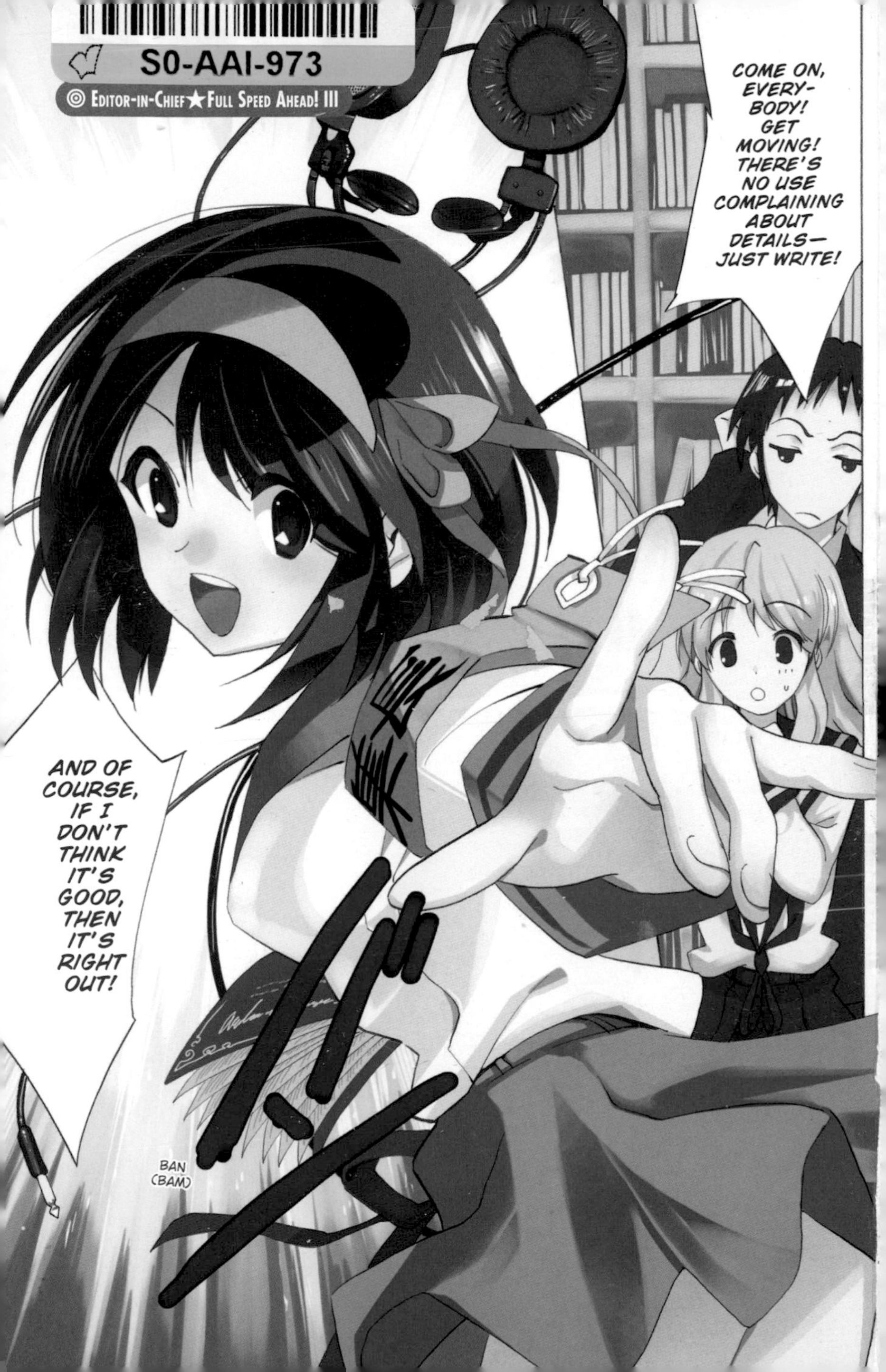
Editor-in-Chief★Full Speed Ahead! III
COME ON, EVERY-BODY! GET MOVING! THERE'S NO USE COMPLAINING ABOUT DETAILS—JUST WRITE!
AND OF COURSE, IF I DON'T THINK IT'S GOOD, THEN IT'S RIGHT OUT!
BAN (BAM)

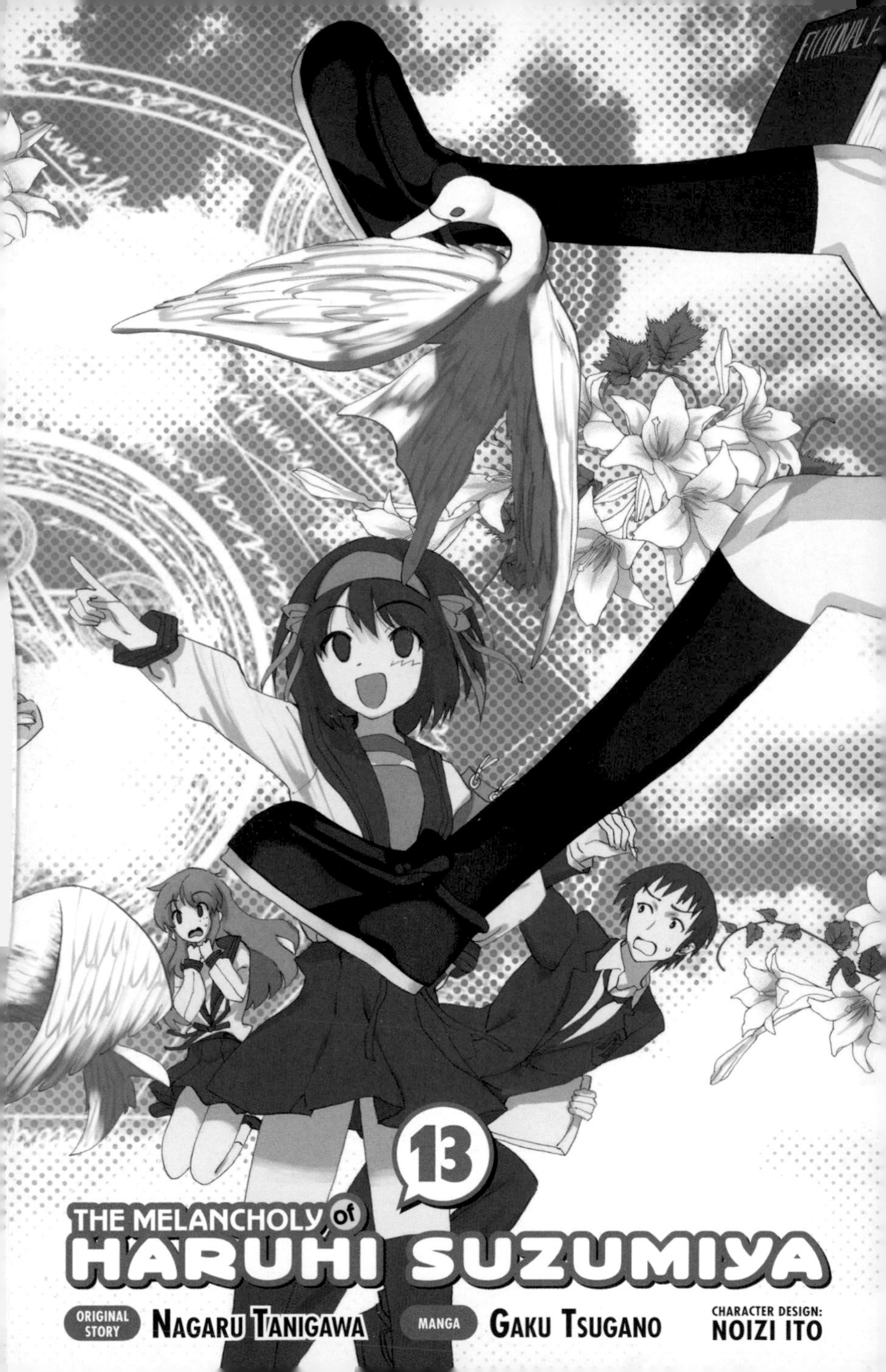
13
THE MELANCHOLY of
HARUHI SUZUMIYA
ORIGINAL STORY
NAGARU TANIGAWA
MANGA
GAKU TSUGANO
CHARACTER DESIGN:
NOIZI ITO

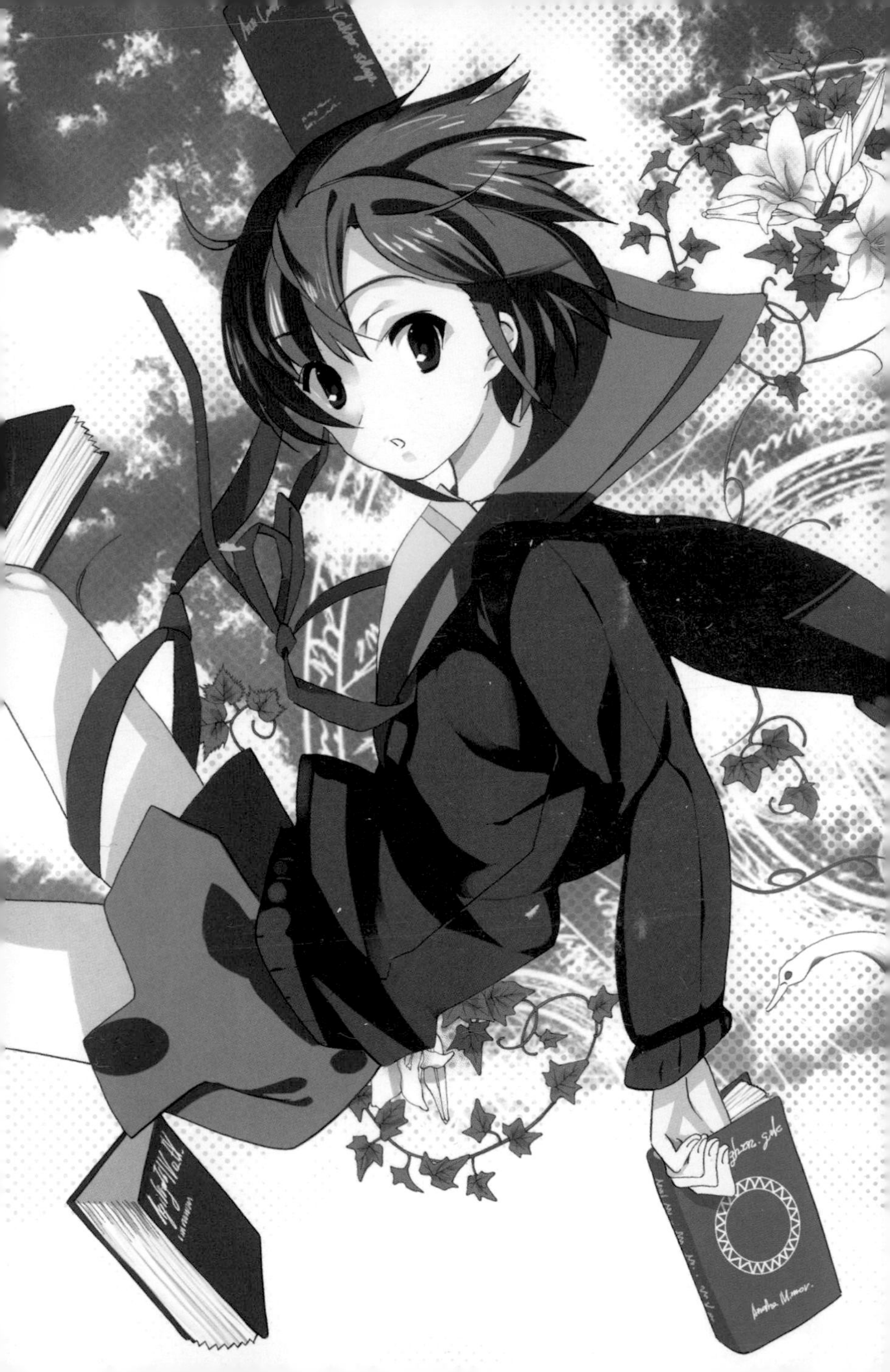

CONTENTS

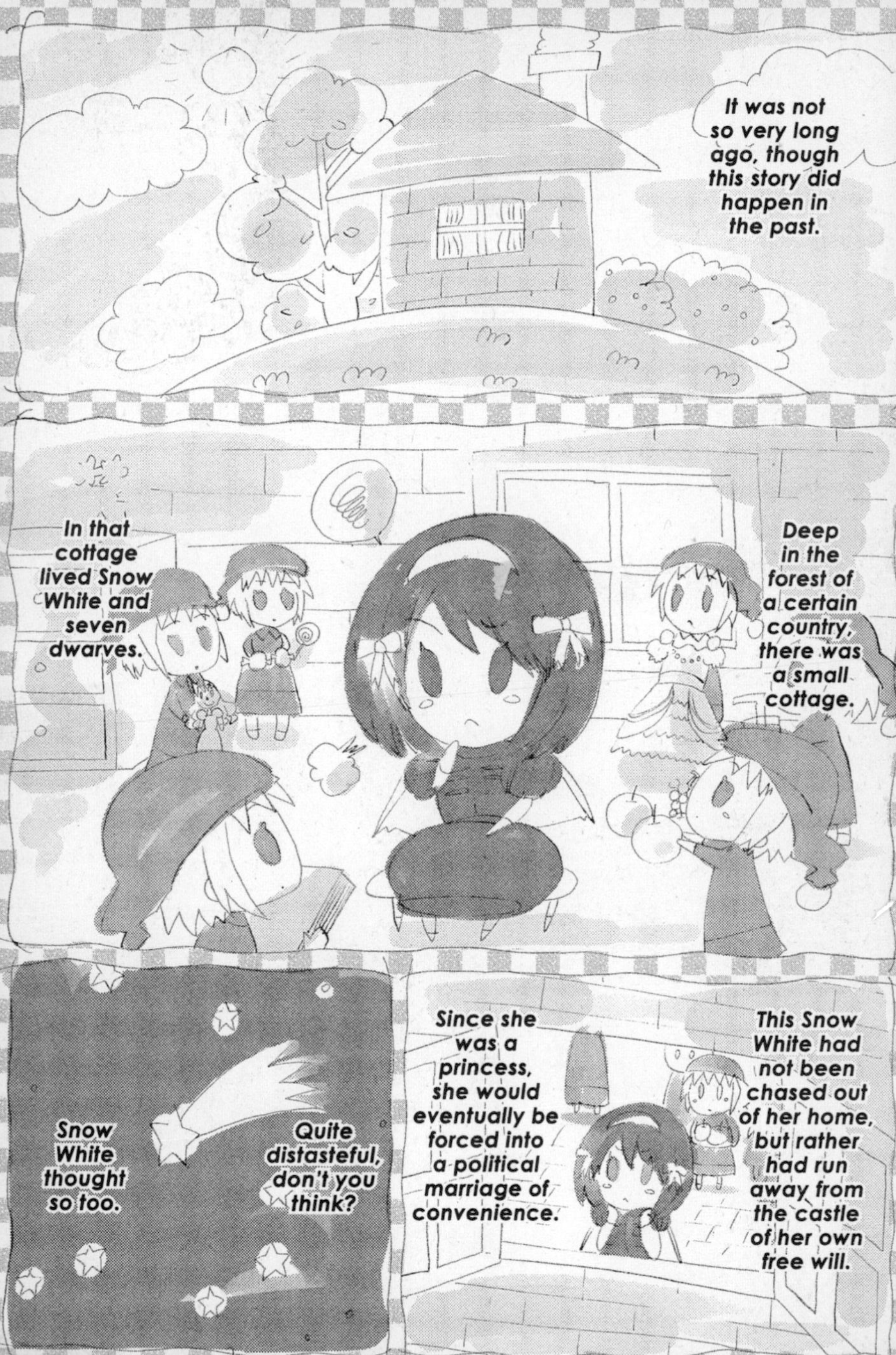
It was not so very long ago, though this story did happen in the past.
Deep in the forest of a certain country, there was a small cottage.
In that cottage lived Snow White and seven dwarves.
This Snow White had not been chased out of her home, but rather had run away from the castle of her own free will.
Since she was a princess, she would eventually be forced into a political marriage of convenience.
Quite distasteful, don't you think?
Snow White thought so too.

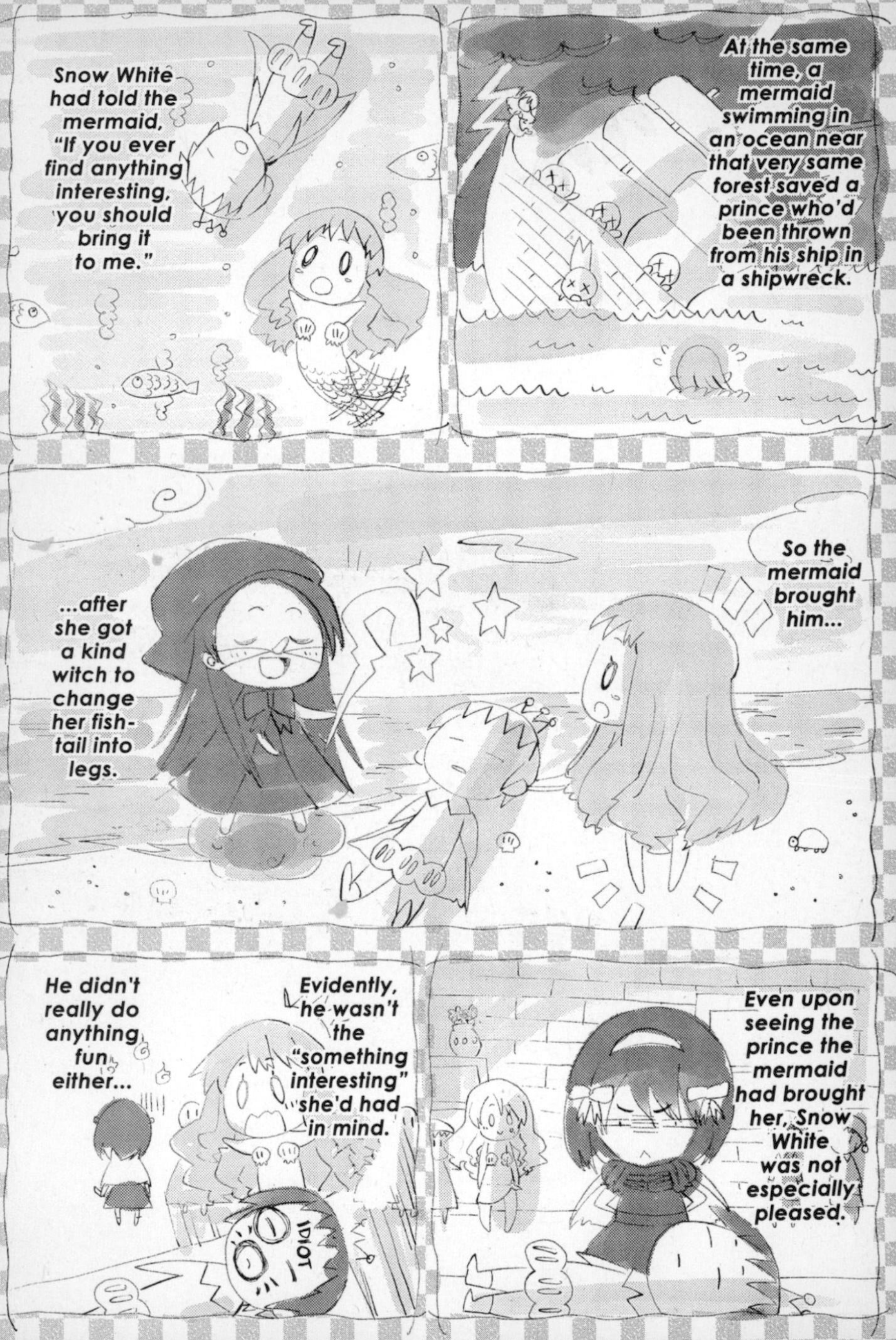
At the same time, a mermaid swimming in an ocean near that very same forest saved a prince who'd been thrown from his ship in a shipwreck.
Snow White had told the mermaid, "If you ever find anything interesting, you should bring it to me."
So the mermaid brought him...
...after she got a kind witch to change her fish-tail into legs.
Even upon seeing the prince the mermaid had brought her, Snow White was not especially pleased.
Evidently, he wasn't the "something interesting" she'd had in mind.
He didn't really do anything fun either...
IDIOT

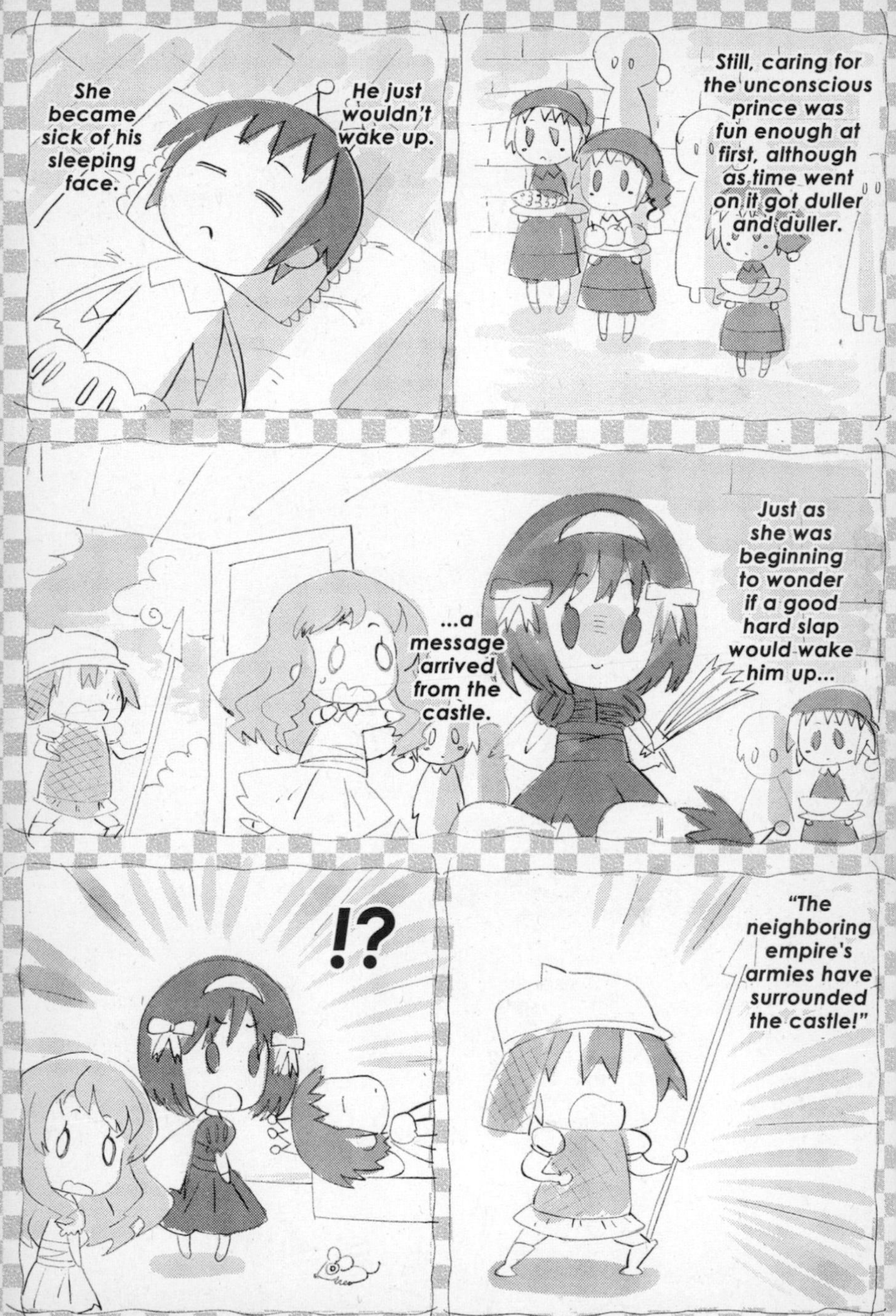
Still, caring for the unconscious prince was fun enough at first, although as time went on it got duller and duller.
He just wouldn't wake up.
She became sick of his sleeping face.
Just as she was beginning to wonder if a good hard slap would wake him up...
...a message arrived from the castle.
"The neighboring empire's armies have surrounded the castle!"
!?

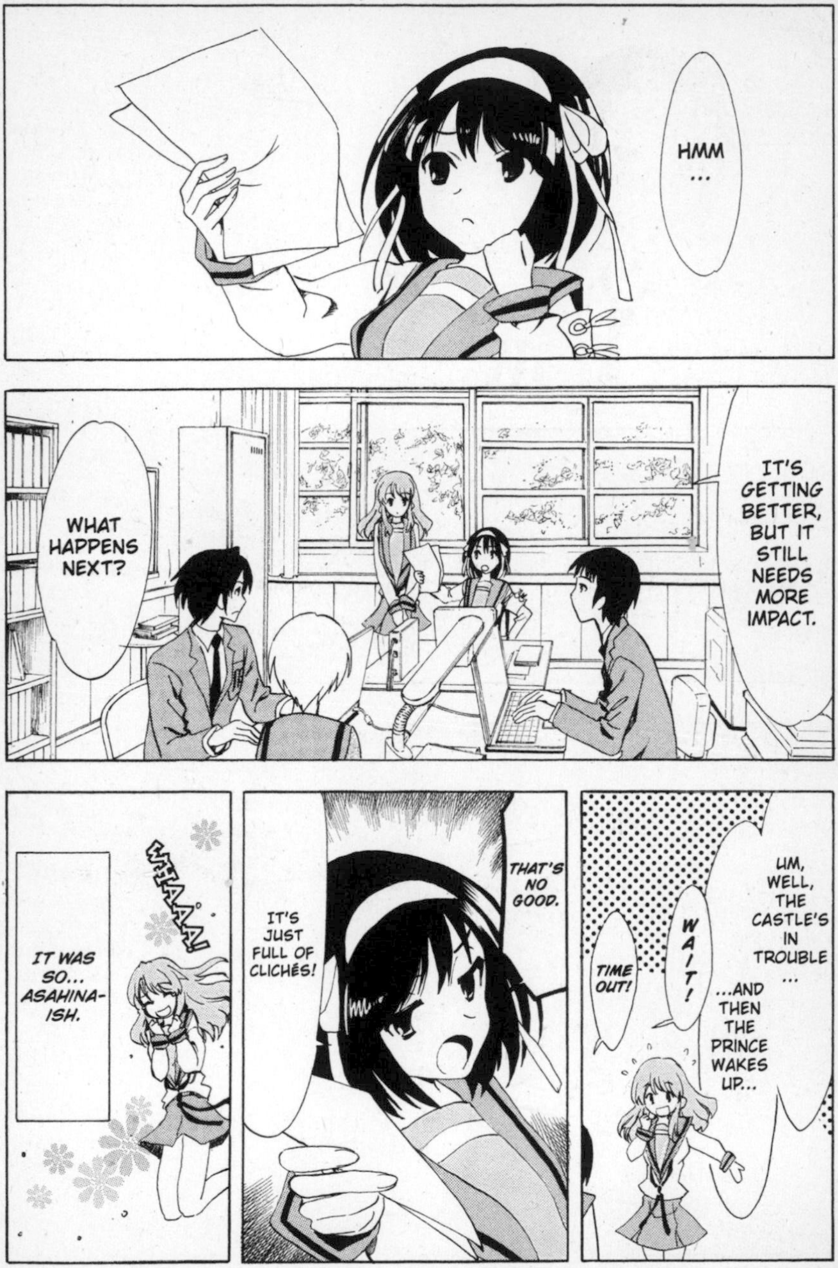
HMM ...
IT'S GETTING BETTER, BUT IT STILL NEEDS MORE IMPACT.
WHAT HAPPENS NEXT?
UM, WELL, THE CASTLE'S IN TROUBLE ...
...AND THEN THE PRINCE WAKES UP...
WAIT!
TIME OUT!
THAT'S NO GOOD.
IT'S JUST FULL OF CLICHÉS!
WHAAA!
IT WAS SO... ASAHINA-ISH.

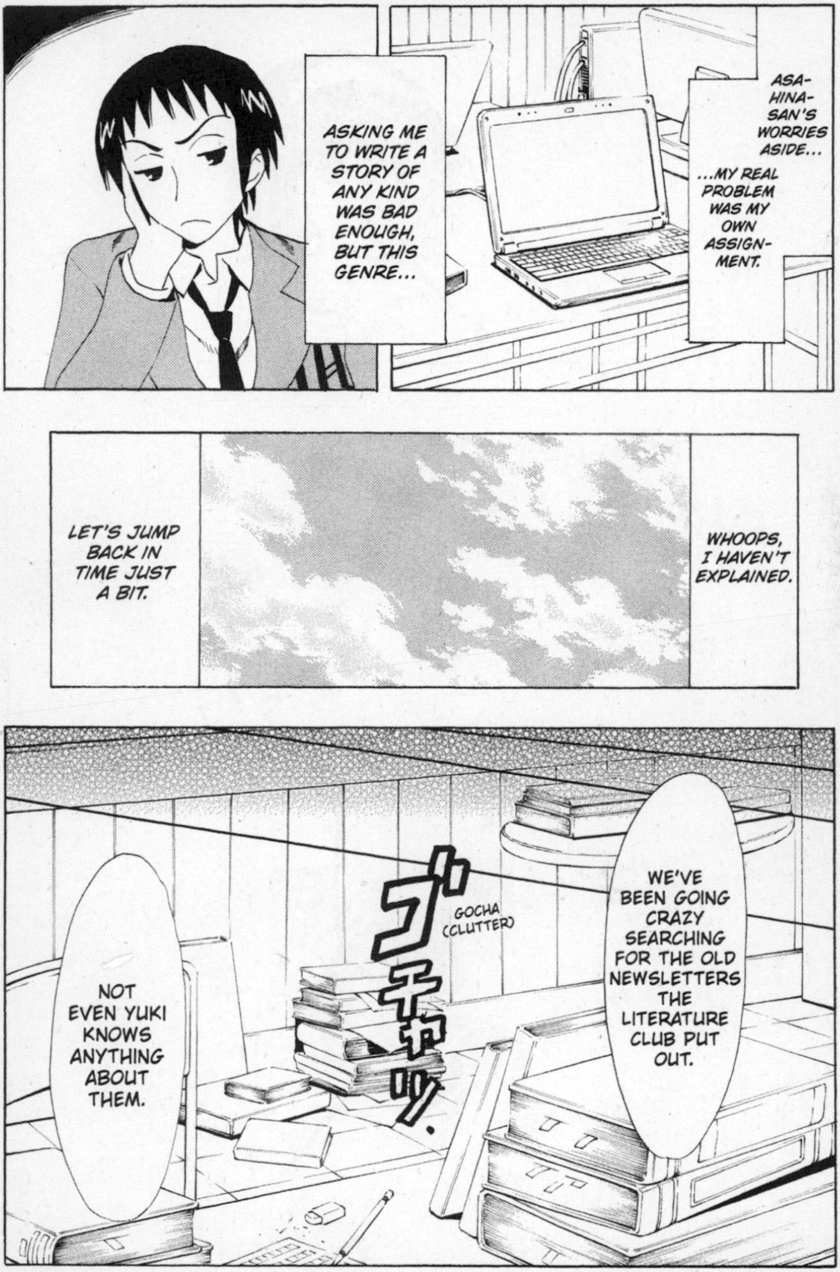

ASA-HINA-SAN'S WORRIES ASIDE...
...MY REAL PROBLEM WAS MY OWN ASSIGN-MENT.
ASKING ME TO WRITE A STORY OF ANY KIND WAS BAD ENOUGH, BUT THIS GENRE...
WHOOPS, I HAVEN'T EXPLAINED.
LET'S JUMP BACK IN TIME JUST A BIT.
WE'VE BEEN GOING CRAZY SEARCHING FOR THE OLD NEWSLETTERS THE LITERATURE CLUB PUT OUT.
ゴチャッ.
GOCHA (CLUTTER)
NOT EVEN YUKI KNOWS ANYTHING ABOUT THEM.

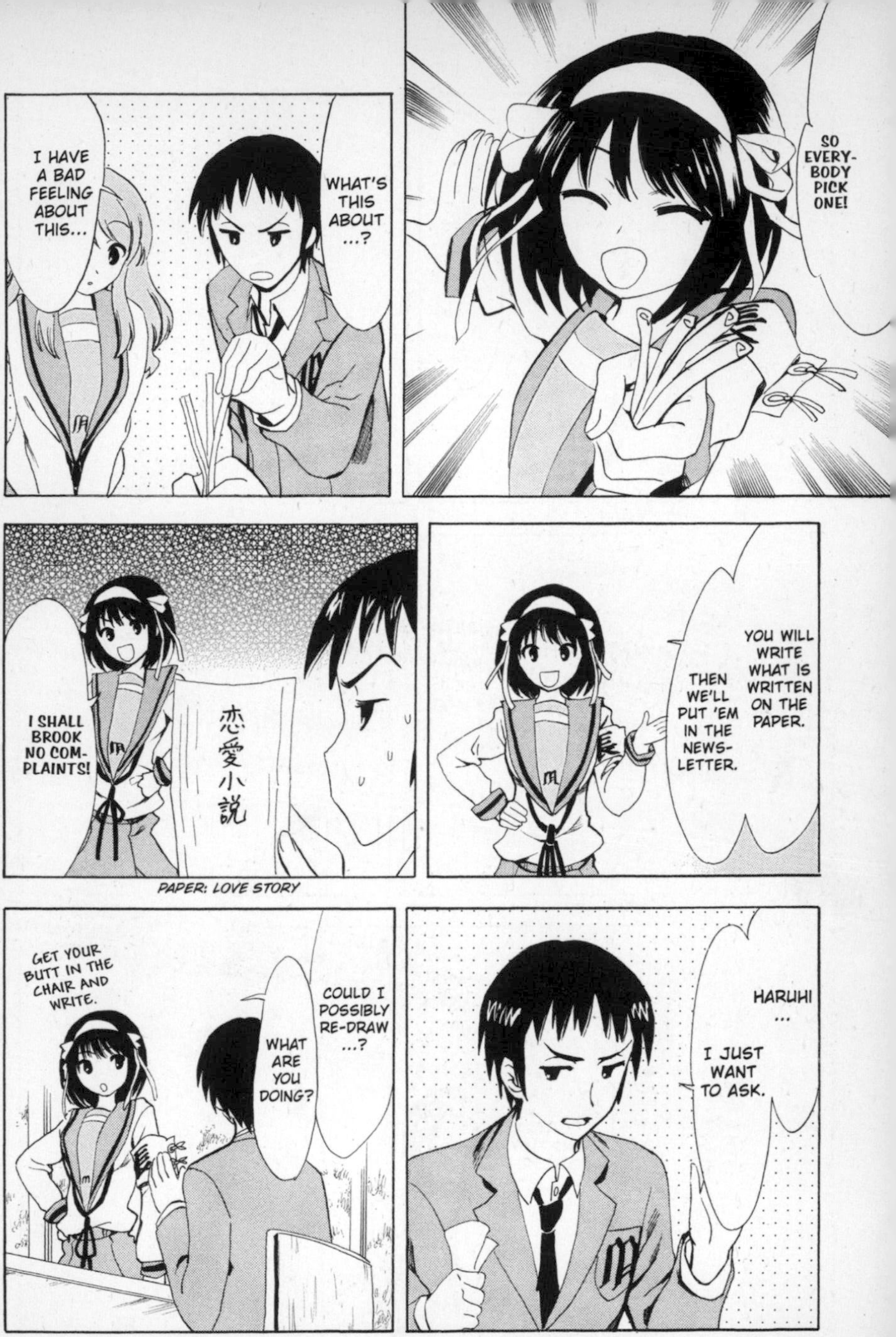
SO EVERYBODY PICK ONE!
WHAT'S THIS ABOUT ...?
I HAVE A BAD FEELING ABOUT THIS...
YOU WILL WRITE WHAT IS WRITTEN ON THE PAPER.
THEN WE'LL PUT 'EM IN THE NEWSLETTER.
恋愛小説
I SHALL BROOK NO COMPLAINTS!
PAPER: LOVE STORY
HARUHI ...
I JUST WANT TO ASK.
COULD I POSSIBLY RE-DRAW ...?
WHAT ARE YOU DOING?
GET YOUR BUTT IN THE CHAIR AND WRITE.

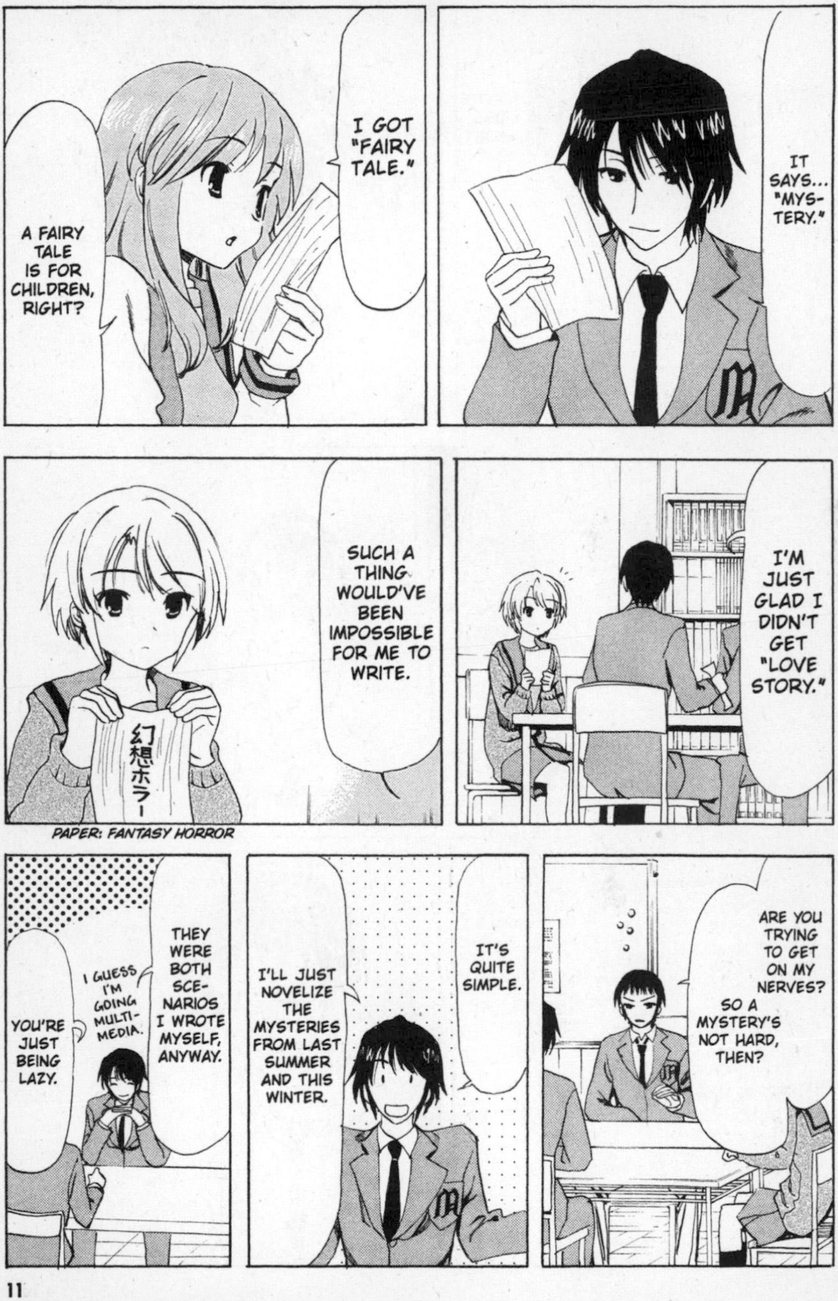
IT SAYS... "MYSTERY."
I GOT "FAIRY TALE."
A FAIRY TALE IS FOR CHILDREN, RIGHT?
I'M JUST GLAD I DIDN'T GET "LOVE STORY."
SUCH A THING WOULD'VE BEEN IMPOSSIBLE FOR ME TO WRITE.
幻想ホラー
ARE YOU TRYING TO GET ON MY NERVES?
SO A MYSTERY'S NOT HARD, THEN?
IT'S QUITE SIMPLE.
I'LL JUST NOVELIZE THE MYSTERIES FROM LAST SUMMER AND THIS WINTER.
THEY WERE BOTH SCENARIOS I WROTE MYSELF, ANYWAY.
I GUESS I'M GOING MULTI-MEDIA.
YOU'RE JUST BEING LAZY.

PAPER: FANTASY HORROR

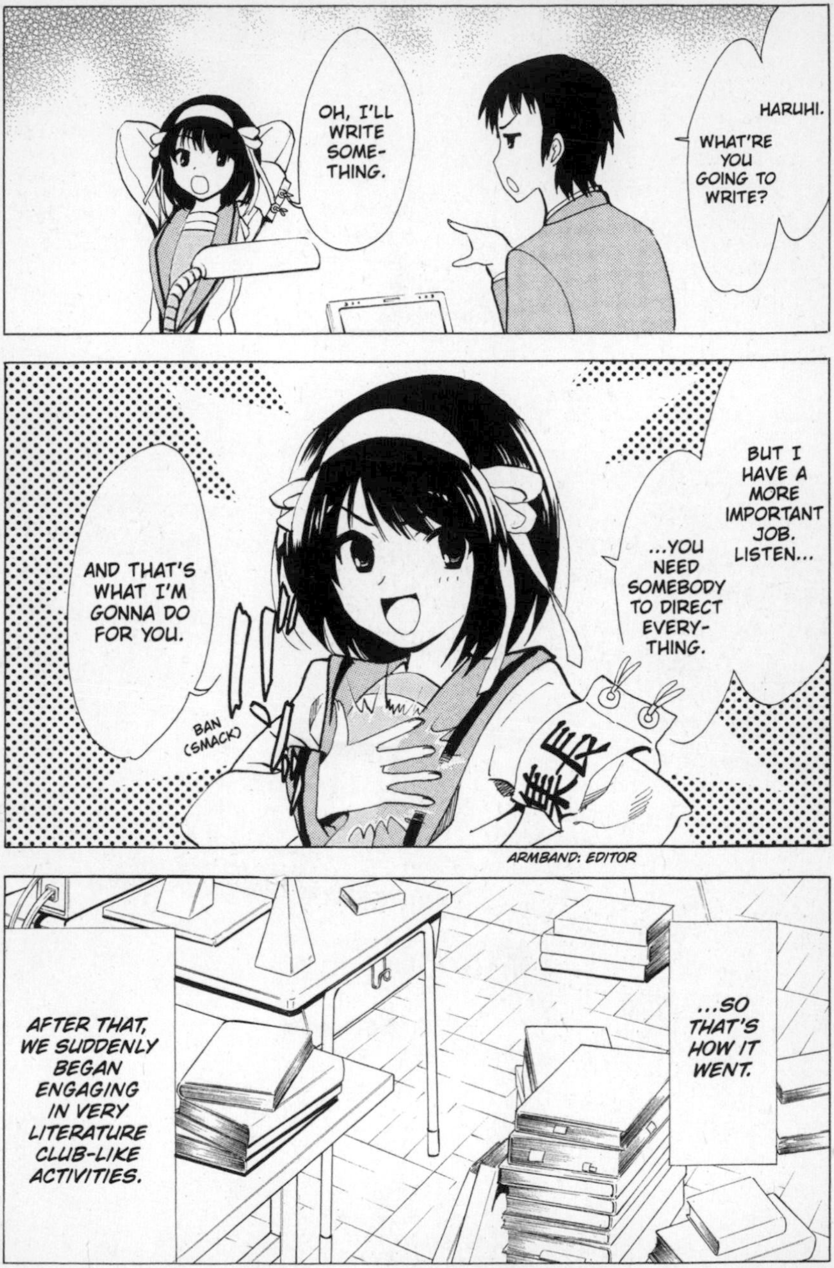
HARUHI.
WHAT'RE YOU GOING TO WRITE?
OH, I'LL WRITE SOME-THING.
BUT I HAVE A MORE IMPORTANT JOB. LISTEN...
...YOU NEED SOMEBODY TO DIRECT EVERY-THING.
AND THAT'S WHAT I'M GONNA DO FOR YOU.
BAN (SMACK)
ARMBAND: EDITOR
...SO THAT'S HOW IT WENT.
AFTER THAT, WE SUDDENLY BEGAN ENGAGING IN VERY LITERATURE CLUB-LIKE ACTIVITIES.

HEADBAND: TRAINING

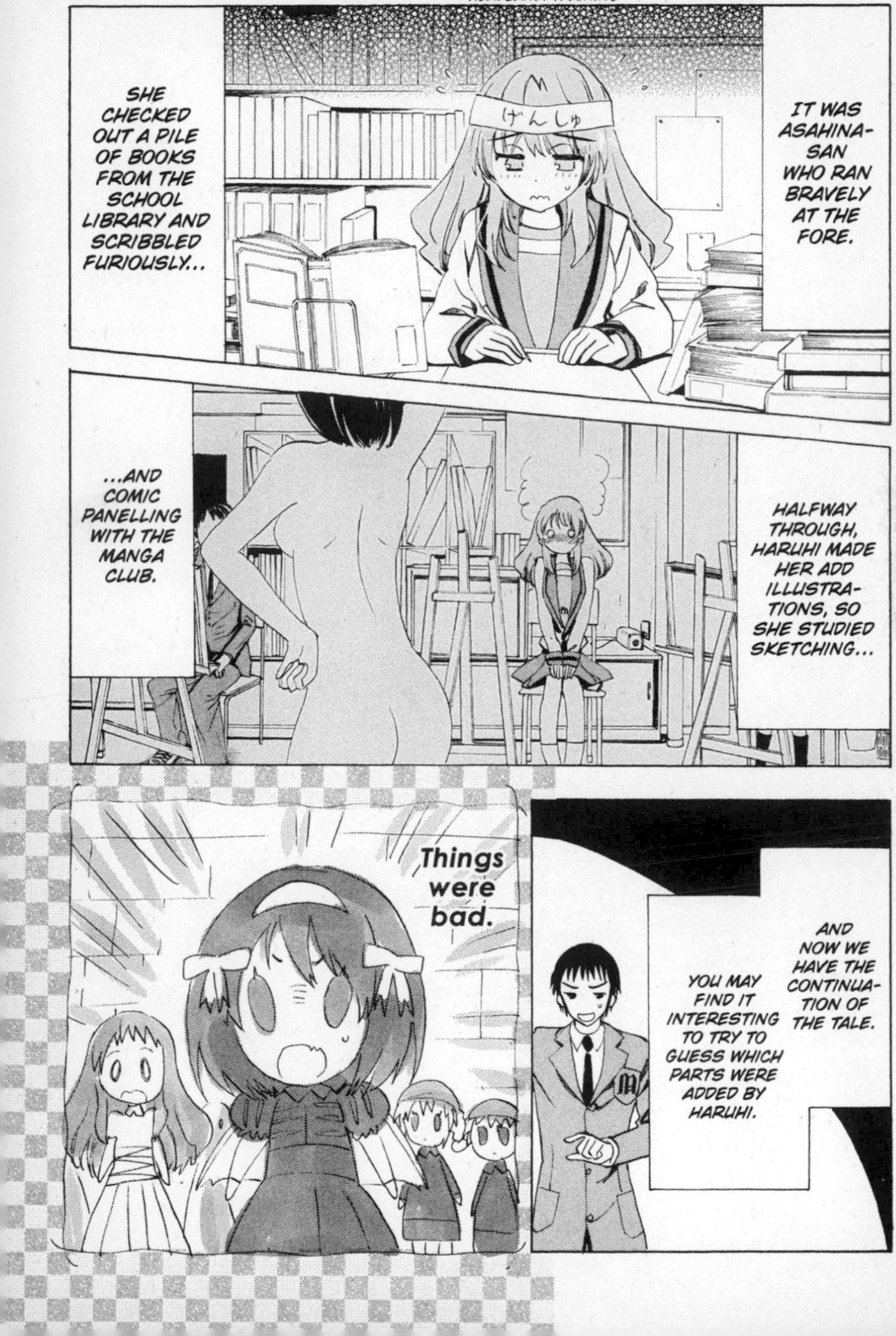

IT WAS ASAHINA-SAN WHO RAN BRAVELY AT THE FORE.
SHE CHECKED OUT A PILE OF BOOKS FROM THE SCHOOL LIBRARY AND SCRIBBLED FURIOUSLY...
HALFWAY THROUGH, HARUHI MADE HER ADD ILLUSTRATIONS, SO SHE STUDIED SKETCHING...
...AND COMIC PANELLING WITH THE MANGA CLUB.
AND NOW WE HAVE THE CONTINUATION OF THE TALE.
YOU MAY FIND IT INTERESTING TO TRY TO GUESS WHICH PARTS WERE ADDED BY HARUHI.
Things were bad.

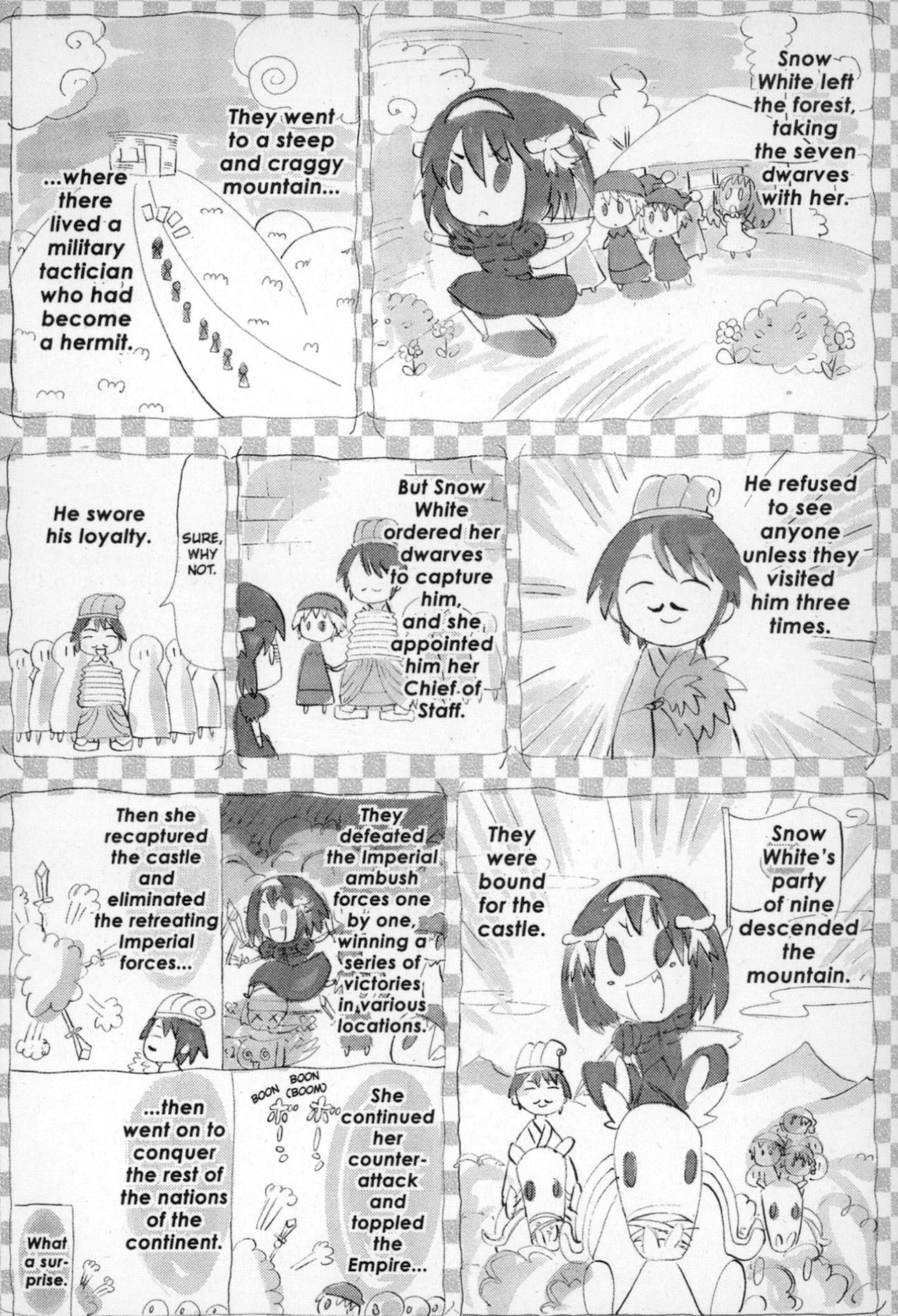

Snow White left the forest, taking the seven dwarves with her.
They went to a steep and craggy mountain...
...where there lived a military tactician who had become a hermit.
He refused to see anyone unless they visited him three times.
But Snow White ordered her dwarves to capture him, and she appointed him her Chief of Staff.
SURE, WHY NOT.
He swore his loyalty.
Snow White's party of nine descended the mountain.
They were bound for the castle.
They defeated the Imperial ambush forces one by one, winning a series of victories in various locations.
Then she recaptured the castle and eliminated the retreating Imperial forces...
BOON BOON (BOOM)
She continued her counter-attack and toppled the Empire...
...then went on to conquer the rest of the nations of the continent.
What a sur-prise.

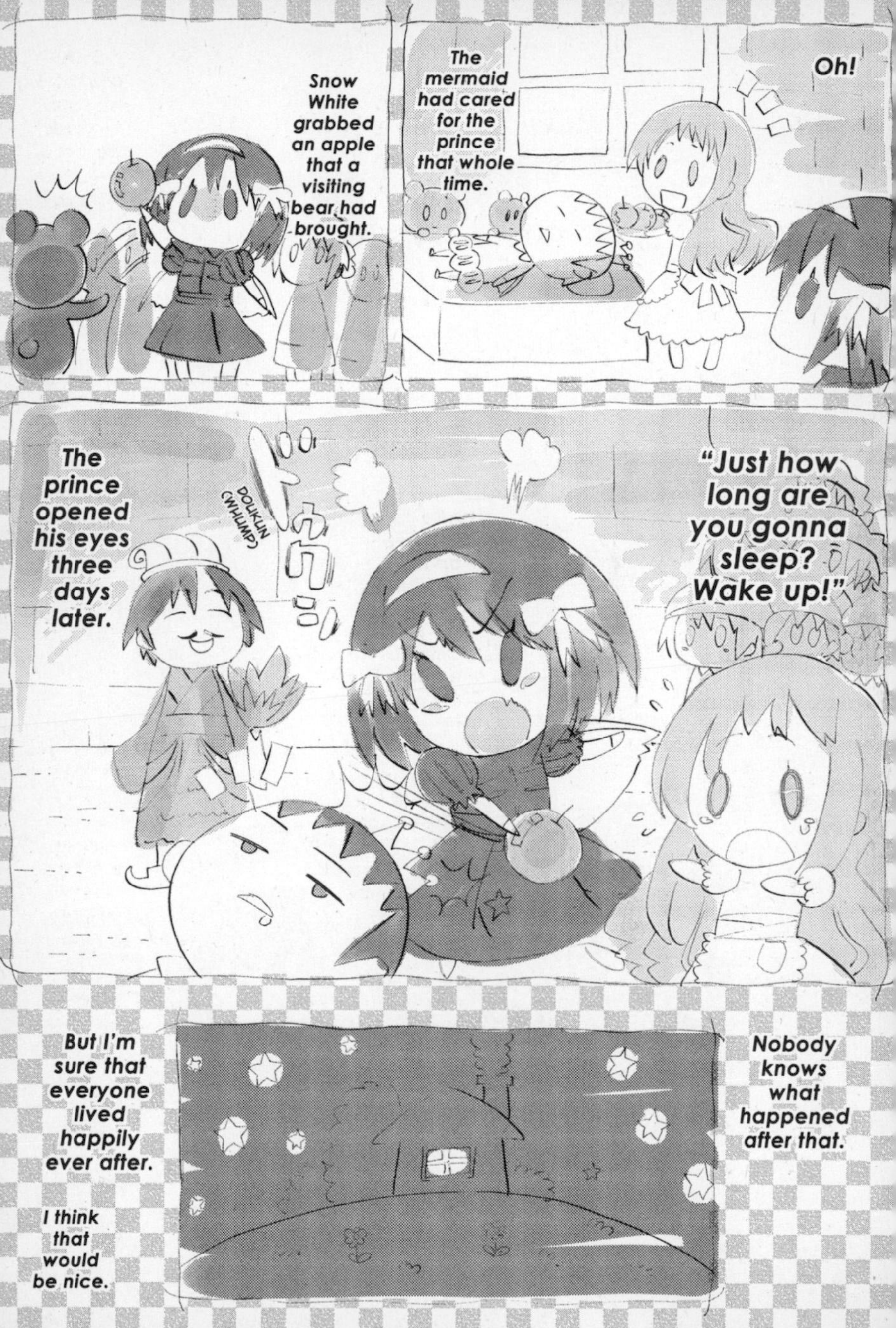
Oh!
The mermaid had cared for the prince that whole time.
Snow White grabbed an apple that a visiting bear had brought.
"Just how long are you gonna sleep? Wake up!"
DOUKUN (WHUMP)
The prince opened his eyes three days later.
Nobody knows what happened after that.
But I'm sure that everyone lived happily ever after.
I think that would be nice.

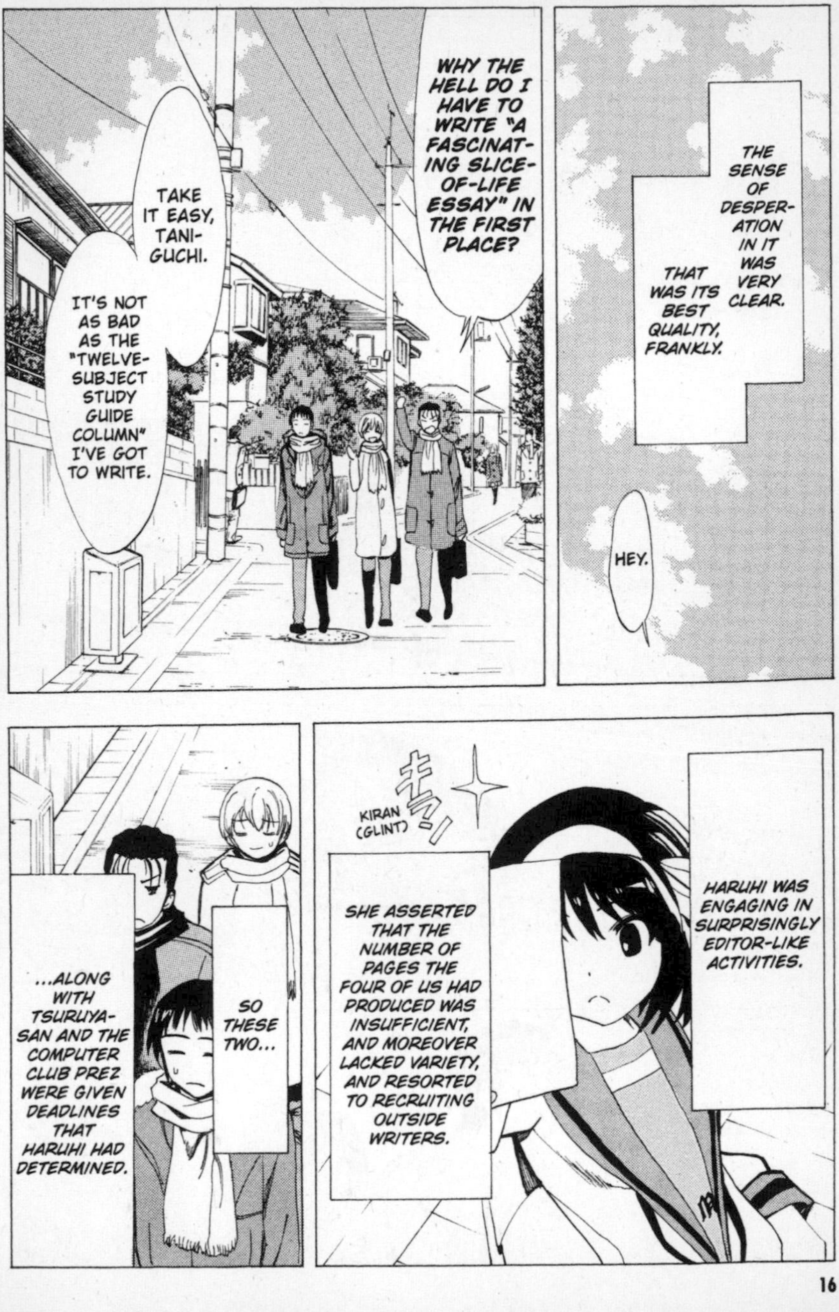
THE SENSE OF DESPERATION IN IT WAS VERY CLEAR.
THAT WAS ITS BEST QUALITY, FRANKLY.
HEY.
WHY THE HELL DO I HAVE TO WRITE "A FASCINATING SLICE-OF-LIFE ESSAY" IN THE FIRST PLACE?
TAKE IT EASY, TANIGUCHI.
IT'S NOT AS BAD AS THE "TWELVE-SUBJECT STUDY GUIDE COLUMN" I'VE GOT TO WRITE.
HARUHI WAS ENGAGING IN SURPRISINGLY EDITOR-LIKE ACTIVITIES.
KIRAN (GLINT)
SHE ASSERTED THAT THE NUMBER OF PAGES THE FOUR OF US HAD PRODUCED WAS INSUFFICIENT, AND MOREOVER LACKED VARIETY, AND RESORTED TO RECRUITING OUTSIDE WRITERS.
SO THESE TWO...
...ALONG WITH TSURUYA-SAN AND THE COMPUTER CLUB PREZ WERE GIVEN DEADLINES THAT HARUHI HAD DETERMINED.

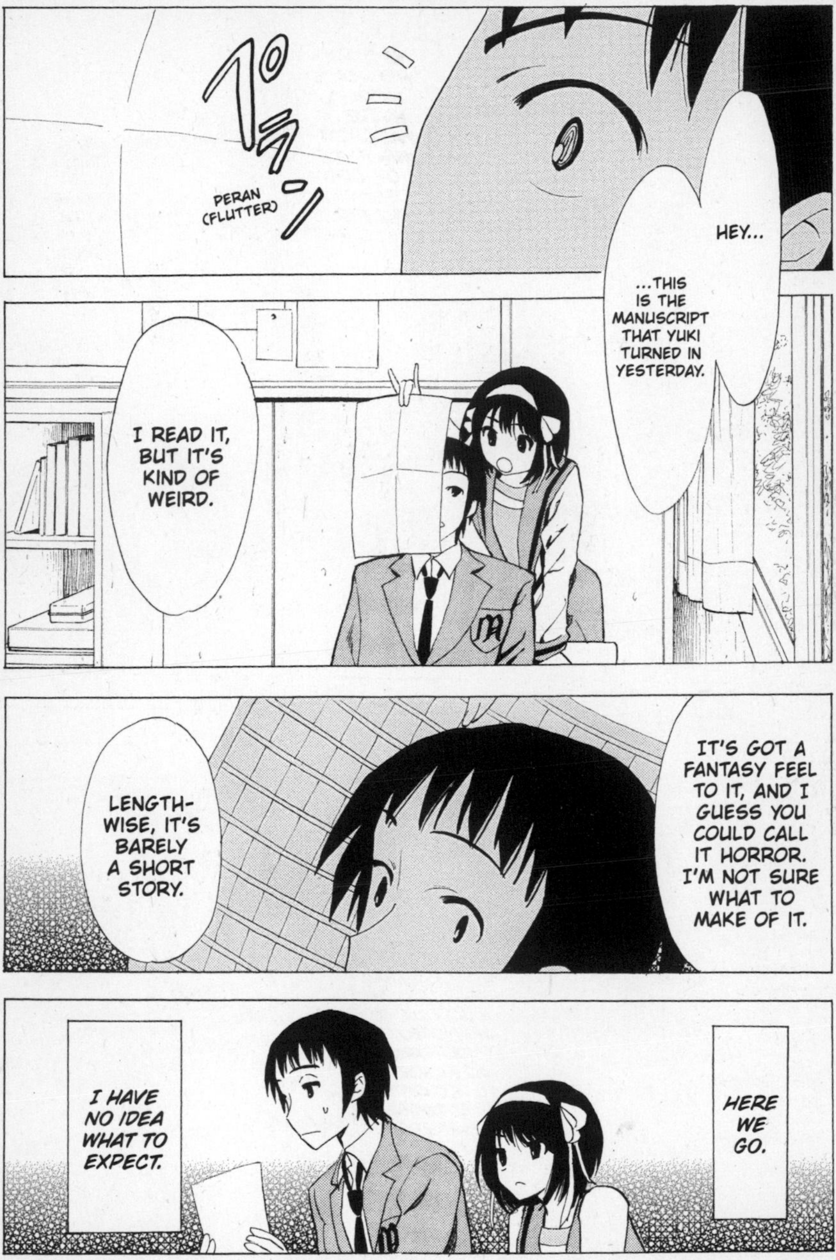
HEY...
...THIS IS THE MANUSCRIPT THAT YUKI TURNED IN YESTERDAY.
PERAN (FLUTTER)
I READ IT, BUT IT'S KIND OF WEIRD.
IT'S GOT A FANTASY FEEL TO IT, AND I GUESS YOU COULD CALL IT HORROR. I'M NOT SURE WHAT TO MAKE OF IT.
LENGTH-WISE, IT'S BARELY A SHORT STORY.
HERE WE GO.
I HAVE NO IDEA WHAT TO EXPECT.

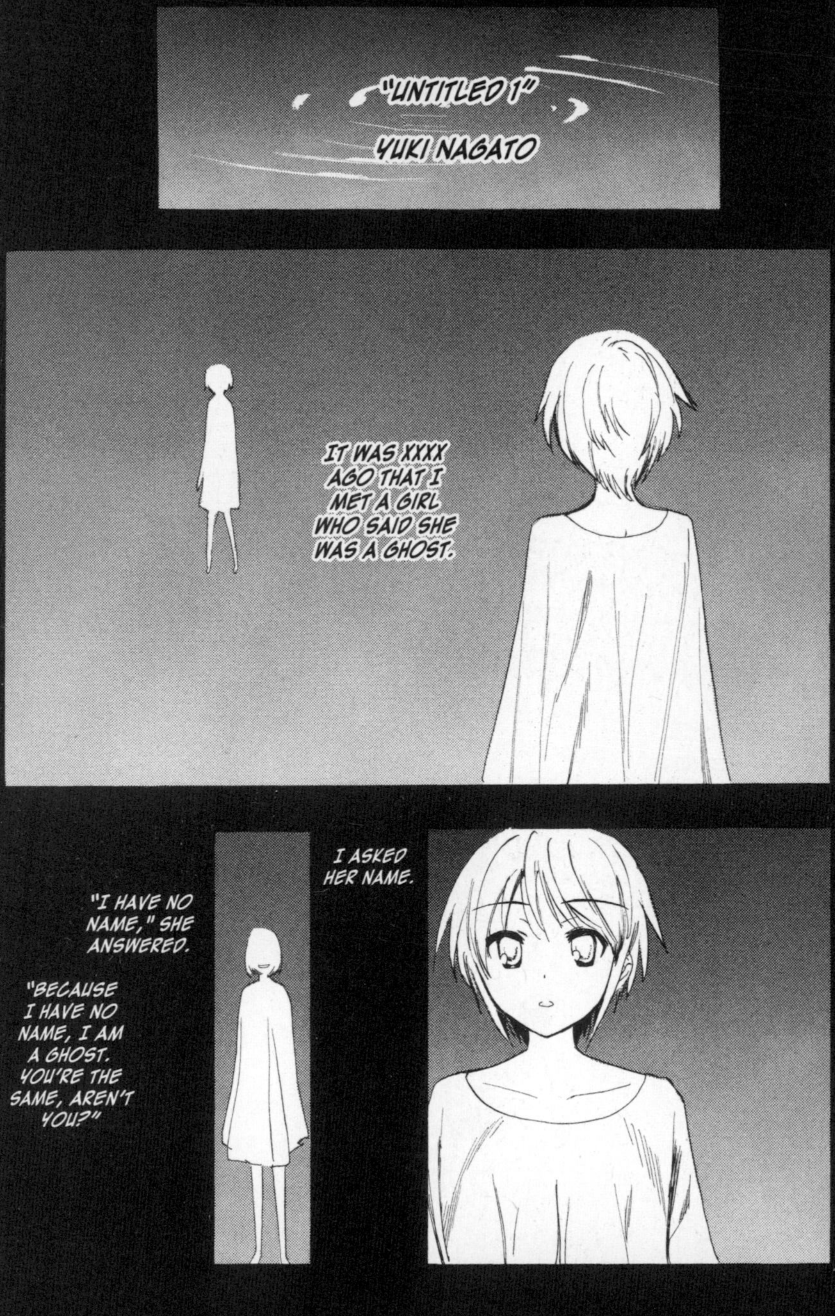
"UNTITLED 1"
YUKI NAGATO
IT WAS XXXX AGO THAT I MET A GIRL WHO SAID SHE WAS A GHOST.
I ASKED HER NAME.
"I HAVE NO NAME," SHE ANSWERED.
"BECAUSE I HAVE NO NAME, I AM A GHOST. YOU'RE THE SAME, AREN'T YOU?"

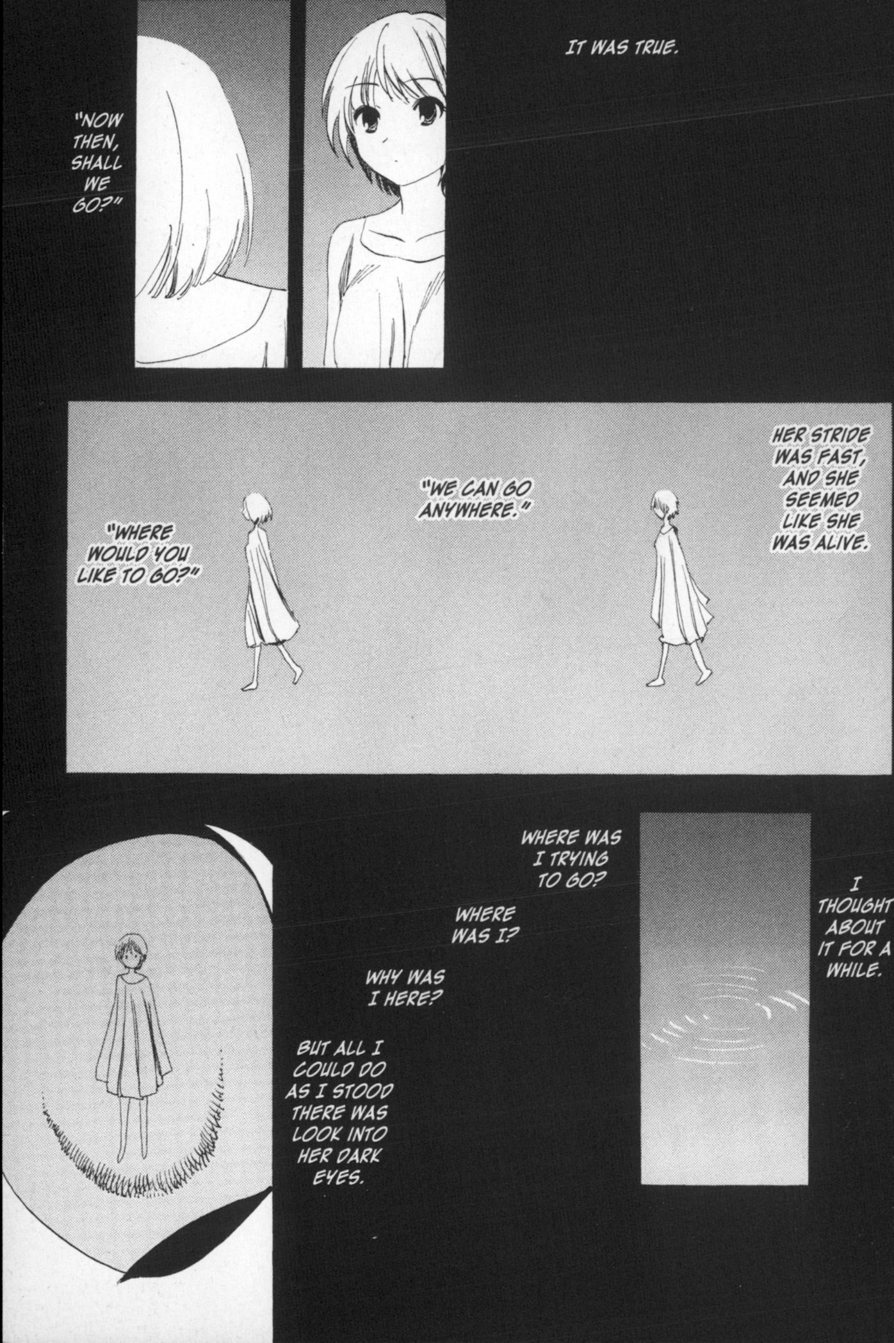
IT WAS TRUE.
"NOW THEN, SHALL WE GO?"
HER STRIDE WAS FAST, AND SHE SEEMED LIKE SHE WAS ALIVE.
"WE CAN GO ANYWHERE."
"WHERE WOULD YOU LIKE TO GO?"
I THOUGHT ABOUT IT FOR A WHILE.
WHERE WAS I TRYING TO GO?
WHERE WAS I?
WHY WAS I HERE?
BUT ALL I COULD DO AS I STOOD THERE WAS LOOK INTO HER DARK EYES.

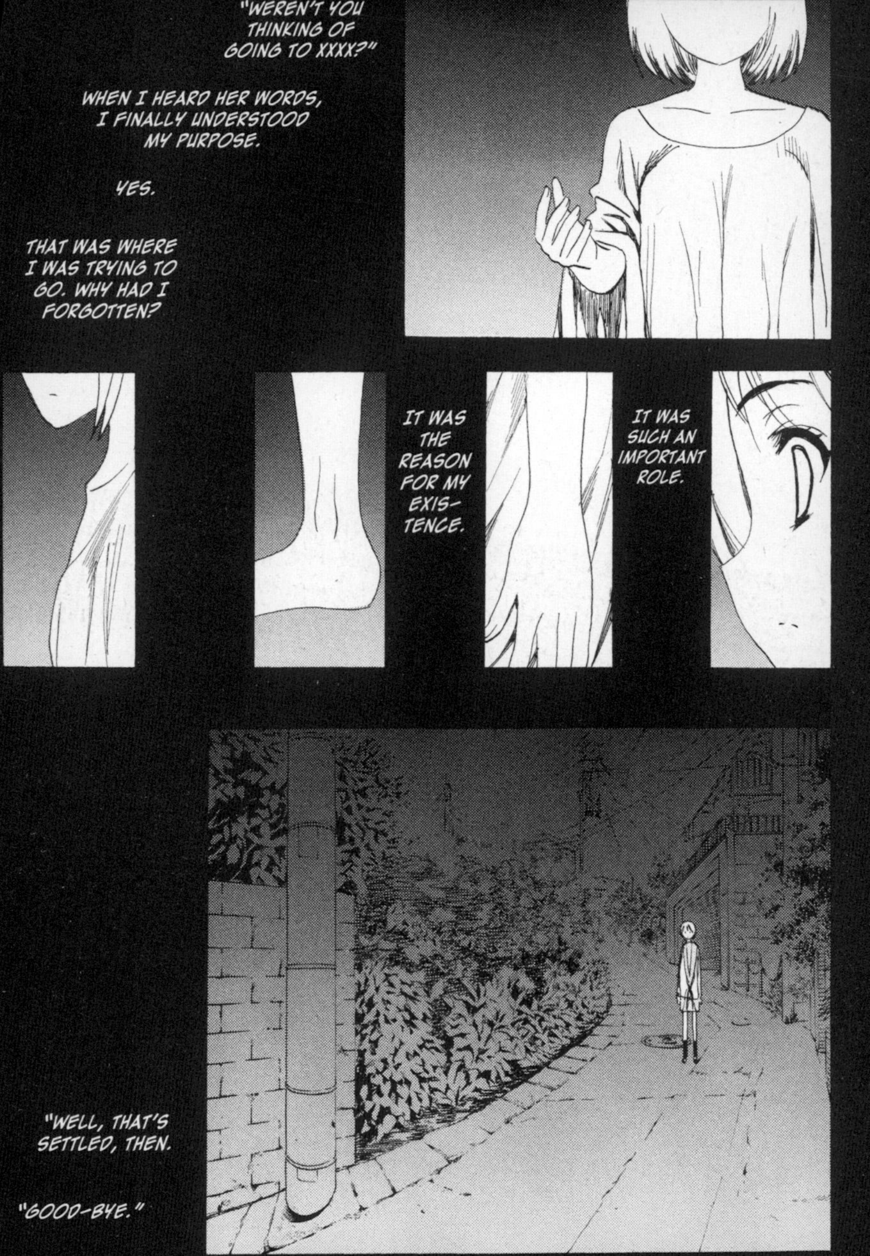
"WEREN'T YOU THINKING OF GOING TO XXXX?"
WHEN I HEARD HER WORDS, I FINALLY UNDERSTOOD MY PURPOSE.
YES.
THAT WAS WHERE I WAS TRYING TO GO. WHY HAD I FORGOTTEN?
IT WAS SUCH AN IMPORTANT ROLE.
IT WAS THE REASON FOR MY EXISTENCE.
"WELL, THAT'S SETTLED, THEN.
"GOOD-BYE."

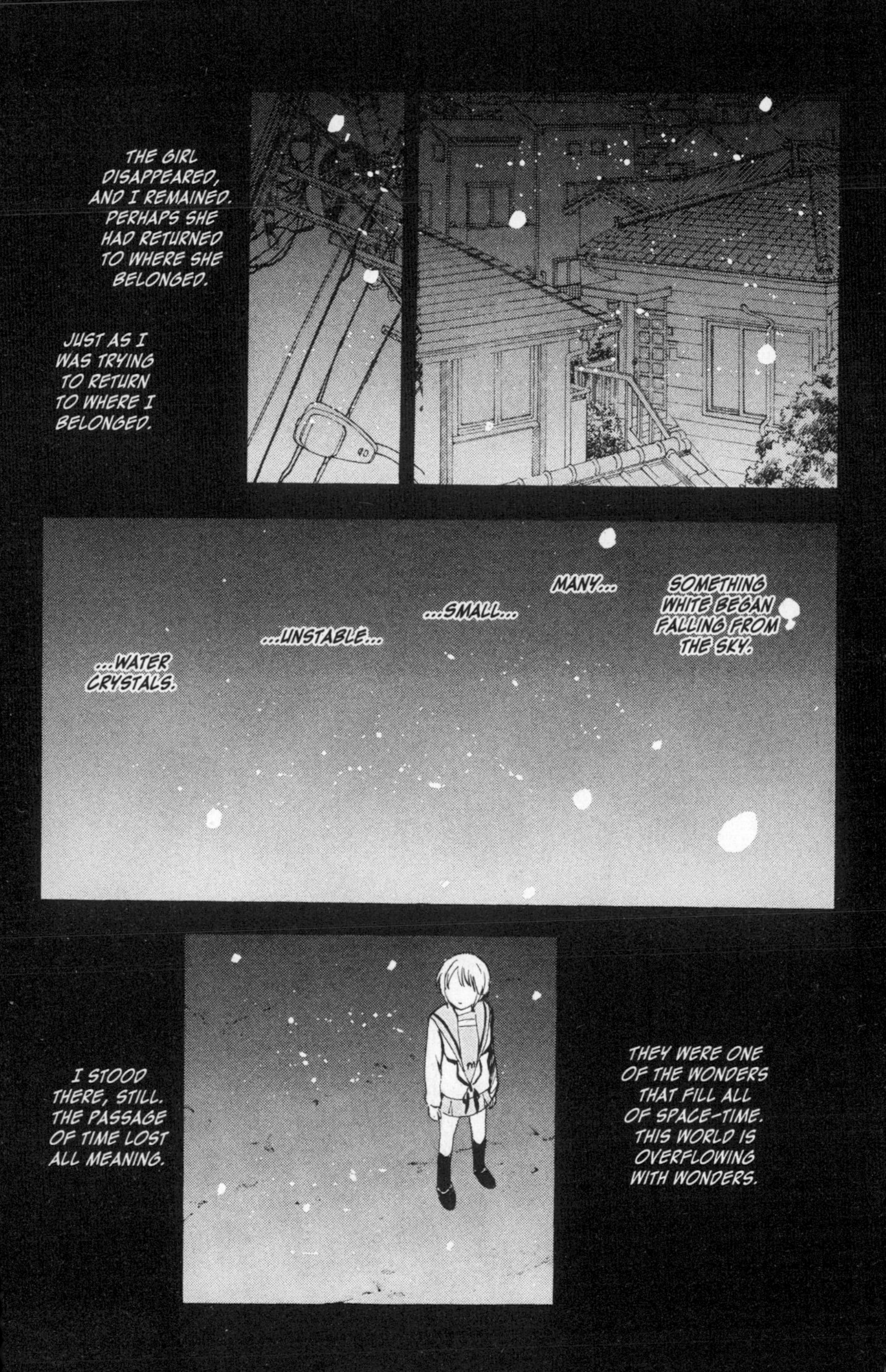
THE GIRL DISAPPEARED, AND I REMAINED. PERHAPS SHE HAD RETURNED TO WHERE SHE BELONGED.
JUST AS I WAS TRYING TO RETURN TO WHERE I BELONGED.
SOMETHING WHITE BEGAN FALLING FROM THE SKY.
MANY...
...SMALL...
...UNSTABLE...
...WATER CRYSTALS.
THEY WERE ONE OF THE WONDERS THAT FILL ALL OF SPACE-TIME. THIS WORLD IS OVERFLOWING WITH WONDERS.
I STOOD THERE, STILL. THE PASSAGE OF TIME LOST ALL MEANING.

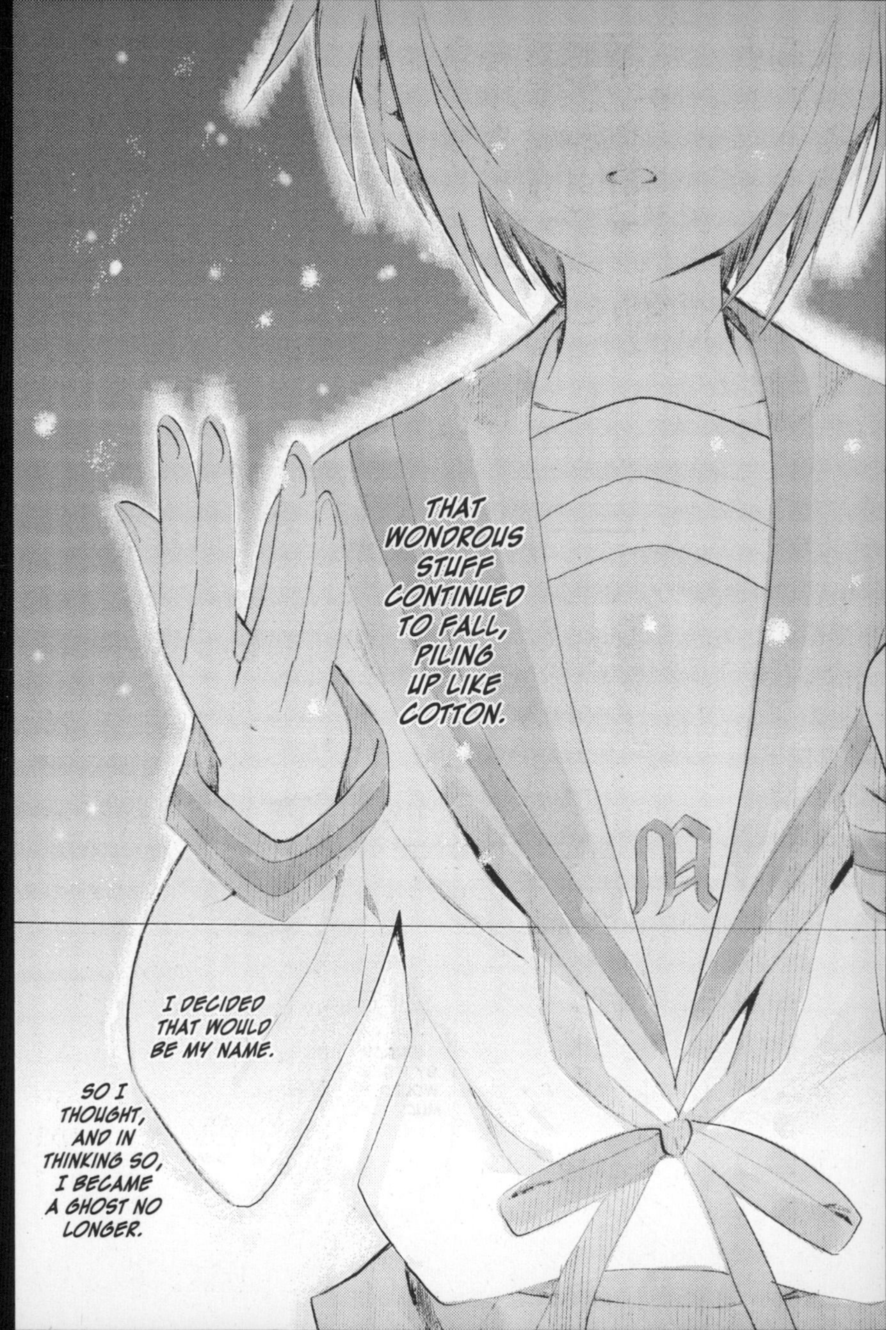
THAT WONDROUS STUFF CONTINUED TO FALL, PILING UP LIKE COTTON.
I DECIDED THAT WOULD BE MY NAME.
SO I THOUGHT, AND IN THINKING SO, I BECAME A GHOST NO LONGER.

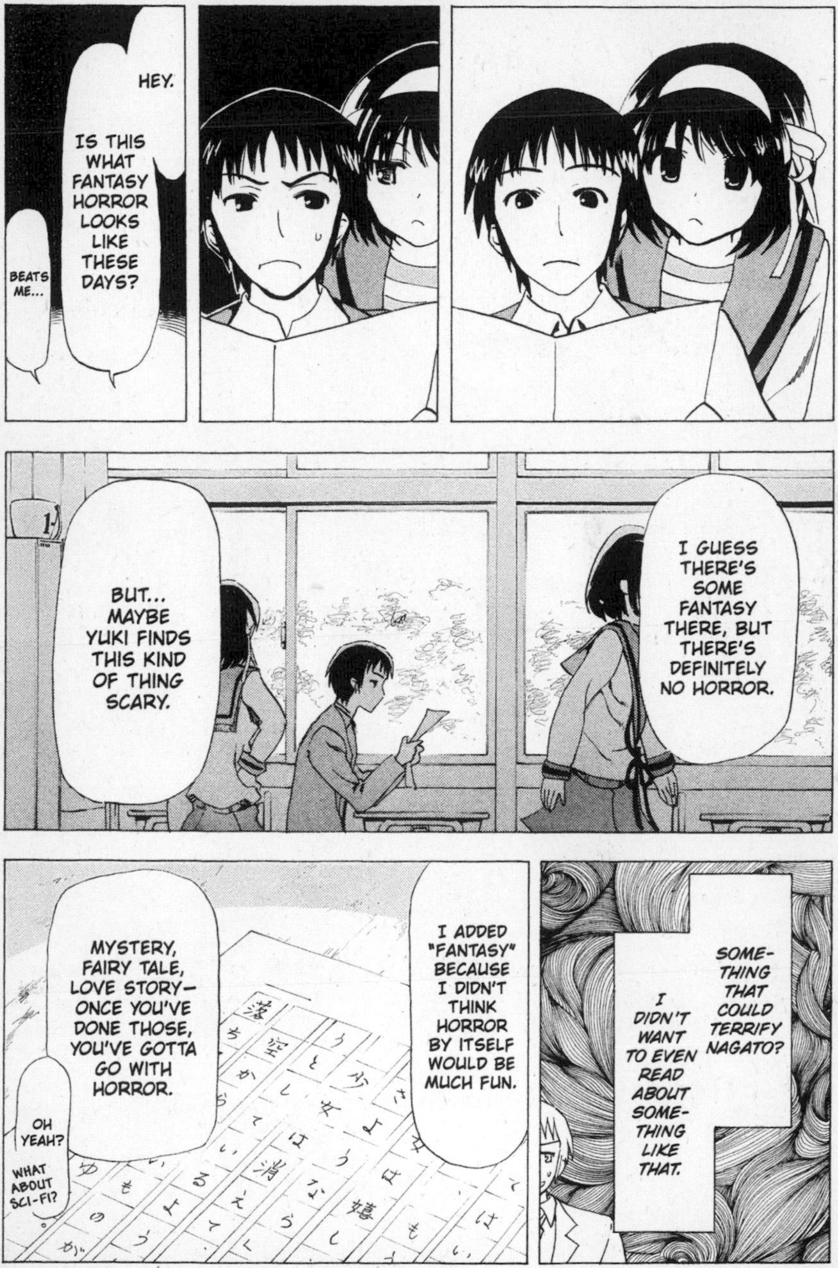
HEY.
IS THIS WHAT FANTASY HORROR LOOKS LIKE THESE DAYS?
BEATS ME...
I GUESS THERE'S SOME FANTASY THERE, BUT THERE'S DEFINITELY NO HORROR.
BUT... MAYBE YUKI FINDS THIS KIND OF THING SCARY.
SOME-THING THAT COULD TERRIFY NAGATO?
I DIDN'T WANT TO EVEN READ ABOUT SOME-THING LIKE THAT.
I ADDED "FANTASY" BECAUSE I DIDN'T THINK HORROR BY ITSELF WOULD BE MUCH FUN.
MYSTERY, FAIRY TALE, LOVE STORY—ONCE YOU'VE DONE THOSE, YOU'VE GOTTA GO WITH HORROR.
OH YEAH?
WHAT ABOUT SCI-FI?

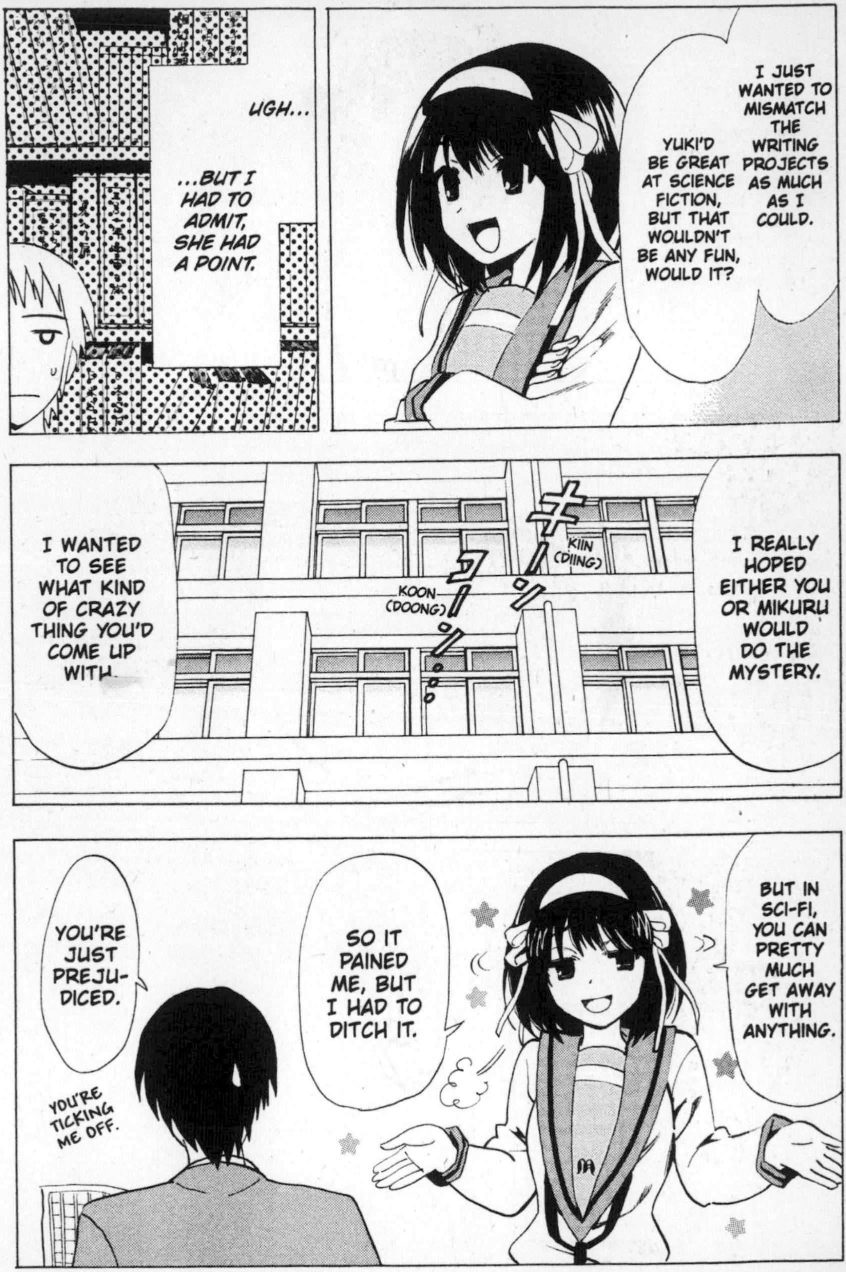
I JUST WANTED TO MISMATCH THE WRITING PROJECTS AS MUCH AS I COULD.
YUKI'D BE GREAT AT SCIENCE FICTION, BUT THAT WOULDN'T BE ANY FUN, WOULD IT?
UGH...
...BUT I HAD TO ADMIT, SHE HAD A POINT.
I REALLY HOPED EITHER YOU OR MIKURU WOULD DO THE MYSTERY.
KIIN (DIING)
KOON (DOONG)
I WANTED TO SEE WHAT KIND OF CRAZY THING YOU'D COME UP WITH.
BUT IN SCI-FI, YOU CAN PRETTY MUCH GET AWAY WITH ANYTHING.
SO IT PAINED ME, BUT I HAD TO DITCH IT.
YOU'RE JUST PREJU-DICED.
YOU'RE TICKING ME OFF.

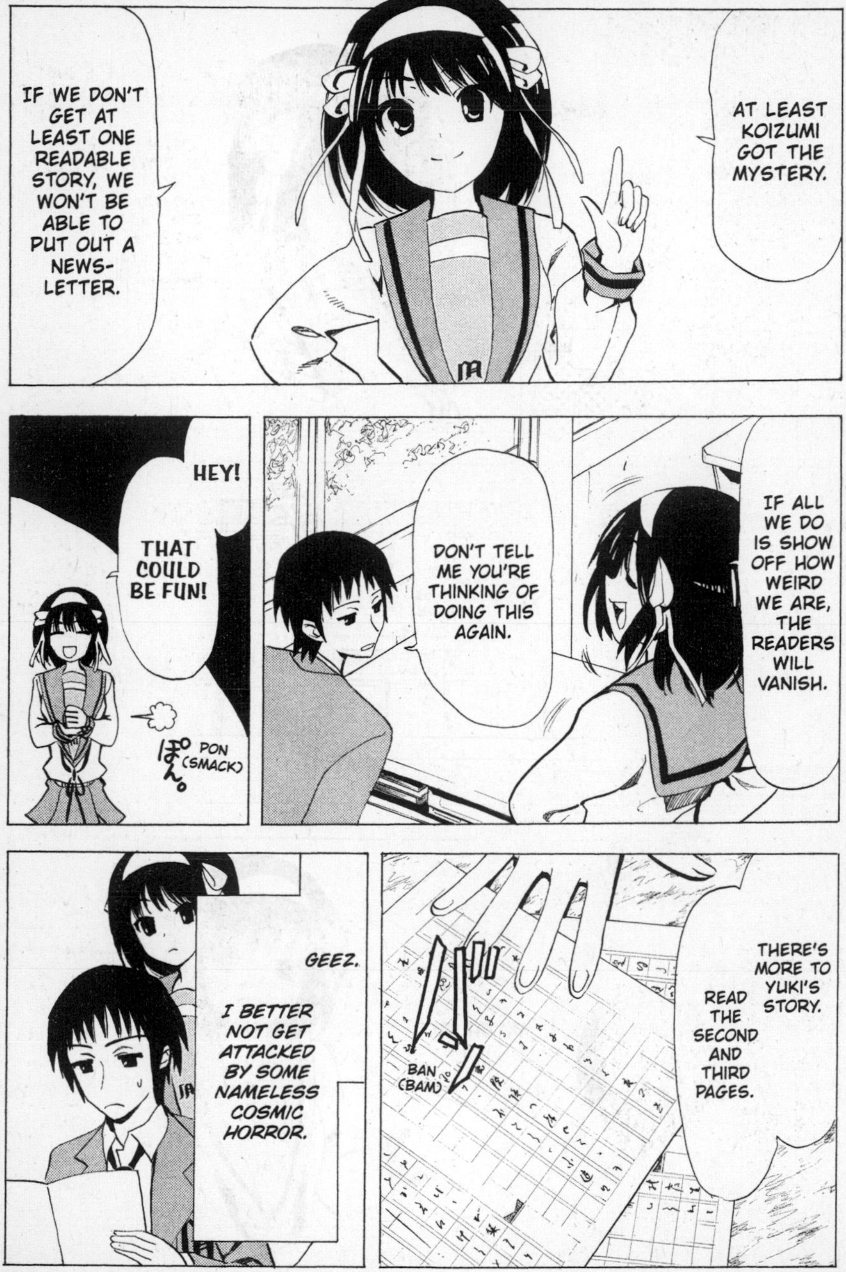
AT LEAST KOIZUMI GOT THE MYSTERY.
IF WE DON'T GET AT LEAST ONE READABLE STORY, WE WON'T BE ABLE TO PUT OUT A NEWS-LETTER.
IF ALL WE DO IS SHOW OFF HOW WEIRD WE ARE, THE READERS WILL VANISH.
DON'T TELL ME YOU'RE THINKING OF DOING THIS AGAIN.
HEY!
THAT COULD BE FUN!
ぽん。
PON (SMACK)
THERE'S MORE TO YUKI'S STORY.
READ THE SECOND AND THIRD PAGES.
BAN (BAM)
GEEZ.
I BETTER NOT GET ATTACKED BY SOME NAMELESS COSMIC HORROR.

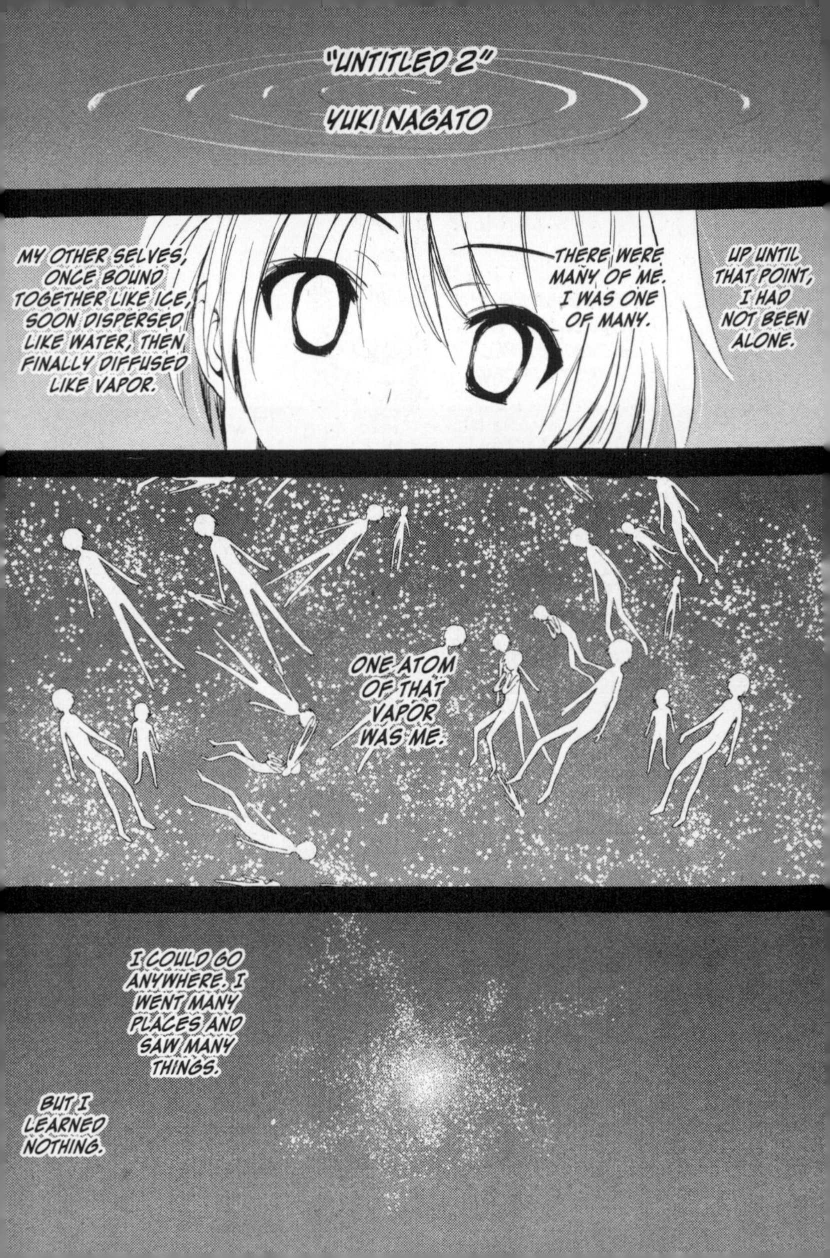
"UNTITLED 2"
YUKI NAGATO
UP UNTIL THAT POINT, I HAD NOT BEEN ALONE.
THERE WERE MANY OF ME. I WAS ONE OF MANY.
MY OTHER SELVES, ONCE BOUND TOGETHER LIKE ICE, SOON DISPERSED LIKE WATER, THEN FINALLY DIFFUSED LIKE VAPOR.
ONE ATOM OF THAT VAPOR WAS ME.
I COULD GO ANYWHERE. I WENT MANY PLACES AND SAW MANY THINGS.
BUT I LEARNED NOTHING.

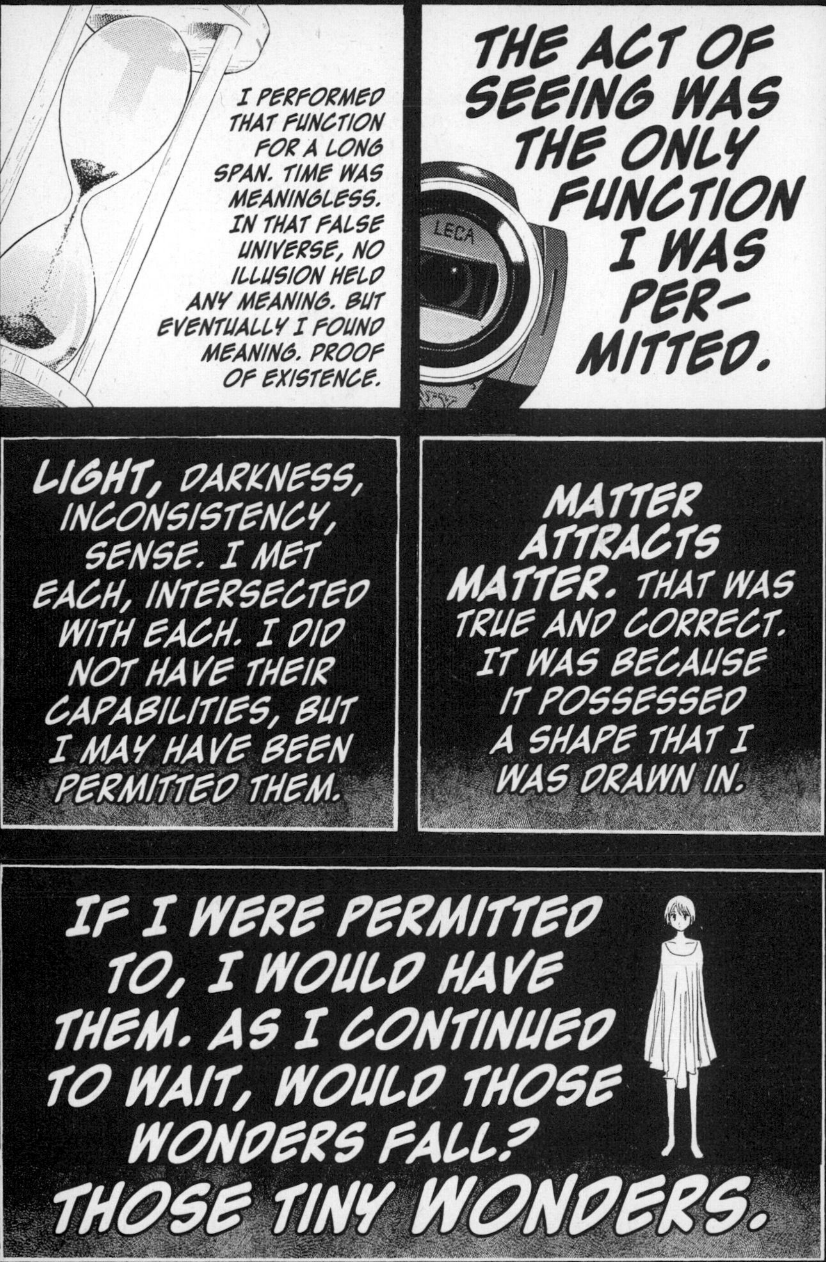
THE ACT OF SEEING WAS THE ONLY FUNCTION I WAS PER- MITTED.
LECA
I PERFORMED THAT FUNCTION FOR A LONG SPAN. TIME WAS MEANINGLESS. IN THAT FALSE UNIVERSE, NO ILLUSION HELD ANY MEANING. BUT EVENTUALLY I FOUND MEANING. PROOF OF EXISTENCE.
MATTER ATTRACTS MATTER. THAT WAS TRUE AND CORRECT. IT WAS BECAUSE IT POSSESSED A SHAPE THAT I WAS DRAWN IN.
LIGHT, DARKNESS, INCONSISTENCY, SENSE. I MET EACH, INTERSECTED WITH EACH. I DID NOT HAVE THEIR CAPABILITIES, BUT I MAY HAVE BEEN PERMITTED THEM.
IF I WERE PERMITTED TO, I WOULD HAVE THEM. AS I CONTINUED TO WAIT, WOULD THOSE WONDERS FALL?
THOSE TINY WONDERS.

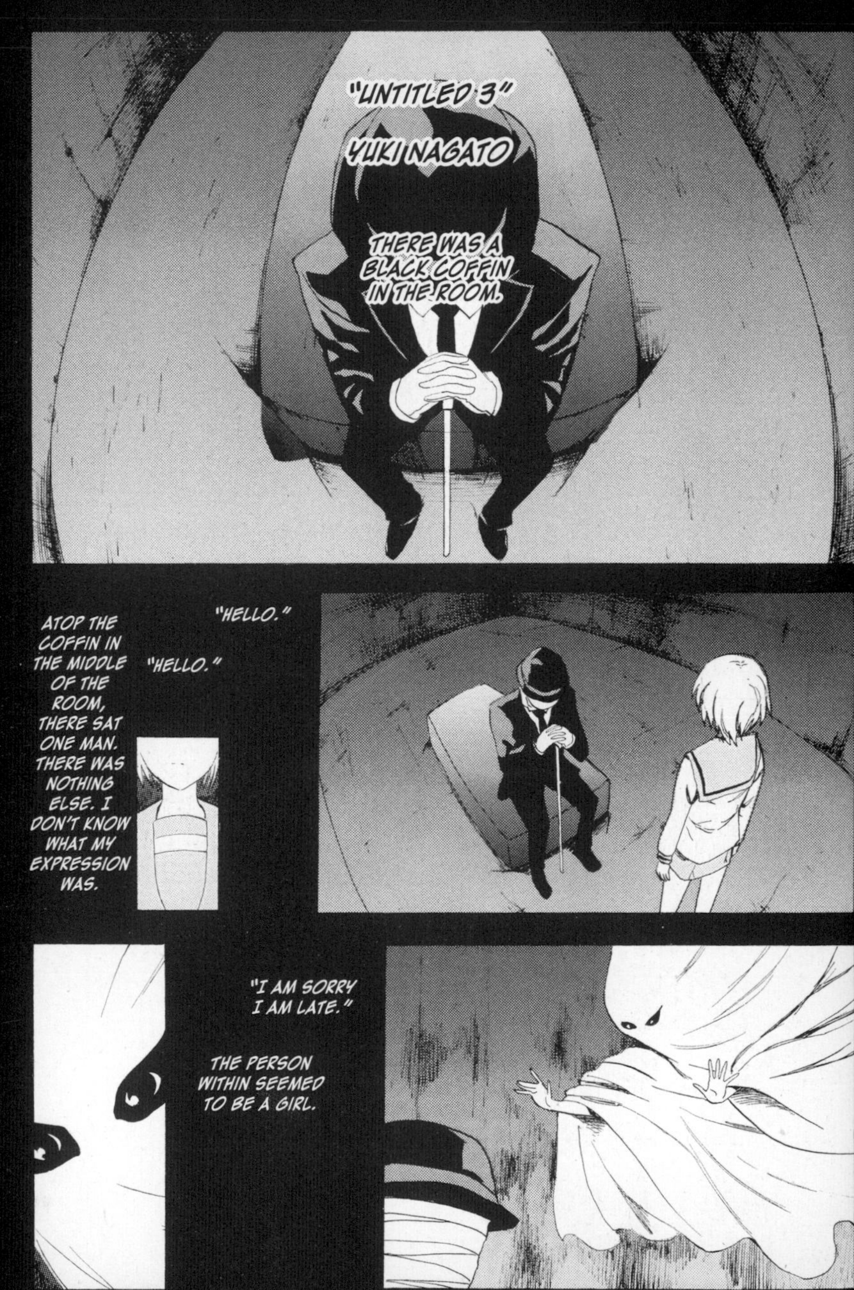
"UNTITLED 3"
YUKI NAGATO
THERE WAS A BLACK COFFIN IN THE ROOM.
"HELLO."
"HELLO."
ATOP THE COFFIN IN THE MIDDLE OF THE ROOM, THERE SAT ONE MAN. THERE WAS NOTHING ELSE. I DON'T KNOW WHAT MY EXPRESSION WAS.
"I AM SORRY I AM LATE."
THE PERSON WITHIN SEEMED TO BE A GIRL.

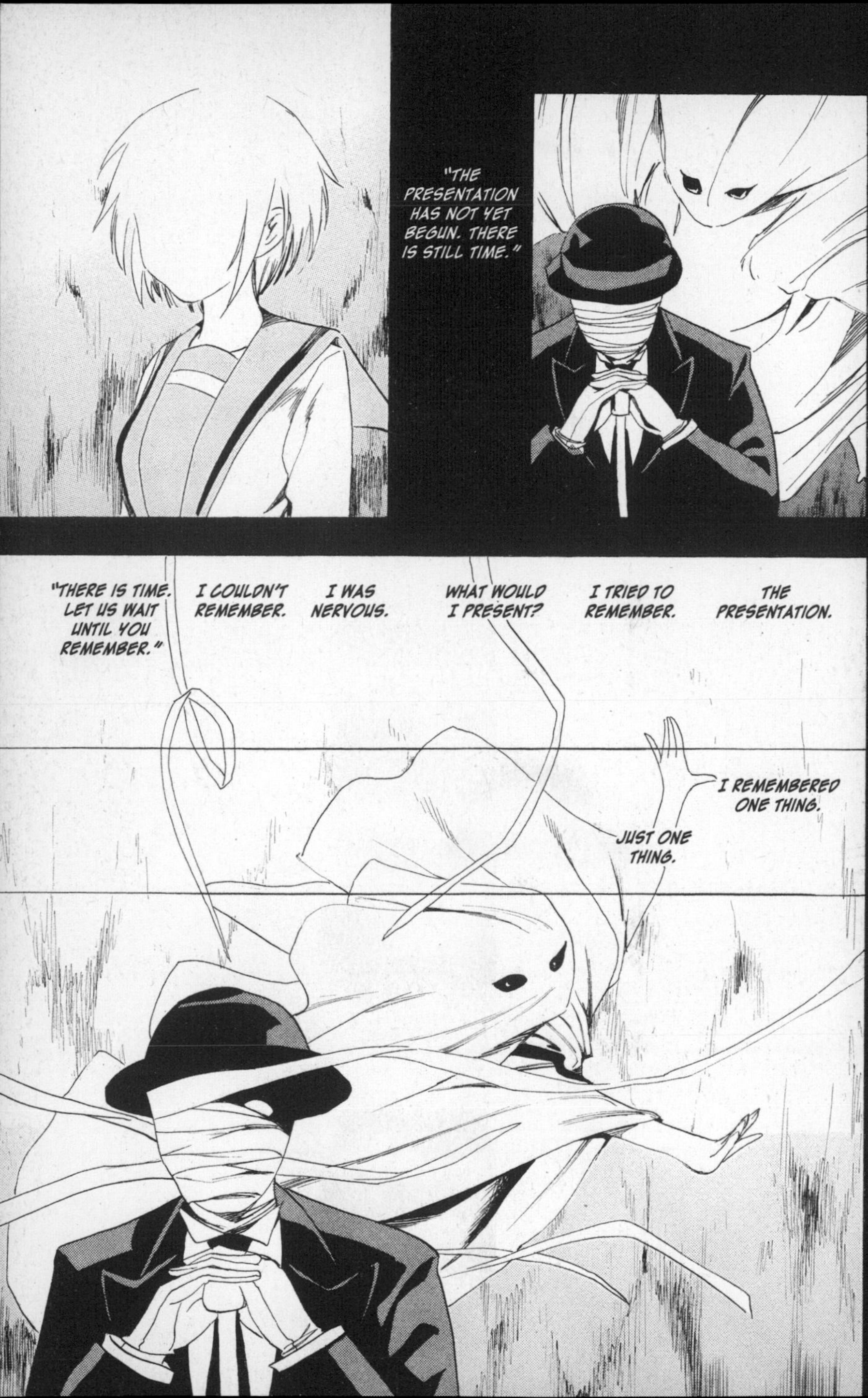
"THE PRESENTATION HAS NOT YET BEGUN. THERE IS STILL TIME."
THE PRESENTATION.
I TRIED TO REMEMBER.
WHAT WOULD I PRESENT?
I WAS NERVOUS.
I COULDN'T REMEMBER.
"THERE IS TIME. LET US WAIT UNTIL YOU REMEMBER."
I REMEMBERED ONE THING.
JUST ONE THING.

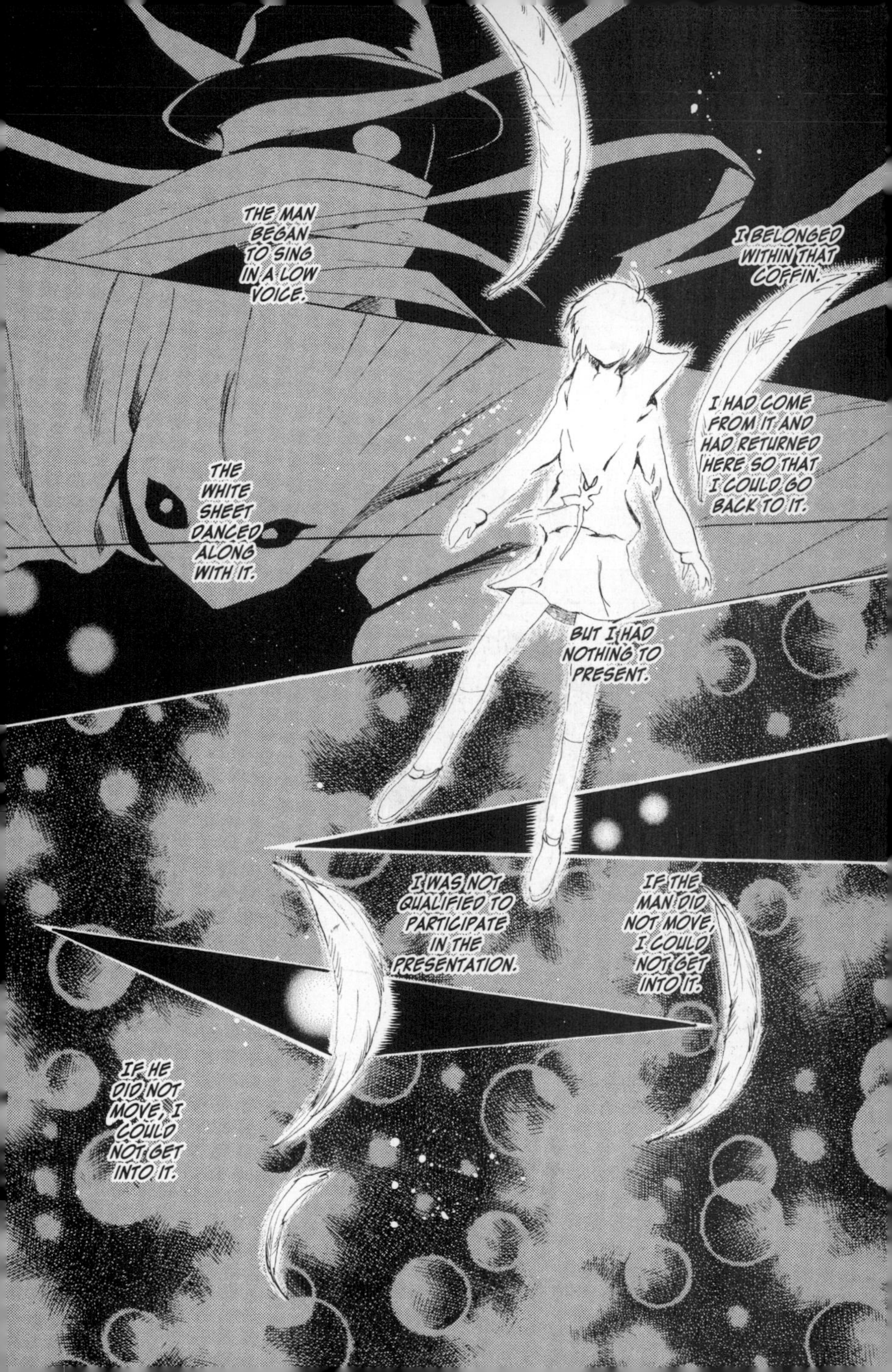
I BELONGED WITHIN THAT COFFIN.
THE MAN BEGAN TO SING IN A LOW VOICE.
I HAD COME FROM IT AND HAD RETURNED HERE SO THAT I COULD GO BACK TO IT.
THE WHITE SHEET DANCED ALONG WITH IT.
BUT I HAD NOTHING TO PRESENT.
IF THE MAN DID NOT MOVE, I COULD NOT GET INTO IT.
I WAS NOT QUALIFIED TO PARTICIPATE IN THE PRESENTATION.
IF HE DID NOT MOVE, I COULD NOT GET INTO IT.

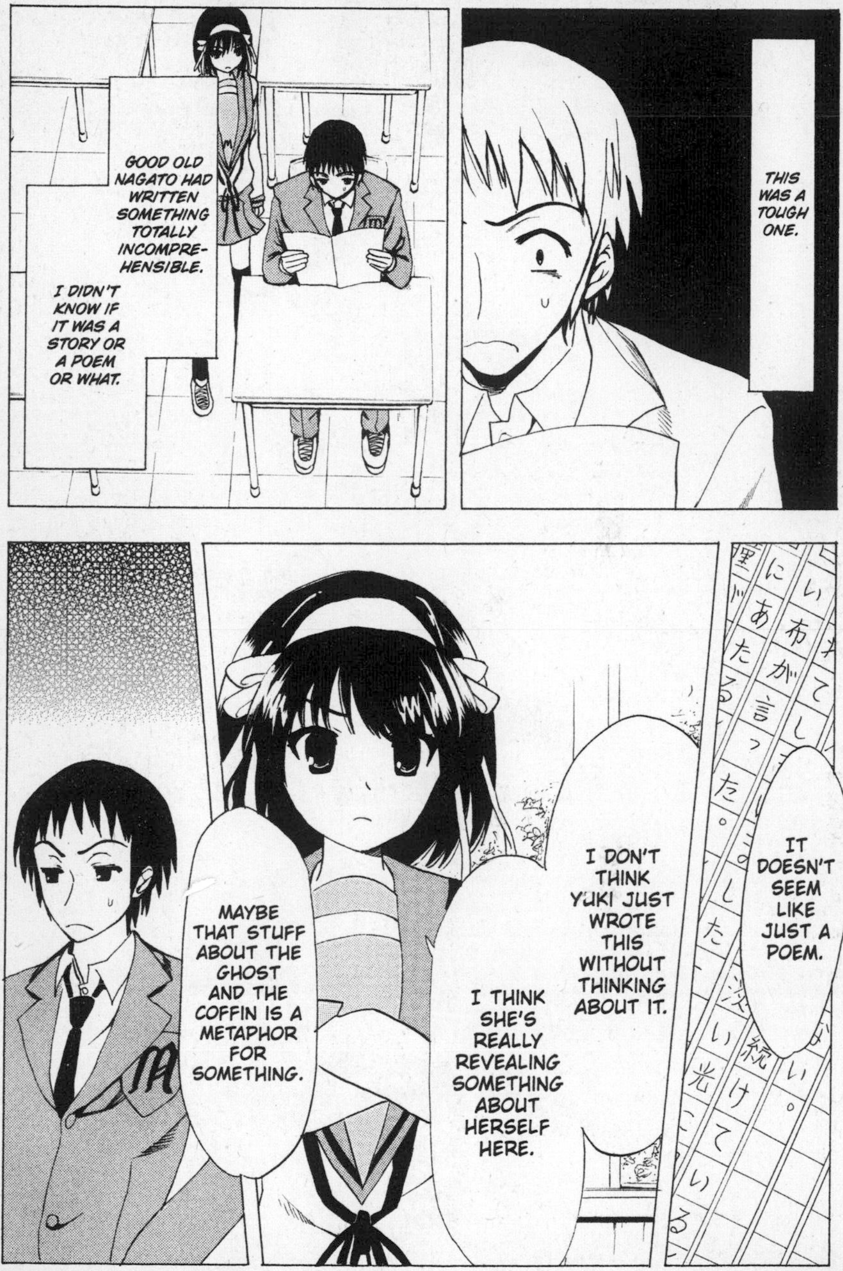
THIS WAS A TOUGH ONE.
GOOD OLD NAGATO HAD WRITTEN SOMETHING TOTALLY INCOMPRE-HENSIBLE.
I DIDN'T KNOW IF IT WAS A STORY OR A POEM OR WHAT.
IT DOESN'T SEEM LIKE JUST A POEM.
I DON'T THINK YUKI JUST WROTE THIS WITHOUT THINKING ABOUT IT.
I THINK SHE'S REALLY REVEALING SOMETHING ABOUT HERSELF HERE.
MAYBE THAT STUFF ABOUT THE GHOST AND THE COFFIN IS A METAPHOR FOR SOMETHING.

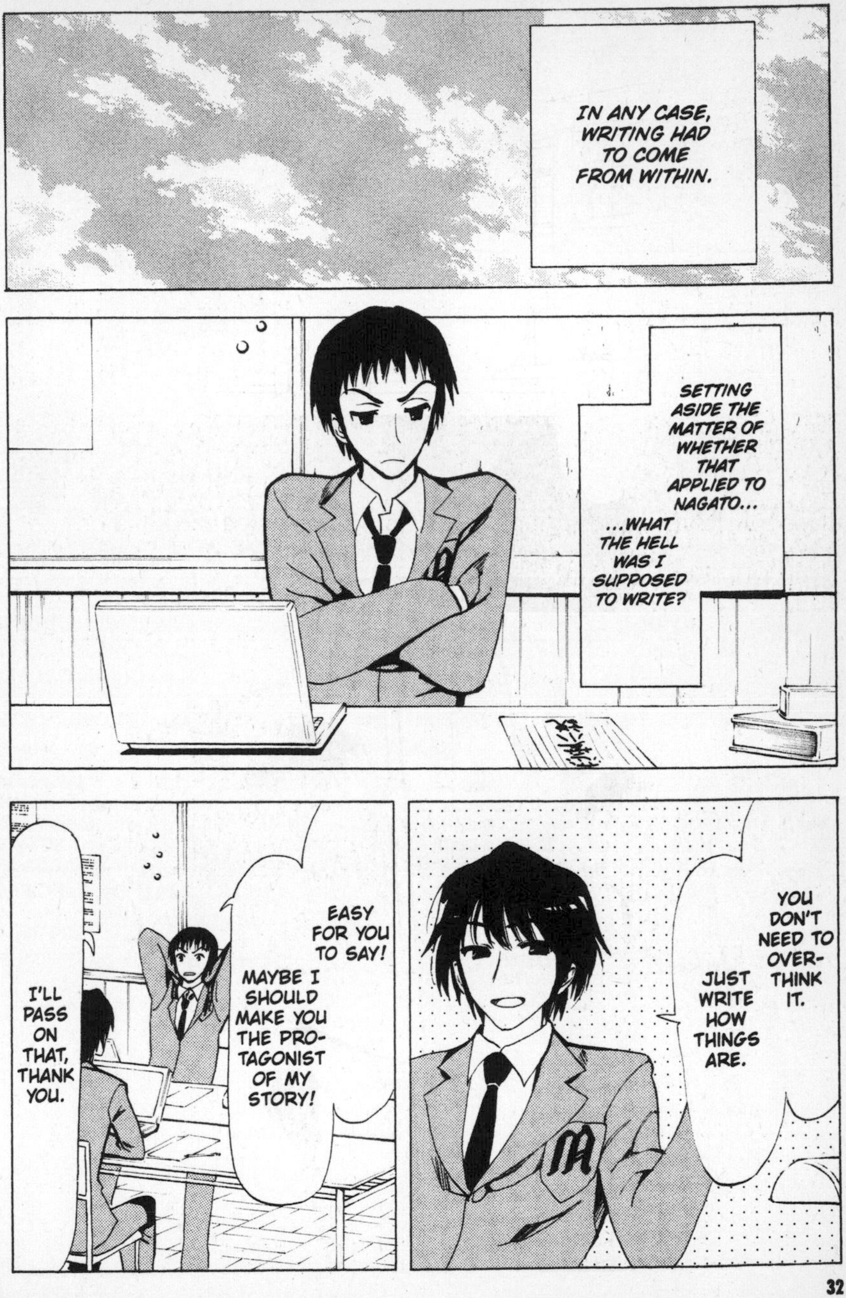
IN ANY CASE, WRITING HAD TO COME FROM WITHIN.
SETTING ASIDE THE MATTER OF WHETHER THAT APPLIED TO NAGATO...
...WHAT THE HELL WAS I SUPPOSED TO WRITE?
YOU DON'T NEED TO OVER-THINK IT.
JUST WRITE HOW THINGS ARE.
EASY FOR YOU TO SAY!
MAYBE I SHOULD MAKE YOU THE PRO-TAGONIST OF MY STORY!
I'LL PASS ON THAT, THANK YOU.

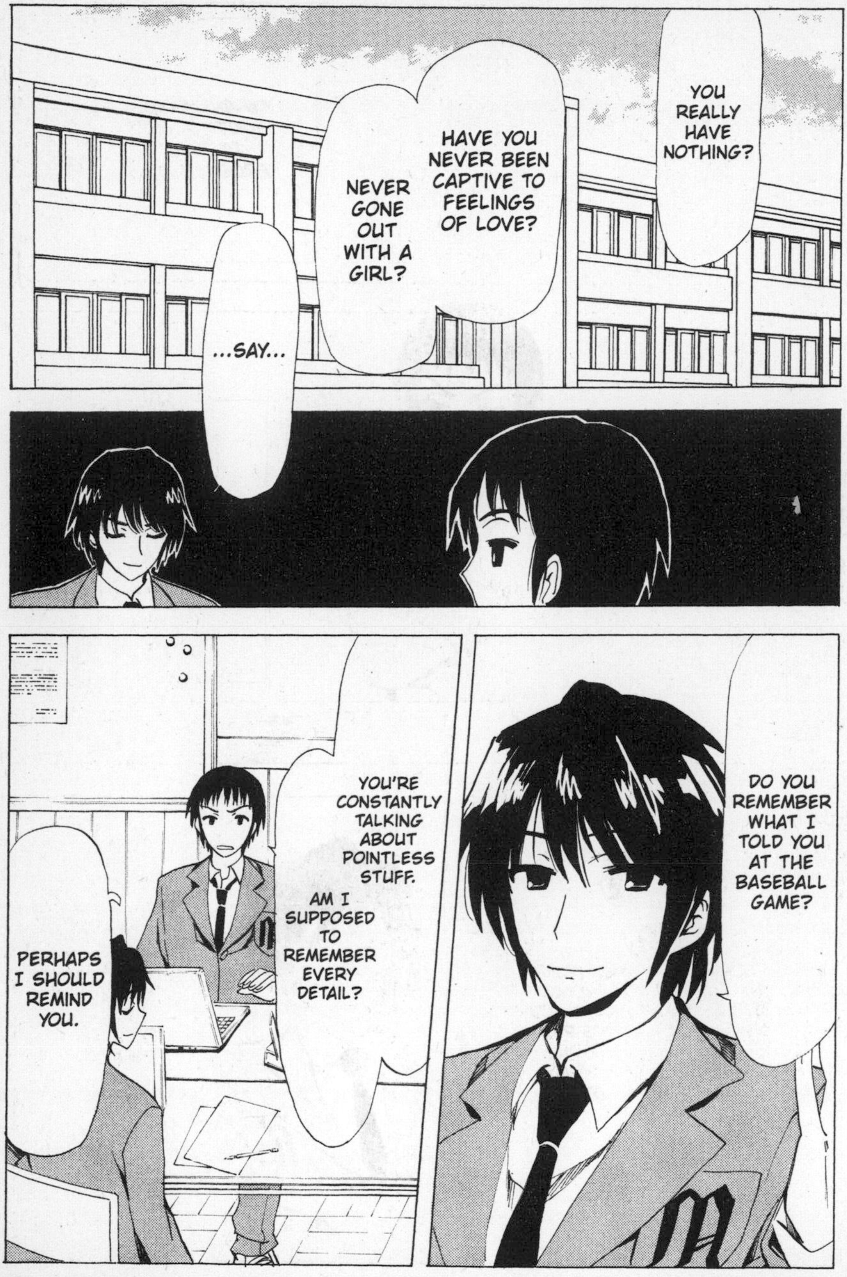
YOU REALLY HAVE NOTHING?
HAVE YOU NEVER BEEN CAPTIVE TO FEELINGS OF LOVE?
NEVER GONE OUT WITH A GIRL?
...SAY...
DO YOU REMEMBER WHAT I TOLD YOU AT THE BASEBALL GAME?
YOU'RE CONSTANTLY TALKING ABOUT POINTLESS STUFF.
AM I SUPPOSED TO REMEMBER EVERY DETAIL?
PERHAPS I SHOULD REMIND YOU.

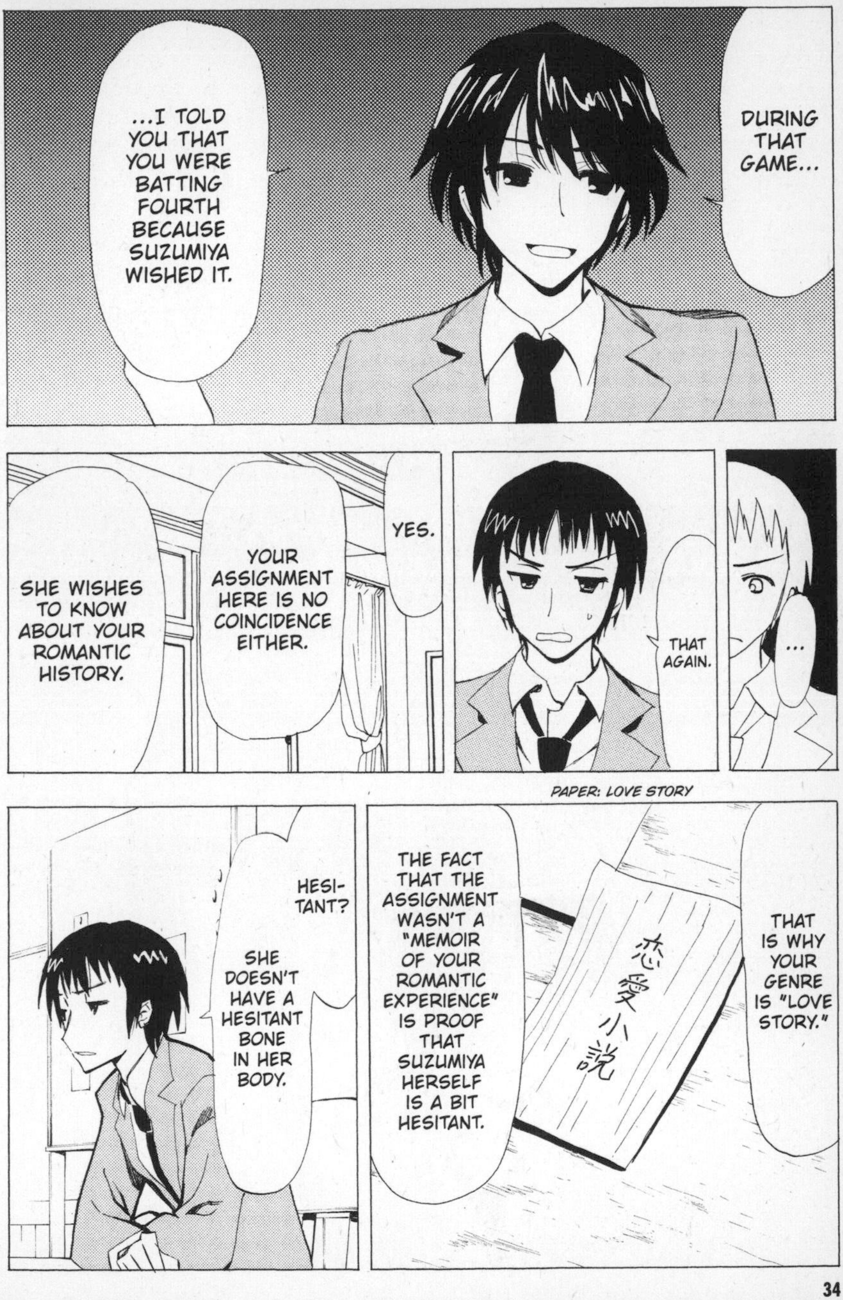
DURING THAT GAME...
...I TOLD YOU THAT YOU WERE BATTING FOURTH BECAUSE SUZUMIYA WISHED IT.
...
THAT AGAIN.
YES.
YOUR ASSIGNMENT HERE IS NO COINCIDENCE EITHER.
SHE WISHES TO KNOW ABOUT YOUR ROMANTIC HISTORY.
PAPER: LOVE STORY
THAT IS WHY YOUR GENRE IS "LOVE STORY."
恋愛小説
THE FACT THAT THE ASSIGNMENT WASN'T A "MEMOIR OF YOUR ROMANTIC EXPERIENCE" IS PROOF THAT SUZUMIYA HERSELF IS A BIT HESITANT.
HESI-TANT?
SHE DOESN'T HAVE A HESITANT BONE IN HER BODY.

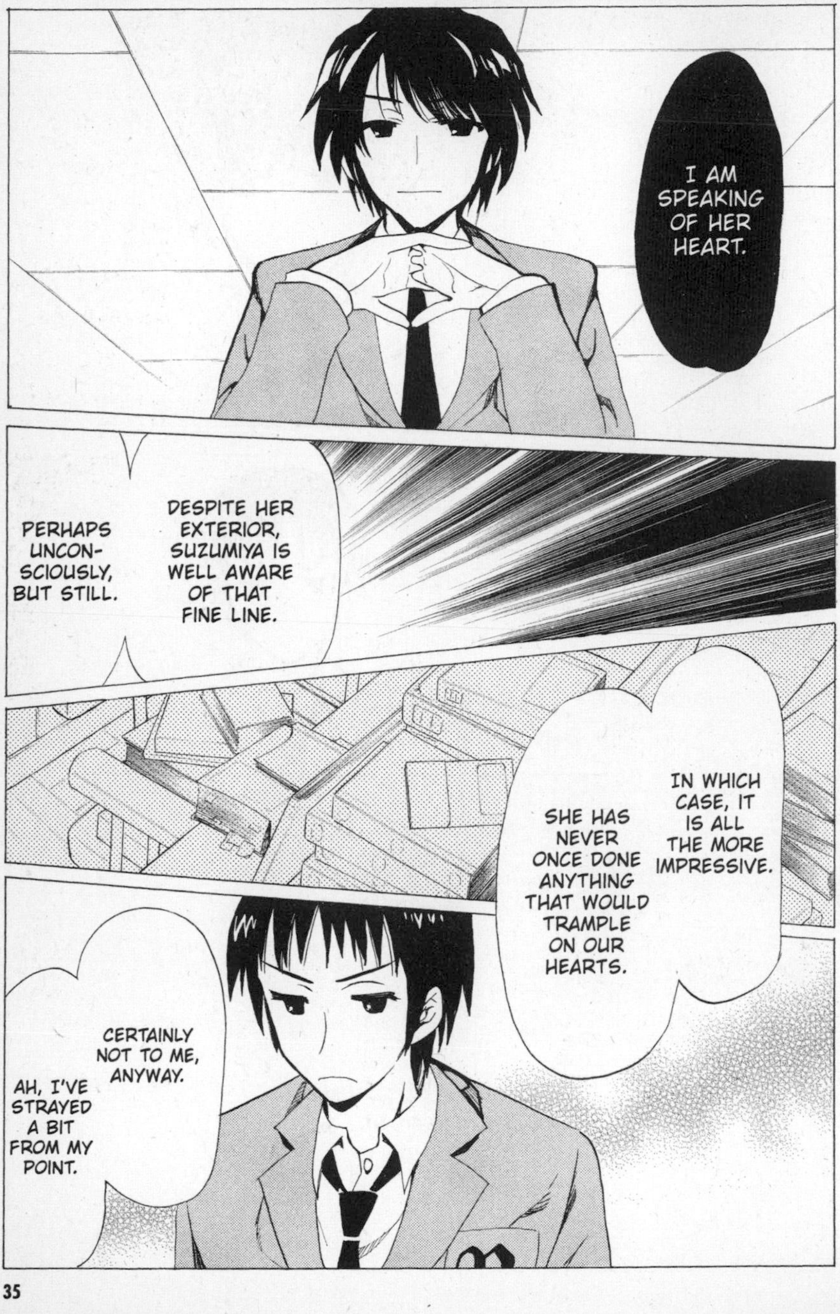
I AM SPEAKING OF HER HEART.
DESPITE HER EXTERIOR, SUZUMIYA IS WELL AWARE OF THAT FINE LINE.
PERHAPS UNCON-SCIOUSLY, BUT STILL.
IN WHICH CASE, IT IS ALL THE MORE IMPRESSIVE.
SHE HAS NEVER ONCE DONE ANYTHING THAT WOULD TRAMPLE ON OUR HEARTS.
CERTAINLY NOT TO ME, ANYWAY.
AH, I'VE STRAYED A BIT FROM MY POINT.

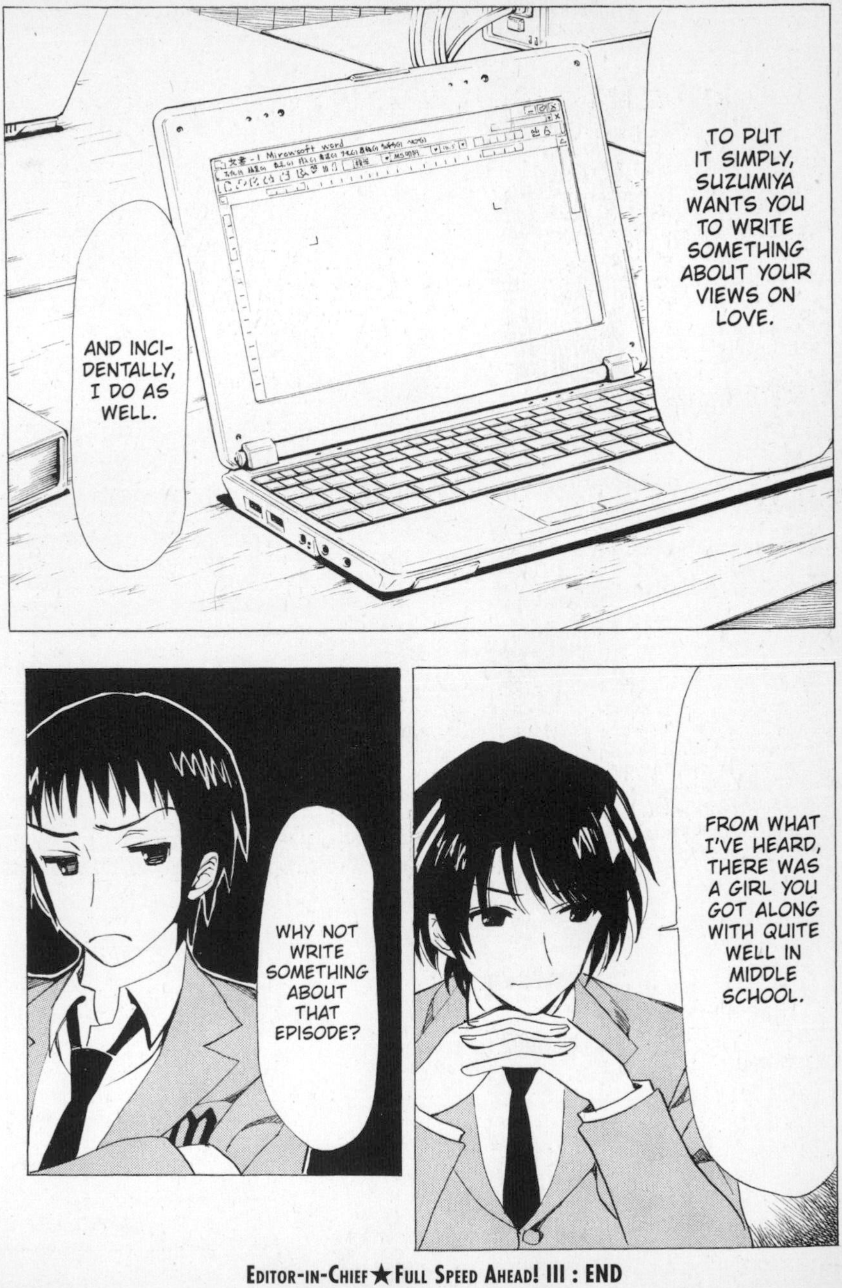
TO PUT IT SIMPLY, SUZUMIYA WANTS YOU TO WRITE SOMETHING ABOUT YOUR VIEWS ON LOVE.
AND INCI-DENTALLY, I DO AS WELL.
FROM WHAT I'VE HEARD, THERE WAS A GIRL YOU GOT ALONG WITH QUITE WELL IN MIDDLE SCHOOL.
WHY NOT WRITE SOMETHING ABOUT THAT EPISODE?

EDITOR-IN-CHIEF★FULL SPEED AHEAD! III : END

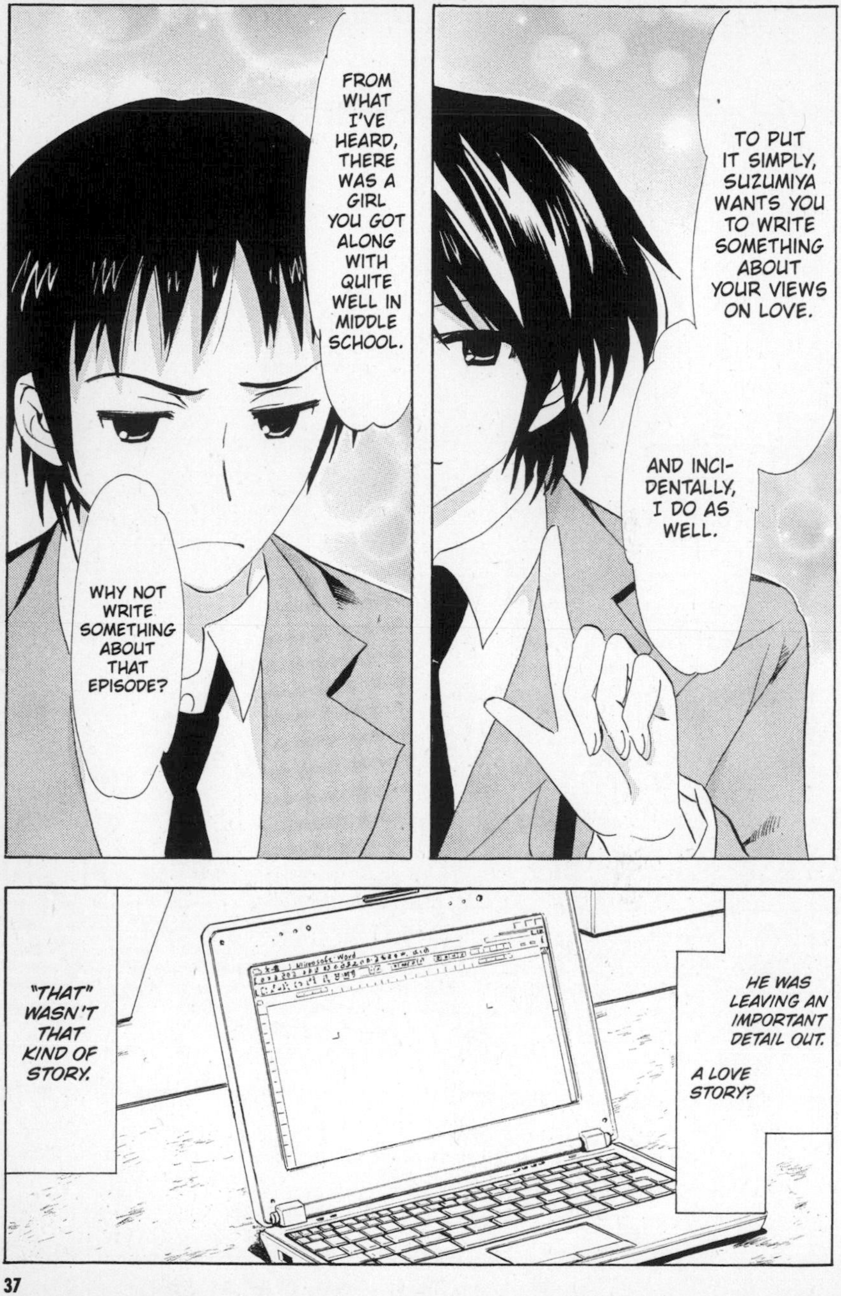
TO PUT IT SIMPLY, SUZUMIYA WANTS YOU TO WRITE SOMETHING ABOUT YOUR VIEWS ON LOVE.
AND INCI-DENTALLY, I DO AS WELL.
FROM WHAT I'VE HEARD, THERE WAS A GIRL YOU GOT ALONG WITH QUITE WELL IN MIDDLE SCHOOL.
WHY NOT WRITE SOMETHING ABOUT THAT EPISODE?
HE WAS LEAVING AN IMPORTANT DETAIL OUT.
A LOVE STORY?
"THAT" WASN'T THAT KIND OF STORY.

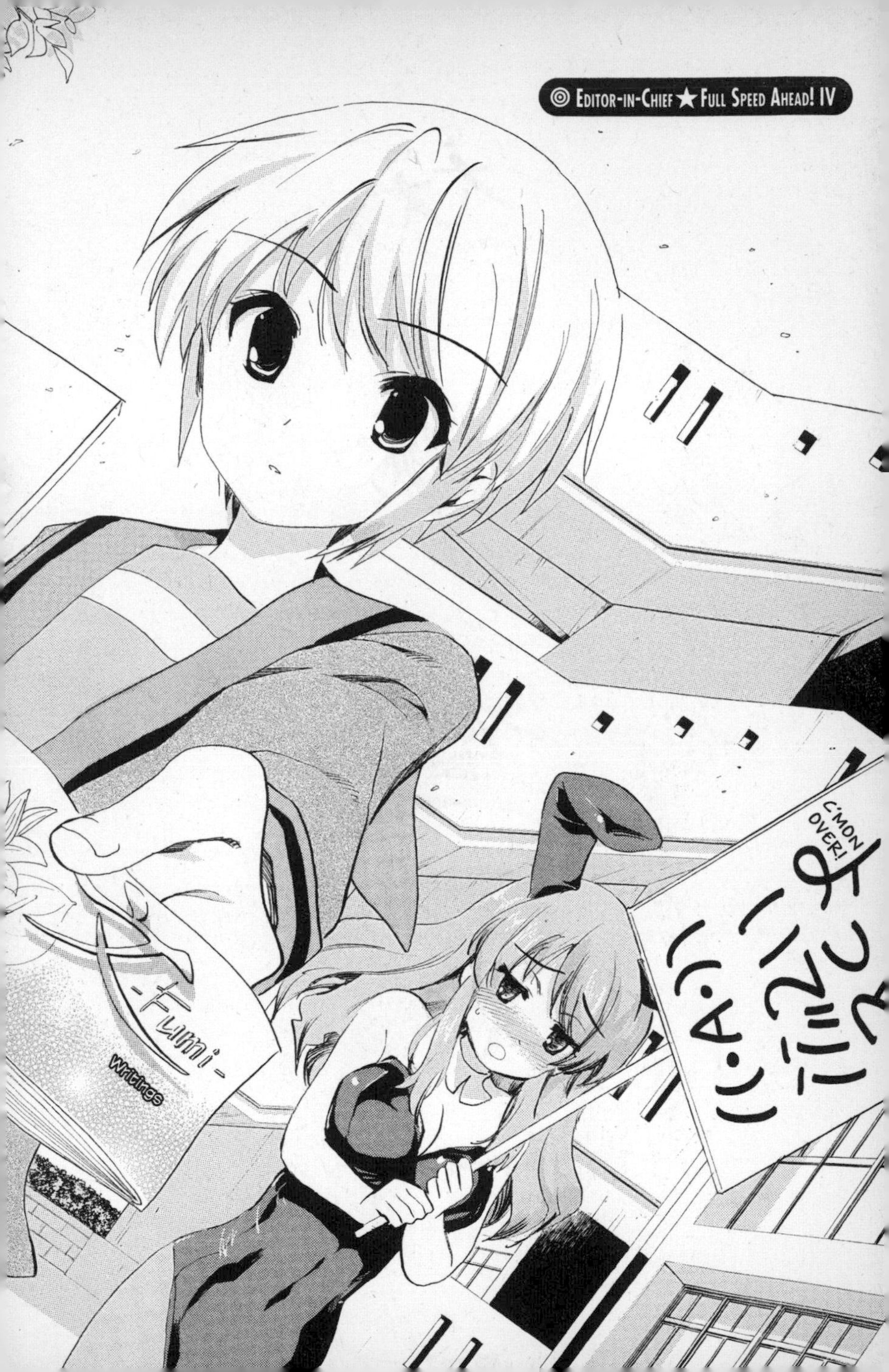
◎ Editor-in-Chief ★ Full Speed Ahead! IV
C'MON OVER!
-Fumi-
Writings

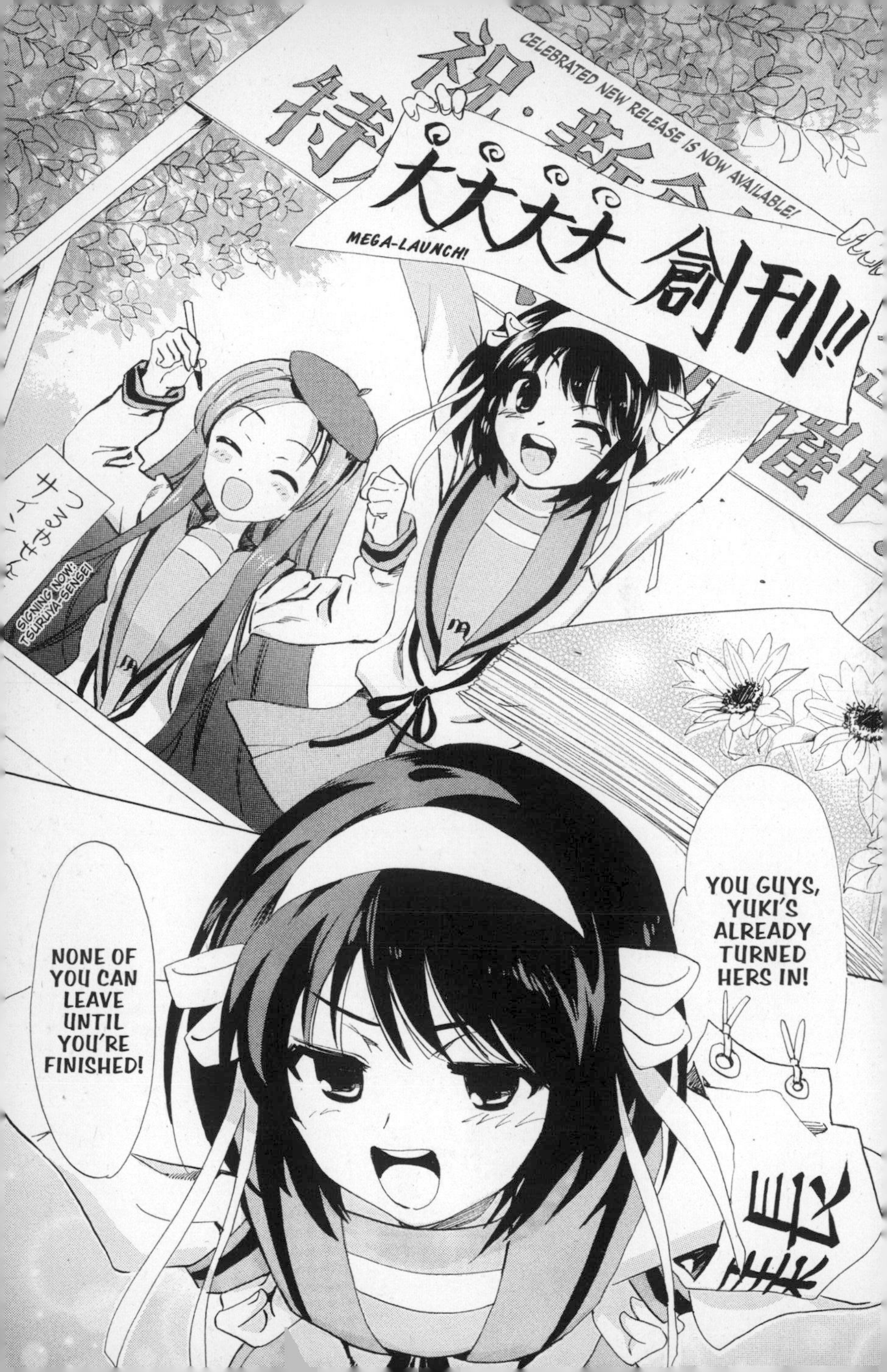
CELEBRATED NEW RELEASE IS NOW AVAILABLE!
大大大大創刊!!
MEGA-LAUNCH!
SIGNING NOW: TSURUYA-SENSEI!
YOU GUYS, YUKI'S ALREADY TURNED HERS IN!
NONE OF YOU CAN LEAVE UNTIL YOU'RE FINISHED!

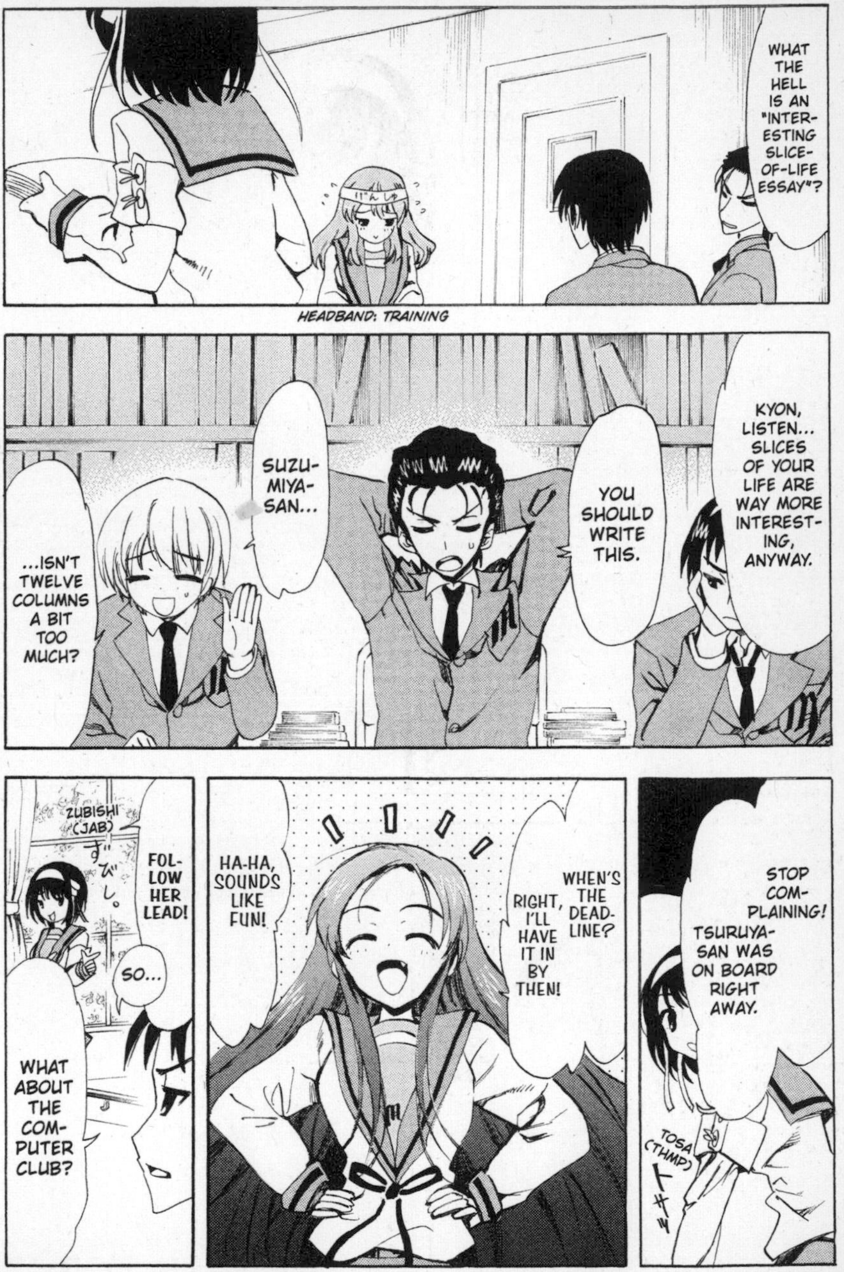
WHAT THE HELL IS AN "INTERESTING SLICE-OF-LIFE ESSAY"?
HEADBAND: TRAINING
KYON, LISTEN... SLICES OF YOUR LIFE ARE WAY MORE INTERESTING, ANYWAY.
YOU SHOULD WRITE THIS.
SUZUMIYA-SAN...
...ISN'T TWELVE COLUMNS A BIT TOO MUCH?
STOP COMPLAINING! TSURUYA-SAN WAS ON BOARD RIGHT AWAY.
TOSA (THMP)
WHEN'S THE DEADLINE?
RIGHT, I'LL HAVE IT IN BY THEN!
HA-HA, SOUNDS LIKE FUN!
FOLLOW HER LEAD!
ZUBISHI (JAB)
SO...
WHAT ABOUT THE COMPUTER CLUB?

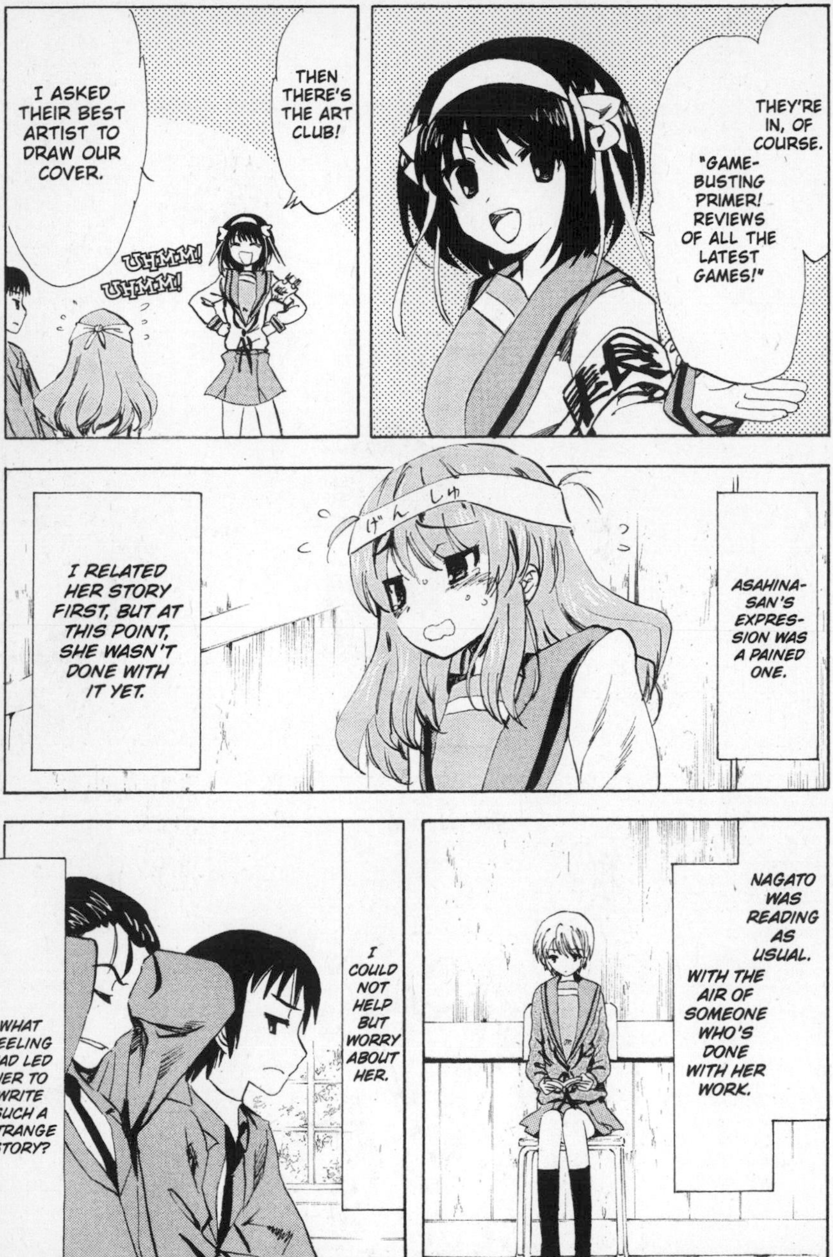
THEY'RE IN, OF COURSE.
"GAME-BUSTING PRIMER! REVIEWS OF ALL THE LATEST GAMES!"
THEN THERE'S THE ART CLUB!
I ASKED THEIR BEST ARTIST TO DRAW OUR COVER.
UHMMM!
UHMMM!
ASAHINA-SAN'S EXPRESSION WAS A PAINED ONE.
げん しゅ
I RELATED HER STORY FIRST, BUT AT THIS POINT, SHE WASN'T DONE WITH IT YET.
NAGATO WAS READING AS USUAL.
WITH THE AIR OF SOMEONE WHO'S DONE WITH HER WORK.
I COULD NOT HELP BUT WORRY ABOUT HER.
WHAT FEELING HAD LED HER TO WRITE SUCH A STRANGE STORY?

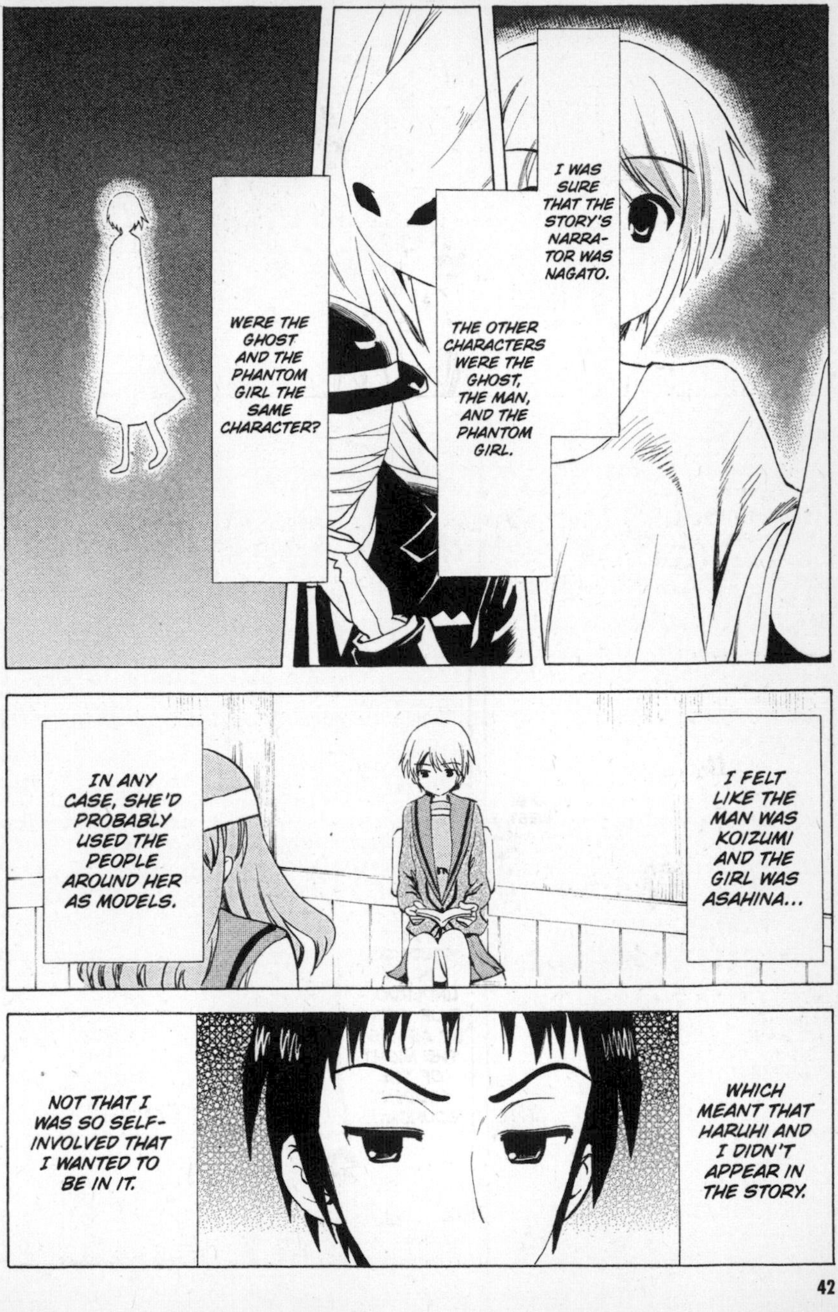
I WAS SURE THAT THE STORY'S NARRATOR WAS NAGATO.
THE OTHER CHARACTERS WERE THE GHOST, THE MAN, AND THE PHANTOM GIRL.
WERE THE GHOST AND THE PHANTOM GIRL THE SAME CHARACTER?
I FELT LIKE THE MAN WAS KOIZUMI AND THE GIRL WAS ASAHINA...
IN ANY CASE, SHE'D PROBABLY USED THE PEOPLE AROUND HER AS MODELS.
WHICH MEANT THAT HARUHI AND I DIDN'T APPEAR IN THE STORY.
NOT THAT I WAS SO SELF-INVOLVED THAT I WANTED TO BE IN IT.

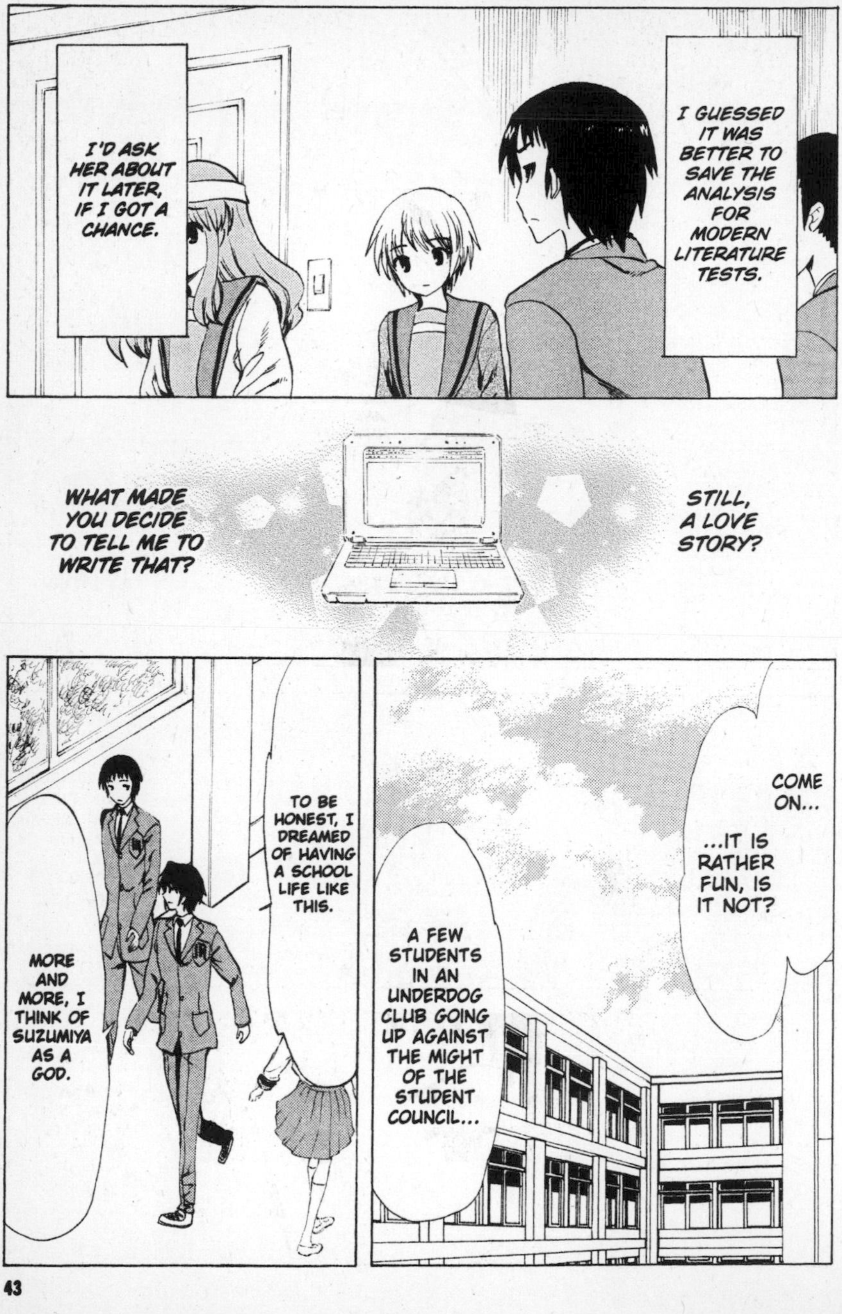
I GUESSED IT WAS BETTER TO SAVE THE ANALYSIS FOR MODERN LITERATURE TESTS.
I'D ASK HER ABOUT IT LATER, IF I GOT A CHANCE.
STILL, A LOVE STORY?
WHAT MADE YOU DECIDE TO TELL ME TO WRITE THAT?
COME ON...
...IT IS RATHER FUN, IS IT NOT?
A FEW STUDENTS IN AN UNDERDOG CLUB GOING UP AGAINST THE MIGHT OF THE STUDENT COUNCIL...
TO BE HONEST, I DREAMED OF HAVING A SCHOOL LIFE LIKE THIS.
MORE AND MORE, I THINK OF SUZUMIYA AS A GOD.

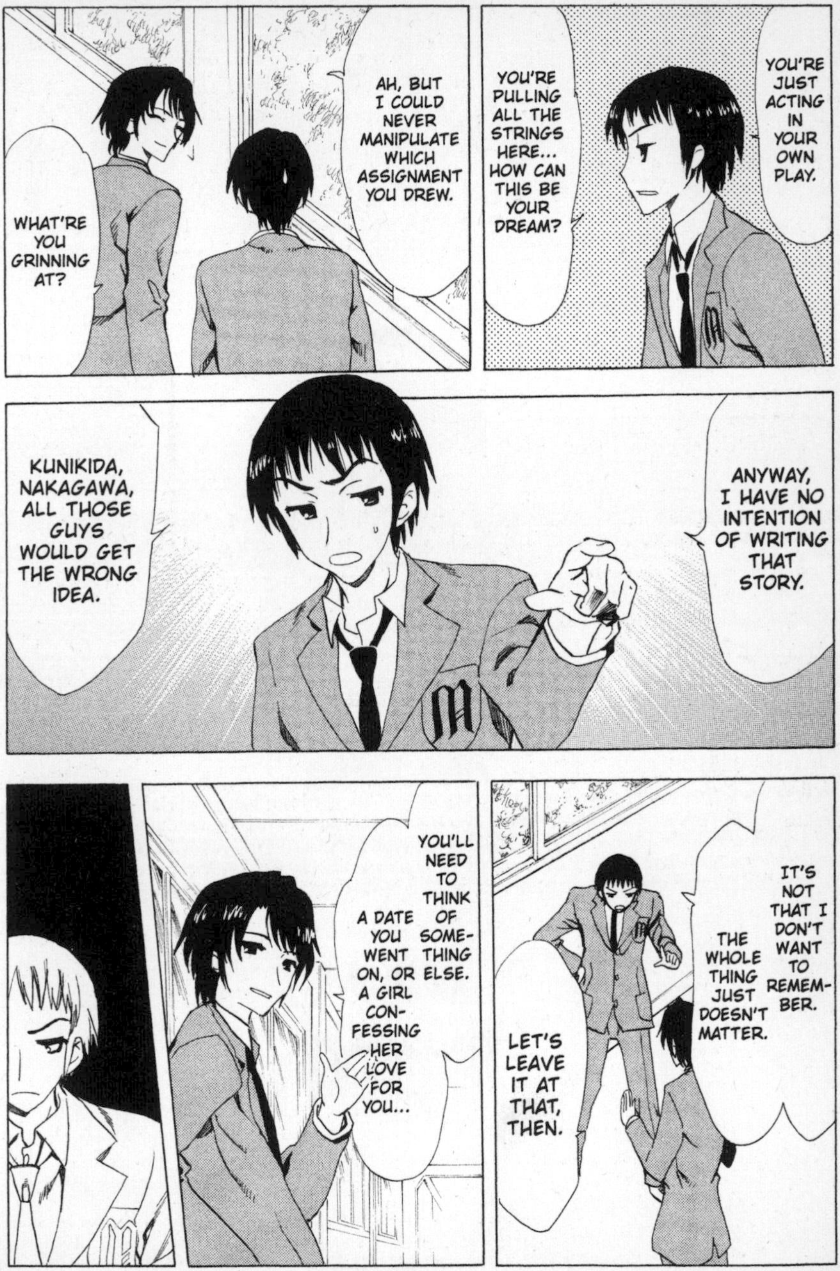
YOU'RE JUST ACTING IN YOUR OWN PLAY.
YOU'RE PULLING ALL THE STRINGS HERE... HOW CAN THIS BE YOUR DREAM?
AH, BUT I COULD NEVER MANIPULATE WHICH ASSIGNMENT YOU DREW.
WHAT'RE YOU GRINNING AT?
ANYWAY, I HAVE NO INTENTION OF WRITING THAT STORY.
KUNIKIDA, NAKAGAWA, ALL THOSE GUYS WOULD GET THE WRONG IDEA.
IT'S NOT THAT I DON'T WANT TO REMEM-BER.
THE WHOLE THING JUST DOESN'T MATTER.
LET'S LEAVE IT AT THAT, THEN.
YOU'LL NEED TO THINK OF SOME-THING ELSE.
A DATE YOU WENT ON, OR A GIRL CON-FESSING HER LOVE FOR YOU...

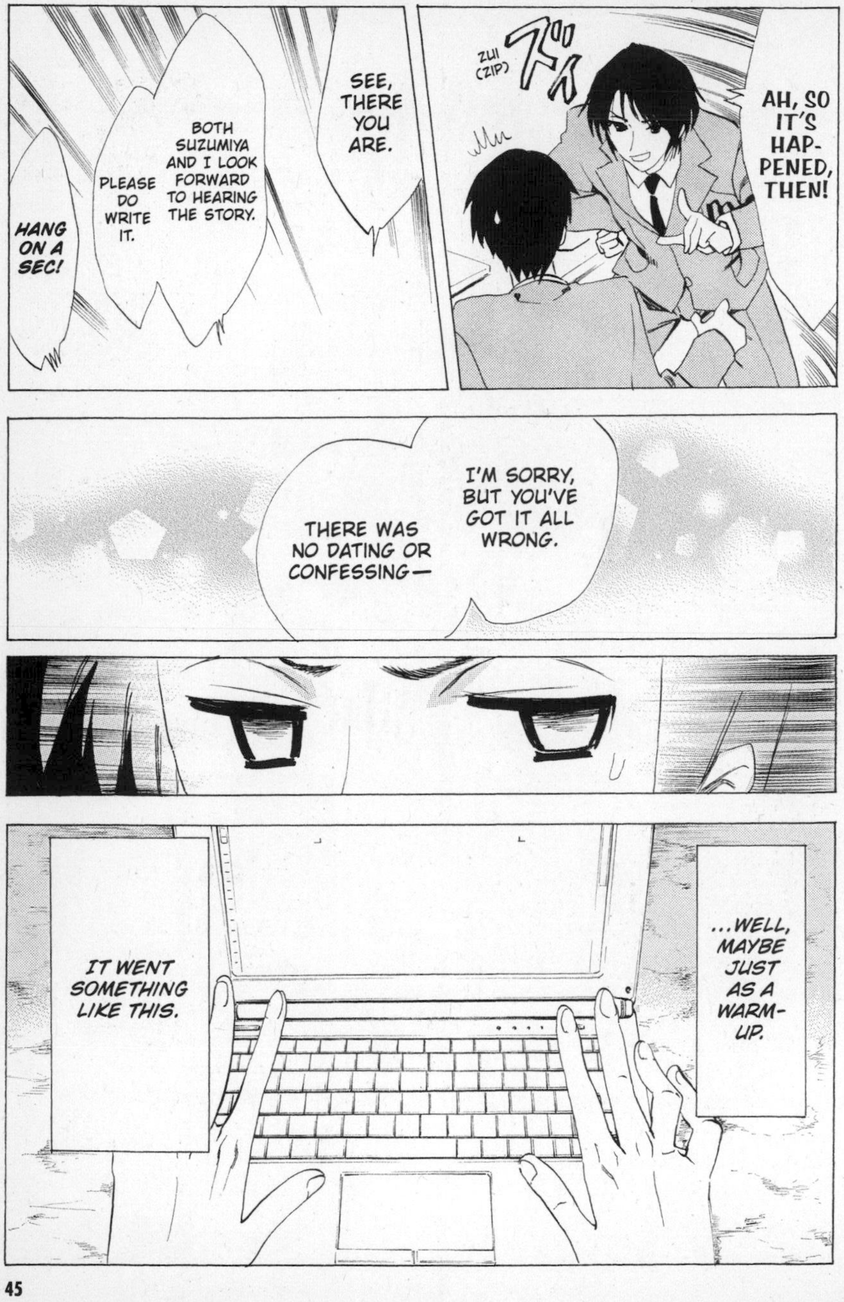
ZUI (ZIP)
AH, SO IT'S HAPPENED, THEN!
SEE, THERE YOU ARE.
BOTH SUZUMIYA AND I LOOK FORWARD TO HEARING THE STORY.
PLEASE DO WRITE IT.
HANG ON A SEC!
I'M SORRY, BUT YOU'VE GOT IT ALL WRONG.
THERE WAS NO DATING OR CONFESSING—
...WELL, MAYBE JUST AS A WARM-UP.
IT WENT SOMETHING LIKE THIS.

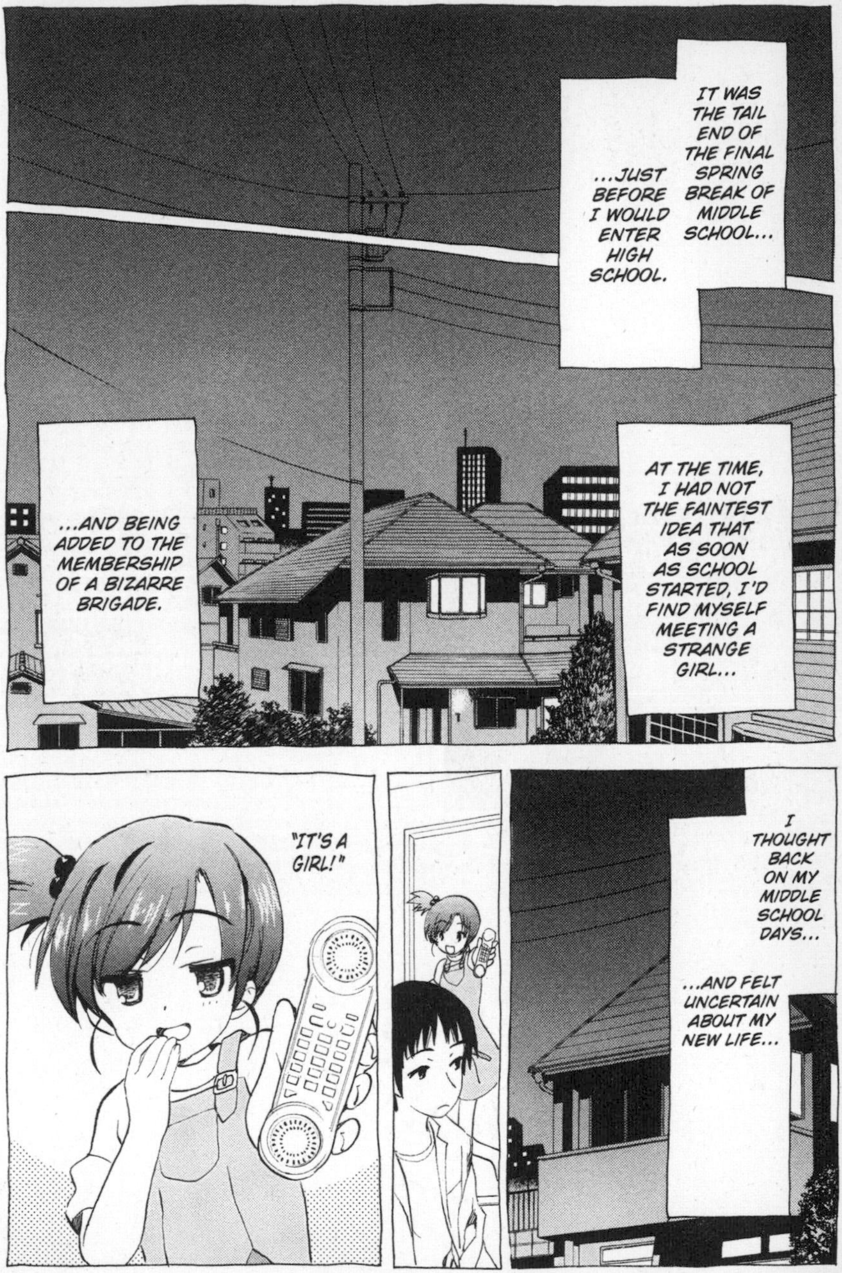
IT WAS THE TAIL END OF THE FINAL SPRING BREAK OF MIDDLE SCHOOL...
...JUST BEFORE I WOULD ENTER HIGH SCHOOL.
AT THE TIME, I HAD NOT THE FAINTEST IDEA THAT AS SOON AS SCHOOL STARTED, I'D FIND MYSELF MEETING A STRANGE GIRL...
...AND BEING ADDED TO THE MEMBERSHIP OF A BIZARRE BRIGADE.
I THOUGHT BACK ON MY MIDDLE SCHOOL DAYS...
...AND FELT UNCERTAIN ABOUT MY NEW LIFE...
"IT'S A GIRL!"

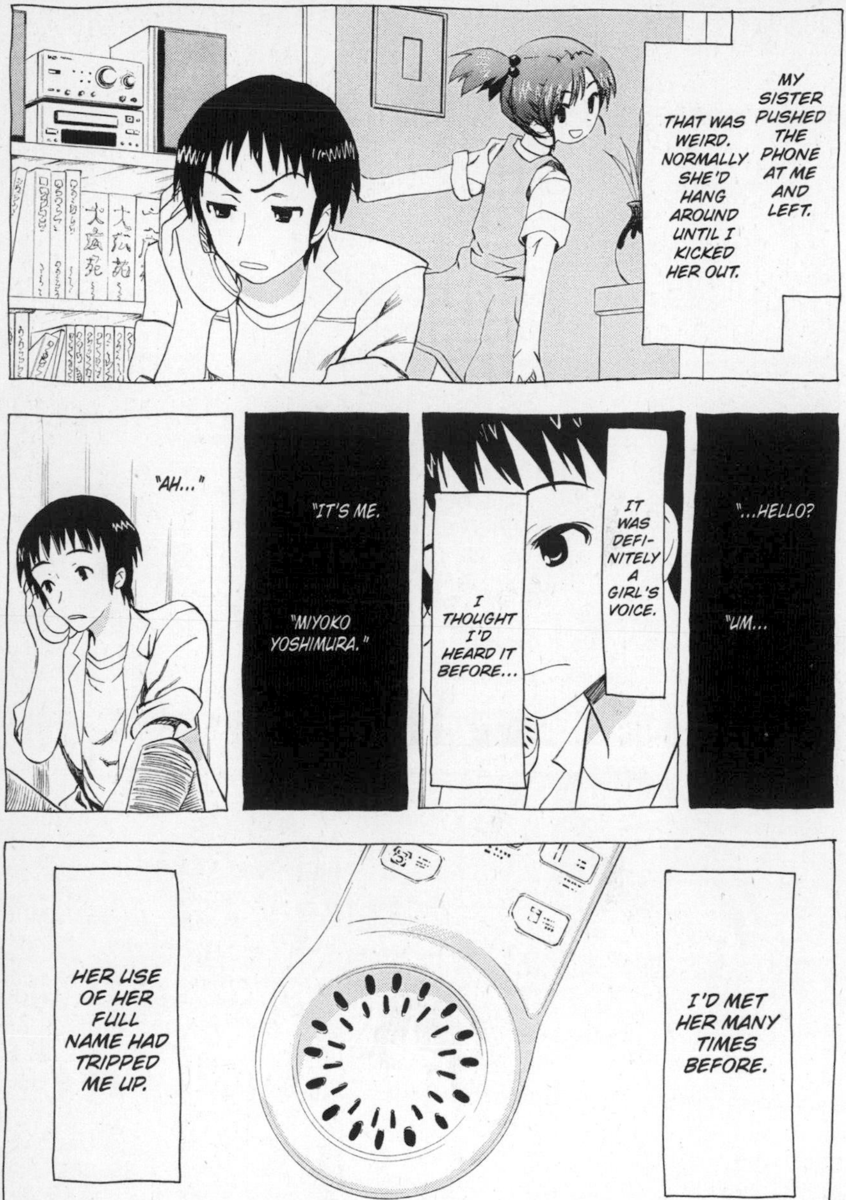
MY SISTER PUSHED THE PHONE AT ME AND LEFT.
THAT WAS WEIRD. NORMALLY SHE'D HANG AROUND UNTIL I KICKED HER OUT.
"...HELLO?
"UM...
IT WAS DEFI-NITELY A GIRL'S VOICE.
I THOUGHT I'D HEARD IT BEFORE...
"IT'S ME.
"MIYOKO YOSHIMURA."
"AH..."
I'D MET HER MANY TIMES BEFORE.
HER USE OF HER FULL NAME HAD TRIPPED ME UP.

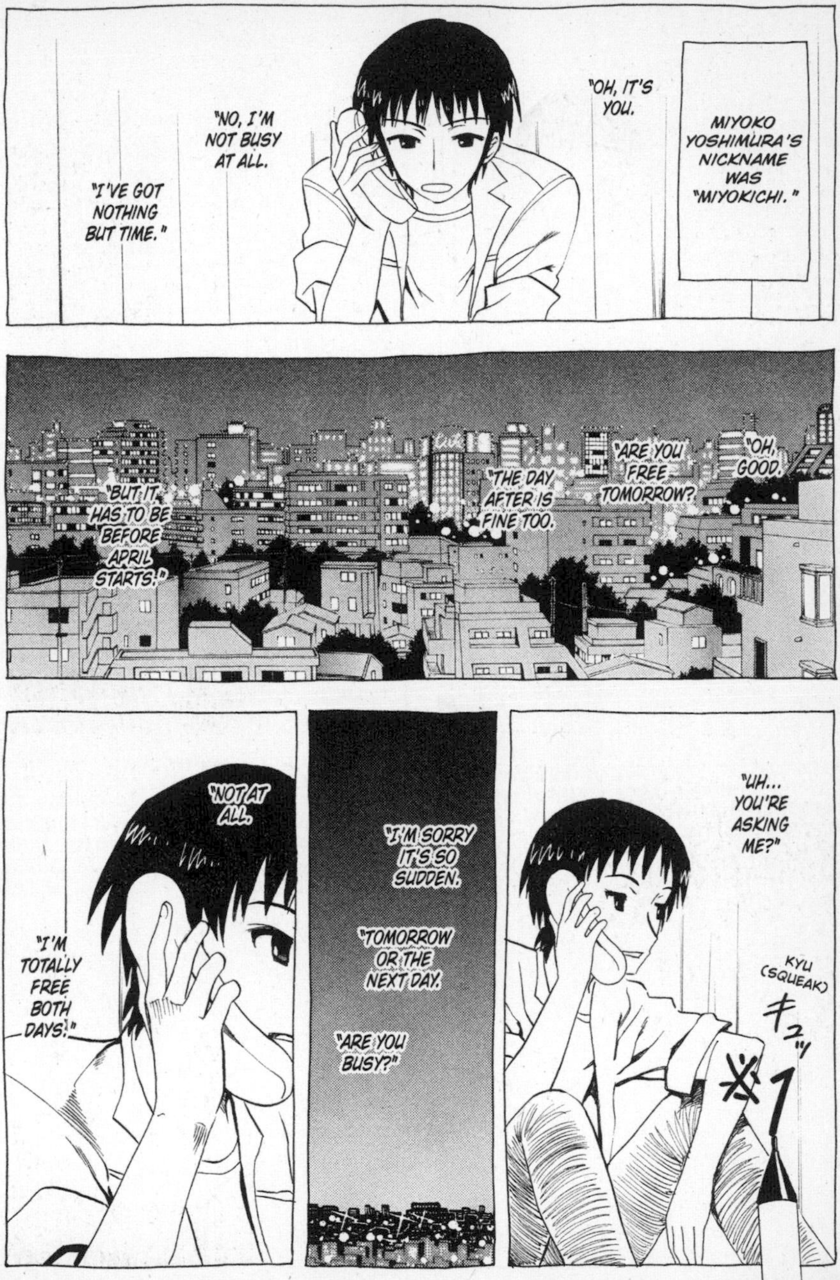
MIYOKO YOSHIMURA'S NICKNAME WAS "MIYOKICHI."
"OH, IT'S YOU.
"NO, I'M NOT BUSY AT ALL.
"I'VE GOT NOTHING BUT TIME."
"OH, GOOD.
"ARE YOU FREE TOMORROW?
"THE DAY AFTER IS FINE TOO.
"BUT IT HAS TO BE BEFORE APRIL STARTS."
"UH... YOU'RE ASKING ME?"
KYU (SQUEAK)
キュッ
※1
"I'M SORRY IT'S SO SUDDEN.
"TOMORROW OR THE NEXT DAY.
"ARE YOU BUSY?"
"NOT AT ALL.
"I'M TOTALLY FREE BOTH DAYS."

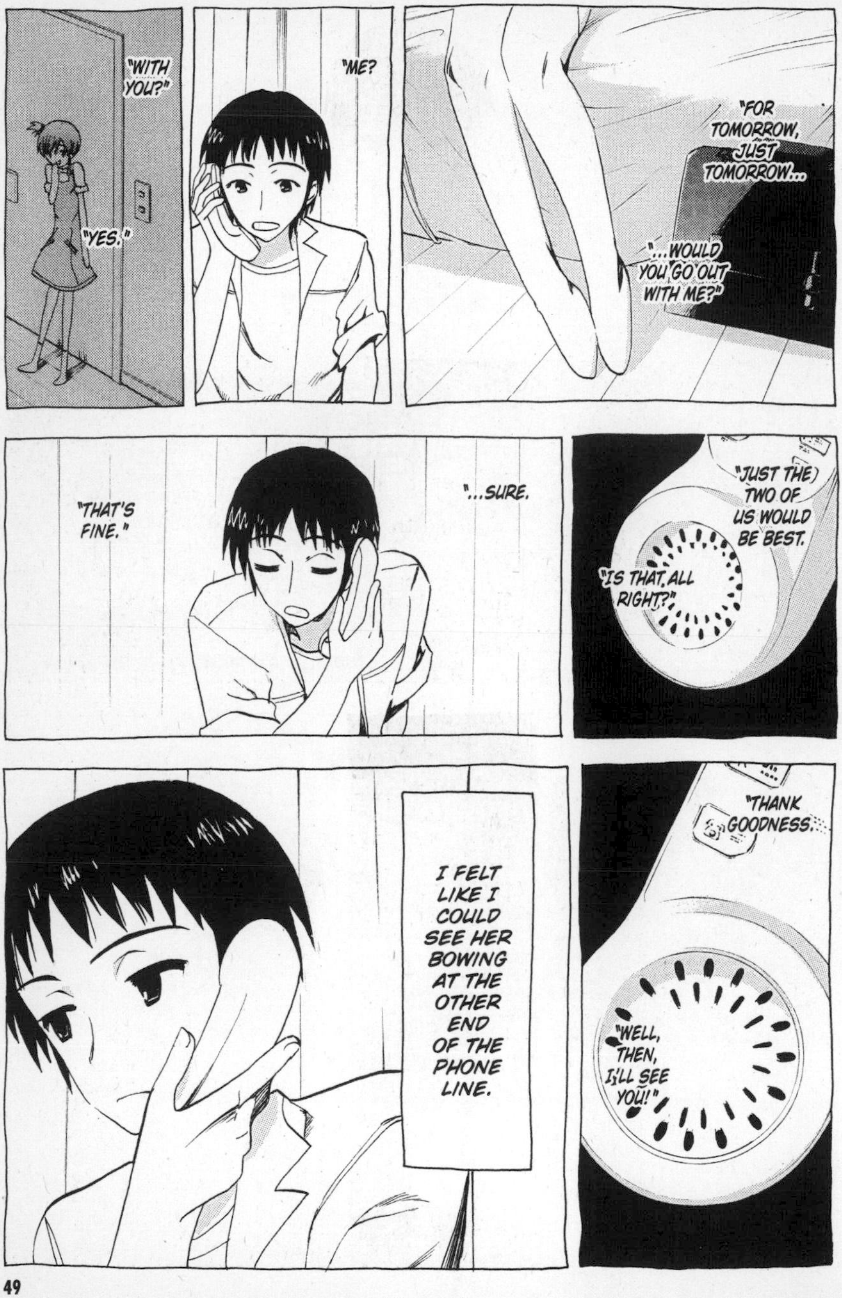
"FOR TOMORROW, JUST TOMORROW...
"...WOULD YOU GO OUT WITH ME?"
"ME?
"WITH YOU?"
"YES."
"JUST THE TWO OF US WOULD BE BEST.
"IS THAT ALL RIGHT?"
"...SURE.
"THAT'S FINE."
"THANK GOODNESS.
"WELL, THEN, I'LL SEE YOU!"
I FELT LIKE I COULD SEE HER BOWING AT THE OTHER END OF THE PHONE LINE.

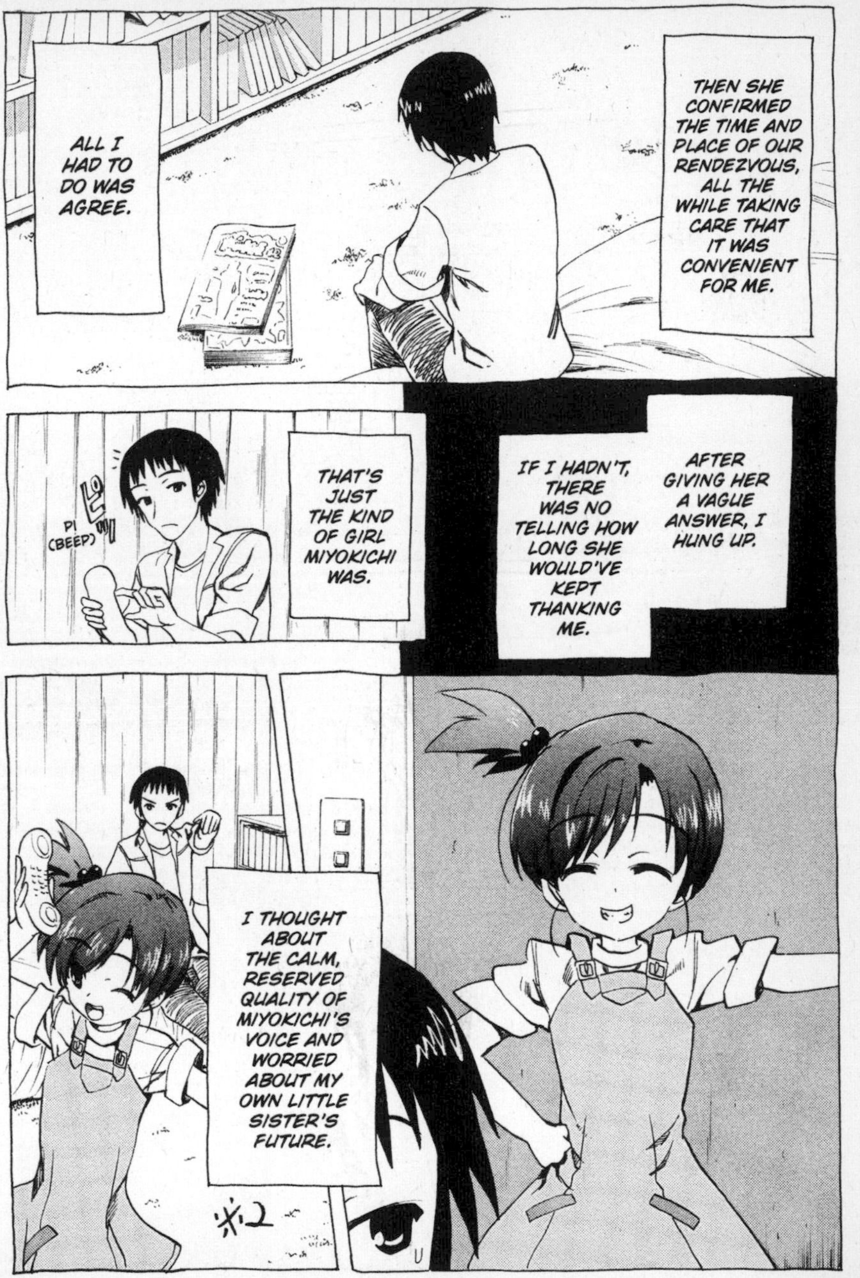
THEN SHE CONFIRMED THE TIME AND PLACE OF OUR RENDEZVOUS, ALL THE WHILE TAKING CARE THAT IT WAS CONVENIENT FOR ME.
ALL I HAD TO DO WAS AGREE.
AFTER GIVING HER A VAGUE ANSWER, I HUNG UP.
IF I HADN'T, THERE WAS NO TELLING HOW LONG SHE WOULD'VE KEPT THANKING ME.
THAT'S JUST THE KIND OF GIRL MIYOKICHI WAS.
PI (BEEP)
I THOUGHT ABOUT THE CALM, RESERVED QUALITY OF MIYOKICHI'S VOICE AND WORRIED ABOUT MY OWN LITTLE SISTER'S FUTURE.
※2

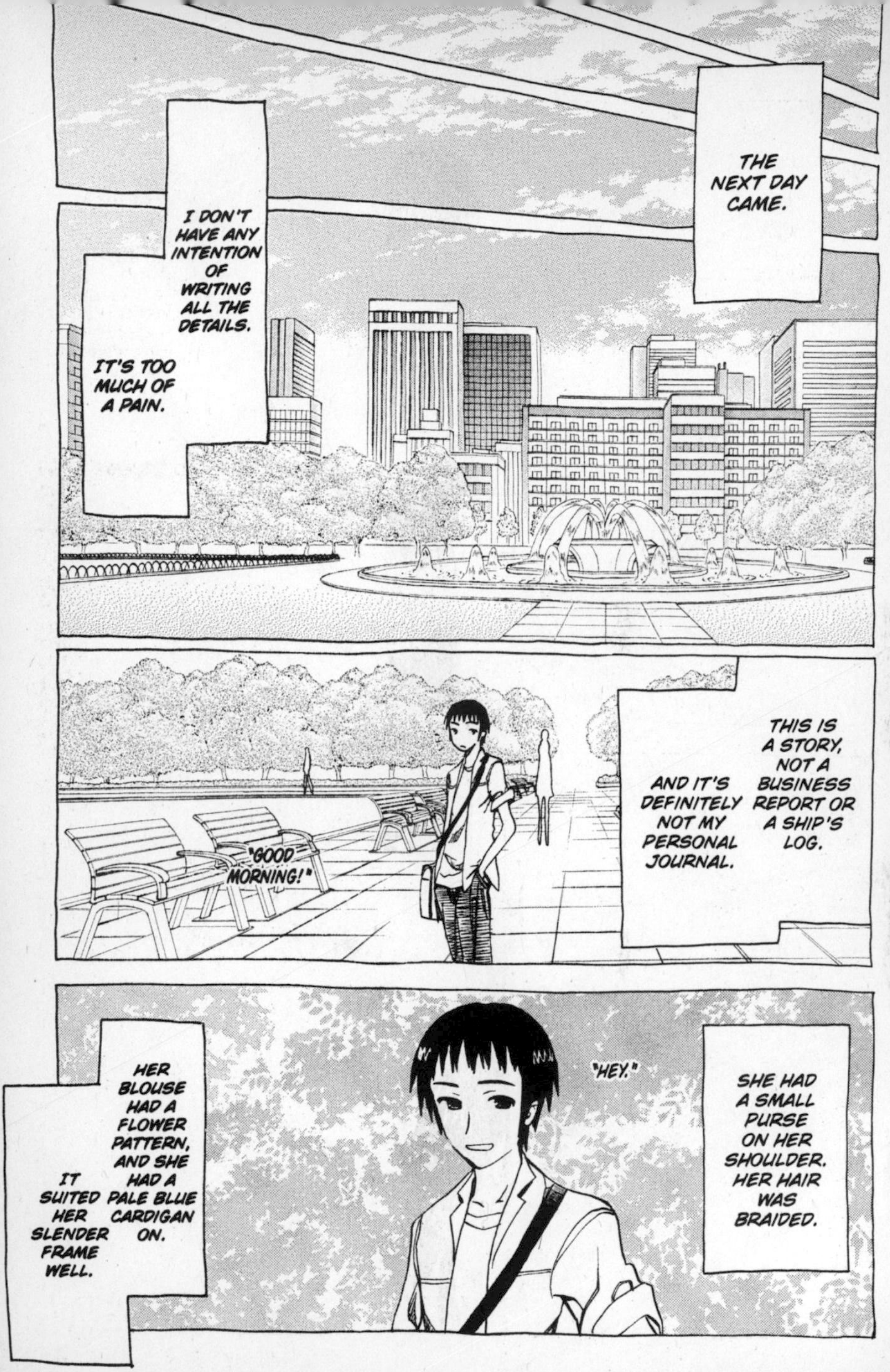
THE NEXT DAY CAME.
I DON'T HAVE ANY INTENTION OF WRITING ALL THE DETAILS.
IT'S TOO MUCH OF A PAIN.
THIS IS A STORY, NOT A BUSINESS REPORT OR A SHIP'S LOG.
AND IT'S DEFINITELY NOT MY PERSONAL JOURNAL.
"GOOD MORNING!"
SHE HAD A SMALL PURSE ON HER SHOULDER. HER HAIR WAS BRAIDED.
"HEY."
HER BLOUSE HAD A FLOWER PATTERN, AND SHE HAD A PALE BLUE CARDIGAN ON.
IT SUITED HER SLENDER FRAME WELL.

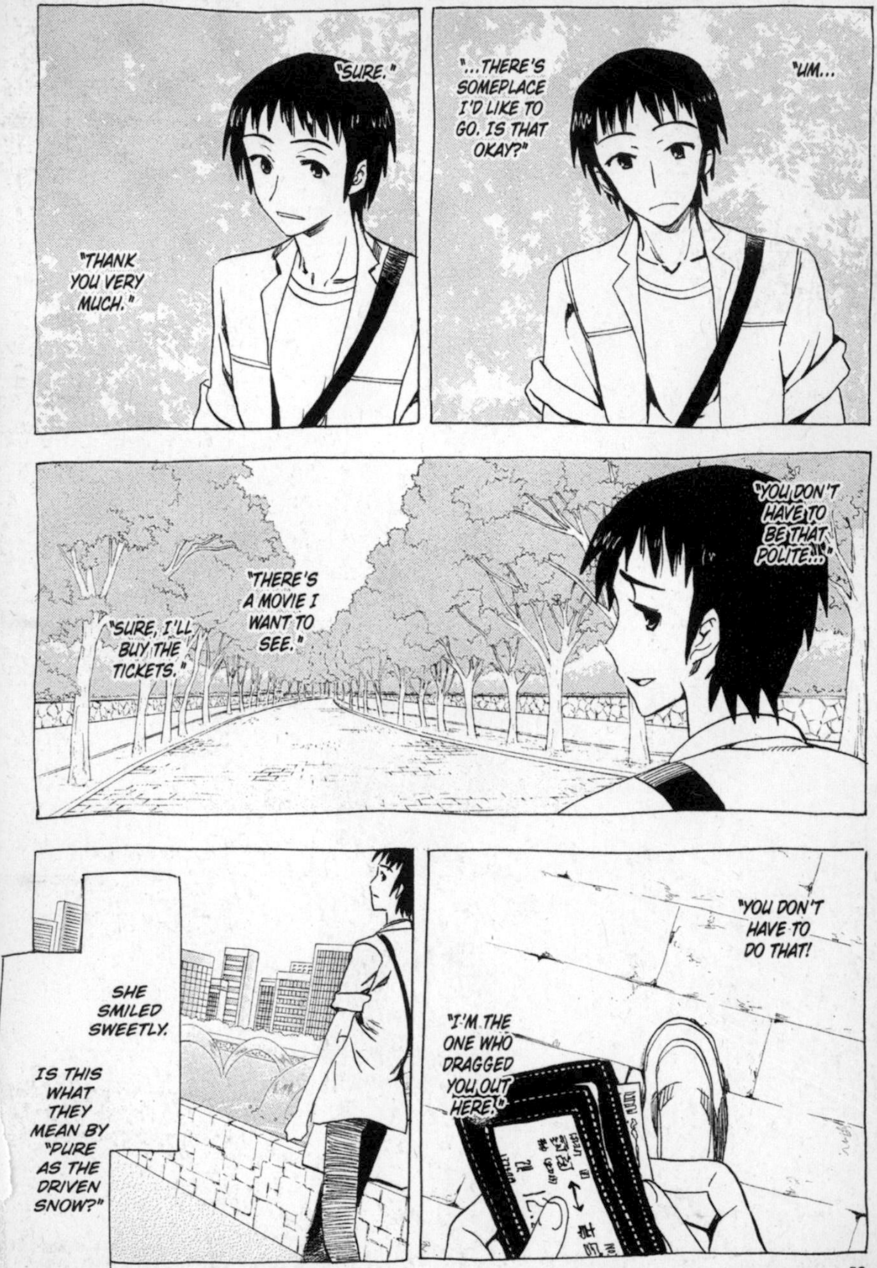
"UM...
"...THERE'S SOMEPLACE I'D LIKE TO GO. IS THAT OKAY?"
"SURE."
"THANK YOU VERY MUCH."
"YOU DON'T HAVE TO BE THAT POLITE..."
"THERE'S A MOVIE I WANT TO SEE."
"SURE, I'LL BUY THE TICKETS."
"YOU DON'T HAVE TO DO THAT!
"I'M THE ONE WHO DRAGGED YOU OUT HERE."
SHE SMILED SWEETLY.
IS THIS WHAT THEY MEAN BY "PURE AS THE DRIVEN SNOW?"

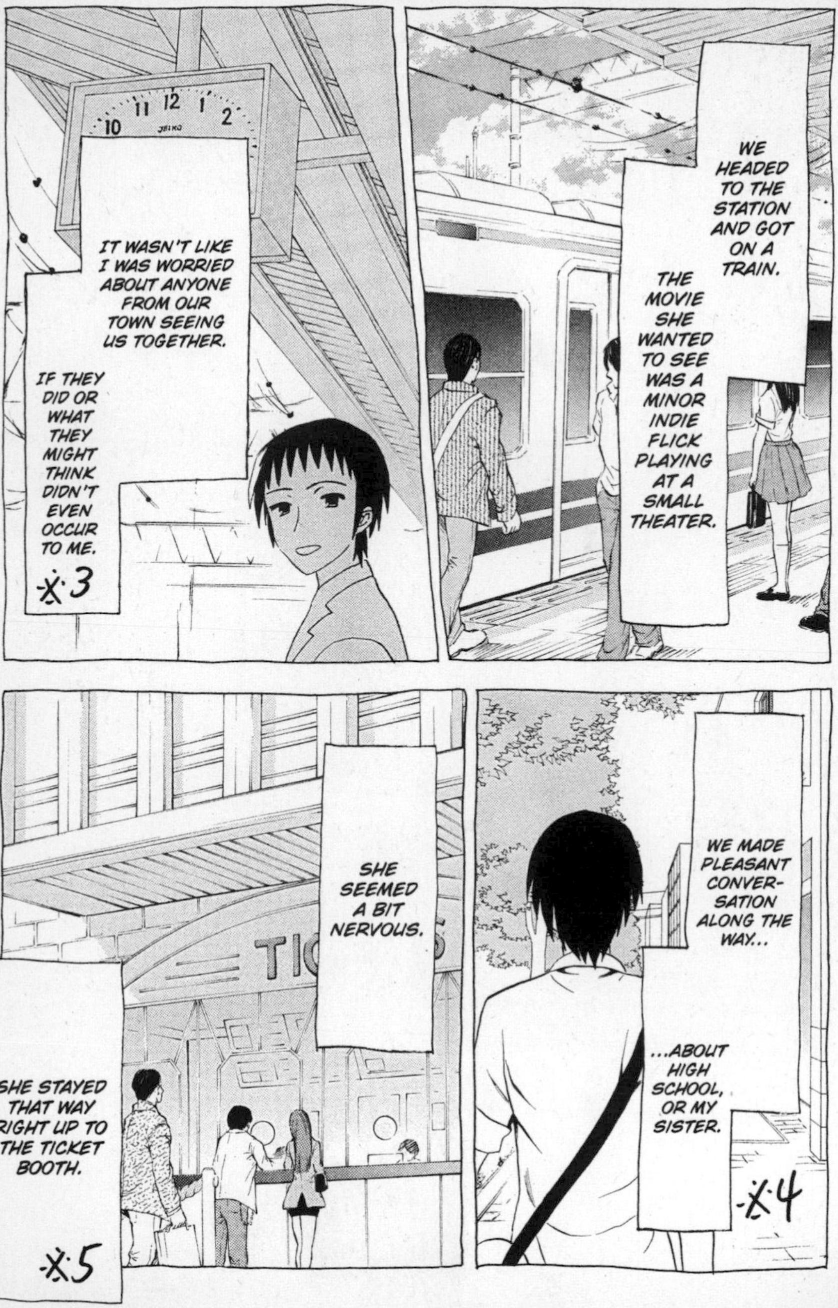
WE HEADED TO THE STATION AND GOT ON A TRAIN.
THE MOVIE SHE WANTED TO SEE WAS A MINOR INDIE FLICK PLAYING AT A SMALL THEATER.
IT WASN'T LIKE I WAS WORRIED ABOUT ANYONE FROM OUR TOWN SEEING US TOGETHER.
IF THEY DID OR WHAT THEY MIGHT THINK DIDN'T EVEN OCCUR TO ME.
※3
WE MADE PLEASANT CONVERSATION ALONG THE WAY...
...ABOUT HIGH SCHOOL, OR MY SISTER.
※4
SHE SEEMED A BIT NERVOUS.
SHE STAYED THAT WAY RIGHT UP TO THE TICKET BOOTH.
※5

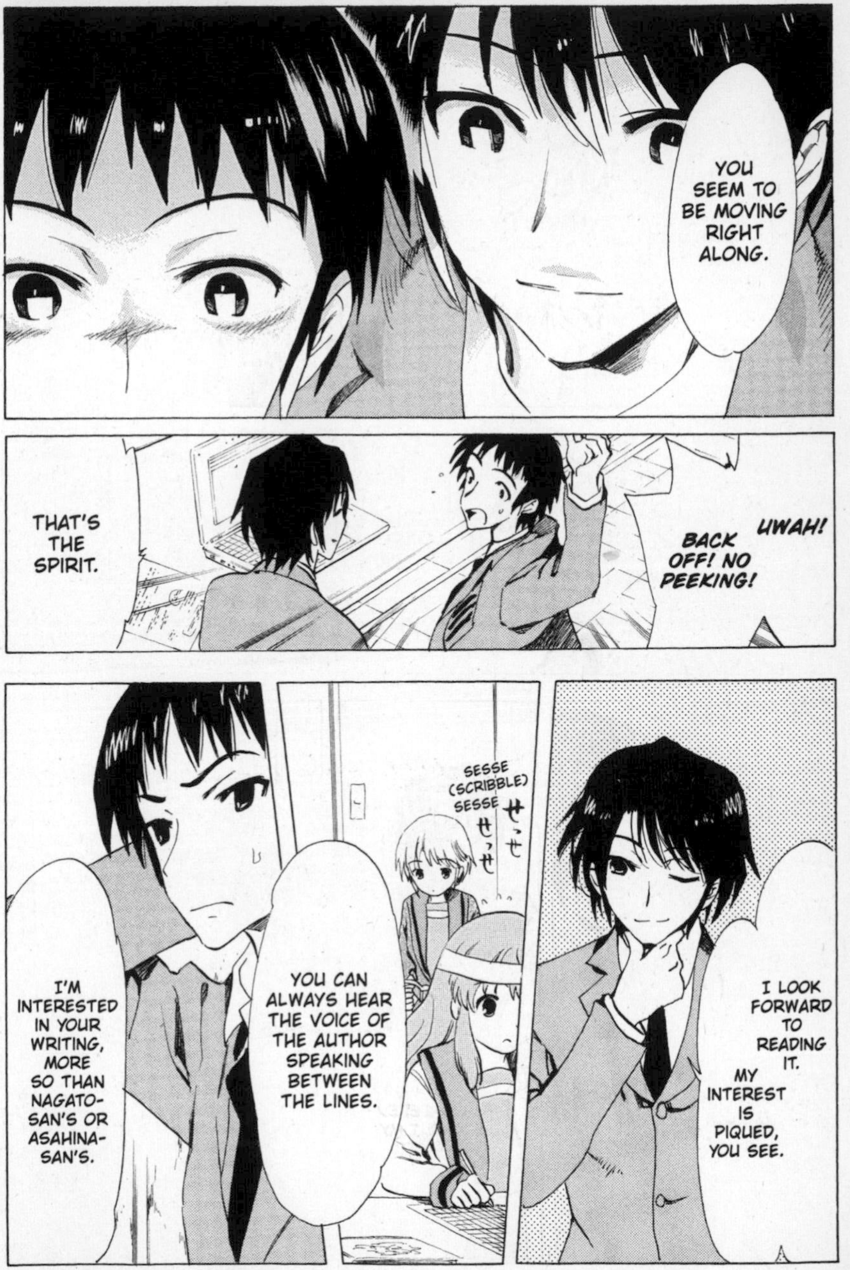
YOU SEEM TO BE MOVING RIGHT ALONG.
UWAH!
BACK OFF! NO PEEKING!
THAT'S THE SPIRIT.
I LOOK FORWARD TO READING IT.
MY INTEREST IS PIQUED, YOU SEE.
SESSE (SCRIBBLE) SESSE
せっせ せっせ
YOU CAN ALWAYS HEAR THE VOICE OF THE AUTHOR SPEAKING BETWEEN THE LINES.
I'M INTERESTED IN YOUR WRITING, MORE SO THAN NAGATO-SAN'S OR ASAHINA-SAN'S.

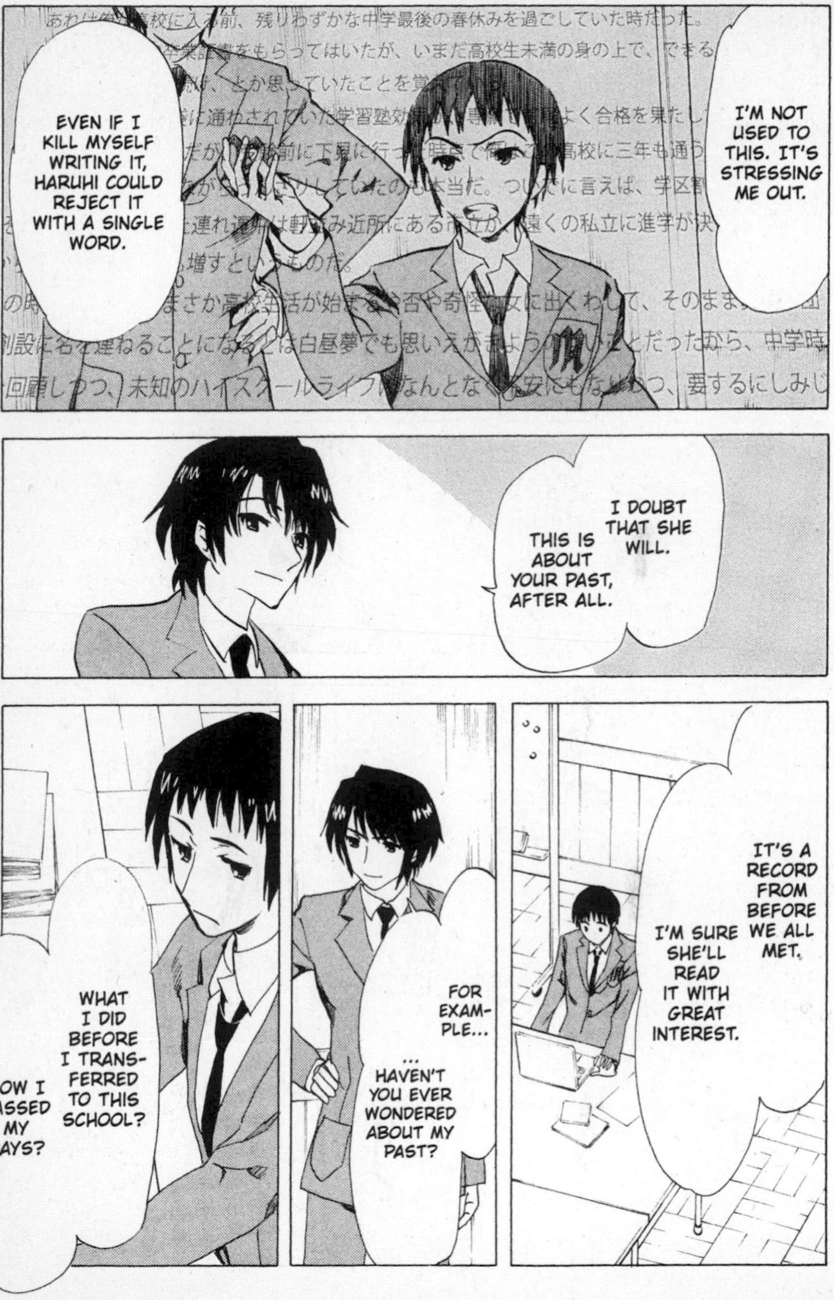
I'M NOT USED TO THIS. IT'S STRESSING ME OUT.
EVEN IF I KILL MYSELF WRITING IT, HARUHI COULD REJECT IT WITH A SINGLE WORD.
I DOUBT THAT SHE WILL.
THIS IS ABOUT YOUR PAST, AFTER ALL.
IT'S A RECORD FROM BEFORE WE ALL MET.
I'M SURE SHE'LL READ IT WITH GREAT INTEREST.
FOR EXAMPLE...
...HAVEN'T YOU EVER WONDERED ABOUT MY PAST?
WHAT I DID BEFORE I TRANSFERRED TO THIS SCHOOL?
HOW I PASSED MY DAYS?

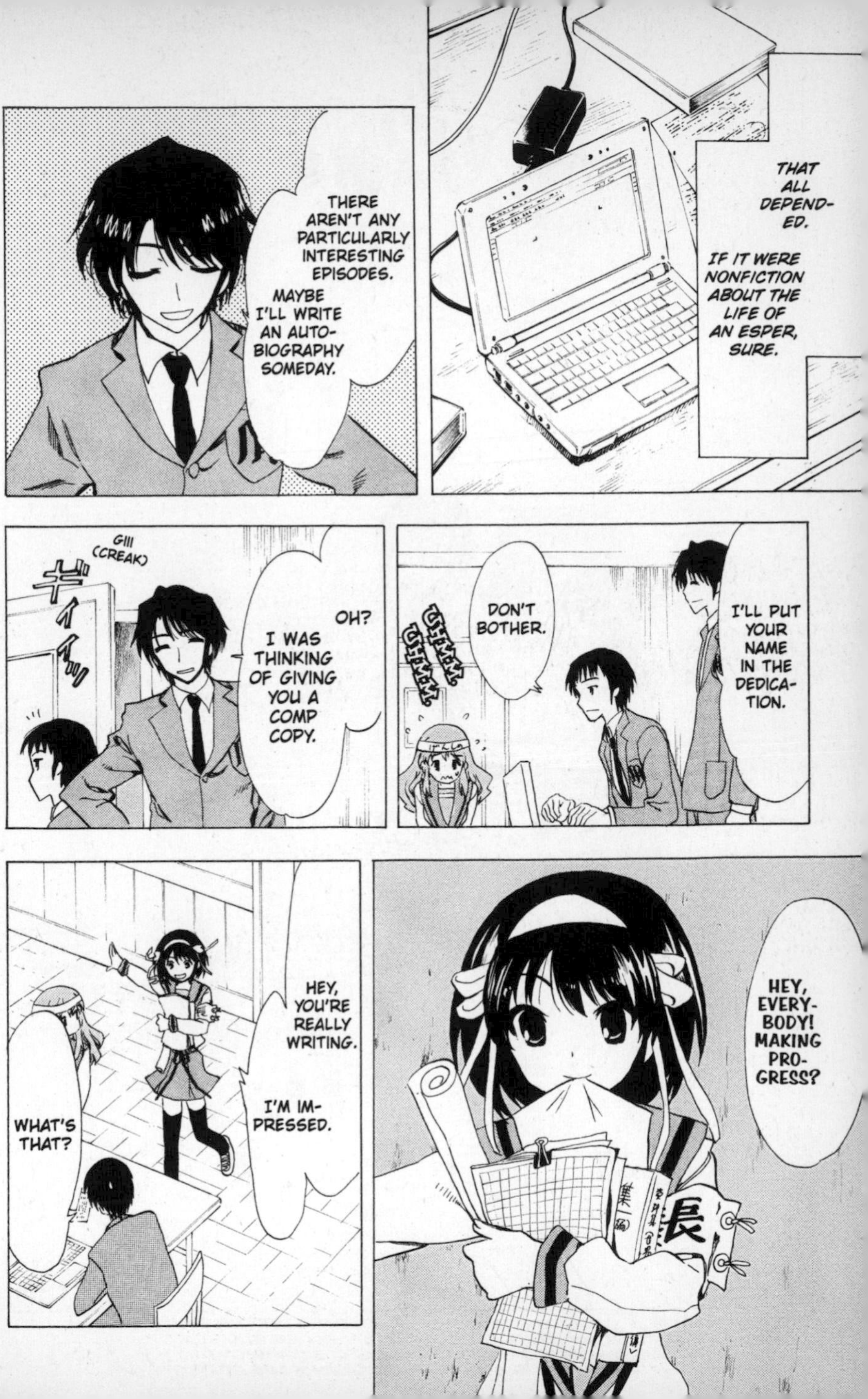
THAT ALL DEPEND-ED.
IF IT WERE NONFICTION ABOUT THE LIFE OF AN ESPER, SURE.
THERE AREN'T ANY PARTICULARLY INTERESTING EPISODES.
MAYBE I'LL WRITE AN AUTO-BIOGRAPHY SOMEDAY.
I'LL PUT YOUR NAME IN THE DEDICA-TION.
DON'T BOTHER.
GIII (CREAK)
OH?
I WAS THINKING OF GIVING YOU A COMP COPY.
HEY, EVERY-BODY! MAKING PRO-GRESS?
HEY, YOU'RE REALLY WRITING.
I'M IM-PRESSED.
WHAT'S THAT?

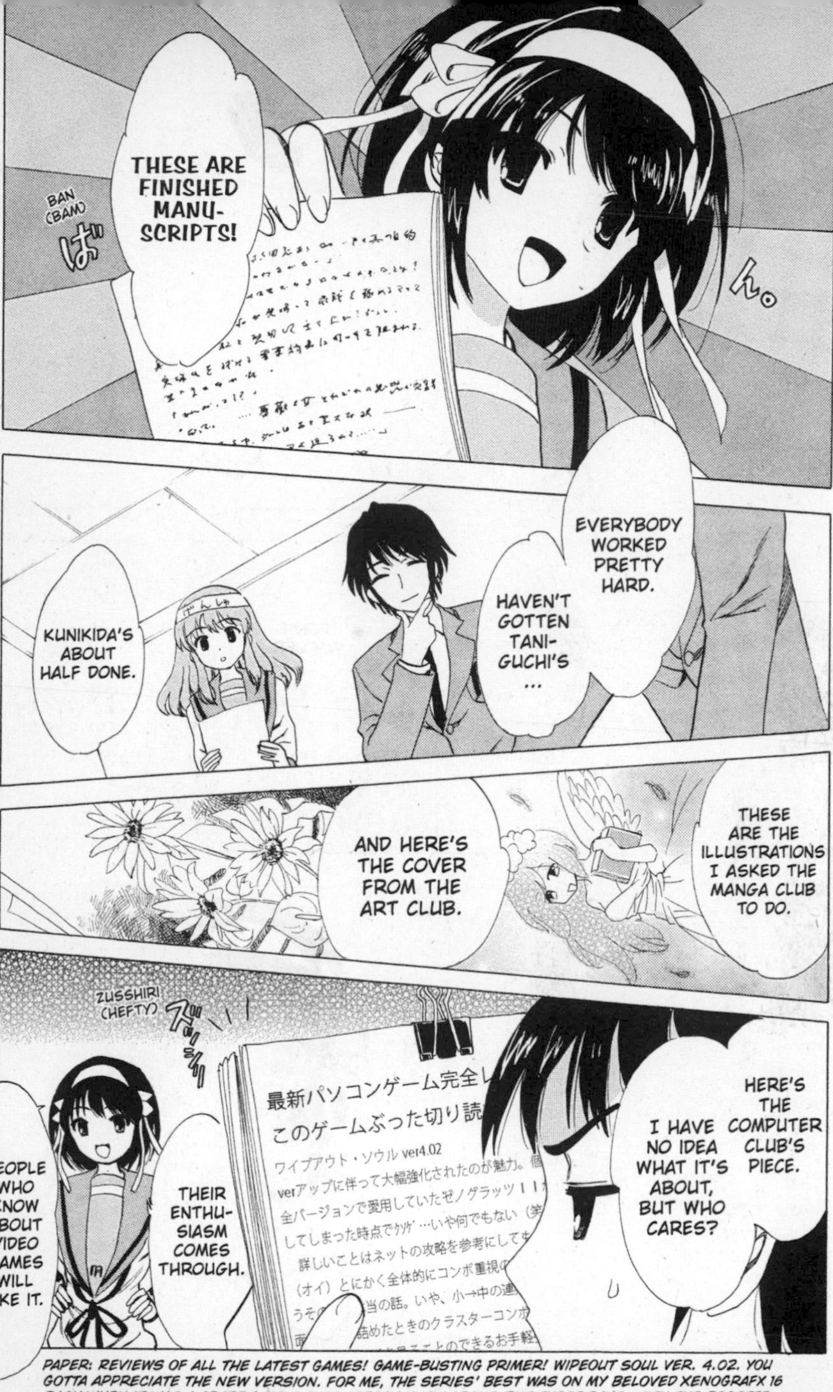
ん。
THESE ARE FINISHED MANU-SCRIPTS!
BAN (BAM)
ば
EVERYBODY WORKED PRETTY HARD.
HAVEN'T GOTTEN TANI-GUCHI'S ...
KUNIKIDA'S ABOUT HALF DONE.
THESE ARE THE ILLUSTRATIONS I ASKED THE MANGA CLUB TO DO.
AND HERE'S THE COVER FROM THE ART CLUB.
ZUSSHIRI (HEFTY)
ズッシリ
HERE'S THE COMPUTER CLUB'S PIECE.
I HAVE NO IDEA WHAT IT'S ABOUT, BUT WHO CARES?
最新パソコンゲーム完全レ
このゲームぶった切り読
ワイプアウト・ソウル ver4.02
THEIR ENTHU-SIASM COMES THROUGH.
PEOPLE WHO KNOW ABOUT VIDEO GAMES WILL LIKE IT.

PAPER: REVIEWS OF ALL THE LATEST GAMES! GAME-BUSTING PRIMER! WIPEOUT SOUL VER. 4.02. YOU GOTTA APPRECIATE THE NEW VERSION. FOR ME, THE SERIES' BEST WAS ON MY BELOVED XENOGRAFX 16 BACK WHEN IT WAS A CRAPPY TITLE THAT NOBODY KNEW ABOUT. BUT THESE DAYS, WITH THE BOOSTED POLY COUNT AND PIXEL SHADERS YOU GET WITH A DECENT GRAPHICS CARD, IT'S PRETTY BADASS...

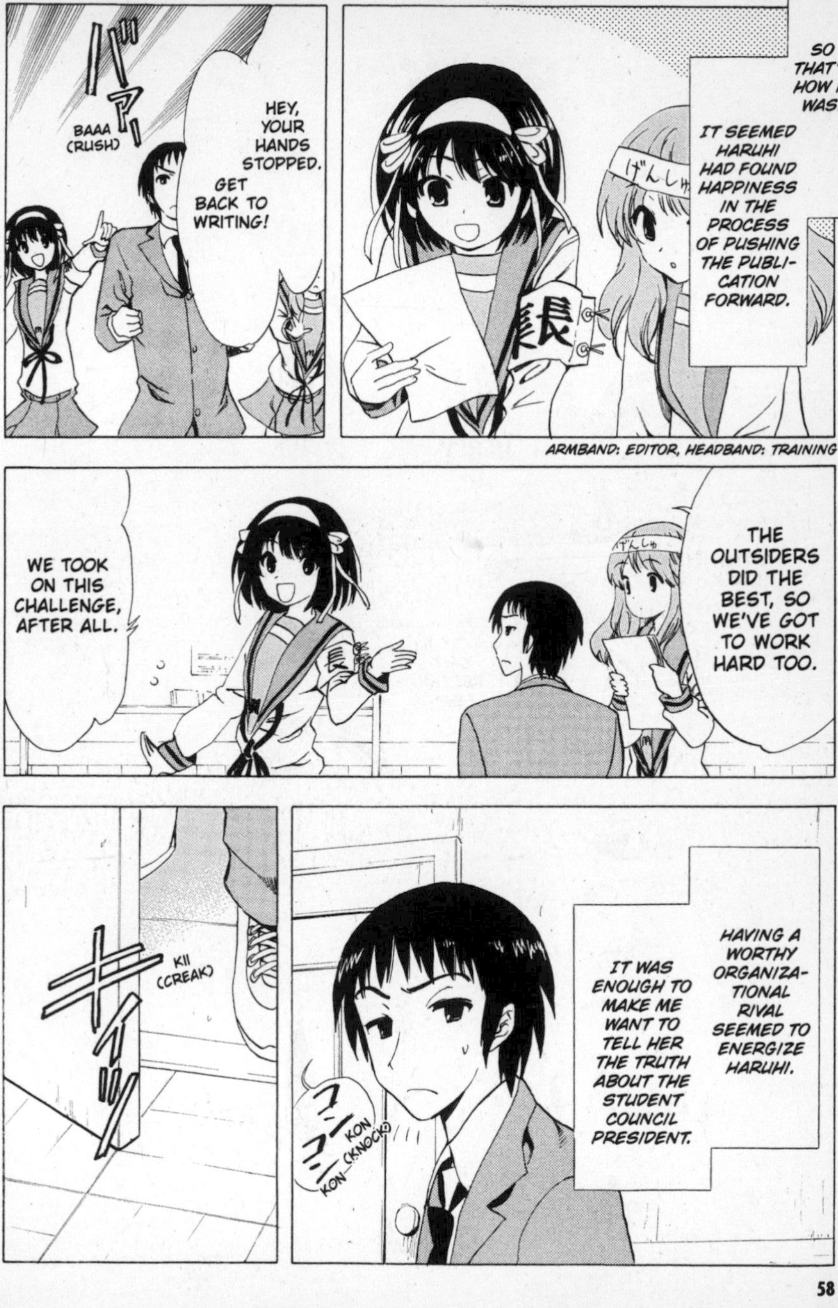
SO THAT'S HOW IT WAS.
IT SEEMED HARUHI HAD FOUND HAPPINESS IN THE PROCESS OF PUSHING THE PUBLICATION FORWARD.
ARMBAND: EDITOR, HEADBAND: TRAINING
HEY, YOUR HANDS STOPPED.
GET BACK TO WRITING!
BAAA (RUSH)
THE OUTSIDERS DID THE BEST, SO WE'VE GOT TO WORK HARD TOO.
WE TOOK ON THIS CHALLENGE, AFTER ALL.
HAVING A WORTHY ORGANIZATIONAL RIVAL SEEMED TO ENERGIZE HARUHI.
IT WAS ENOUGH TO MAKE ME WANT TO TELL HER THE TRUTH ABOUT THE STUDENT COUNCIL PRESIDENT.
KON KON (KNOCK)
KII (CREAK)

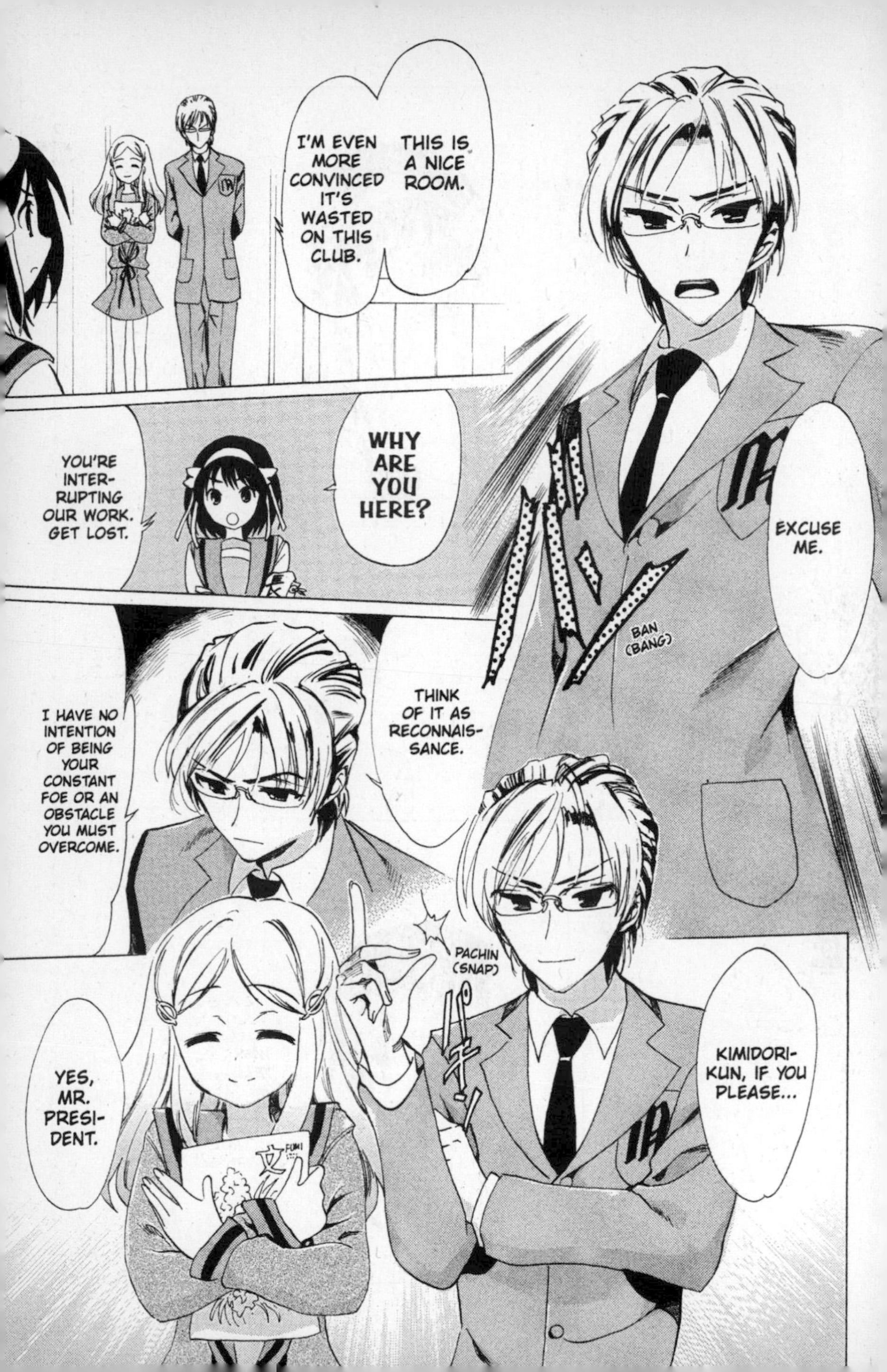
EXCUSE ME.
BAN (BANG)
THIS IS A NICE ROOM.
I'M EVEN MORE CONVINCED IT'S WASTED ON THIS CLUB.
WHY ARE YOU HERE?
YOU'RE INTER-RUPTING OUR WORK. GET LOST.
THINK OF IT AS RECONNAIS-SANCE.
I HAVE NO INTENTION OF BEING YOUR CONSTANT FOE OR AN OBSTACLE YOU MUST OVERCOME.
KIMIDORI-KUN, IF YOU PLEASE...
PACHIN (SNAP)
YES, MR. PRESI-DENT.

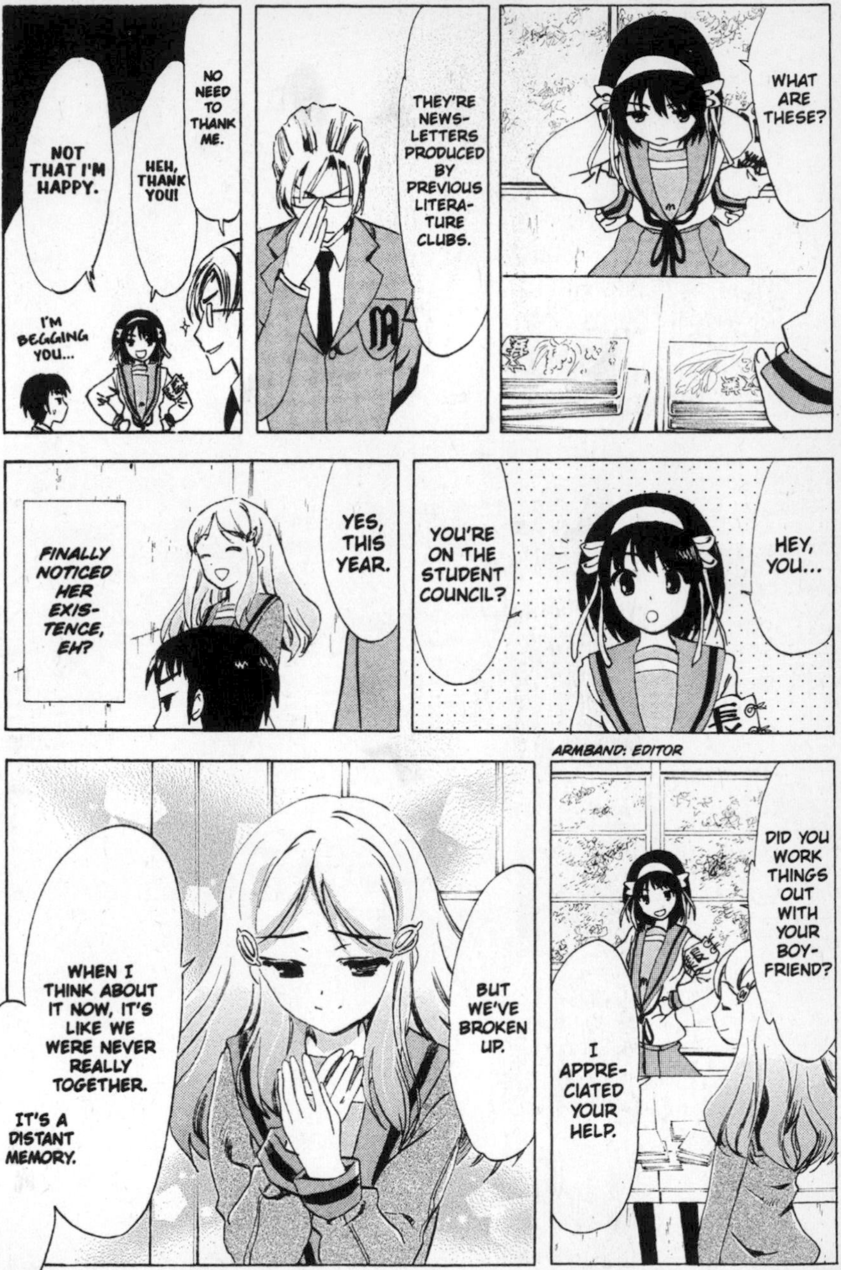
WHAT ARE THESE?
THEY'RE NEWS-LETTERS PRODUCED BY PREVIOUS LITERA-TURE CLUBS.
NO NEED TO THANK ME.
HEH, THANK YOU!
NOT THAT I'M HAPPY.
I'M BEGGING YOU...
HEY, YOU...
YOU'RE ON THE STUDENT COUNCIL?
ARMBAND: EDITOR
YES, THIS YEAR.
FINALLY NOTICED HER EXISTENCE, EH?
DID YOU WORK THINGS OUT WITH YOUR BOY-FRIEND?
I APPRECIATED YOUR HELP.
BUT WE'VE BROKEN UP.
WHEN I THINK ABOUT IT NOW, IT'S LIKE WE WERE NEVER REALLY TOGETHER.
IT'S A DISTANT MEMORY.

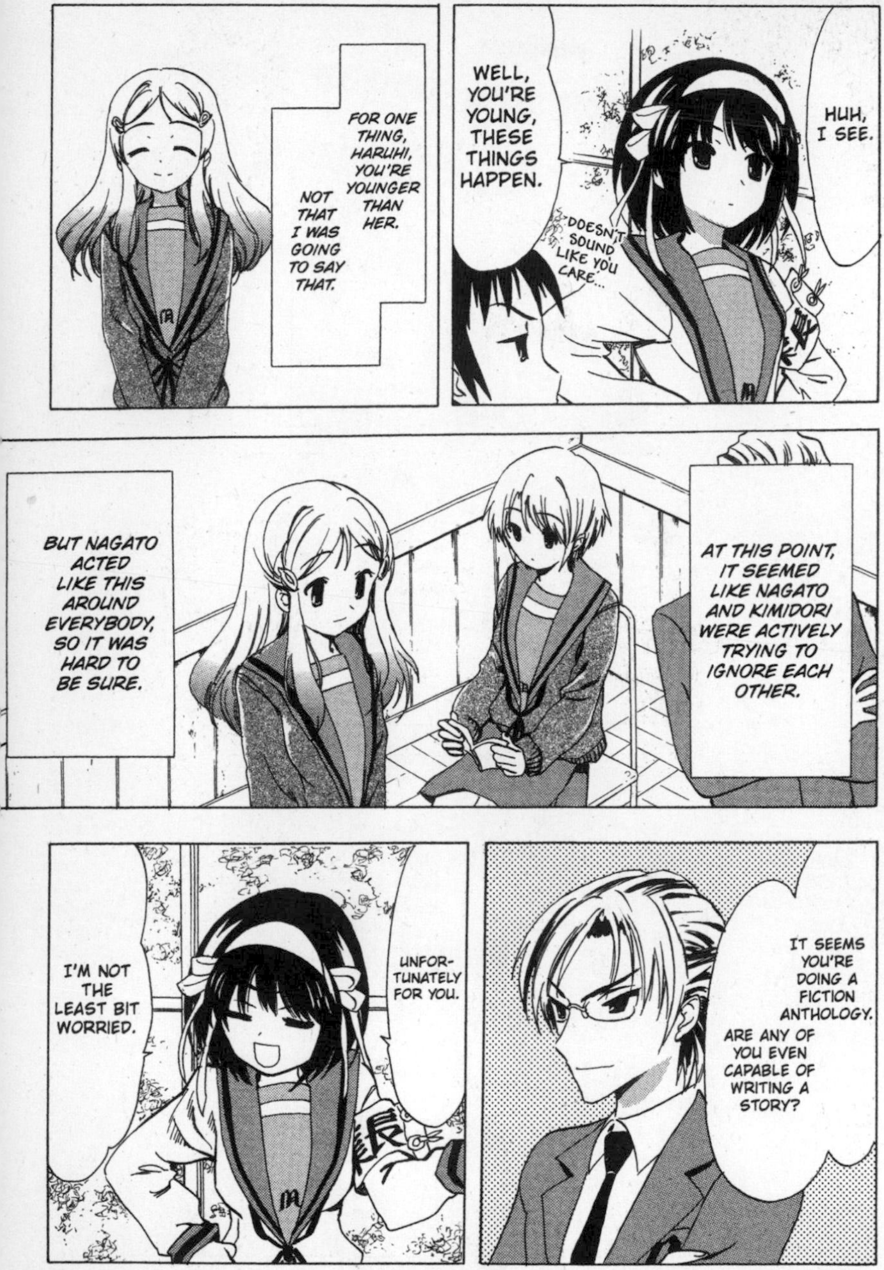
HUH, I SEE.
WELL, YOU'RE YOUNG, THESE THINGS HAPPEN.
DOESN'T SOUND LIKE YOU CARE...
FOR ONE THING, HARUHI, YOU'RE YOUNGER THAN HER.
NOT THAT I WAS GOING TO SAY THAT.
AT THIS POINT, IT SEEMED LIKE NAGATO AND KIMIDORI WERE ACTIVELY TRYING TO IGNORE EACH OTHER.
BUT NAGATO ACTED LIKE THIS AROUND EVERYBODY, SO IT WAS HARD TO BE SURE.
IT SEEMS YOU'RE DOING A FICTION ANTHOLOGY.
ARE ANY OF YOU EVEN CAPABLE OF WRITING A STORY?
UNFOR-TUNATELY FOR YOU.
I'M NOT THE LEAST BIT WORRIED.

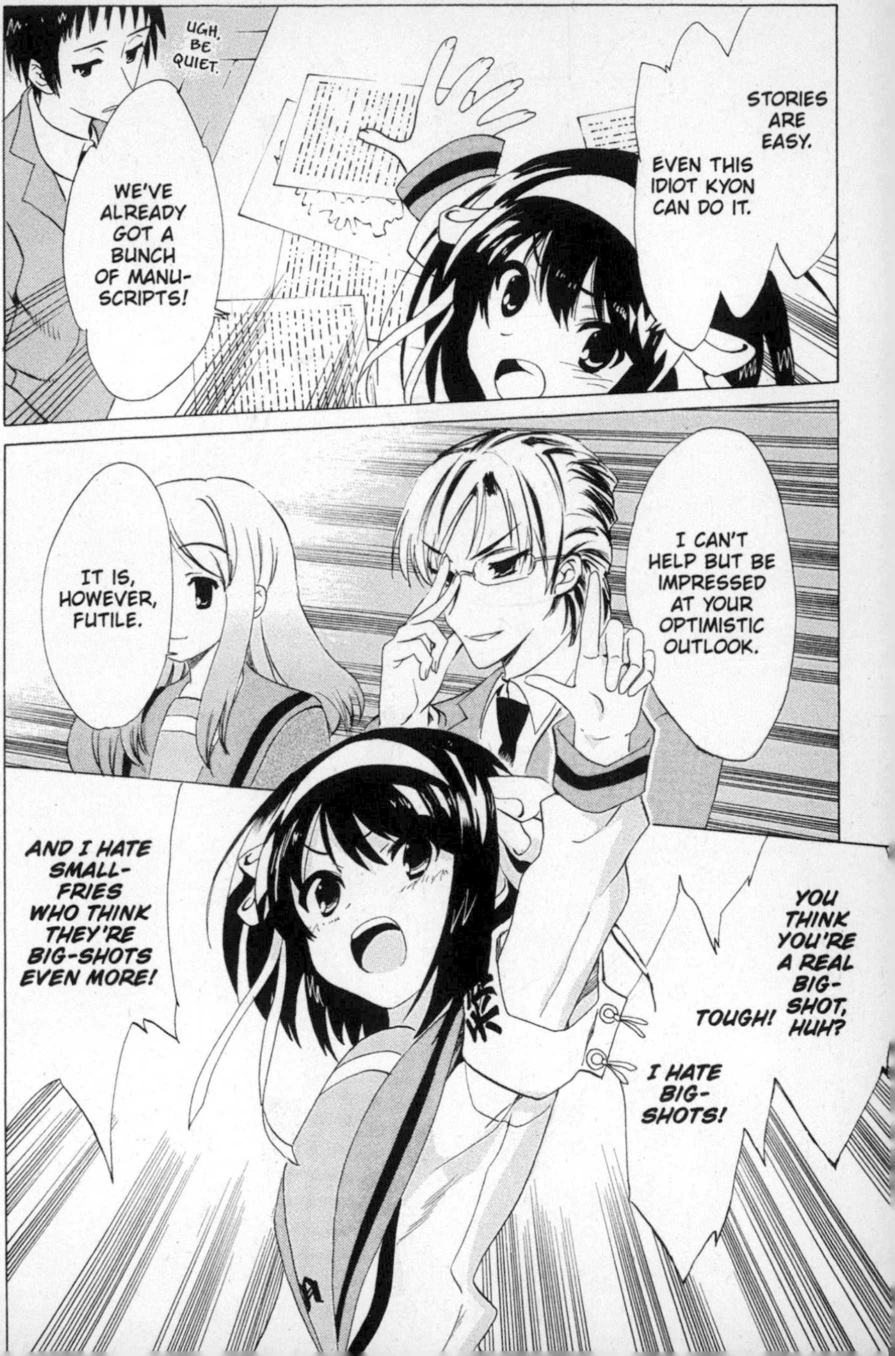
STORIES ARE EASY.
EVEN THIS IDIOT KYON CAN DO IT.
WE'VE ALREADY GOT A BUNCH OF MANU-SCRIPTS!
UGH, BE QUIET.
I CAN'T HELP BUT BE IMPRESSED AT YOUR OPTIMISTIC OUTLOOK.
IT IS, HOWEVER, FUTILE.
YOU THINK YOU'RE A REAL BIG-SHOT, HUH?
TOUGH!
I HATE BIG-SHOTS!
AND I HATE SMALL-FRIES WHO THINK THEY'RE BIG-SHOTS EVEN MORE!

HEADBAND: TRAINING

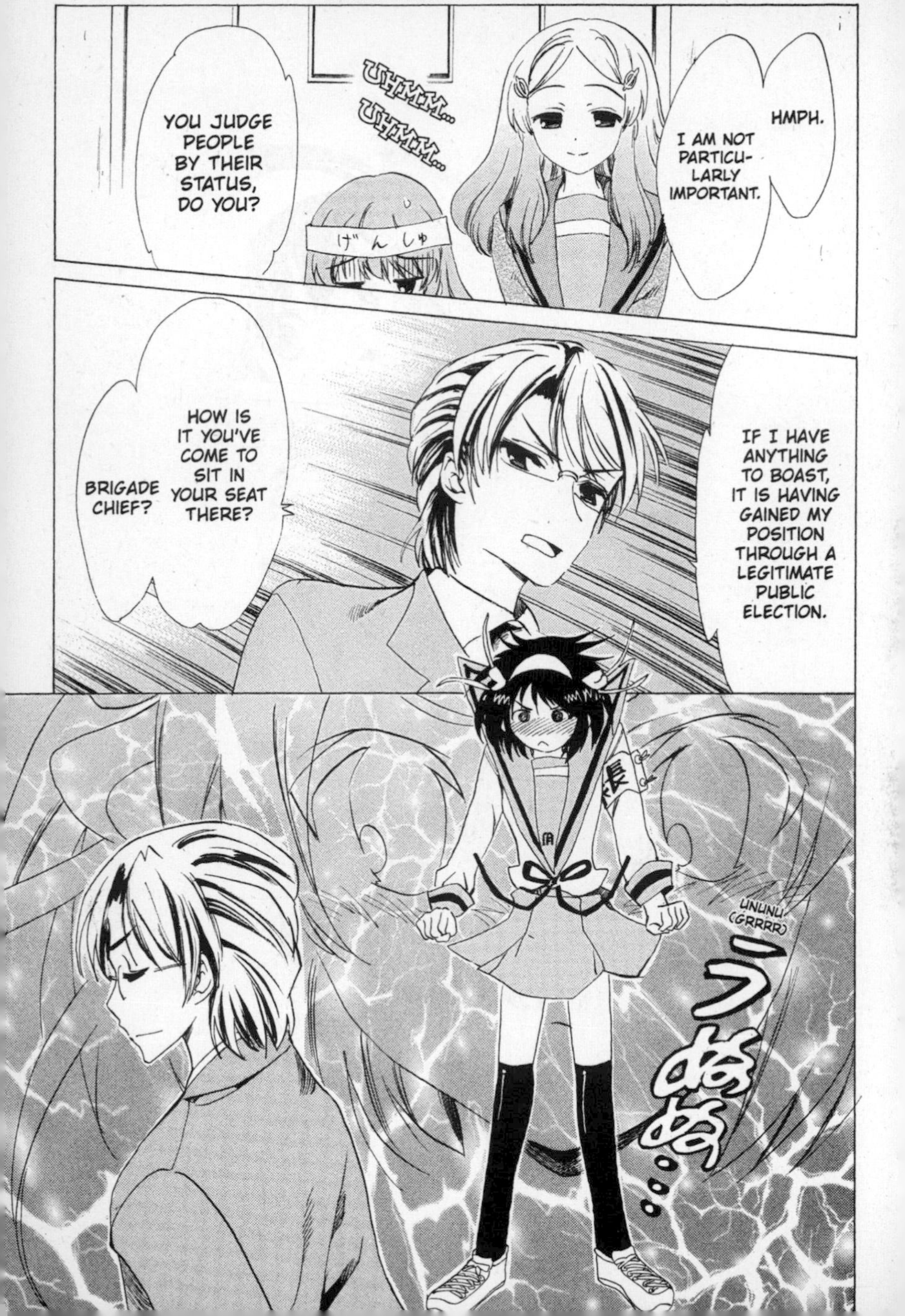
HMPH.
I AM NOT PARTICU-LARLY IMPORTANT.
UHMMM... UHMMM...
げんしゅ
YOU JUDGE PEOPLE BY THEIR STATUS, DO YOU?
IF I HAVE ANYTHING TO BOAST, IT IS HAVING GAINED MY POSITION THROUGH A LEGITIMATE PUBLIC ELECTION.
HOW IS IT YOU'VE COME TO SIT IN YOUR SEAT THERE?
BRIGADE CHIEF?
長
うぬぬ...
UNUNU (GRRRR)

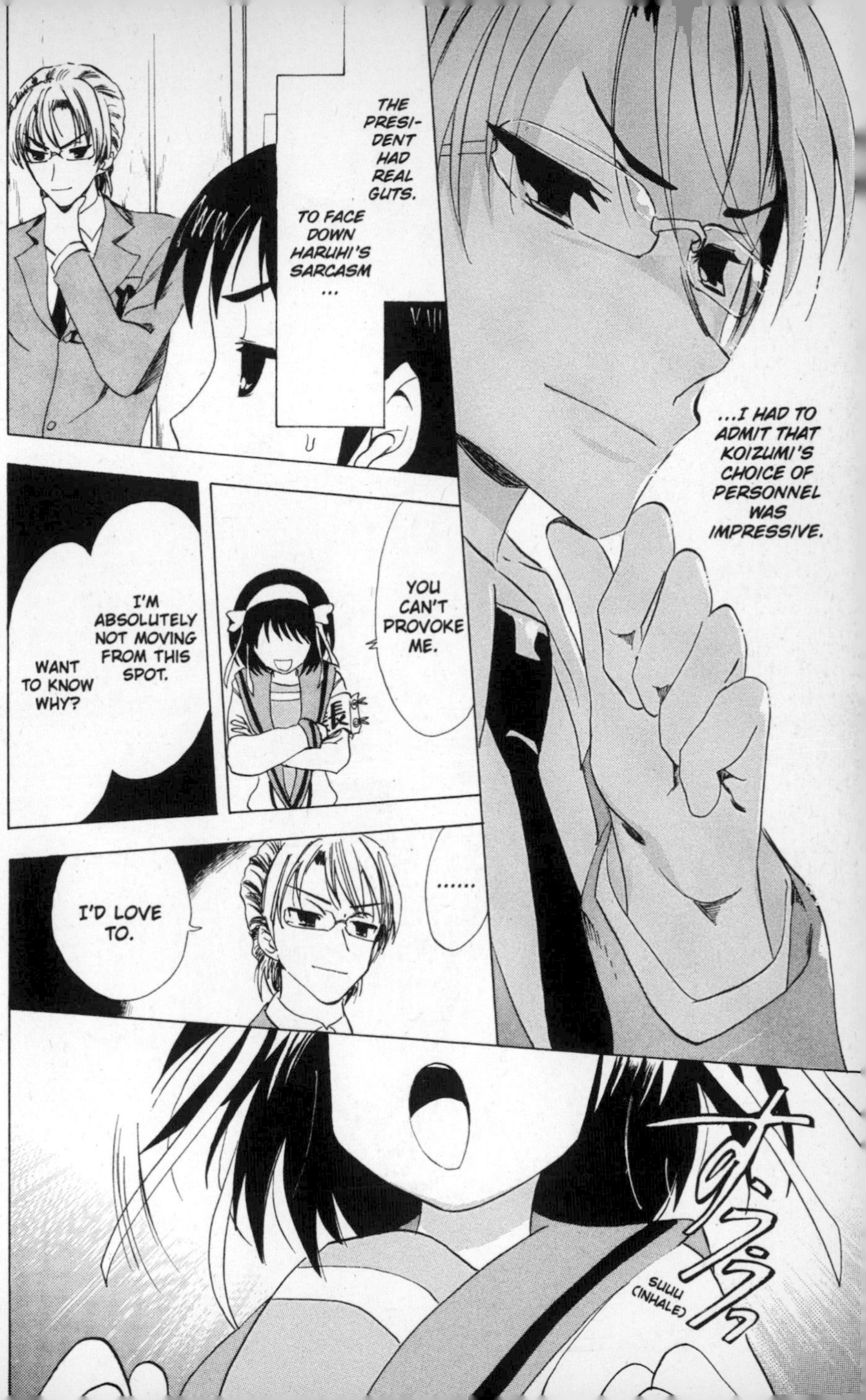
THE PRESIDENT HAD REAL GUTS.
TO FACE DOWN HARUHI'S SARCASM ...
...I HAD TO ADMIT THAT KOIZUMI'S CHOICE OF PERSONNEL WAS IMPRESSIVE.
YOU CAN'T PROVOKE ME.
I'M ABSOLUTELY NOT MOVING FROM THIS SPOT.
WANT TO KNOW WHY?
......
I'D LOVE TO.
SUUU (INHALE)

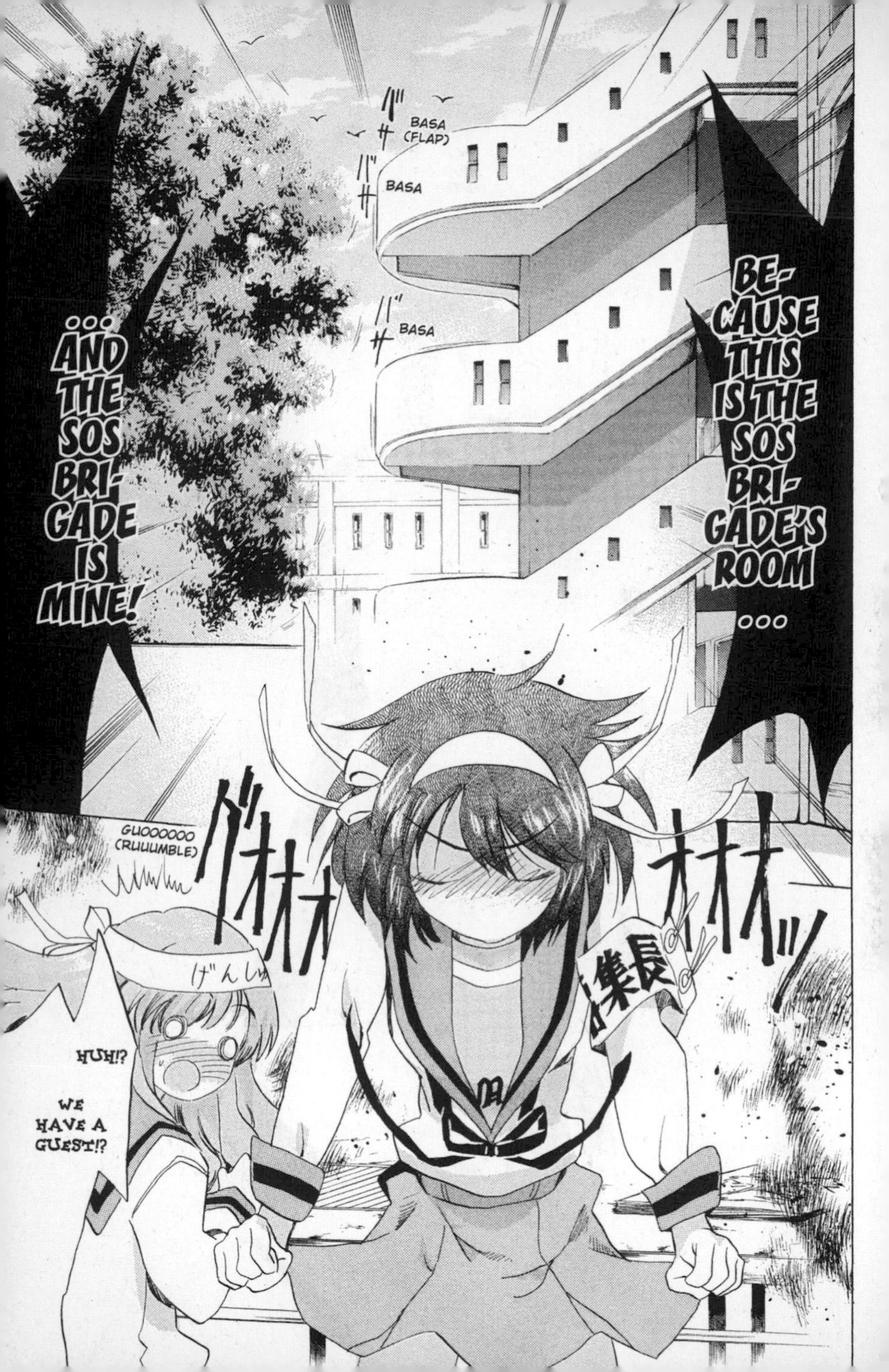

BASA (FLAP)
BASA
BASA
BE-CAUSE THIS IS THE SOS BRI-GADE'S ROOM...
...AND THE SOS BRI-GADE IS MINE!
グオオオオオオッ
GUOOOOOO (RUUUMBLE)
HUH!?
WE HAVE A GUEST!?

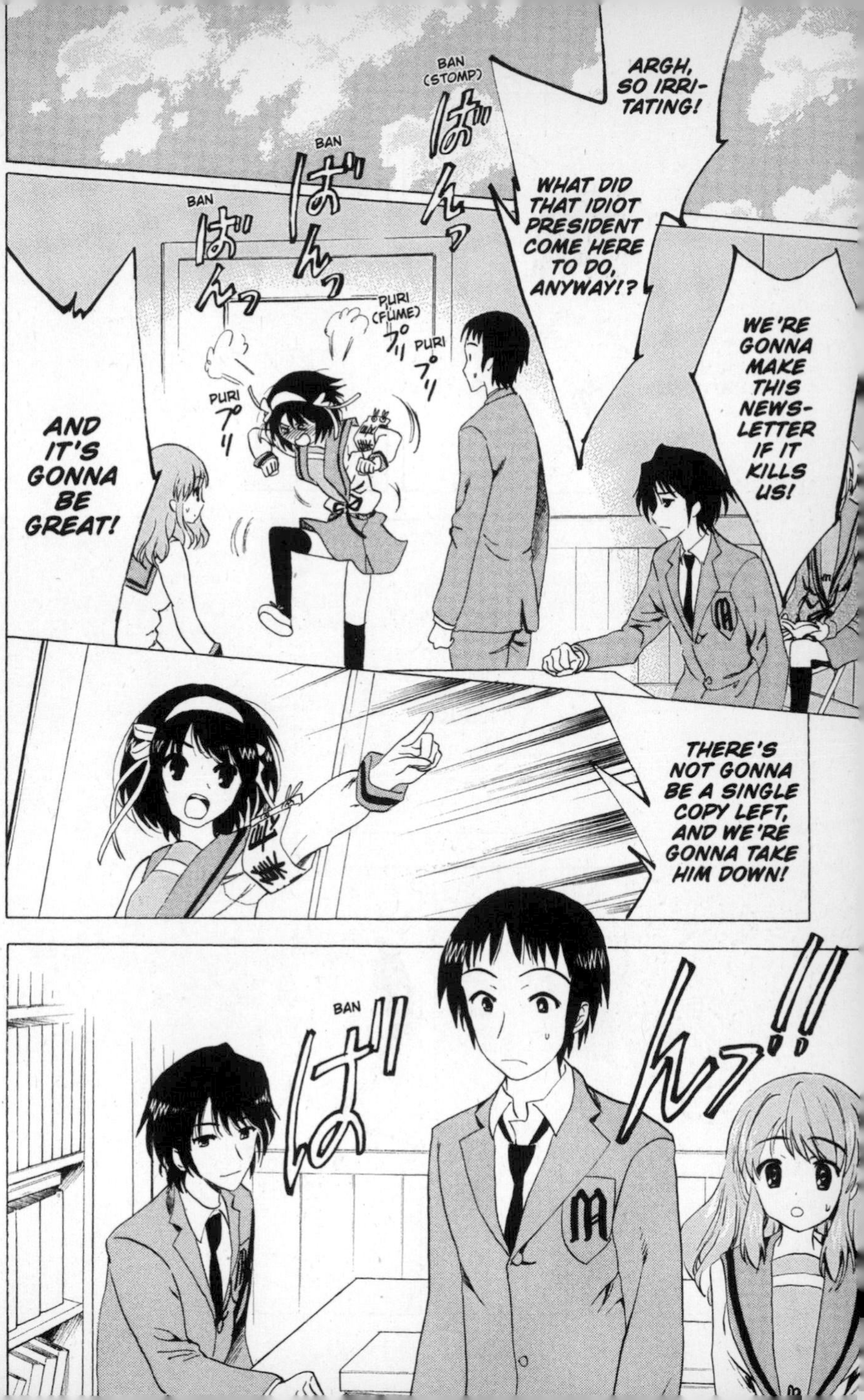
ARGH, SO IRRITATING!
BAN (STOMP)
ばんっ
BAN
ばんっ
BAN
ばんっ
WHAT DID THAT IDIOT PRESIDENT COME HERE TO DO, ANYWAY!?
WE'RE GONNA MAKE THIS NEWSLETTER IF IT KILLS US!
PURI (FUME)
プリ
PURI
プリ
PURI
プリ
AND IT'S GONNA BE GREAT!
THERE'S NOT GONNA BE A SINGLE COPY LEFT, AND WE'RE GONNA TAKE HIM DOWN!
BAN
ばんっ!!

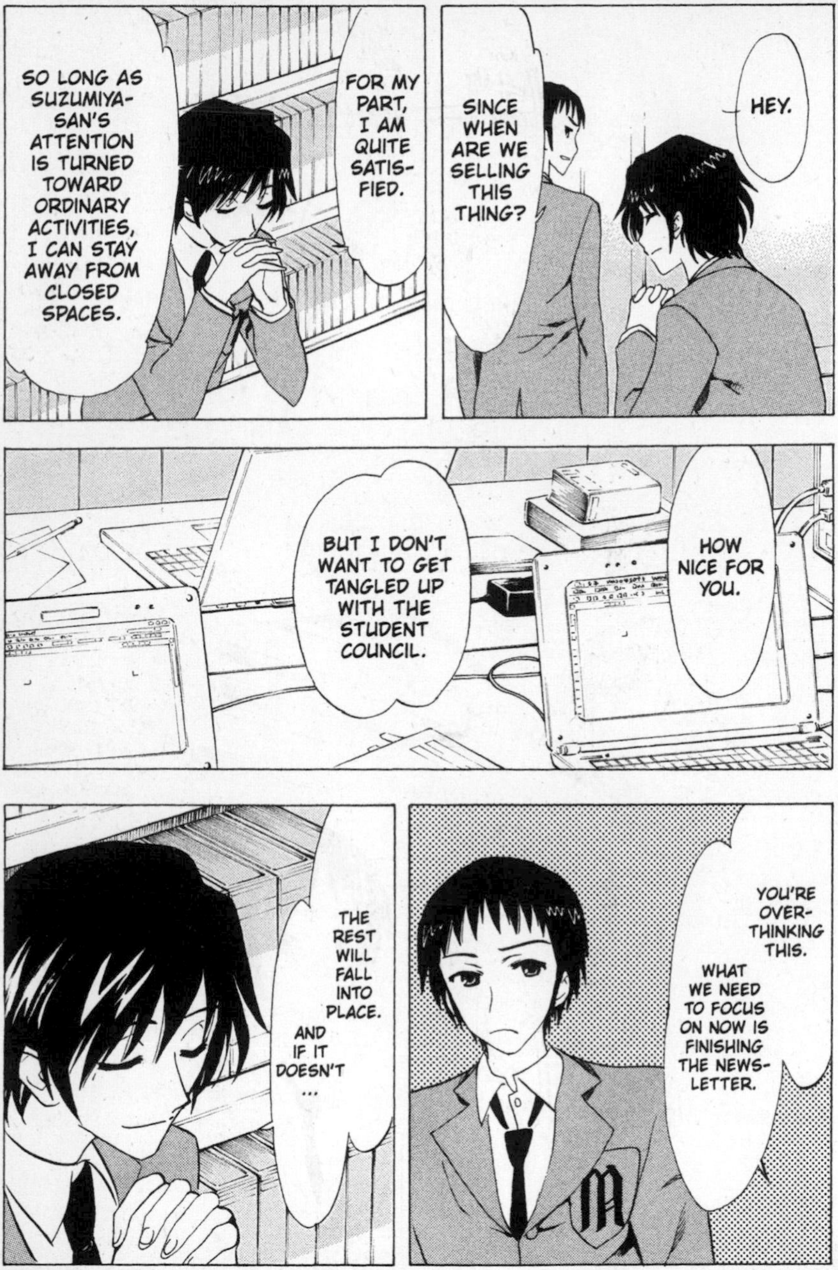
HEY.
SINCE WHEN ARE WE SELLING THIS THING?
FOR MY PART, I AM QUITE SATIS-FIED.
SO LONG AS SUZUMIYA-SAN'S ATTENTION IS TURNED TOWARD ORDINARY ACTIVITIES, I CAN STAY AWAY FROM CLOSED SPACES.
HOW NICE FOR YOU.
BUT I DON'T WANT TO GET TANGLED UP WITH THE STUDENT COUNCIL.
YOU'RE OVER-THINKING THIS.
WHAT WE NEED TO FOCUS ON NOW IS FINISHING THE NEWS-LETTER.
THE REST WILL FALL INTO PLACE.
AND IF IT DOESN'T ...

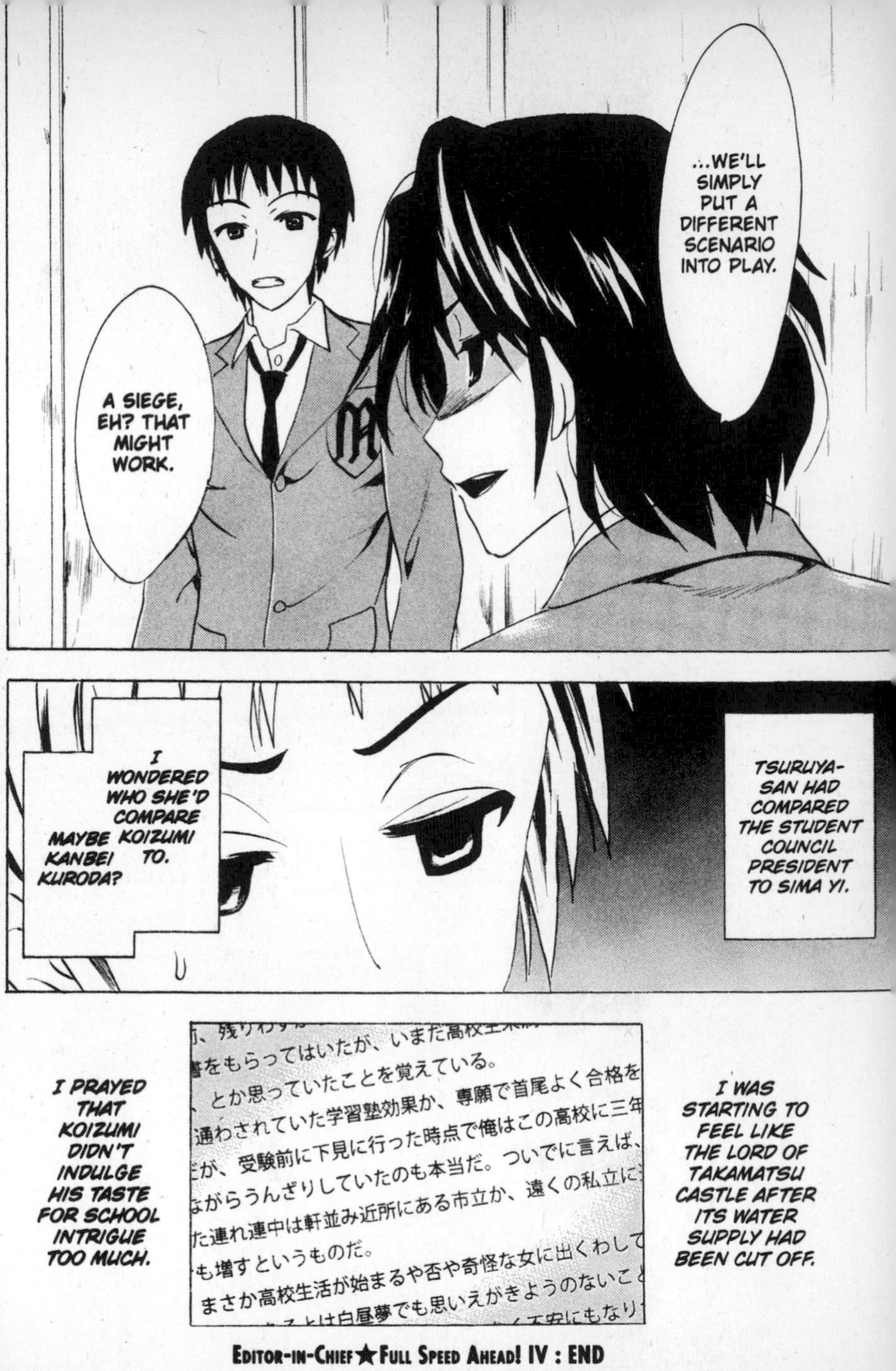
...WE'LL SIMPLY PUT A DIFFERENT SCENARIO INTO PLAY.
A SIEGE, EH? THAT MIGHT WORK.
TSURUYA-SAN HAD COMPARED THE STUDENT COUNCIL PRESIDENT TO SIMA YI.
I WONDERED WHO SHE'D COMPARE KOIZUMI TO.
MAYBE KANBEI KURODA?
I WAS STARTING TO FEEL LIKE THE LORD OF TAKAMATSU CASTLE AFTER ITS WATER SUPPLY HAD BEEN CUT OFF.
書をもらってはいたが、いまだ高校生
、とか思っていたことを覚えている。
通わされていた学習塾効果か、専願で首尾よく合格を
だが、受験前に下見に行った時点で俺はこの高校に三年
ながらうんざりしていたのも本当だ。ついでに言えば、
た連れ連中は軒並み近所にある市立か、遠くの私立に
も増すというものだ。
まさか高校生活が始まるや否や奇怪な女に出くわして
まさか高校生活が始まるや否や奇怪な女に出くわして
I PRAYED THAT KOIZUMI DIDN'T INDULGE HIS TASTE FOR SCHOOL INTRIGUE TOO MUCH.

EDITOR-IN-CHIEF★FULL SPEED AHEAD! IV : END

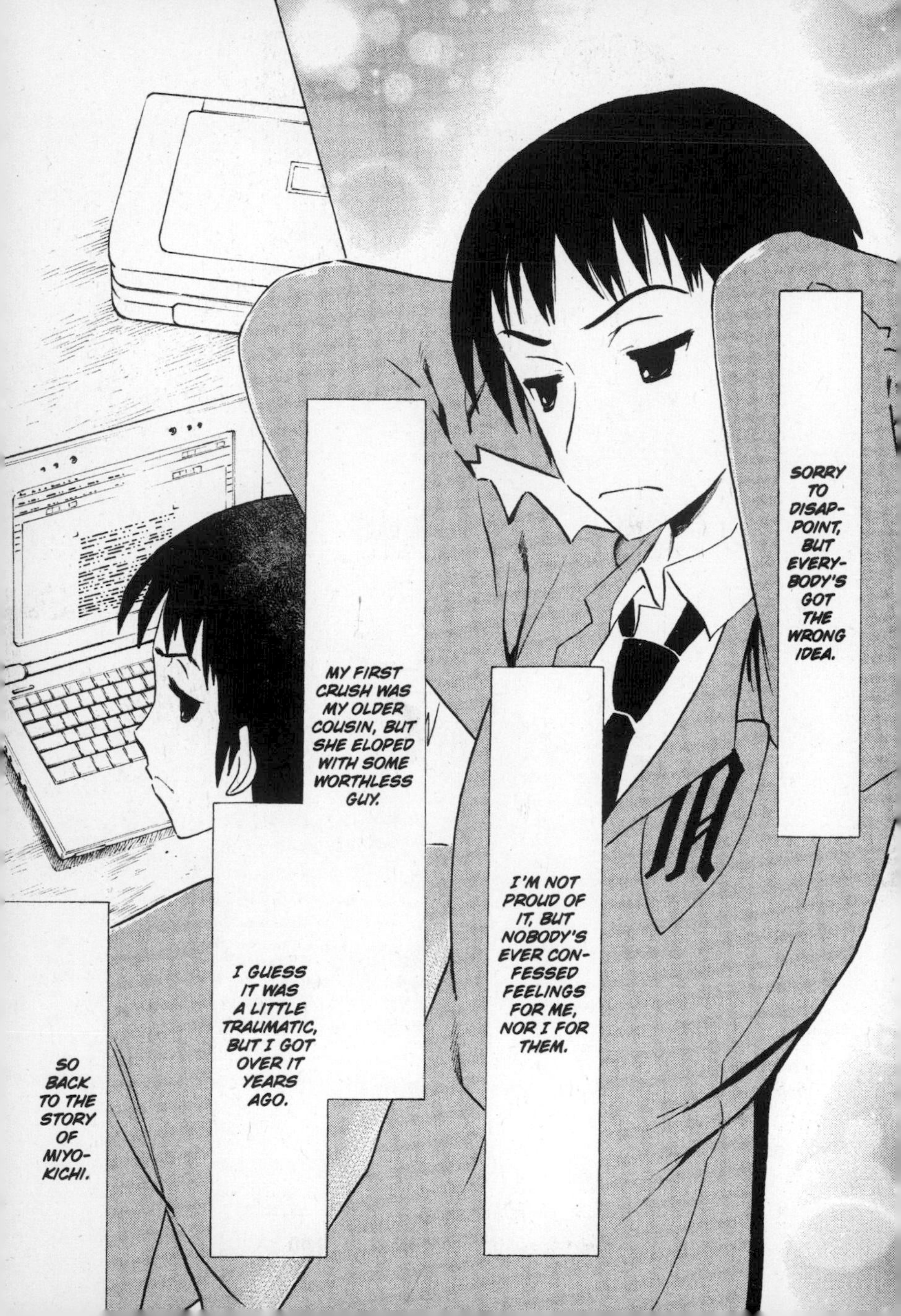
SORRY TO DISAPPOINT, BUT EVERYBODY'S GOT THE WRONG IDEA.
I'M NOT PROUD OF IT, BUT NOBODY'S EVER CONFESSED FEELINGS FOR ME, NOR I FOR THEM.
MY FIRST CRUSH WAS MY OLDER COUSIN, BUT SHE ELOPED WITH SOME WORTHLESS GUY.
I GUESS IT WAS A LITTLE TRAUMATIC, BUT I GOT OVER IT YEARS AGO.
SO BACK TO THE STORY OF MIYOKICHI.

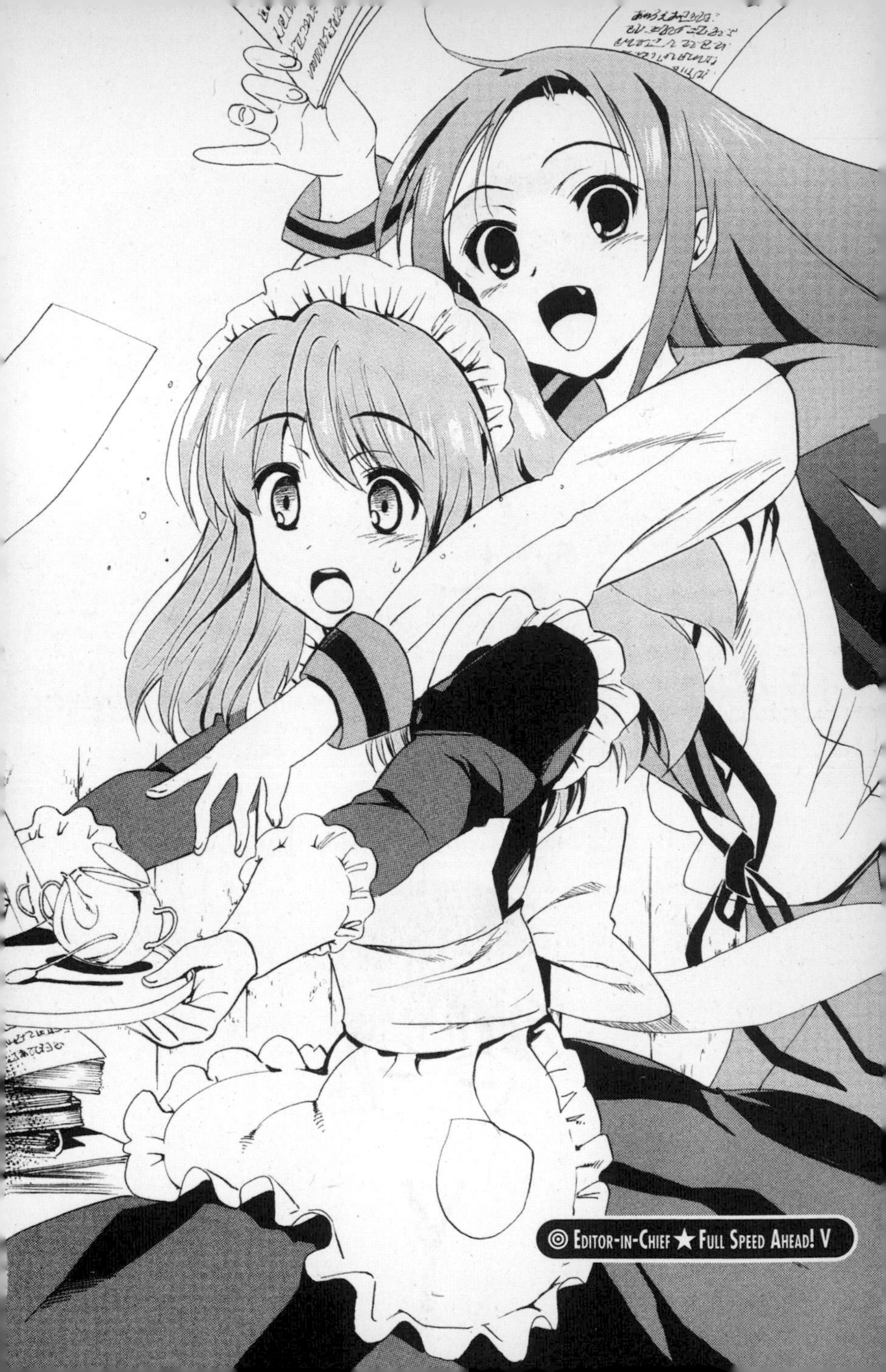
◎ Editor-in-Chief★Full Speed Ahead! V

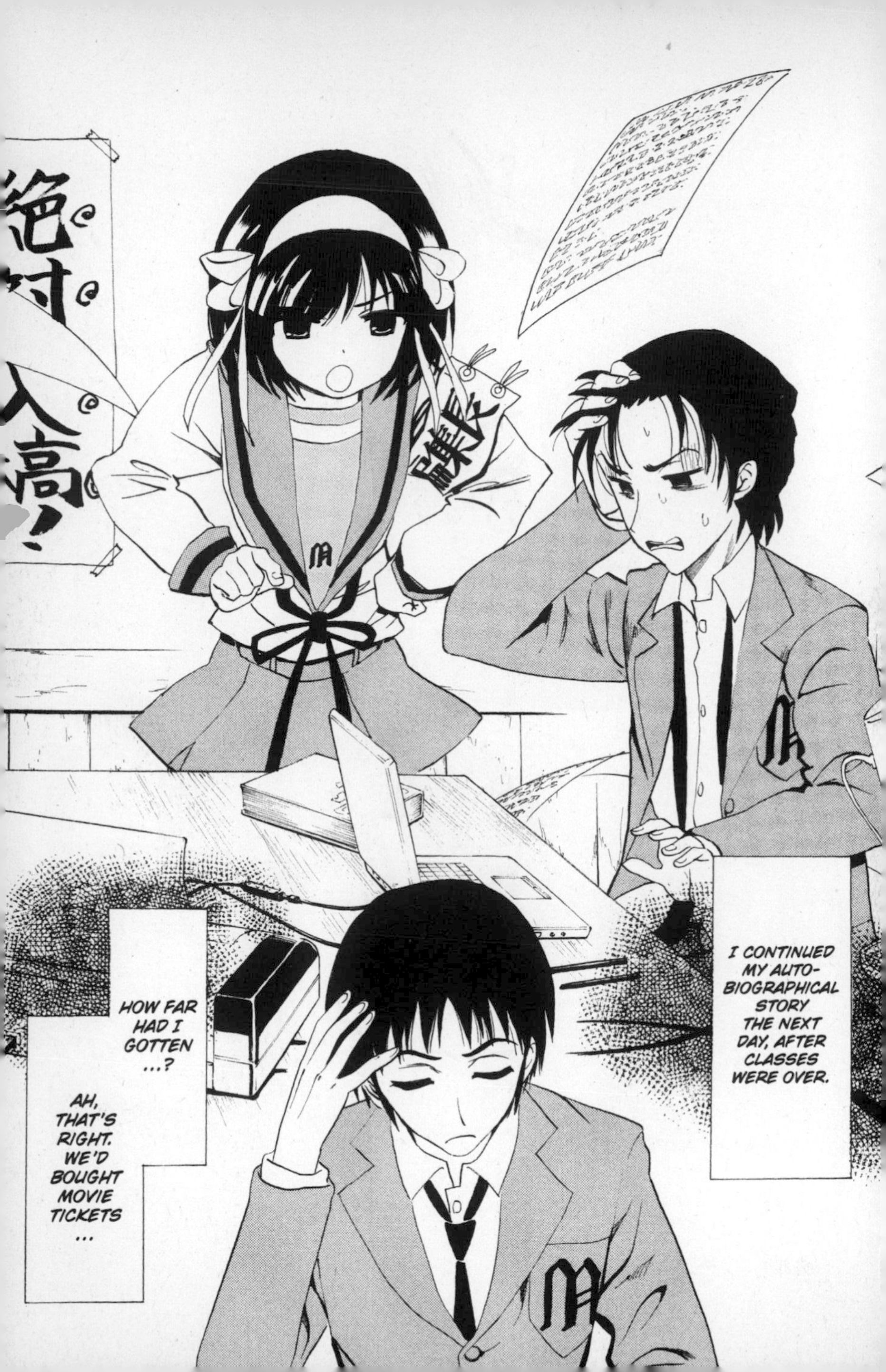
I CONTINUED MY AUTO-BIOGRAPHICAL STORY THE NEXT DAY, AFTER CLASSES WERE OVER.
絶対入稿!
HOW FAR HAD I GOTTEN ...?
AH, THAT'S RIGHT. WE'D BOUGHT MOVIE TICKETS ...

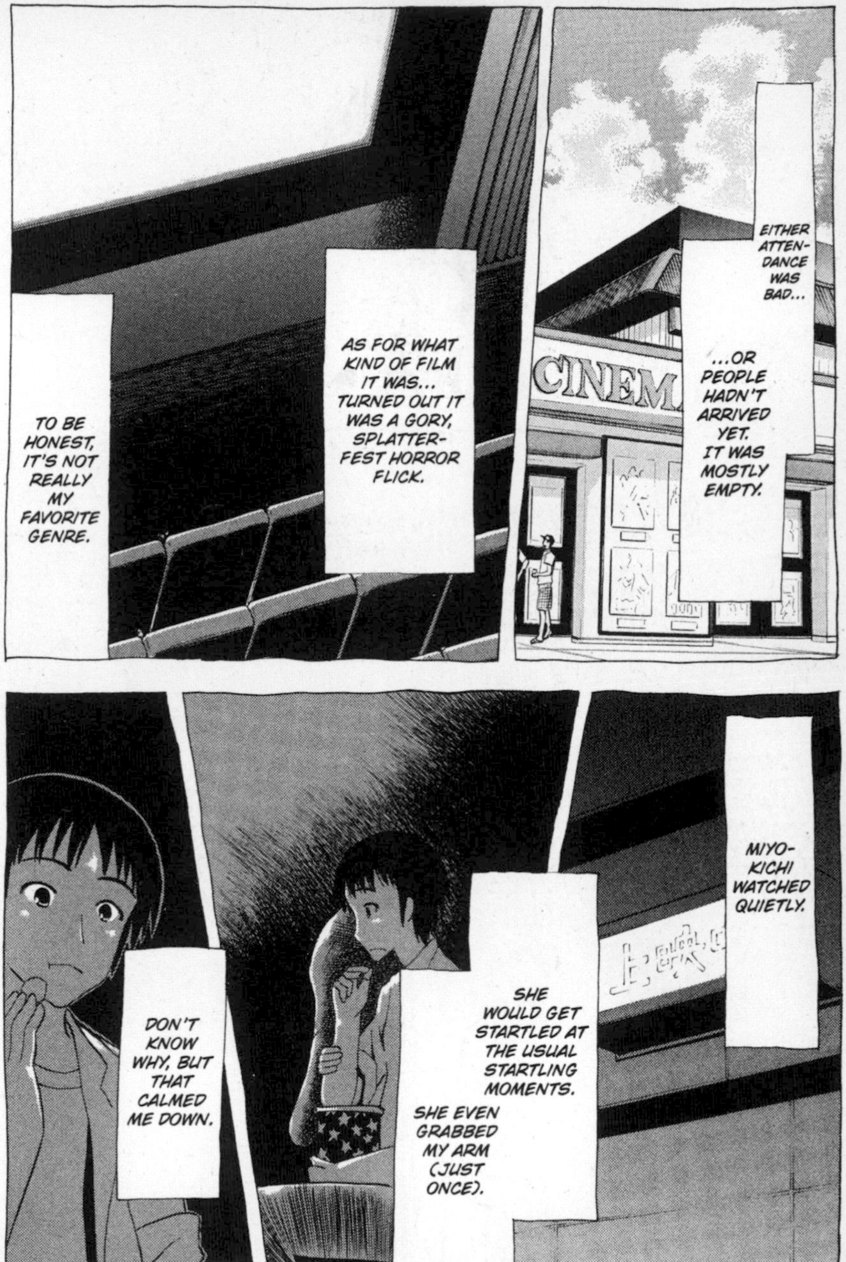
EITHER ATTEN-DANCE WAS BAD...
...OR PEOPLE HADN'T ARRIVED YET. IT WAS MOSTLY EMPTY.
AS FOR WHAT KIND OF FILM IT WAS... TURNED OUT IT WAS A GORY, SPLATTER-FEST HORROR FLICK.
TO BE HONEST, IT'S NOT REALLY MY FAVORITE GENRE.
MIYO-KICHI WATCHED QUIETLY.
SHE WOULD GET STARTLED AT THE USUAL STARTLING MOMENTS.
SHE EVEN GRABBED MY ARM (JUST ONCE).
DON'T KNOW WHY, BUT THAT CALMED ME DOWN.

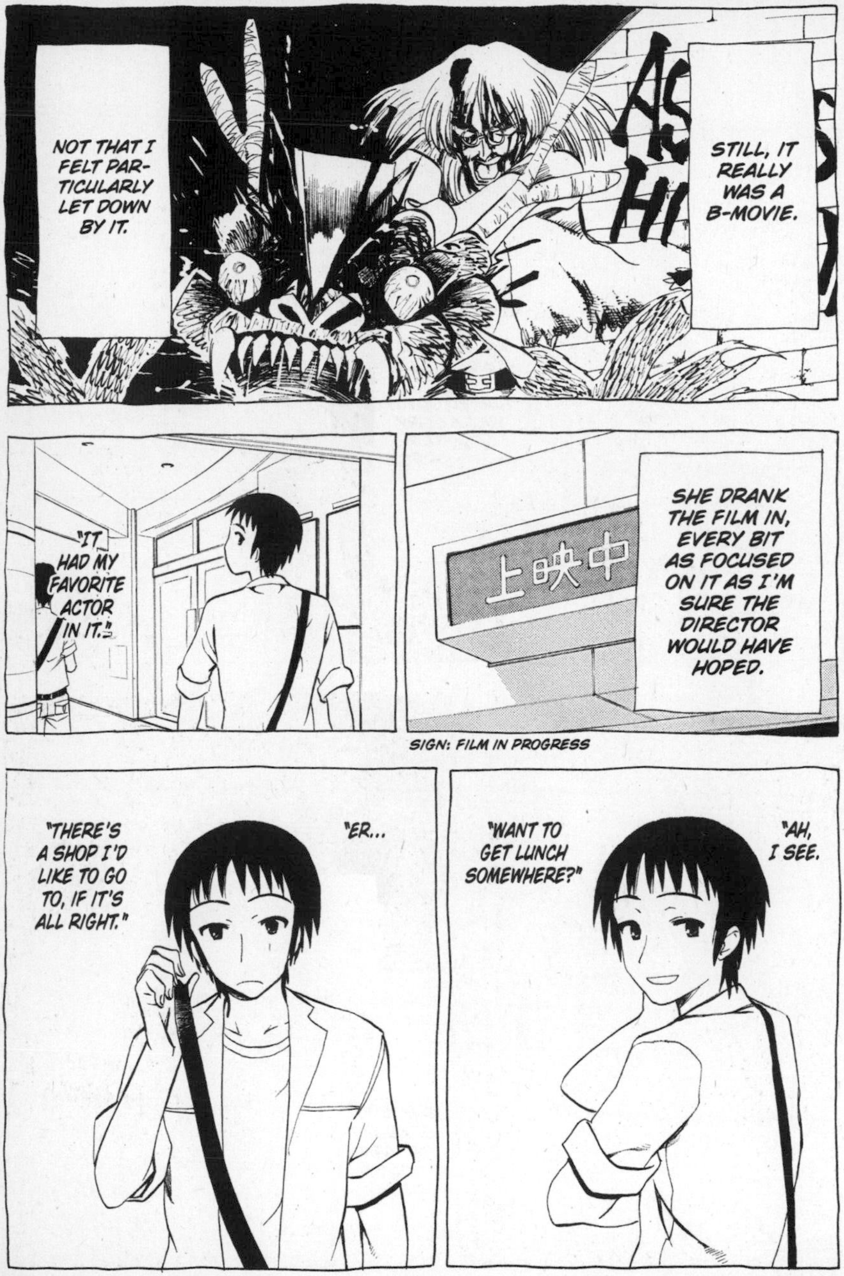
STILL, IT REALLY WAS A B-MOVIE.
NOT THAT I FELT PAR-TICULARLY LET DOWN BY IT.
SHE DRANK THE FILM IN, EVERY BIT AS FOCUSED ON IT AS I'M SURE THE DIRECTOR WOULD HAVE HOPED.
上映中
SIGN: FILM IN PROGRESS
"IT HAD MY FAVORITE ACTOR IN IT."
"AH, I SEE.
"WANT TO GET LUNCH SOMEWHERE?"
"ER...
"THERE'S A SHOP I'D LIKE TO GO TO, IF IT'S ALL RIGHT."

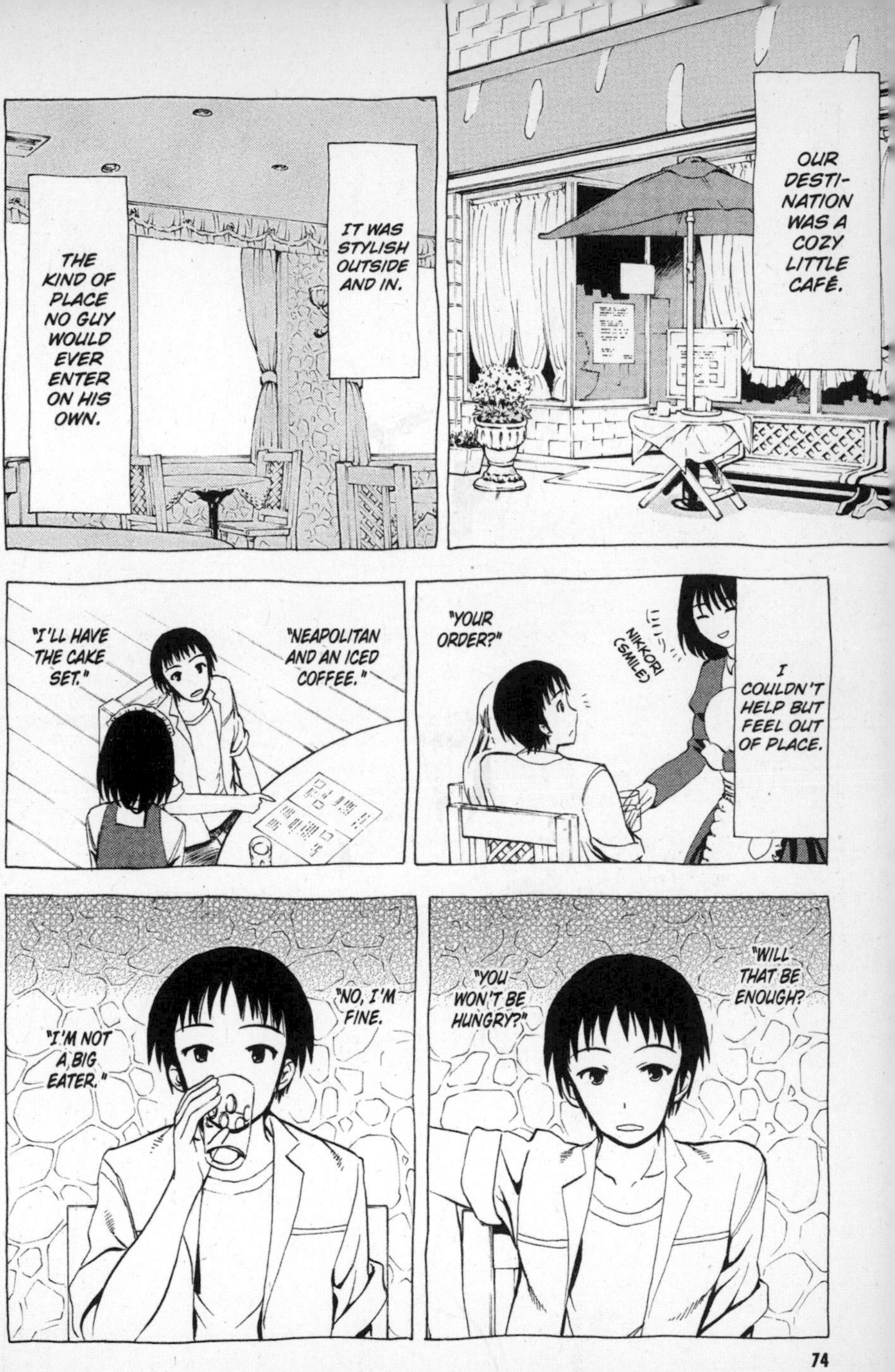
OUR DESTINATION WAS A COZY LITTLE CAFÉ.
IT WAS STYLISH OUTSIDE AND IN.
THE KIND OF PLACE NO GUY WOULD EVER ENTER ON HIS OWN.
I COULDN'T HELP BUT FEEL OUT OF PLACE.
NIKKORI (SMILE)
"YOUR ORDER?"
"NEAPOLITAN AND AN ICED COFFEE."
"I'LL HAVE THE CAKE SET."
"WILL THAT BE ENOUGH?
"YOU WON'T BE HUNGRY?"
"NO, I'M FINE.
"I'M NOT A BIG EATER."

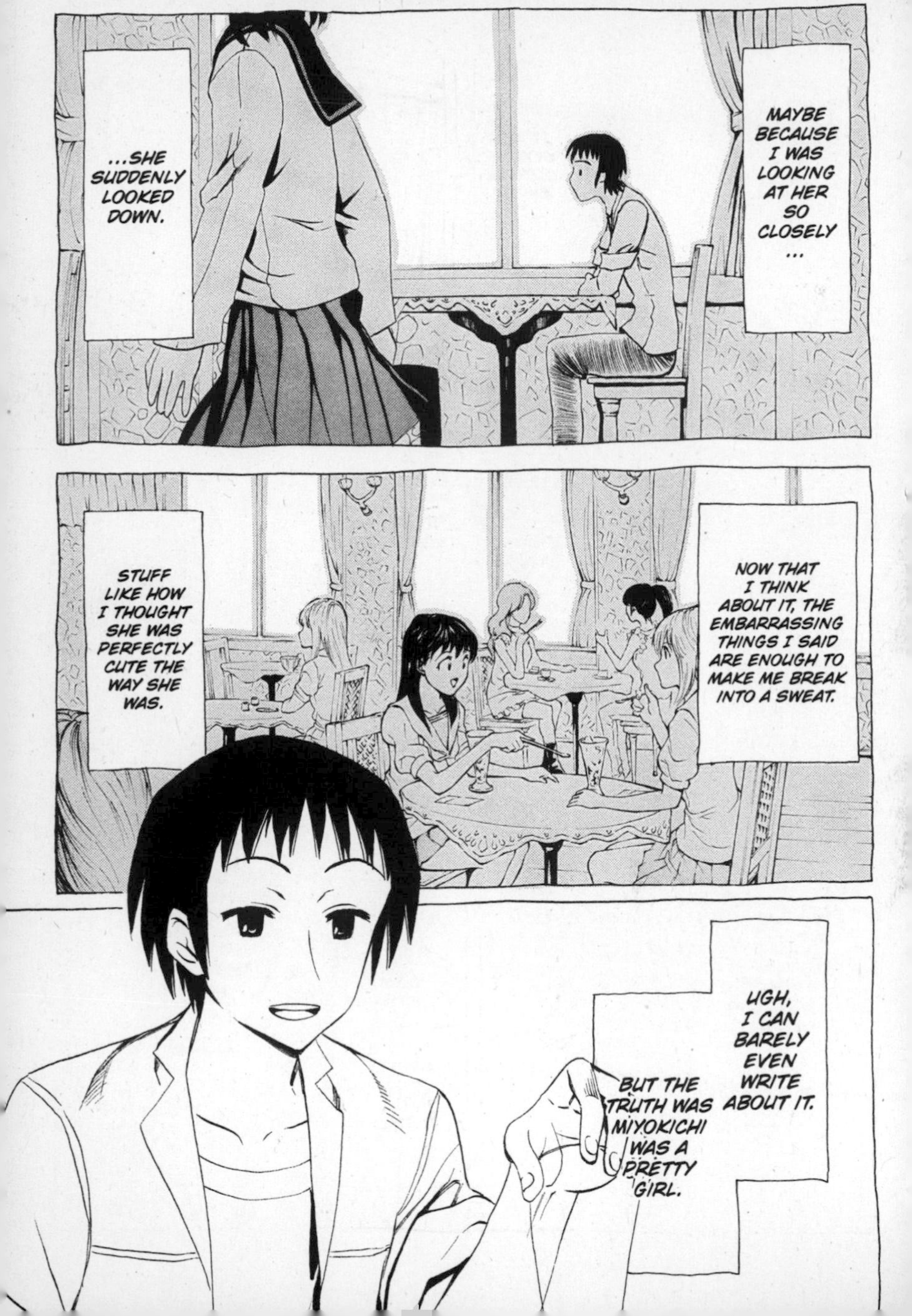
MAYBE BECAUSE I WAS LOOKING AT HER SO CLOSELY ...
...SHE SUDDENLY LOOKED DOWN.
NOW THAT I THINK ABOUT IT, THE EMBARRASSING THINGS I SAID ARE ENOUGH TO MAKE ME BREAK INTO A SWEAT.
STUFF LIKE HOW I THOUGHT SHE WAS PERFECTLY CUTE THE WAY SHE WAS.
UGH, I CAN BARELY EVEN WRITE ABOUT IT.
BUT THE TRUTH WAS MIYOKICHI WAS A PRETTY GIRL.

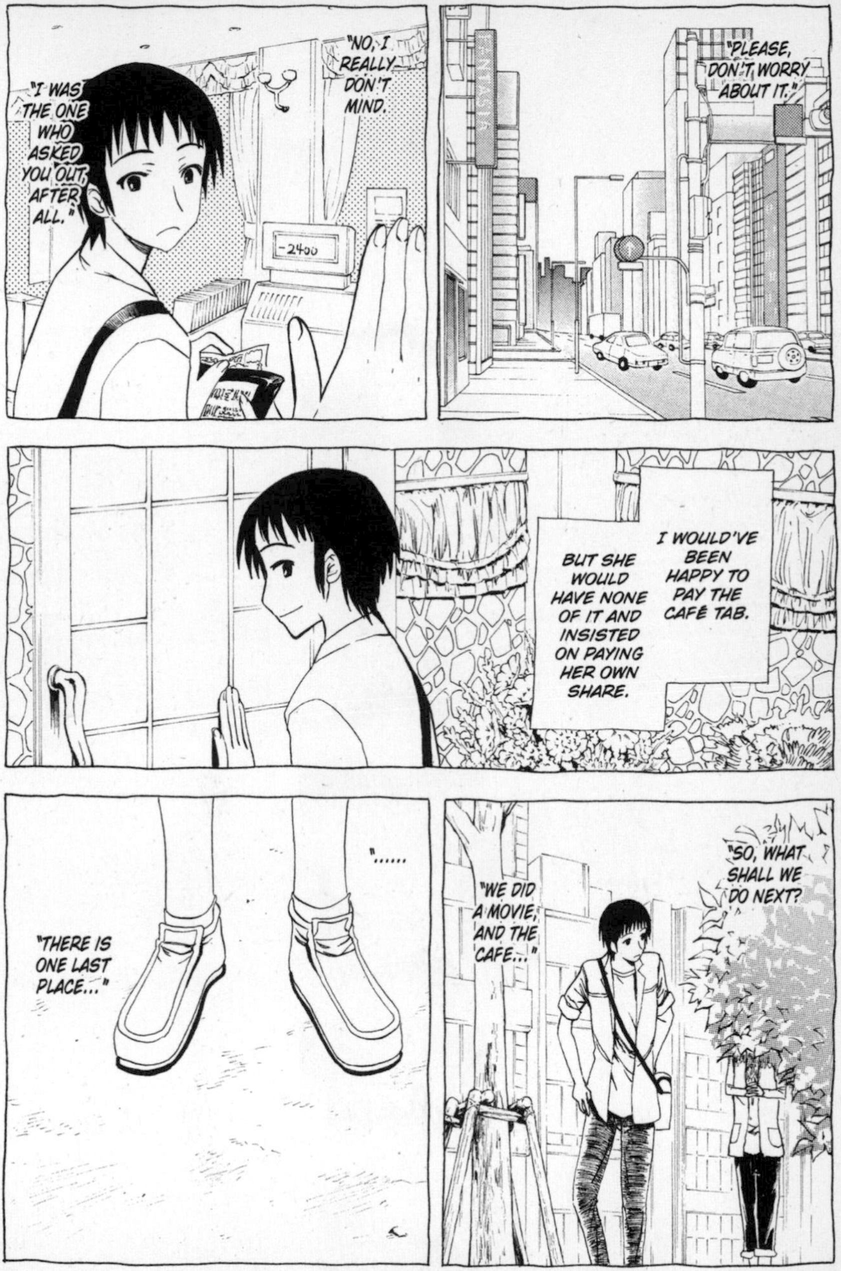
"PLEASE, DON'T WORRY ABOUT IT."
"NO, I REALLY DON'T MIND.
"I WAS THE ONE WHO ASKED YOU OUT, AFTER ALL."
I WOULD'VE BEEN HAPPY TO PAY THE CAFÉ TAB.
BUT SHE WOULD HAVE NONE OF IT AND INSISTED ON PAYING HER OWN SHARE.
"SO, WHAT SHALL WE DO NEXT?
"WE DID A MOVIE, AND THE CAFE..."
"......
"THERE IS ONE LAST PLACE..."

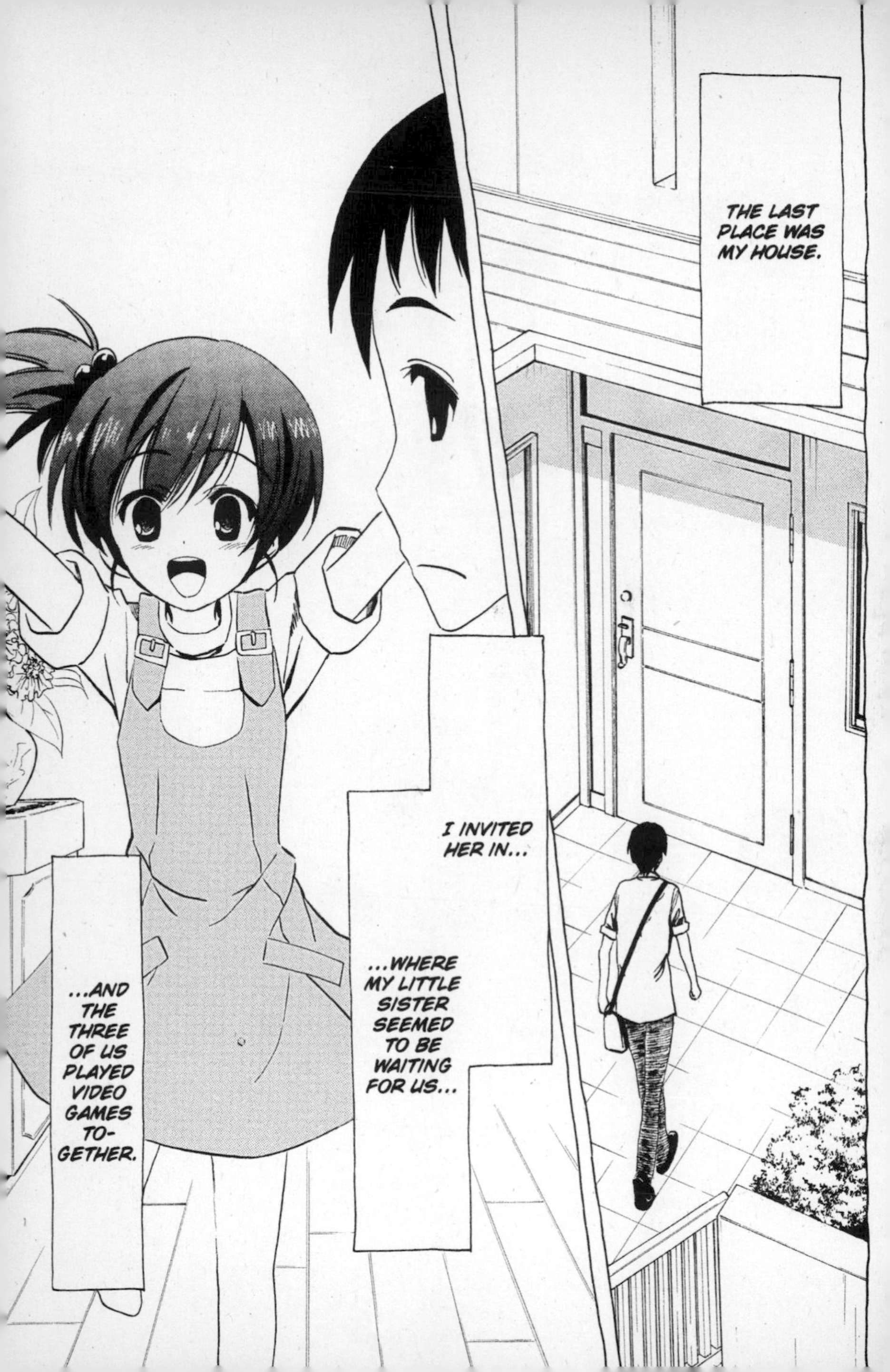
THE LAST PLACE WAS MY HOUSE.
I INVITED HER IN...
...WHERE MY LITTLE SISTER SEEMED TO BE WAITING FOR US...
...AND THE THREE OF US PLAYED VIDEO GAMES TOGETHER.

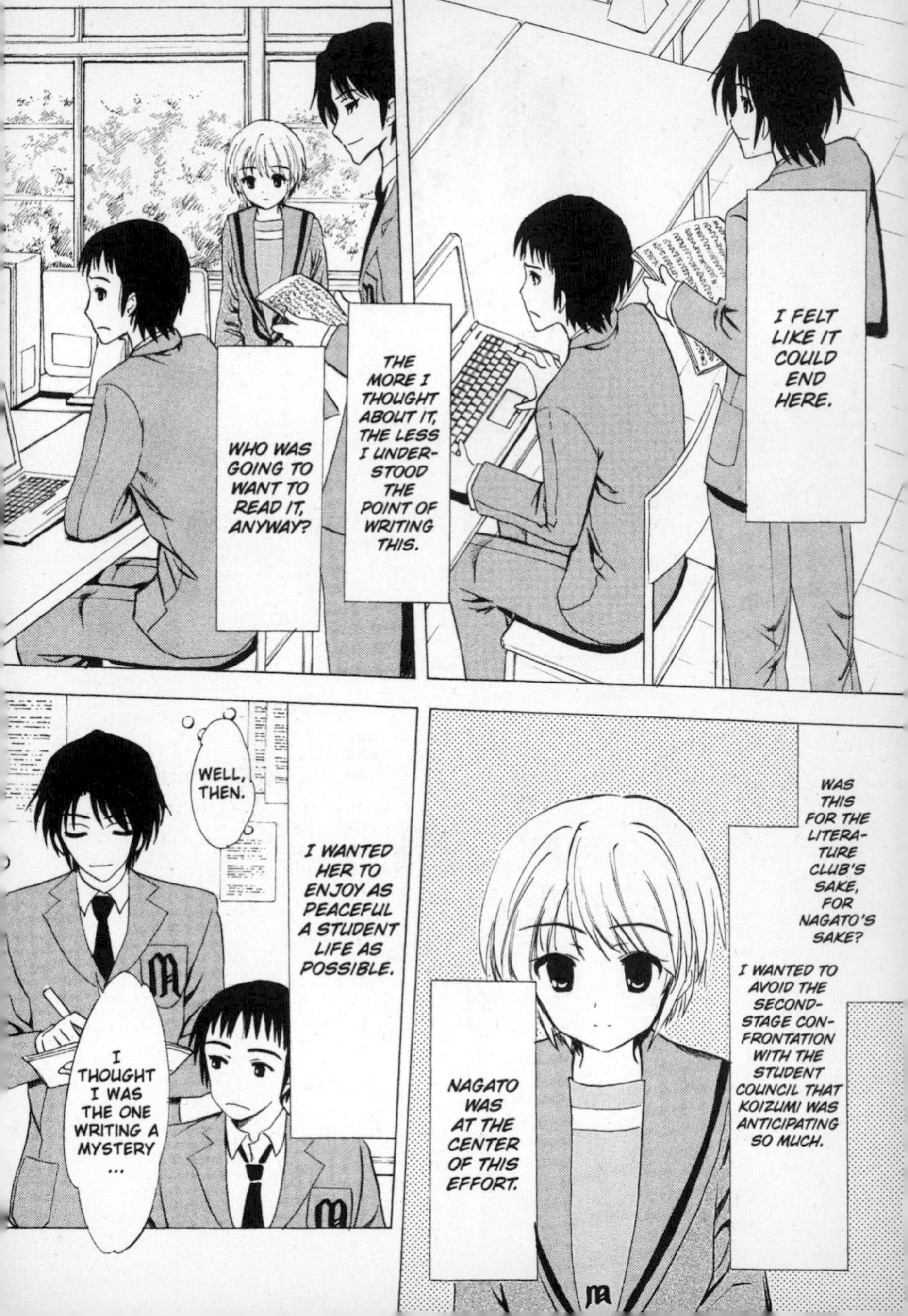
I FELT LIKE IT COULD END HERE.
THE MORE I THOUGHT ABOUT IT, THE LESS I UNDERSTOOD THE POINT OF WRITING THIS.
WHO WAS GOING TO WANT TO READ IT, ANYWAY?
WAS THIS FOR THE LITERATURE CLUB'S SAKE, FOR NAGATO'S SAKE?
I WANTED TO AVOID THE SECOND-STAGE CONFRONTATION WITH THE STUDENT COUNCIL THAT KOIZUMI WAS ANTICIPATING SO MUCH.
NAGATO WAS AT THE CENTER OF THIS EFFORT.
I WANTED HER TO ENJOY AS PEACEFUL A STUDENT LIFE AS POSSIBLE.
WELL, THEN.
I THOUGHT I WAS THE ONE WRITING A MYSTERY...

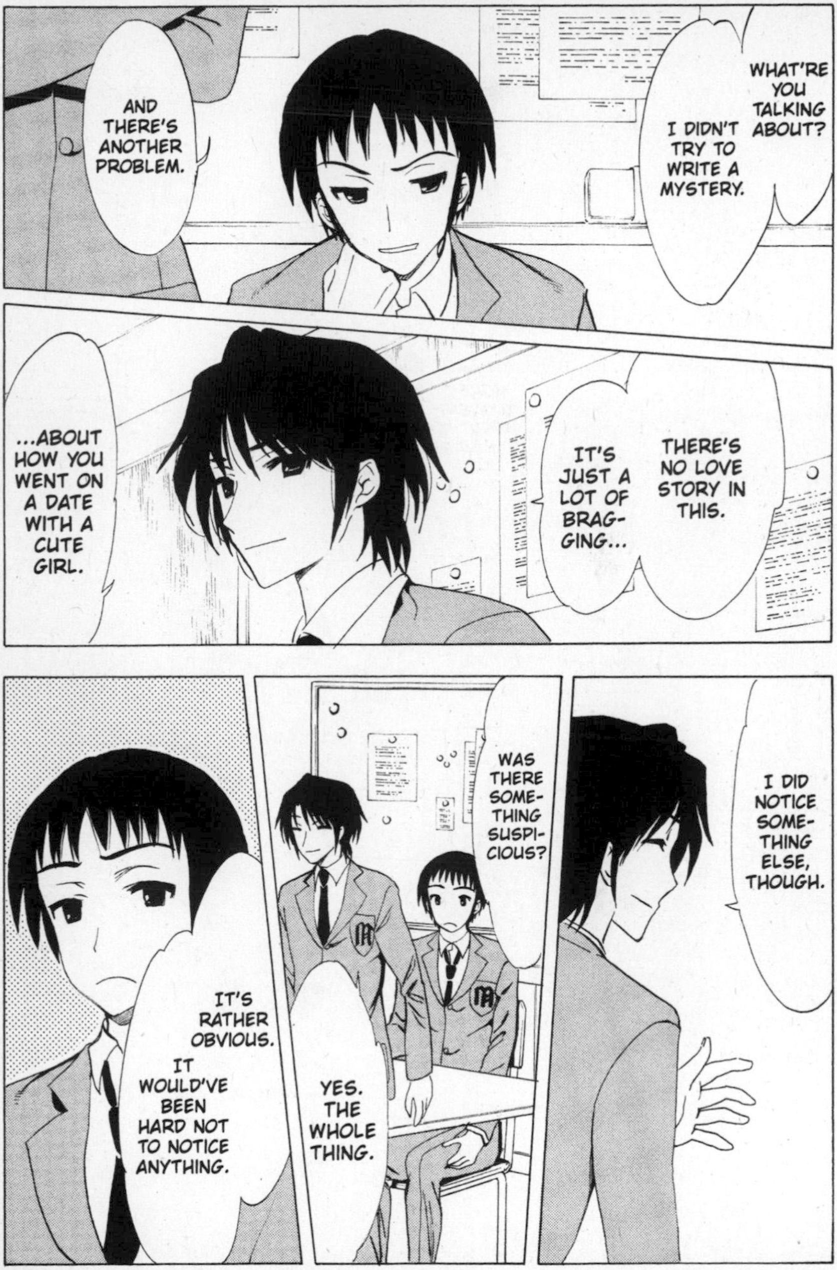
WHAT'RE YOU TALKING ABOUT?
I DIDN'T TRY TO WRITE A MYSTERY.
AND THERE'S ANOTHER PROBLEM.
THERE'S NO LOVE STORY IN THIS.
IT'S JUST A LOT OF BRAG-GING...
...ABOUT HOW YOU WENT ON A DATE WITH A CUTE GIRL.
I DID NOTICE SOME-THING ELSE, THOUGH.
WAS THERE SOME-THING SUSPICIOUS?
YES. THE WHOLE THING.
IT'S RATHER OBVIOUS.
IT WOULD'VE BEEN HARD NOT TO NOTICE ANYTHING.

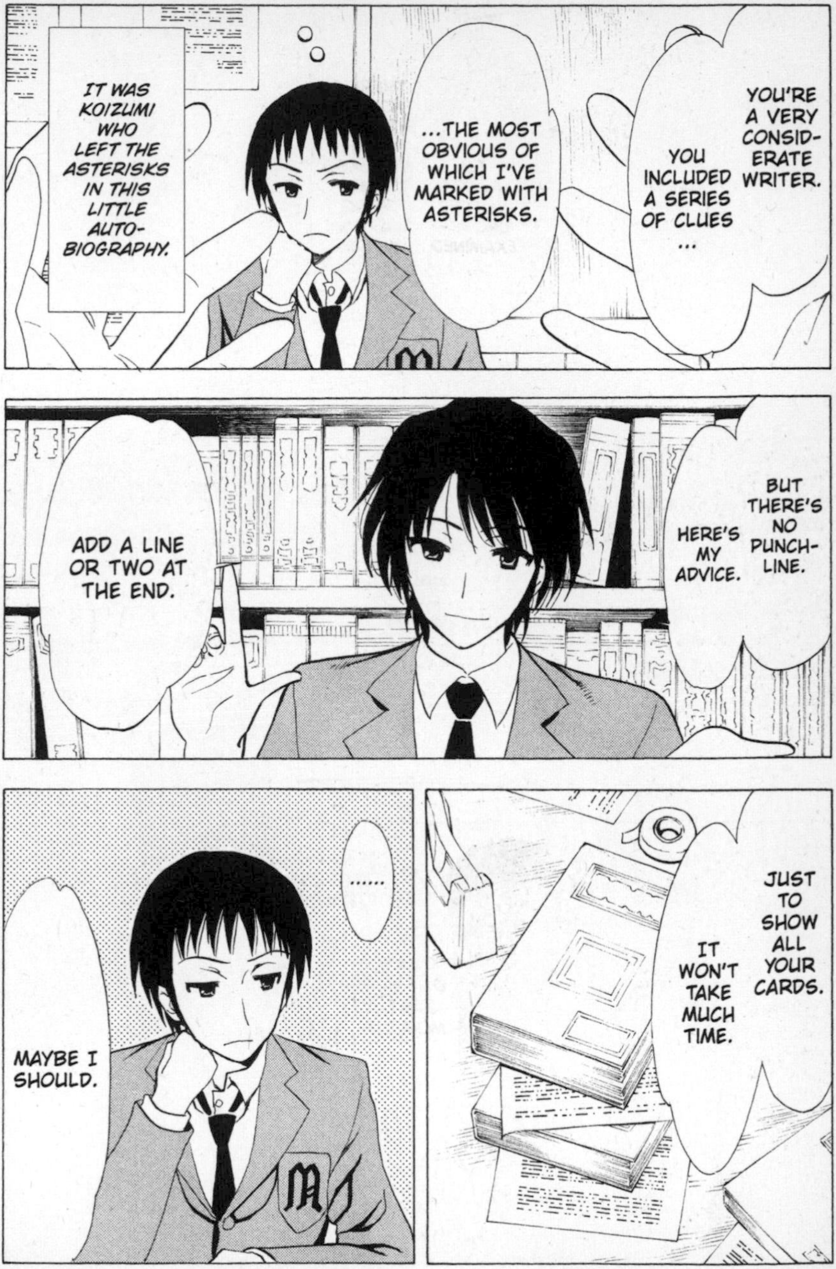
YOU'RE A VERY CONSIDERATE WRITER.
YOU INCLUDED A SERIES OF CLUES ...
...THE MOST OBVIOUS OF WHICH I'VE MARKED WITH ASTERISKS.
IT WAS KOIZUMI WHO LEFT THE ASTERISKS IN THIS LITTLE AUTOBIOGRAPHY.
BUT THERE'S NO PUNCHLINE.
HERE'S MY ADVICE.
ADD A LINE OR TWO AT THE END.
JUST TO SHOW ALL YOUR CARDS.
IT WON'T TAKE MUCH TIME.
......
MAYBE I SHOULD.

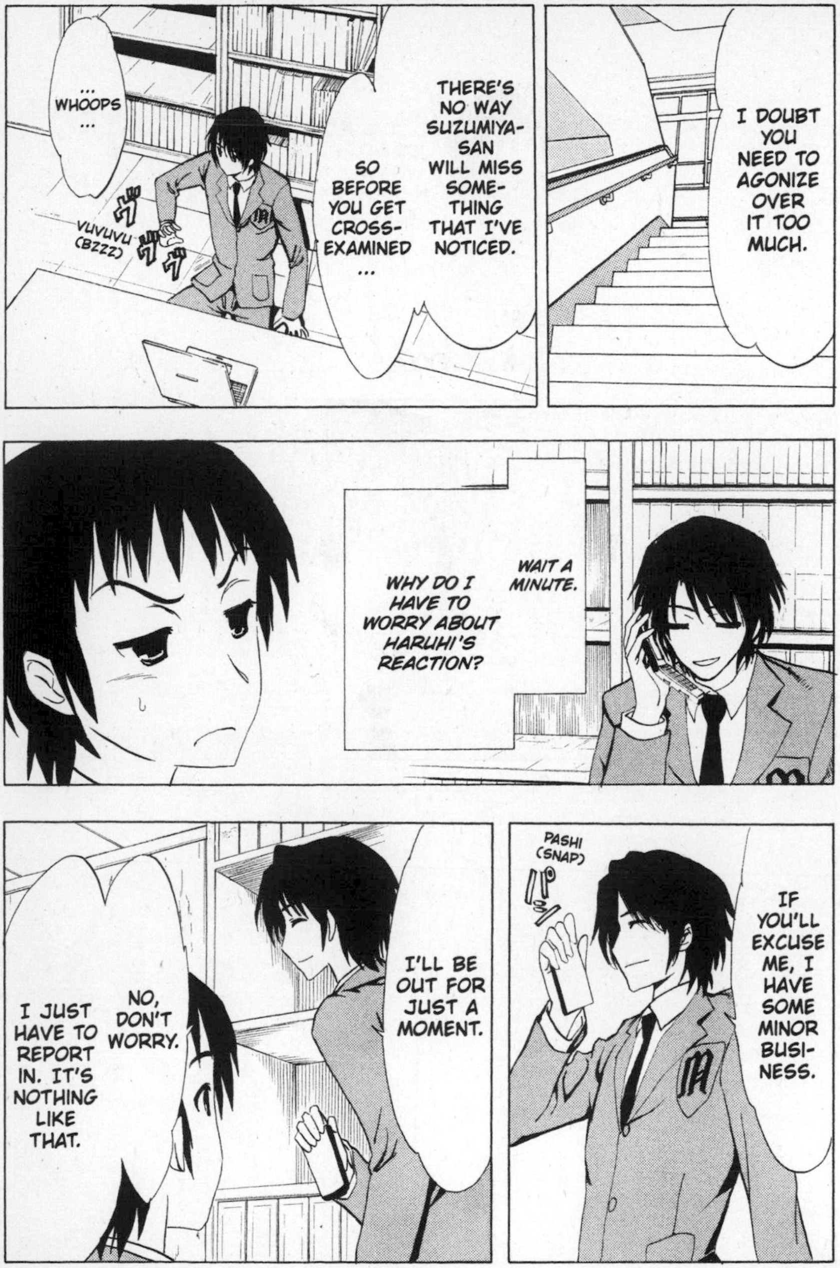
I DOUBT YOU NEED TO AGONIZE OVER IT TOO MUCH.
THERE'S NO WAY SUZUMIYA-SAN WILL MISS SOMETHING THAT I'VE NOTICED.
SO BEFORE YOU GET CROSS-EXAMINED ...
... WHOOPS ...
VUVUVU (BZZZ)
WAIT A MINUTE.
WHY DO I HAVE TO WORRY ABOUT HARUHI'S REACTION?
PASHI (SNAP)
IF YOU'LL EXCUSE ME, I HAVE SOME MINOR BUSINESS.
I'LL BE OUT FOR JUST A MOMENT.
NO, DON'T WORRY.
I JUST HAVE TO REPORT IN. IT'S NOTHING LIKE THAT.

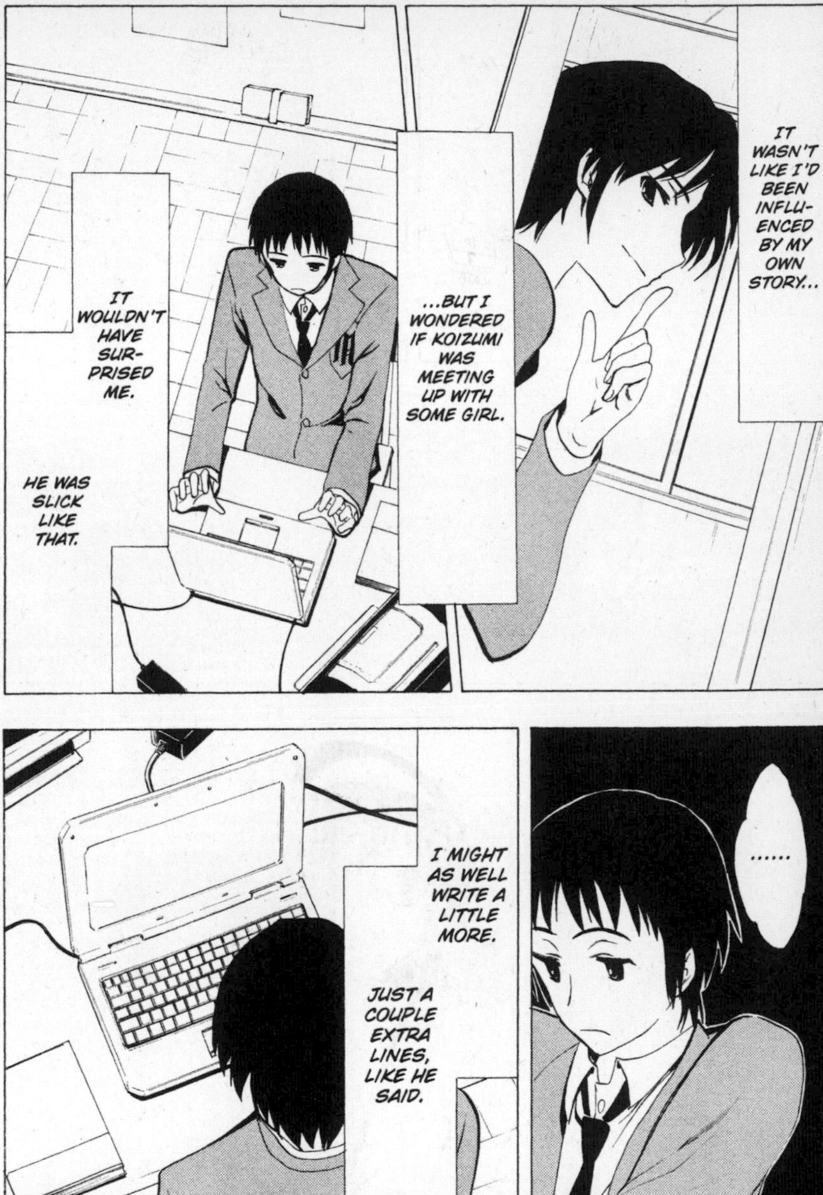
IT WASN'T LIKE I'D BEEN INFLUENCED BY MY OWN STORY...
...BUT I WONDERED IF KOIZUMI WAS MEETING UP WITH SOME GIRL.
IT WOULDN'T HAVE SURPRISED ME.
HE WAS SLICK LIKE THAT.
......
I MIGHT AS WELL WRITE A LITTLE MORE.
JUST A COUPLE EXTRA LINES, LIKE HE SAID.

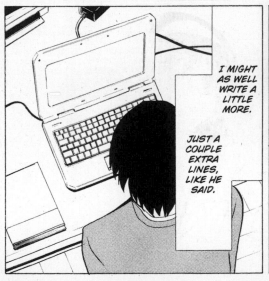

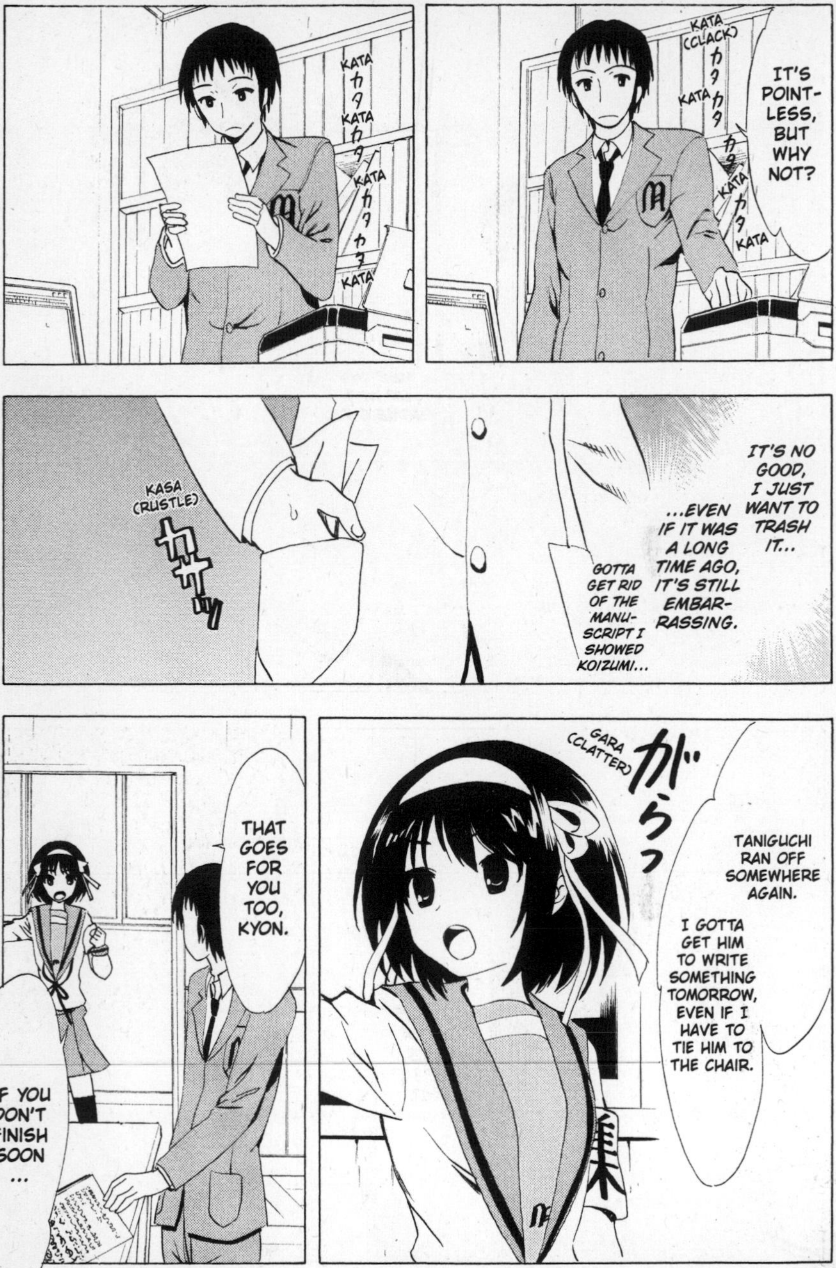
KATA (CLACK)
KATA
KATA
KATA
IT'S POINTLESS, BUT WHY NOT?
KATA
KATA
KATA
KATA
IT'S NO GOOD, I JUST WANT TO TRASH IT...
...EVEN IF IT WAS A LONG TIME AGO, IT'S STILL EMBARRASSING.
GOTTA GET RID OF THE MANUSCRIPT I SHOWED KOIZUMI...
KASA (RUSTLE)
GARA (CLATTER)
TANIGUCHI RAN OFF SOMEWHERE AGAIN.
I GOTTA GET HIM TO WRITE SOMETHING TOMORROW, EVEN IF I HAVE TO TIE HIM TO THE CHAIR.
THAT GOES FOR YOU TOO, KYON.
IF YOU DON'T FINISH SOON ...

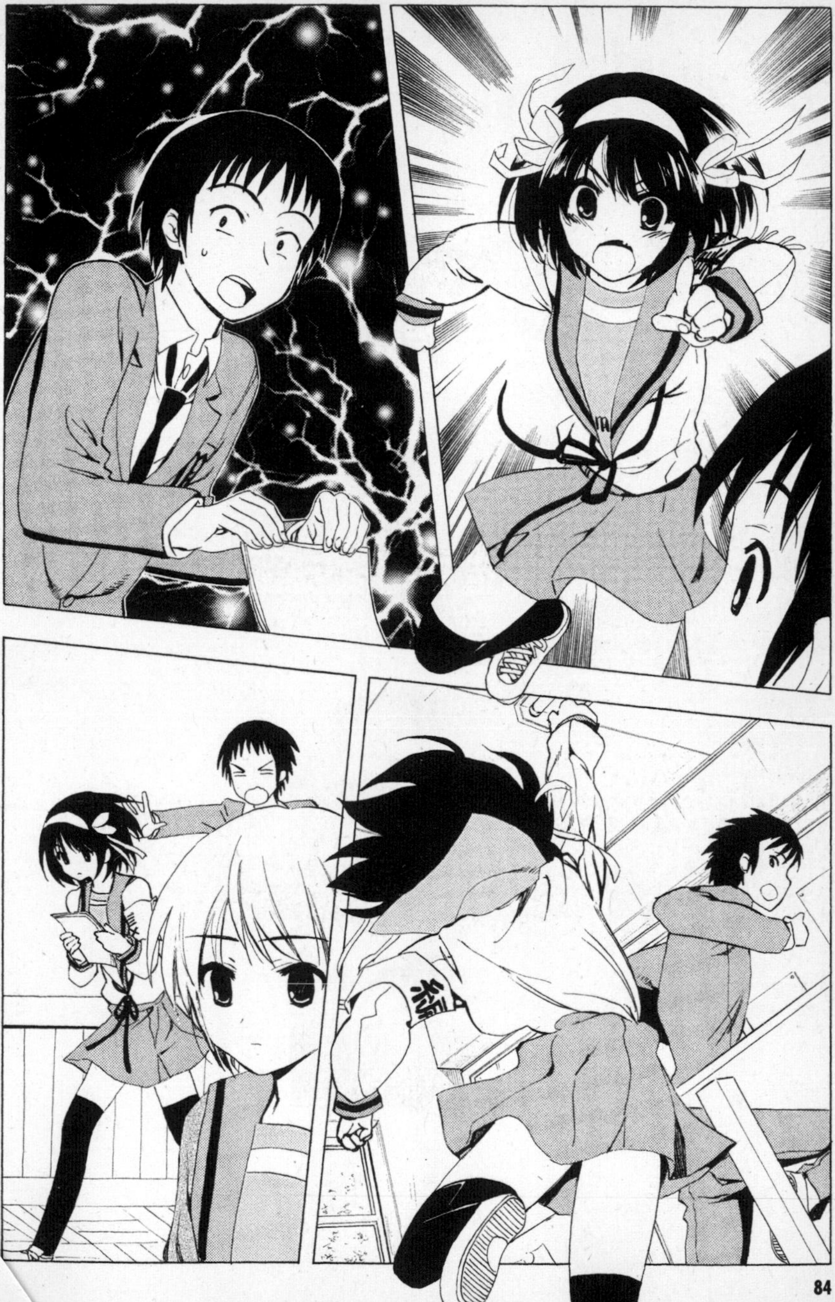

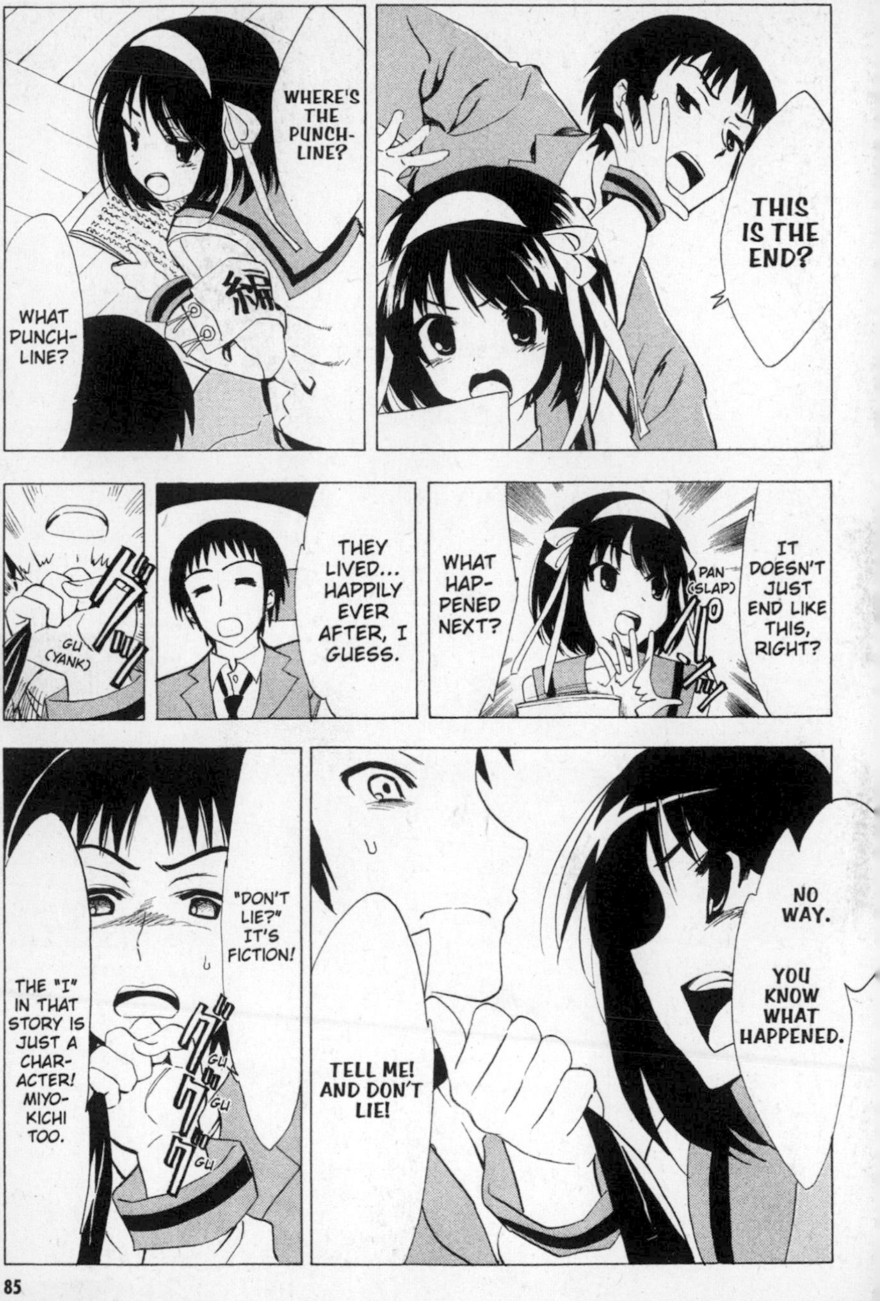
THIS IS THE END?
WHERE'S THE PUNCH-LINE?
WHAT PUNCH-LINE?
IT DOESN'T JUST END LIKE THIS, RIGHT?
PAN (SLAP)
WHAT HAP-PENED NEXT?
THEY LIVED... HAPPILY EVER AFTER, I GUESS.
GU (YANK)
NO WAY.
YOU KNOW WHAT HAPPENED.
TELL ME! AND DON'T LIE!
"DON'T LIE?" IT'S FICTION!
THE "I" IN THAT STORY IS JUST A CHAR-ACTER! MIYO-KICHI TOO.
GU GU GU

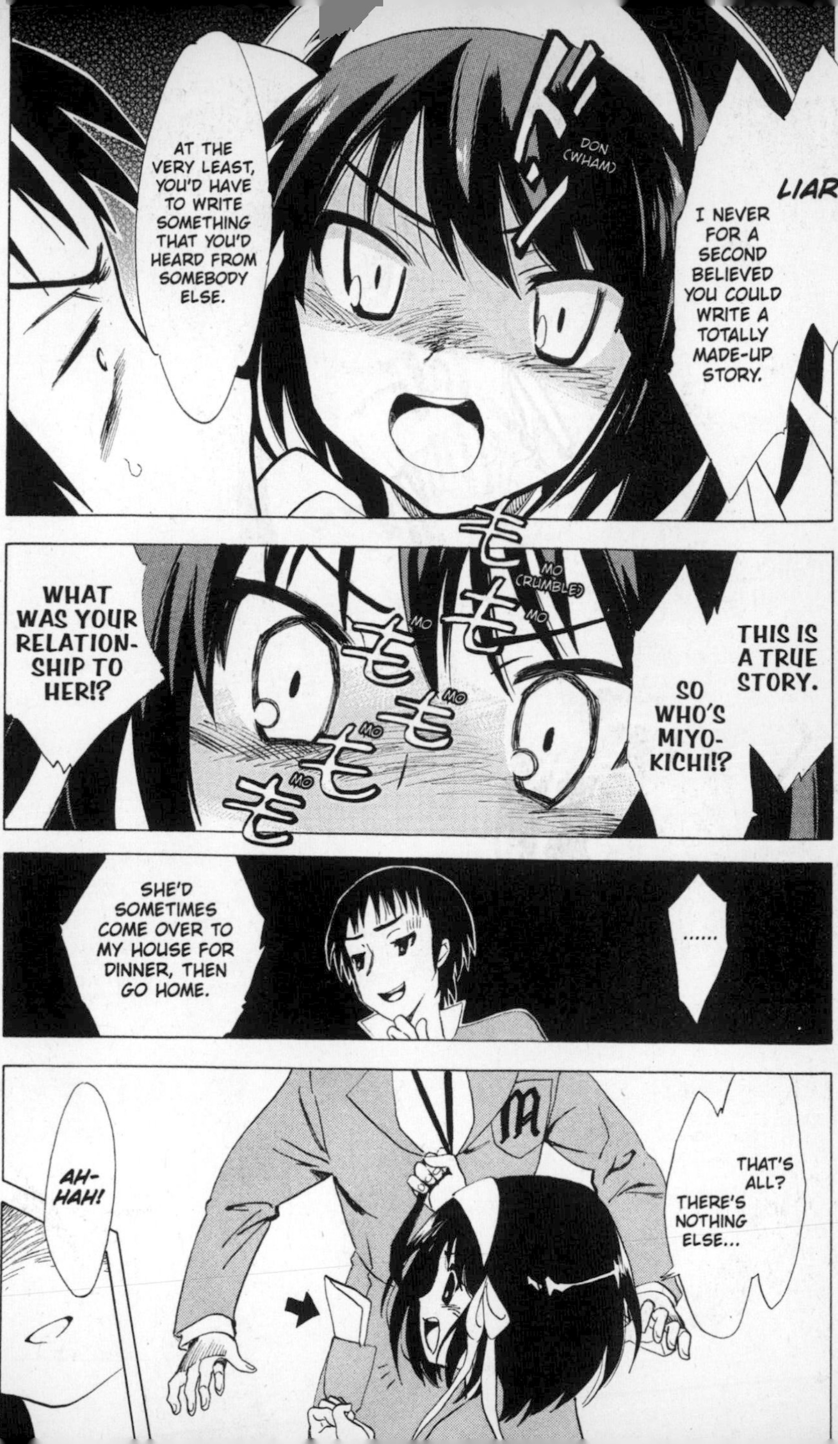
LIAR!
I NEVER FOR A SECOND BELIEVED YOU COULD WRITE A TOTALLY MADE-UP STORY.
DON (WHAM)
AT THE VERY LEAST, YOU'D HAVE TO WRITE SOMETHING THAT YOU'D HEARD FROM SOMEBODY ELSE.
THIS IS A TRUE STORY.
SO WHO'S MIYO-KICHI!?
MO (RUMBLE) MO MO MO MO MO
WHAT WAS YOUR RELATION-SHIP TO HER!?
......
SHE'D SOMETIMES COME OVER TO MY HOUSE FOR DINNER, THEN GO HOME.
THAT'S ALL? THERE'S NOTHING ELSE...
AH-HAH!

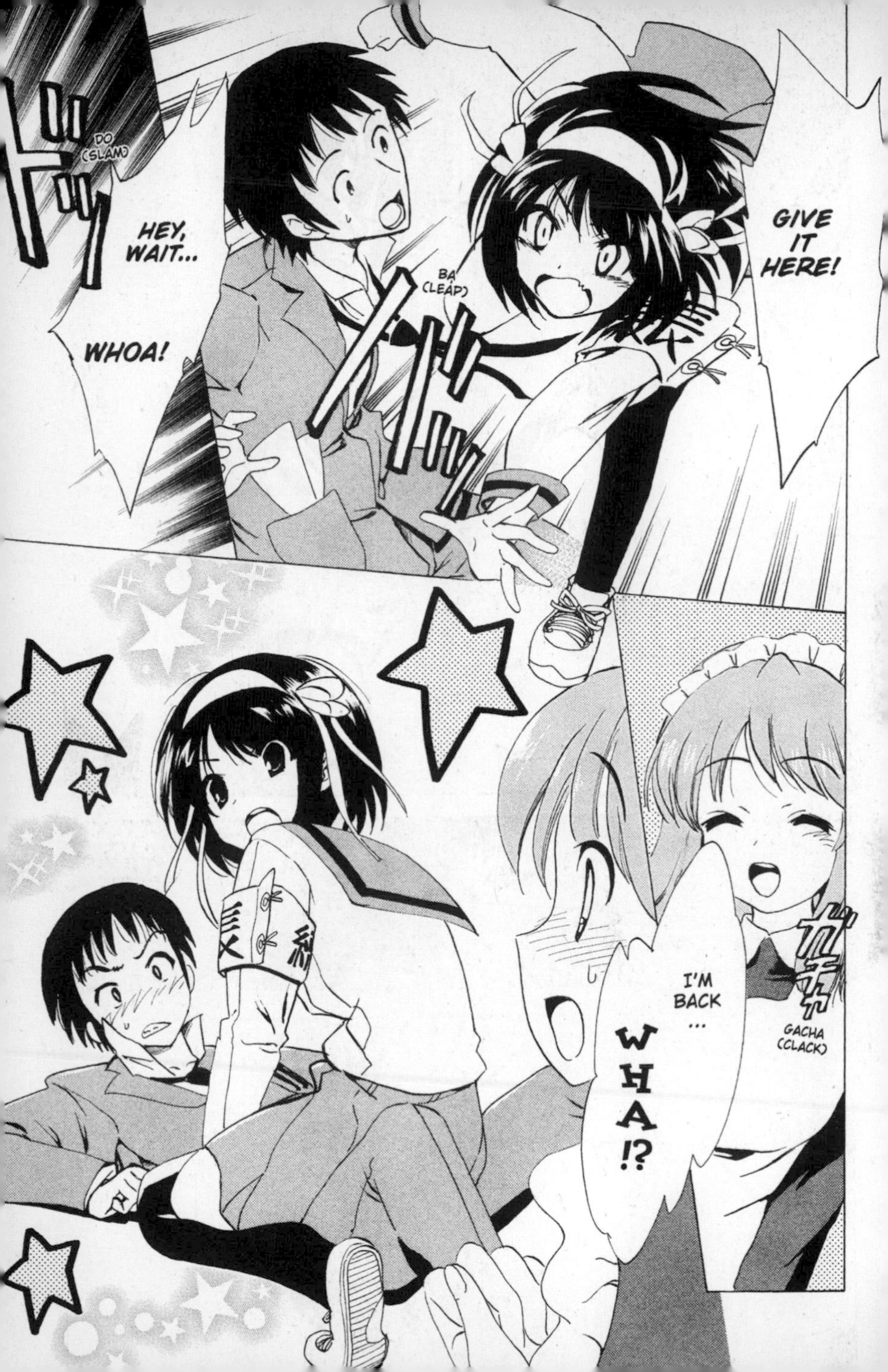
GIVE IT HERE!
BA (LEAP)
DO (SLAM)
HEY, WAIT...
WHOA!
GACHA (CLACK)
I'M BACK...
WHA!?

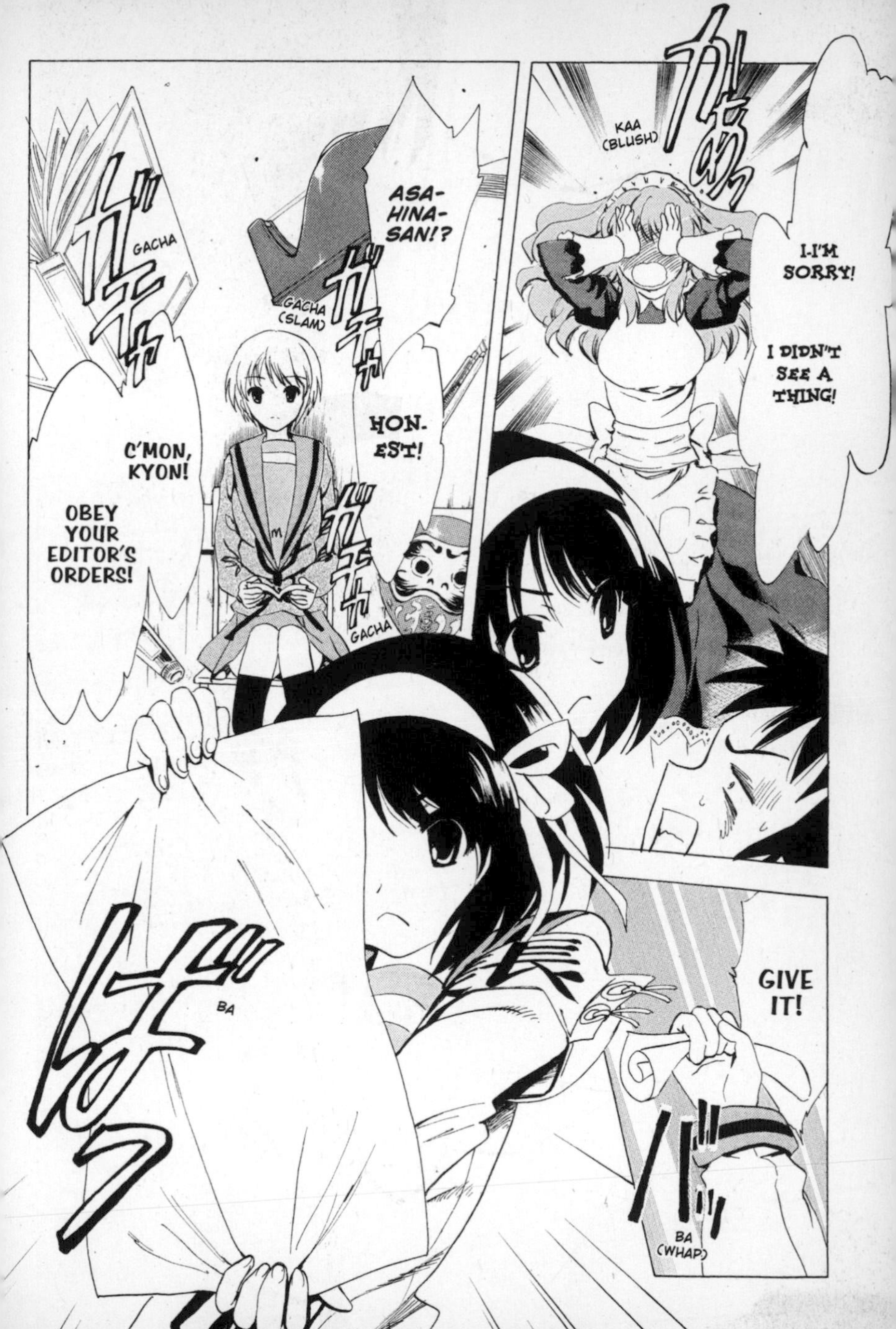
KAA (BLUSH)
I-I'M SORRY!
I DIDN'T SEE A THING!
ASA-HINA-SAN!?
GACHA (SLAM)
GACHA
HON-EST!
GACHA
C'MON, KYON!
OBEY YOUR EDITOR'S ORDERS!
GIVE IT!
BA (WHAP)
BA

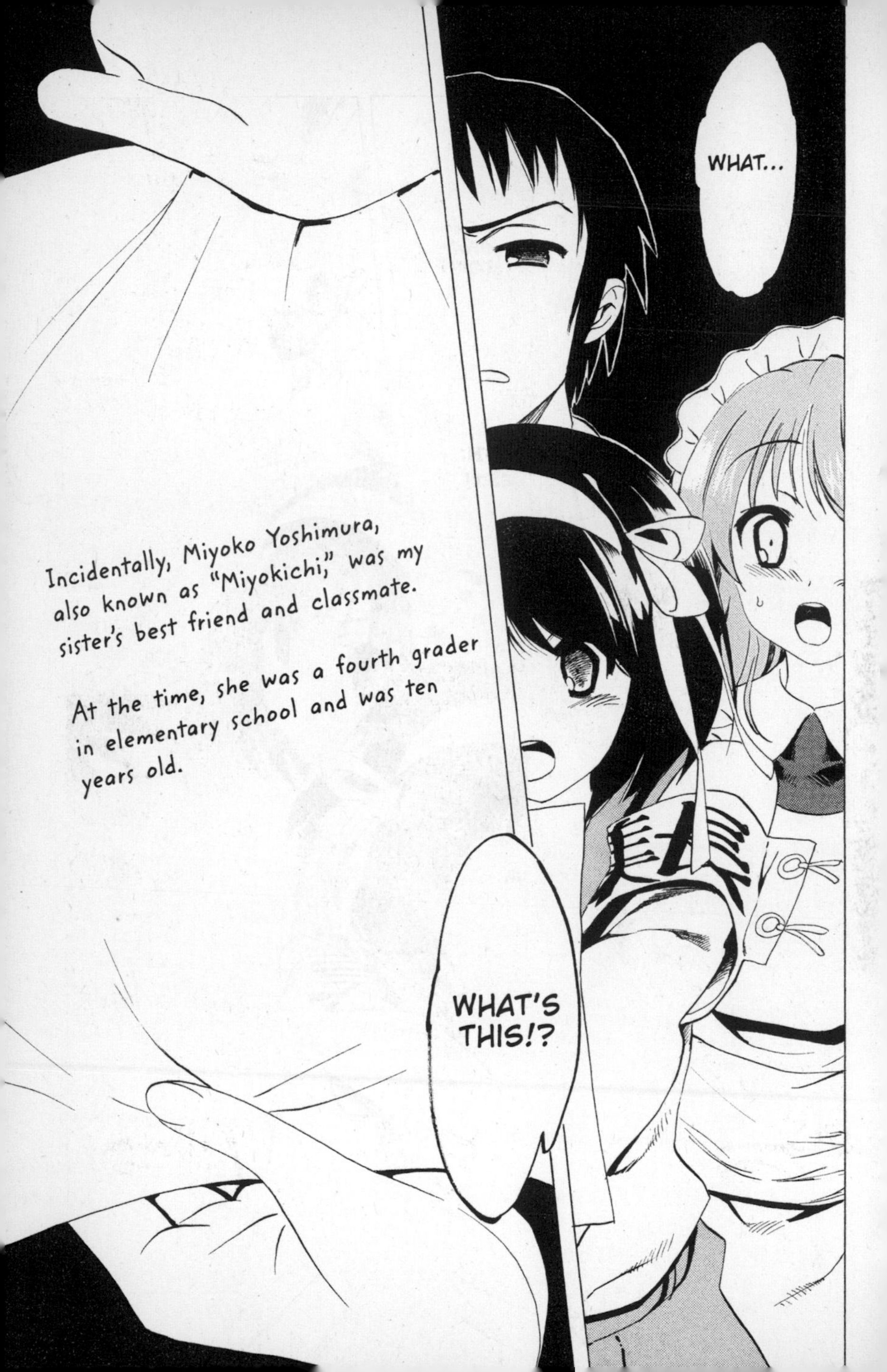
WHAT...
WHAT'S THIS!?
Incidentally, Miyoko Yoshimura, also known as "Miyokichi," was my sister's best friend and classmate.
At the time, she was a fourth grader in elementary school and was ten years old.

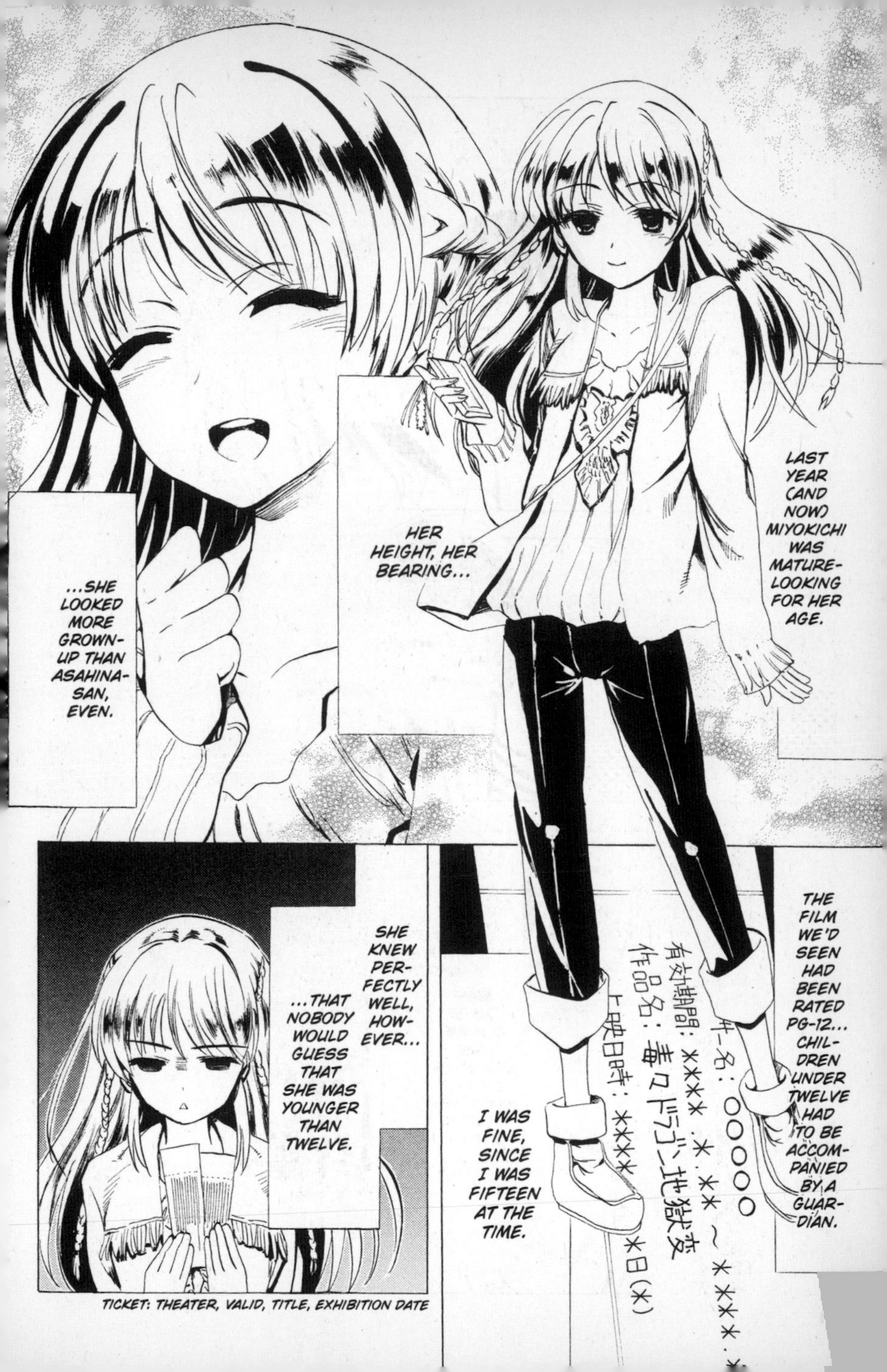
LAST YEAR (AND NOW) MIYOKICHI WAS MATURE-LOOKING FOR HER AGE.
HER HEIGHT, HER BEARING...
...SHE LOOKED MORE GROWN-UP THAN ASAHINA-SAN, EVEN.
THE FILM WE'D SEEN HAD BEEN RATED PG-12... CHILDREN UNDER TWELVE HAD TO BE ACCOMPANIED BY A GUARDIAN.
作品名：毒々ドラゴン地獄変
I WAS FINE, SINCE I WAS FIFTEEN AT THE TIME.
SHE KNEW PERFECTLY WELL, HOWEVER...
...THAT NOBODY WOULD GUESS THAT SHE WAS YOUNGER THAN TWELVE.
TICKET: THEATER, VALID, TITLE, EXHIBITION DATE

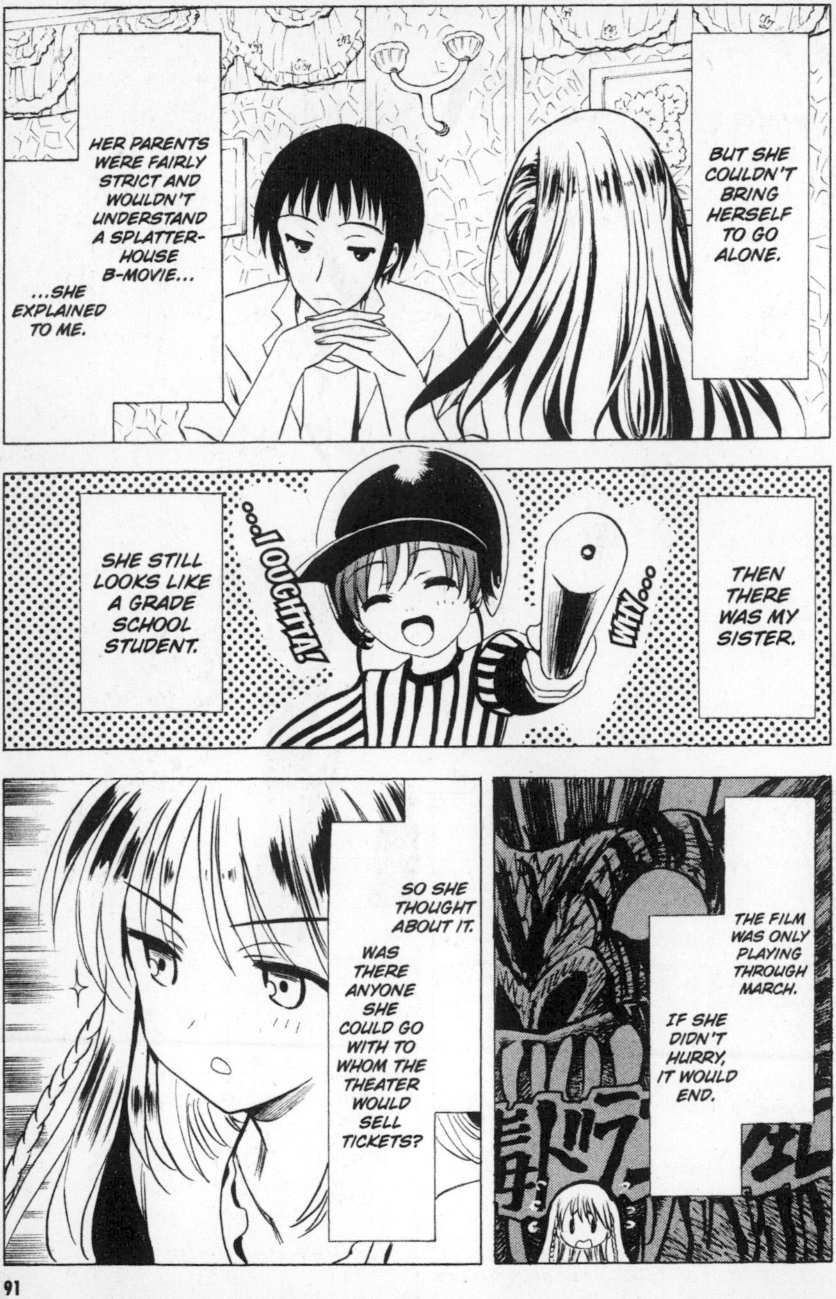
BUT SHE COULDN'T BRING HERSELF TO GO ALONE.
HER PARENTS WERE FAIRLY STRICT AND WOULDN'T UNDERSTAND A SPLATTER-HOUSE B-MOVIE...
...SHE EXPLAINED TO ME.
THEN THERE WAS MY SISTER.
WHY
OUCHITA!
SHE STILL LOOKS LIKE A GRADE SCHOOL STUDENT.
THE FILM WAS ONLY PLAYING THROUGH MARCH.
IF SHE DIDN'T HURRY, IT WOULD END.
SO SHE THOUGHT ABOUT IT.
WAS THERE ANYONE SHE COULD GO WITH TO WHOM THE THEATER WOULD SELL TICKETS?

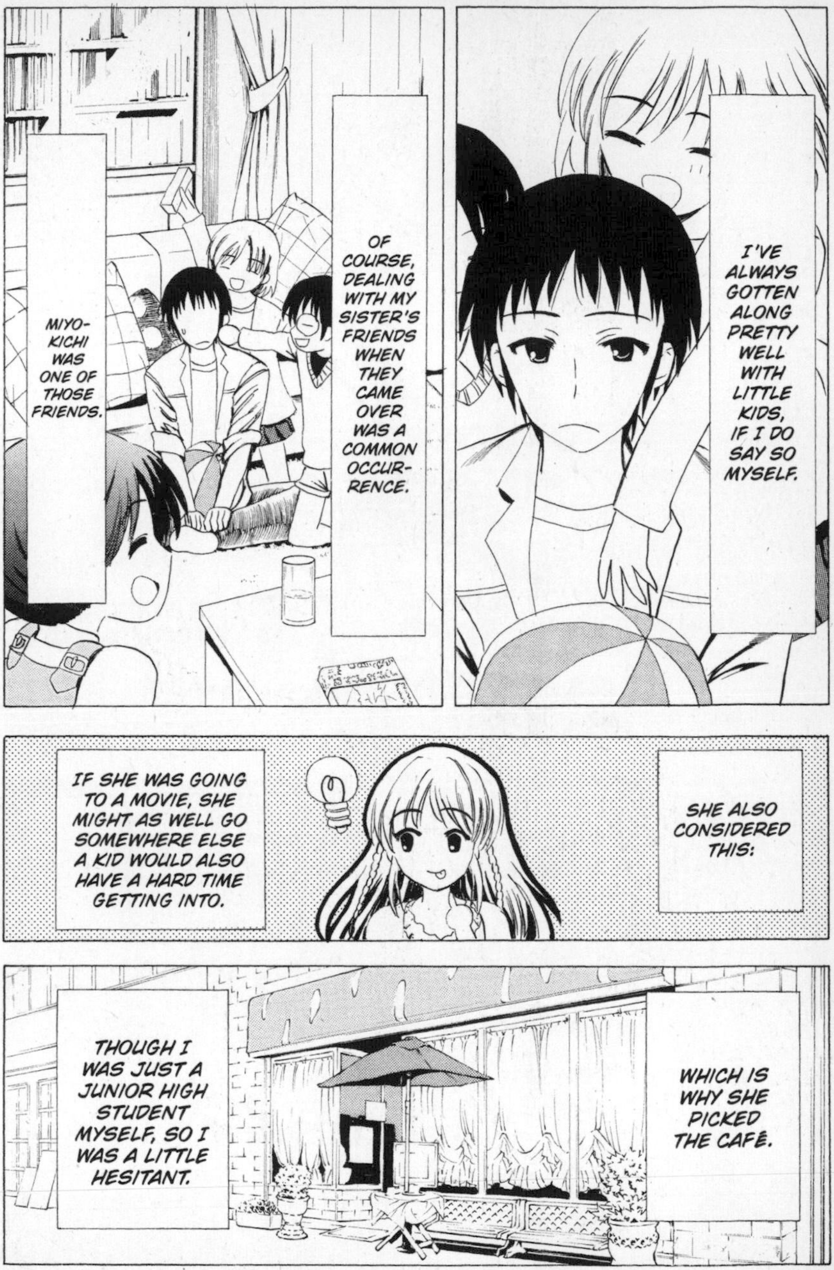

I'VE ALWAYS GOTTEN ALONG PRETTY WELL WITH LITTLE KIDS, IF I DO SAY SO MYSELF.
OF COURSE, DEALING WITH MY SISTER'S FRIENDS WHEN THEY CAME OVER WAS A COMMON OCCURRENCE.
MIYOKICHI WAS ONE OF THOSE FRIENDS.
SHE ALSO CONSIDERED THIS:
IF SHE WAS GOING TO A MOVIE, SHE MIGHT AS WELL GO SOMEWHERE ELSE A KID WOULD ALSO HAVE A HARD TIME GETTING INTO.
WHICH IS WHY SHE PICKED THE CAFÉ.
THOUGH I WAS JUST A JUNIOR HIGH STUDENT MYSELF, SO I WAS A LITTLE HESITANT.

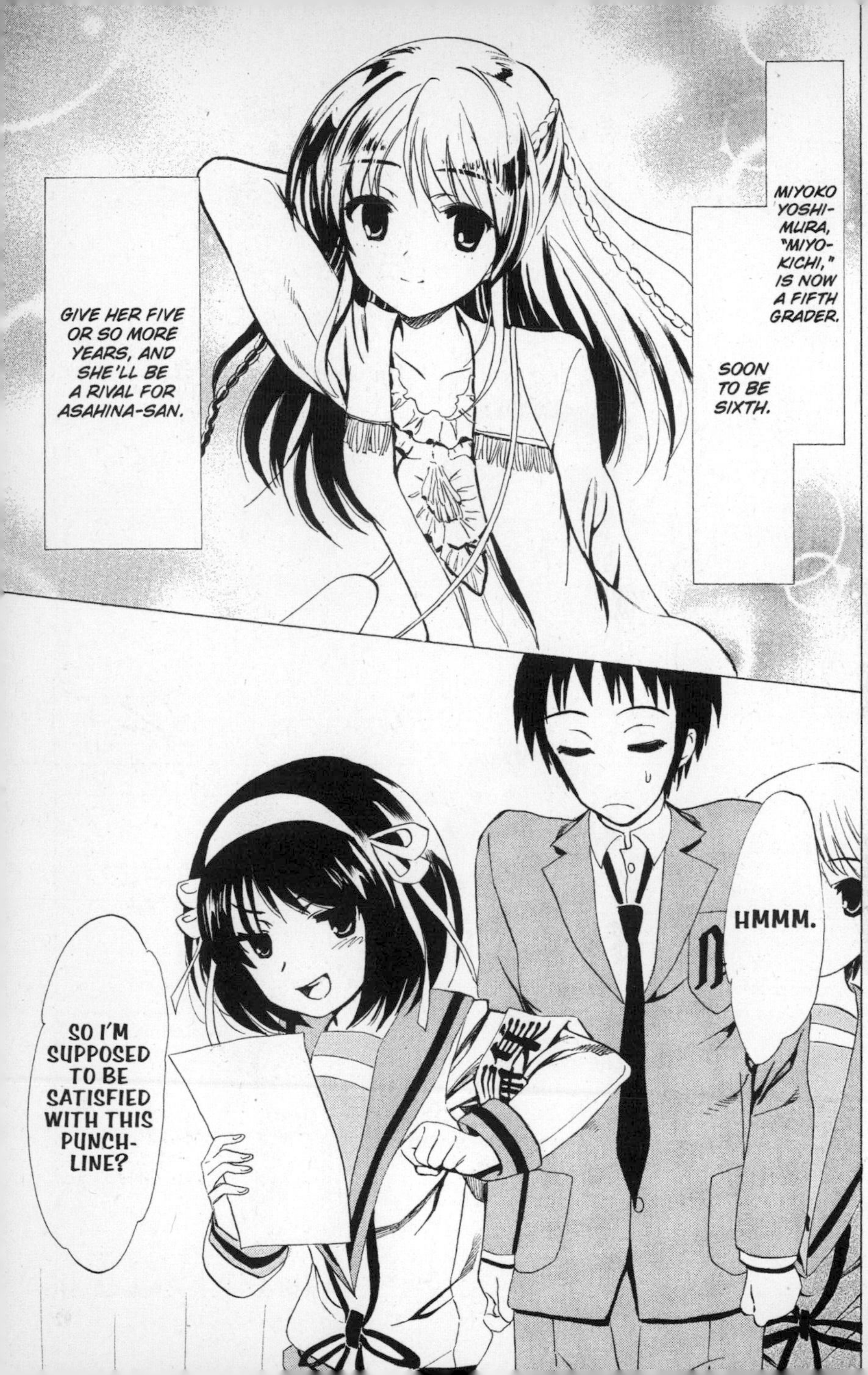
MIYOKO YOSHIMURA, "MIYOKICHI," IS NOW A FIFTH GRADER.
SOON TO BE SIXTH.
GIVE HER FIVE OR SO MORE YEARS, AND SHE'LL BE A RIVAL FOR ASAHINA-SAN.
HMMM.
SO I'M SUPPOSED TO BE SATISFIED WITH THIS PUNCHLINE?

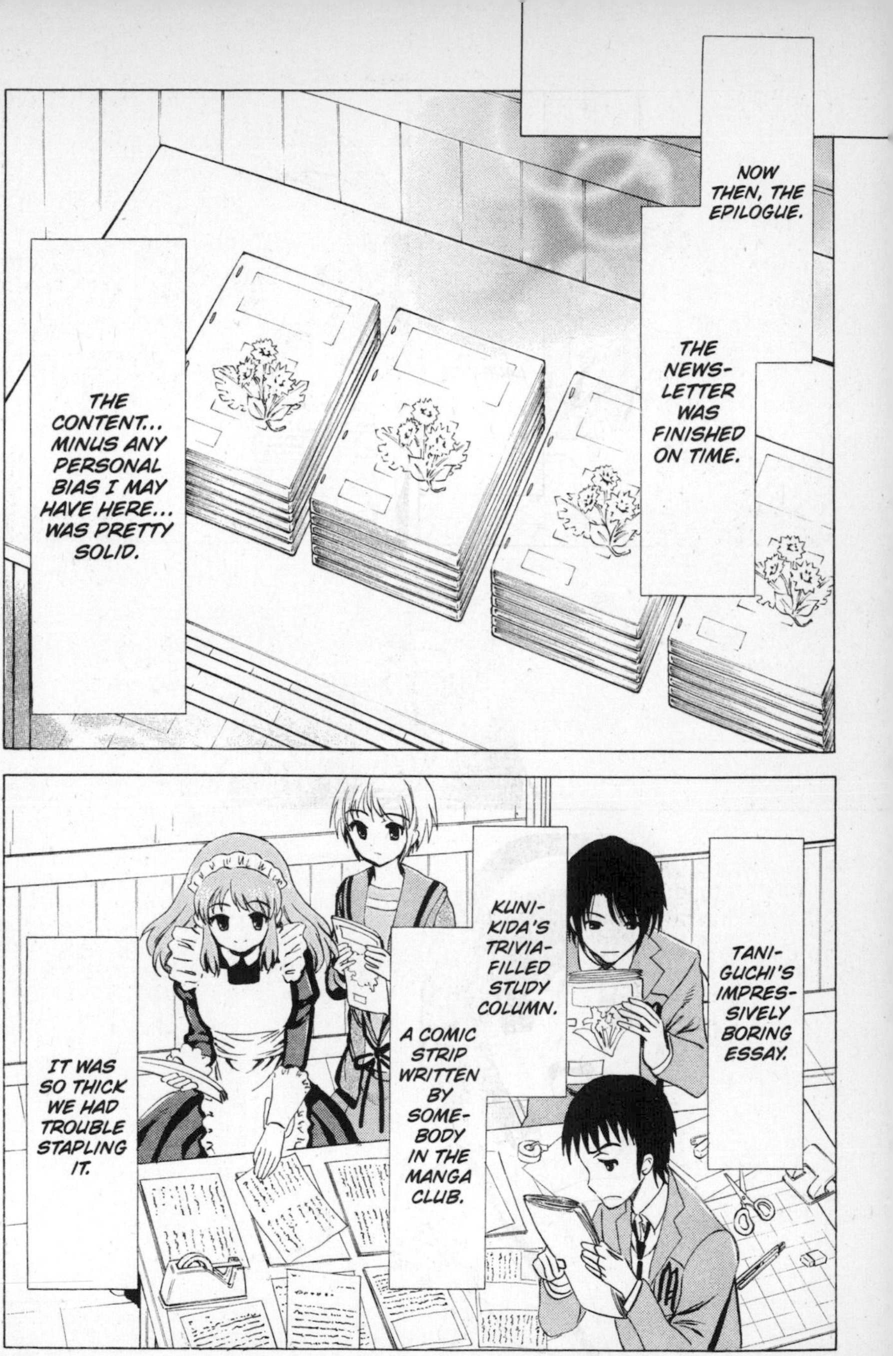
NOW THEN, THE EPILOGUE.
THE NEWSLETTER WAS FINISHED ON TIME.
THE CONTENT... MINUS ANY PERSONAL BIAS I MAY HAVE HERE... WAS PRETTY SOLID.
TANIGUCHI'S IMPRESSIVELY BORING ESSAY.
KUNIKIDA'S TRIVIA-FILLED STUDY COLUMN.
A COMIC STRIP WRITTEN BY SOMEBODY IN THE MANGA CLUB.
IT WAS SO THICK WE HAD TROUBLE STAPLING IT.

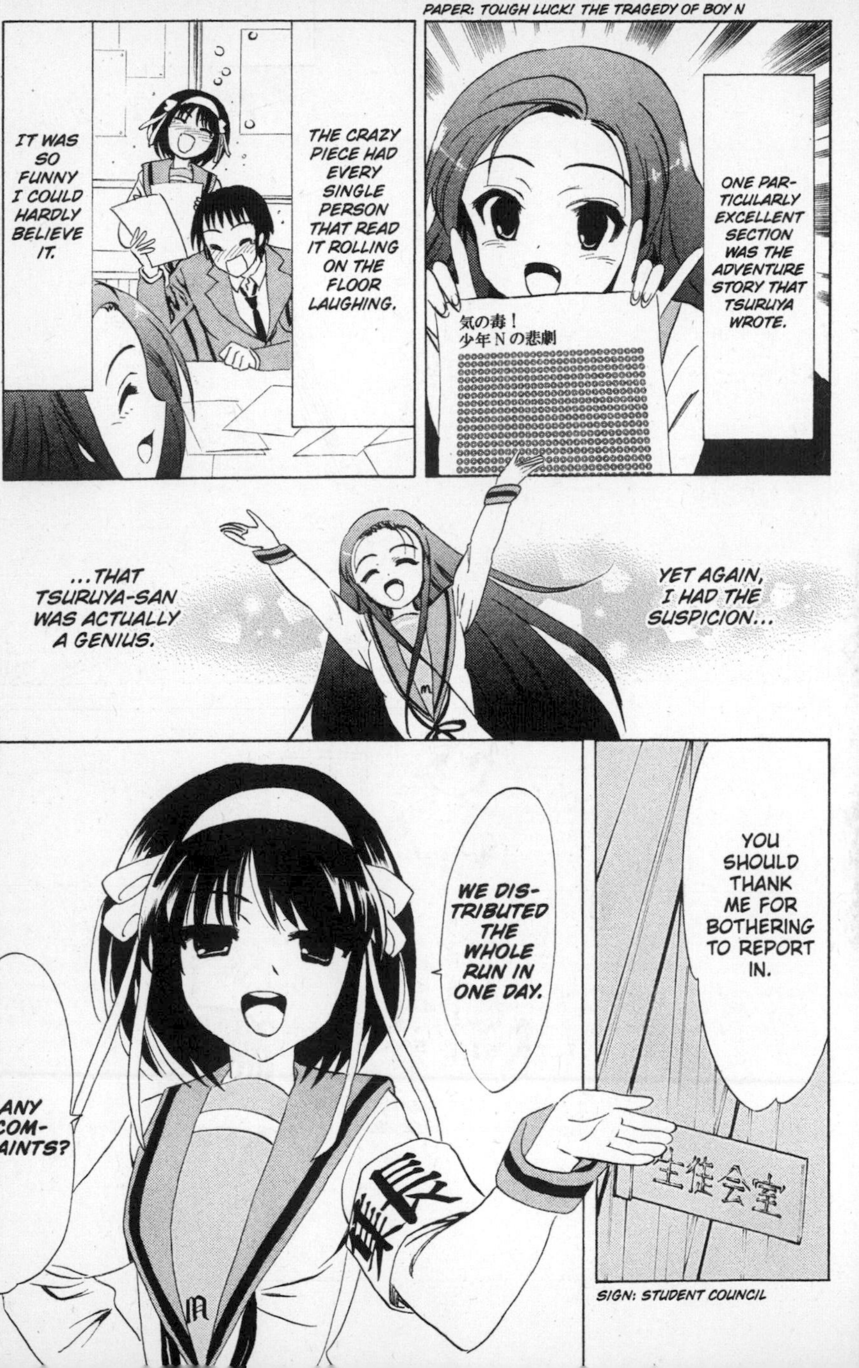
PAPER: TOUGH LUCK! THE TRAGEDY OF BOY N
ONE PARTICULARLY EXCELLENT SECTION WAS THE ADVENTURE STORY THAT TSURUYA WROTE.
気の毒！少年Nの悲劇
THE CRAZY PIECE HAD EVERY SINGLE PERSON THAT READ IT ROLLING ON THE FLOOR LAUGHING.
IT WAS SO FUNNY I COULD HARDLY BELIEVE IT.
YET AGAIN, I HAD THE SUSPICION...
...THAT TSURUYA-SAN WAS ACTUALLY A GENIUS.
YOU SHOULD THANK ME FOR BOTHERING TO REPORT IN.
生徒会室
SIGN: STUDENT COUNCIL
WE DISTRIBUTED THE WHOLE RUN IN ONE DAY.
ANY COMPLAINTS?

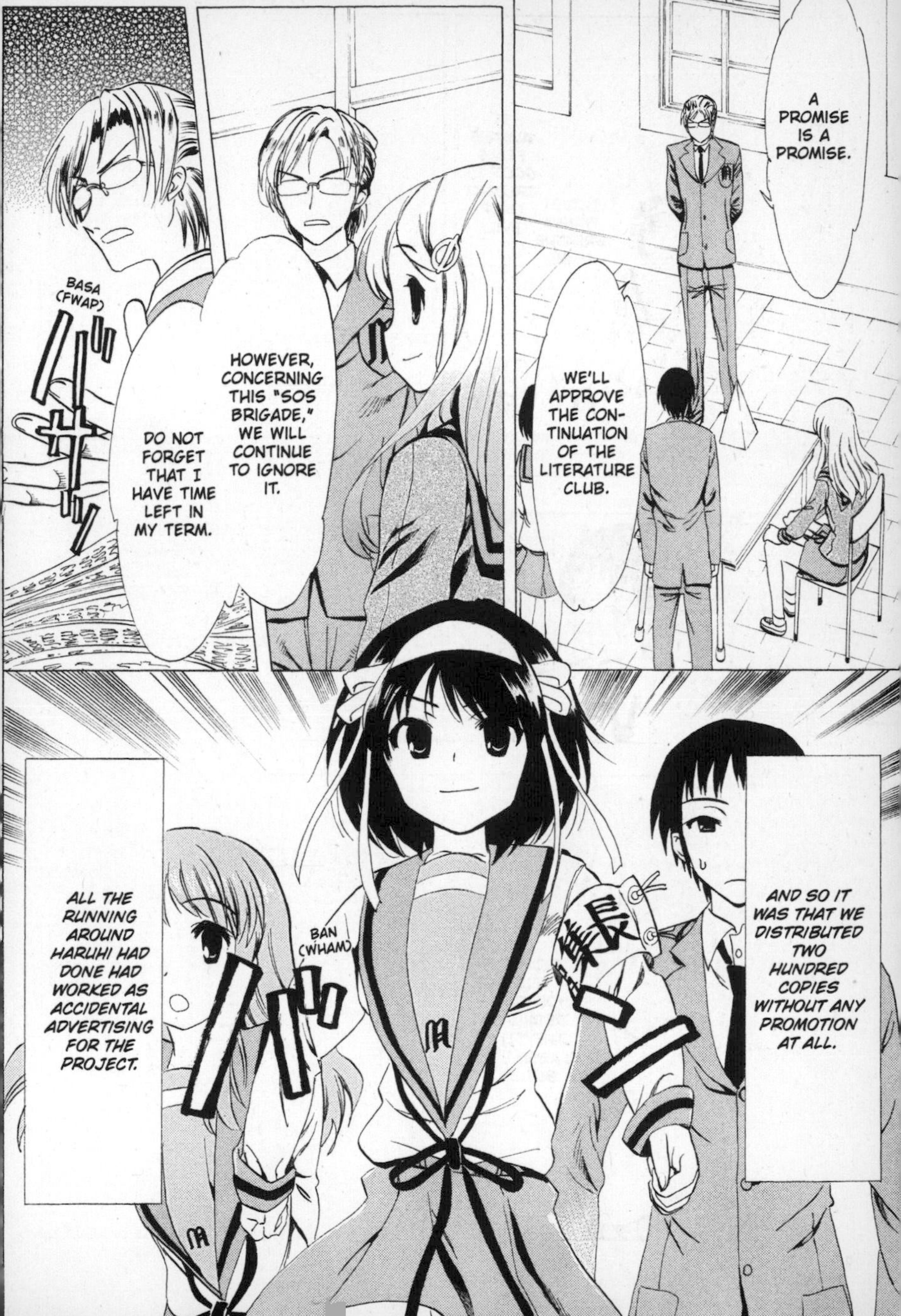
A PROMISE IS A PROMISE.
WE'LL APPROVE THE CONTINUATION OF THE LITERATURE CLUB.
HOWEVER, CONCERNING THIS "SOS BRIGADE," WE WILL CONTINUE TO IGNORE IT.
DO NOT FORGET THAT I HAVE TIME LEFT IN MY TERM.
BASA (FWAP)
AND SO IT WAS THAT WE DISTRIBUTED TWO HUNDRED COPIES WITHOUT ANY PROMOTION AT ALL.
BAN (WHAM)
ALL THE RUNNING AROUND HARUHI HAD DONE HAD WORKED AS ACCIDENTAL ADVERTISING FOR THE PROJECT.

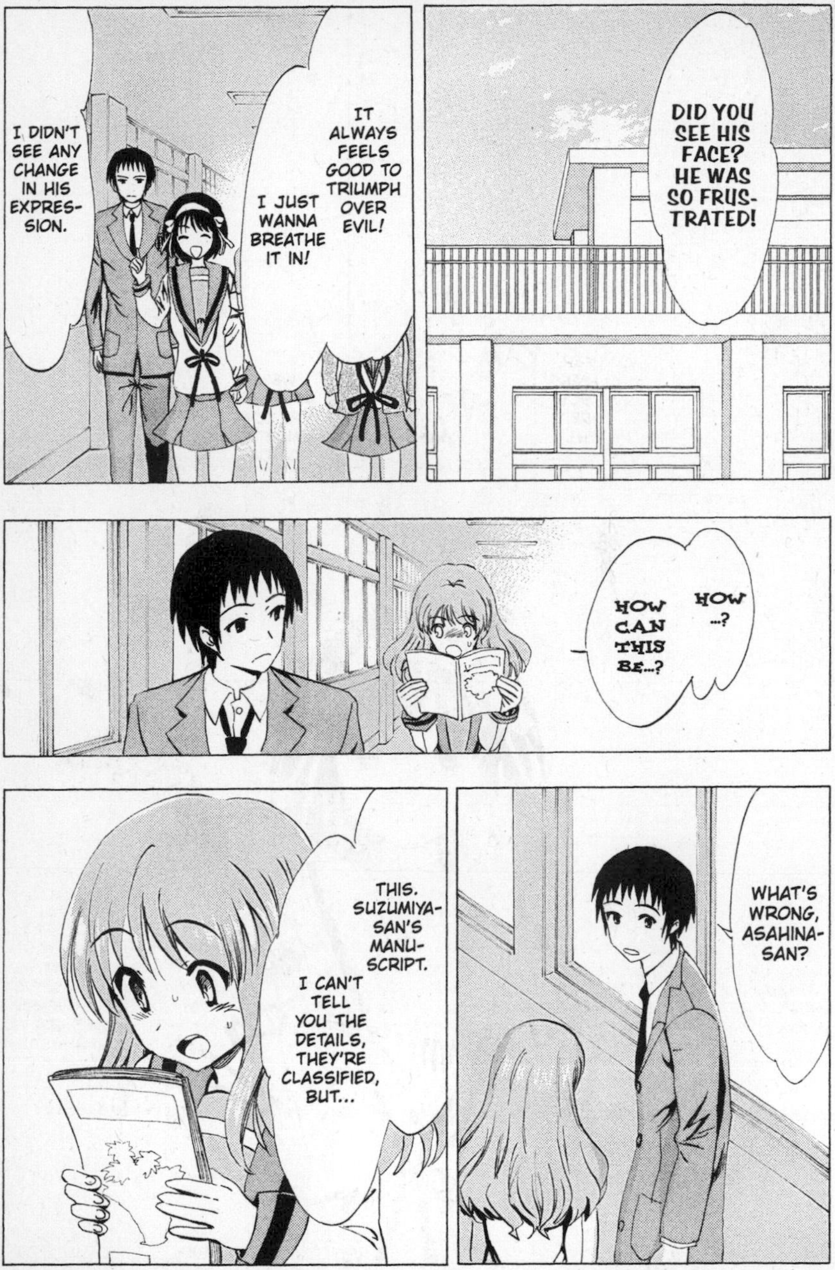
DID YOU SEE HIS FACE? HE WAS SO FRUS-TRATED!
IT ALWAYS FEELS GOOD TO TRIUMPH OVER EVIL!
I JUST WANNA BREATHE IT IN!
I DIDN'T SEE ANY CHANGE IN HIS EXPRES-SION.
HOW ...?
HOW CAN THIS BE...?
WHAT'S WRONG, ASAHINA-SAN?
THIS. SUZUMIYA-SAN'S MANU-SCRIPT.
I CAN'T TELL YOU THE DETAILS, THEY'RE CLASSIFIED, BUT...

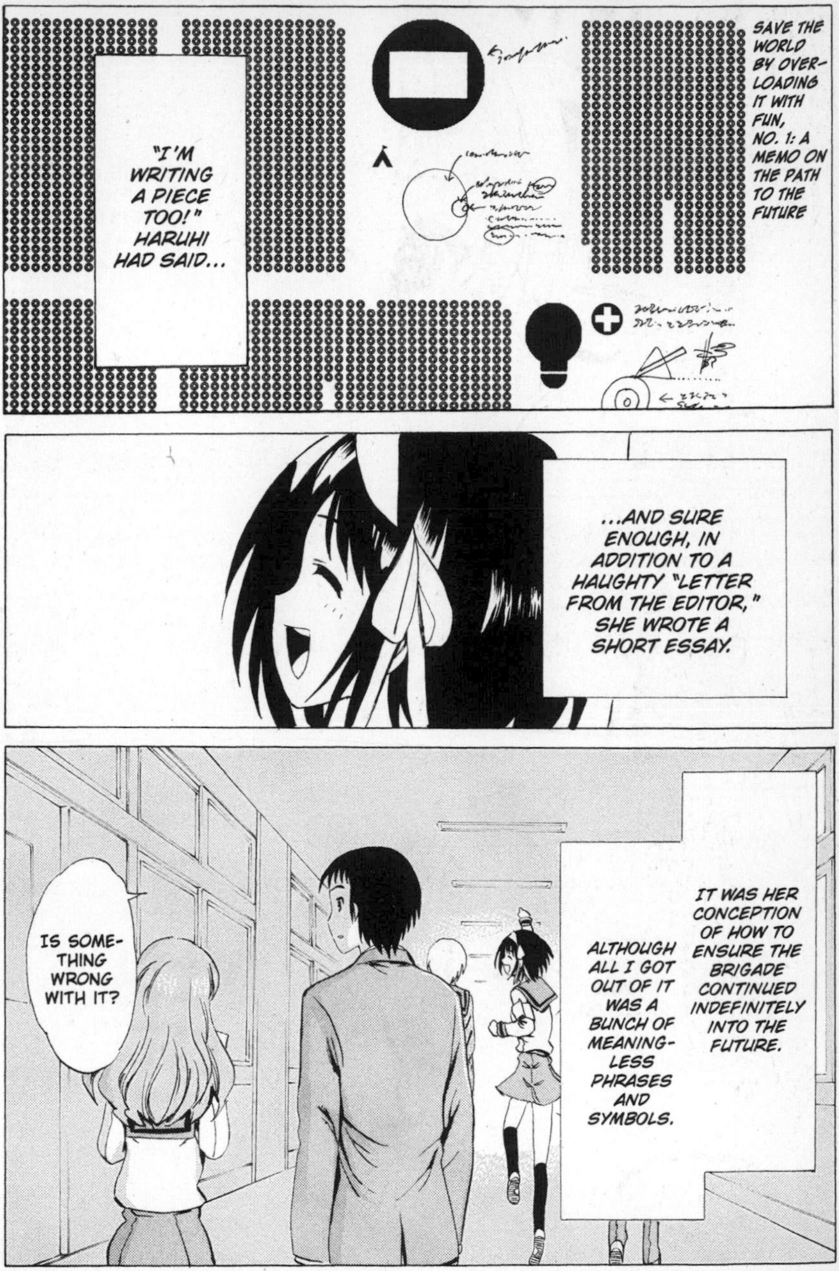
SAVE THE WORLD BY OVER-LOADING IT WITH FUN, NO. 1: A MEMO ON THE PATH TO THE FUTURE
"I'M WRITING A PIECE TOO!" HARUHI HAD SAID...
...AND SURE ENOUGH, IN ADDITION TO A HAUGHTY "LETTER FROM THE EDITOR," SHE WROTE A SHORT ESSAY.
IT WAS HER CONCEPTION OF HOW TO ENSURE THE BRIGADE CONTINUED INDEFINITELY INTO THE FUTURE.
ALTHOUGH ALL I GOT OUT OF IT WAS A BUNCH OF MEANING-LESS PHRASES AND SYMBOLS.
IS SOME-THING WRONG WITH IT?

PAPER: WHEN THE QUANTUM ELECTRODYNAMIC EFFECTS OF TIME-SPACE DILATION ARE PROJECTED ONTO AN N-DIMENSIONAL MANIFOLD THUSLY, WE SEE THAT...
SPECIAL RELATIVITY SHOWS HOW LORENTZ TRANSFORMATIONS CAN BE DERIVED VIA THE FOLLOWING EQUATION...

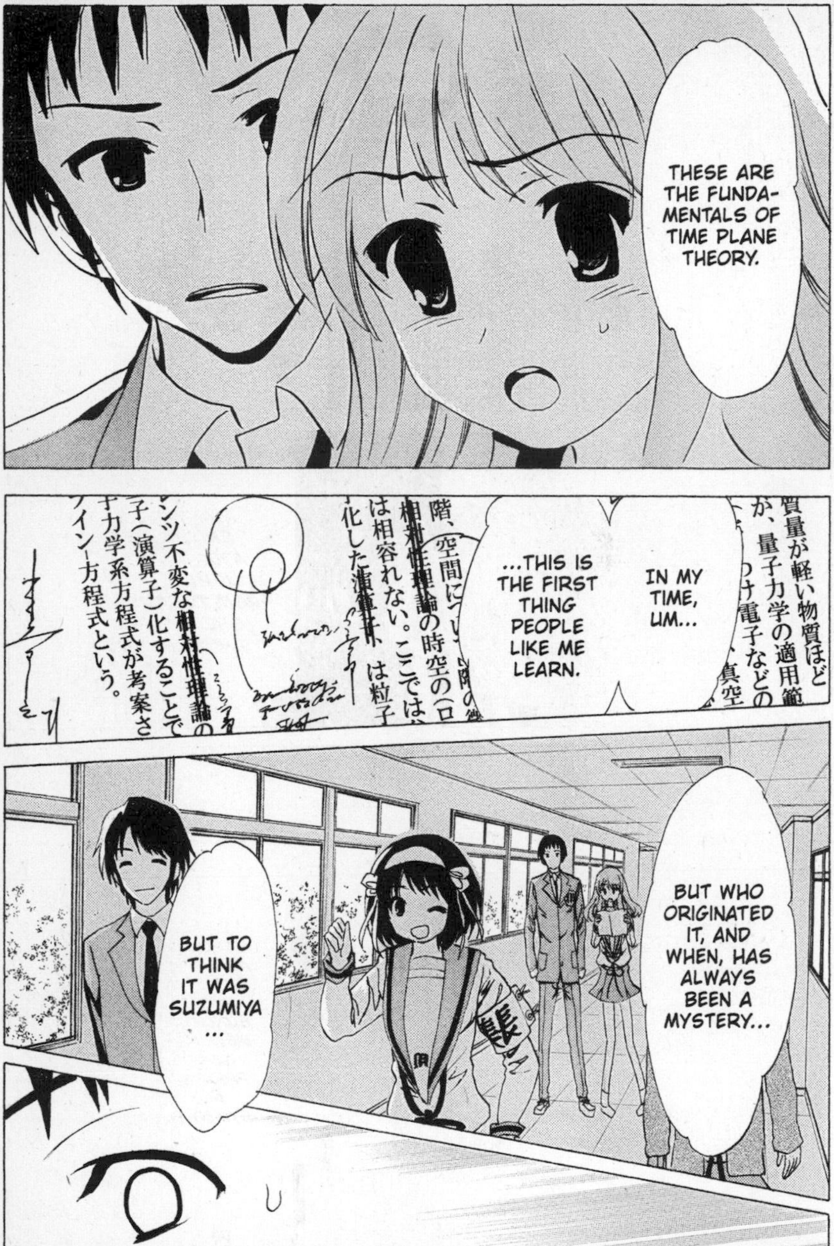
THESE ARE THE FUNDAMENTALS OF TIME PLANE THEORY.
IN MY TIME, UM...
...THIS IS THE FIRST THING PEOPLE LIKE ME LEARN.
BUT WHO ORIGINATED IT, AND WHEN, HAS ALWAYS BEEN A MYSTERY...
BUT TO THINK IT WAS SUZUMIYA ...

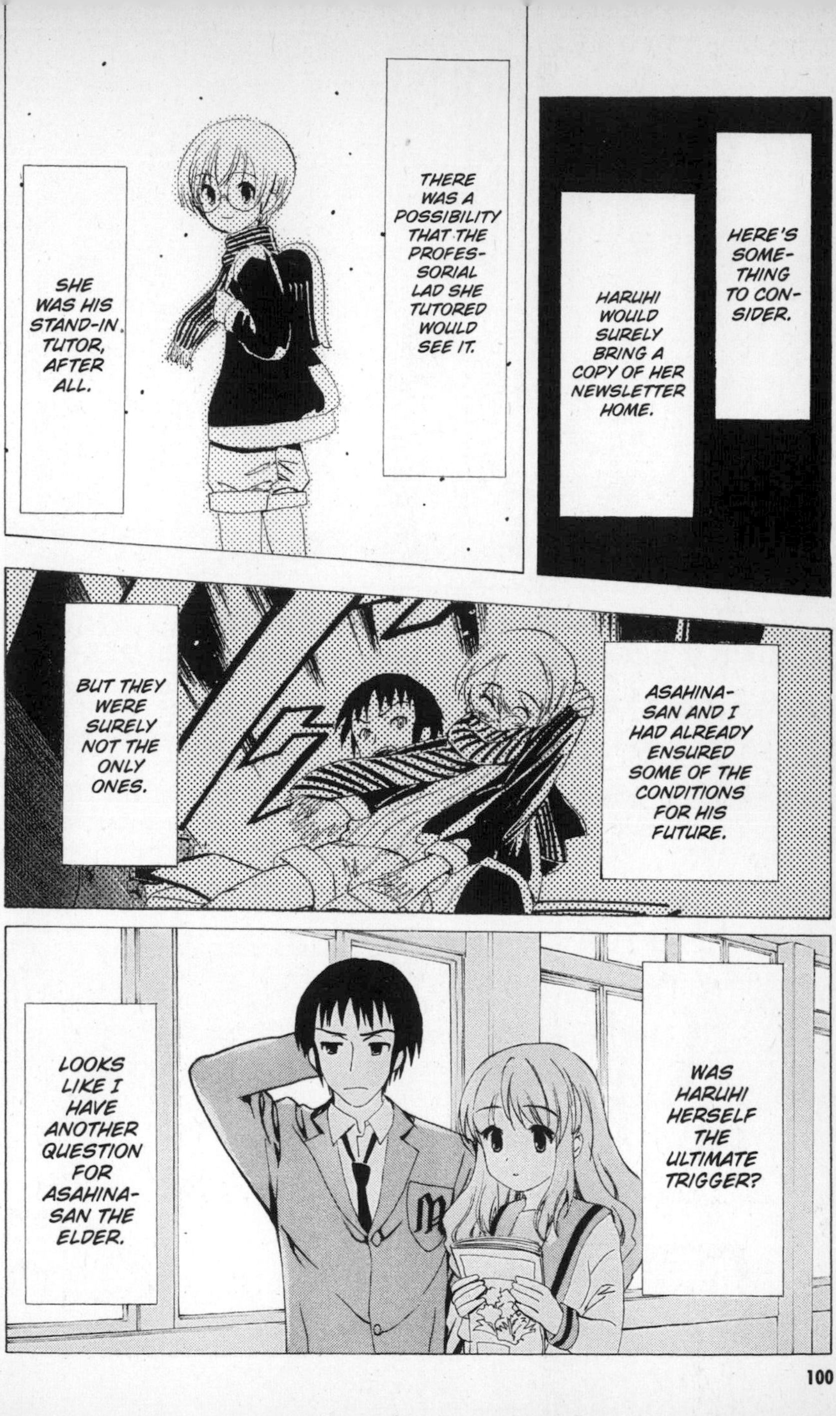
HERE'S SOMETHING TO CONSIDER.
HARUHI WOULD SURELY BRING A COPY OF HER NEWSLETTER HOME.
THERE WAS A POSSIBILITY THAT THE PROFESSORIAL LAD SHE TUTORED WOULD SEE IT.
SHE WAS HIS STAND-IN TUTOR, AFTER ALL.
ASAHINA-SAN AND I HAD ALREADY ENSURED SOME OF THE CONDITIONS FOR HIS FUTURE.
BUT THEY WERE SURELY NOT THE ONLY ONES.
WAS HARUHI HERSELF THE ULTIMATE TRIGGER?
LOOKS LIKE I HAVE ANOTHER QUESTION FOR ASAHINA-SAN THE ELDER.

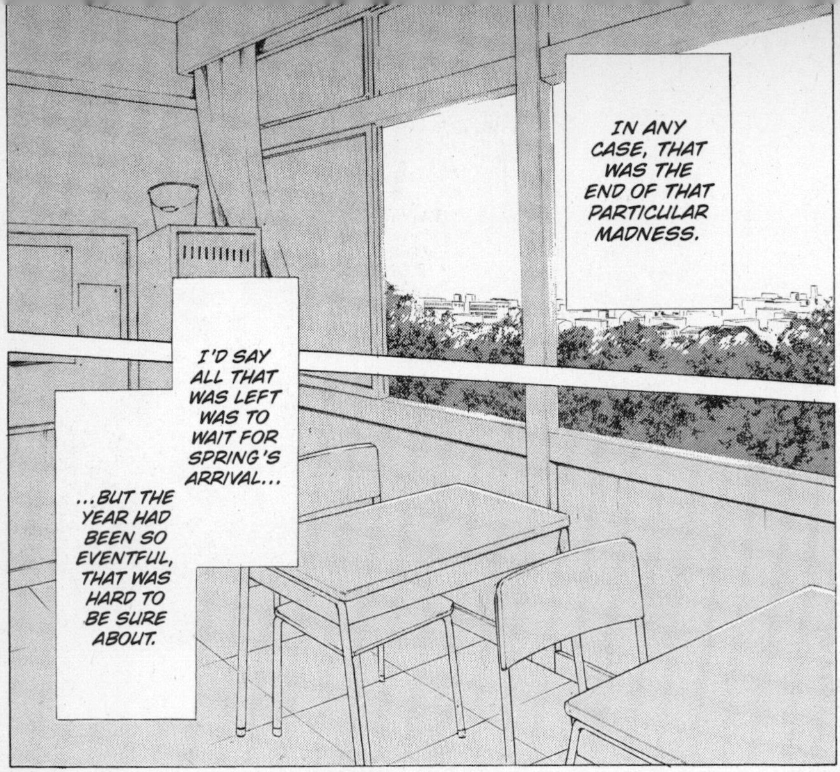
IN ANY CASE, THAT WAS THE END OF THAT PARTICULAR MADNESS.
I'D SAY ALL THAT WAS LEFT WAS TO WAIT FOR SPRING'S ARRIVAL...
...BUT THE YEAR HAD BEEN SO EVENTFUL, THAT WAS HARD TO BE SURE ABOUT.

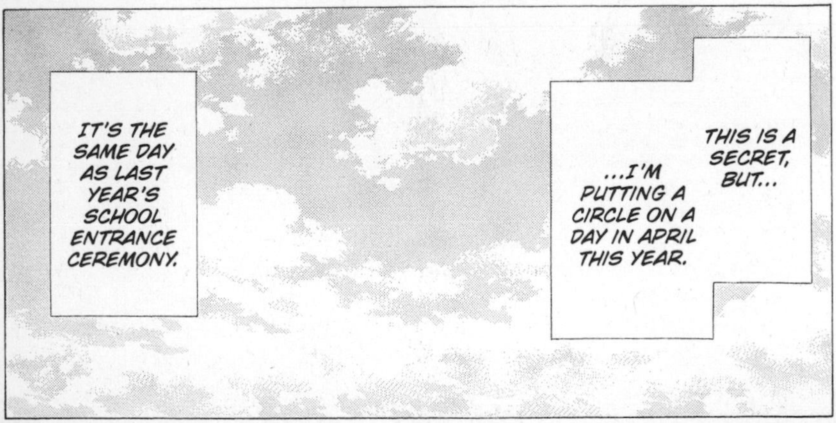
THIS IS A SECRET, BUT...
...I'M PUTTING A CIRCLE ON A DAY IN APRIL THIS YEAR.
IT'S THE SAME DAY AS LAST YEAR'S SCHOOL ENTRANCE CEREMONY.

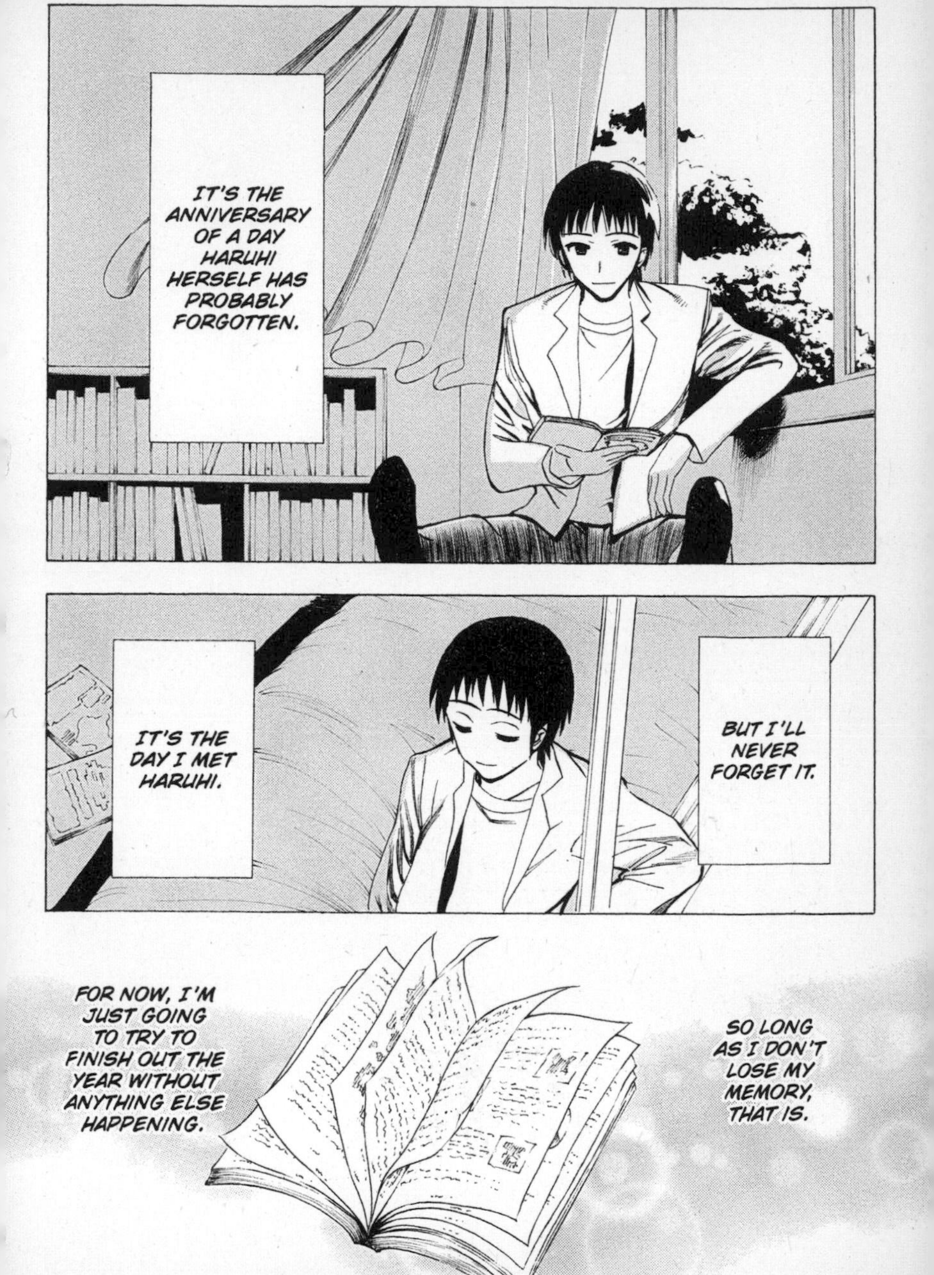
IT'S THE ANNIVERSARY OF A DAY HARUHI HERSELF HAS PROBABLY FORGOTTEN.
IT'S THE DAY I MET HARUHI.
BUT I'LL NEVER FORGET IT.
FOR NOW, I'M JUST GOING TO TRY TO FINISH OUT THE YEAR WITHOUT ANYTHING ELSE HAPPENING.
SO LONG AS I DON'T LOSE MY MEMORY, THAT IS.

EDITOR-IN-CHIEF★FULL SPEED AHEAD! V : END

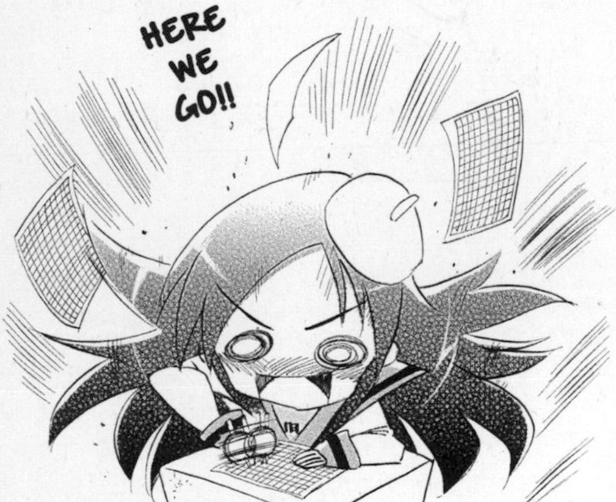
HERE WE GO!!
みかん
BOX: ORANGES

THE MELANCHOLY OF HARUHI SUZUMIYA

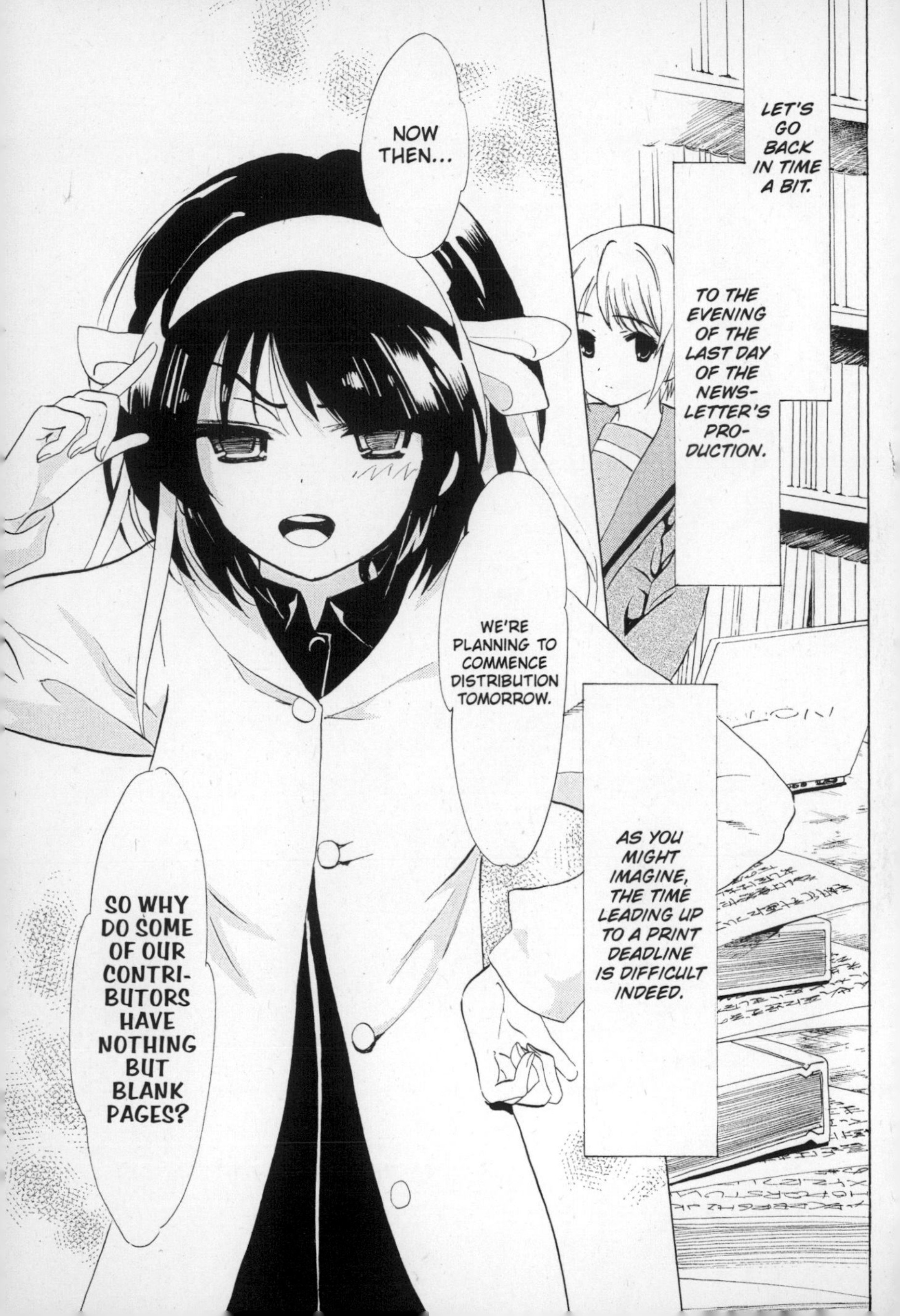
LET'S GO BACK IN TIME A BIT.
TO THE EVENING OF THE LAST DAY OF THE NEWS-LETTER'S PRO-DUCTION.
NOW THEN...
WE'RE PLANNING TO COMMENCE DISTRIBUTION TOMORROW.
AS YOU MIGHT IMAGINE, THE TIME LEADING UP TO A PRINT DEADLINE IS DIFFICULT INDEED.
SO WHY DO SOME OF OUR CONTRI-BUTORS HAVE NOTHING BUT BLANK PAGES?

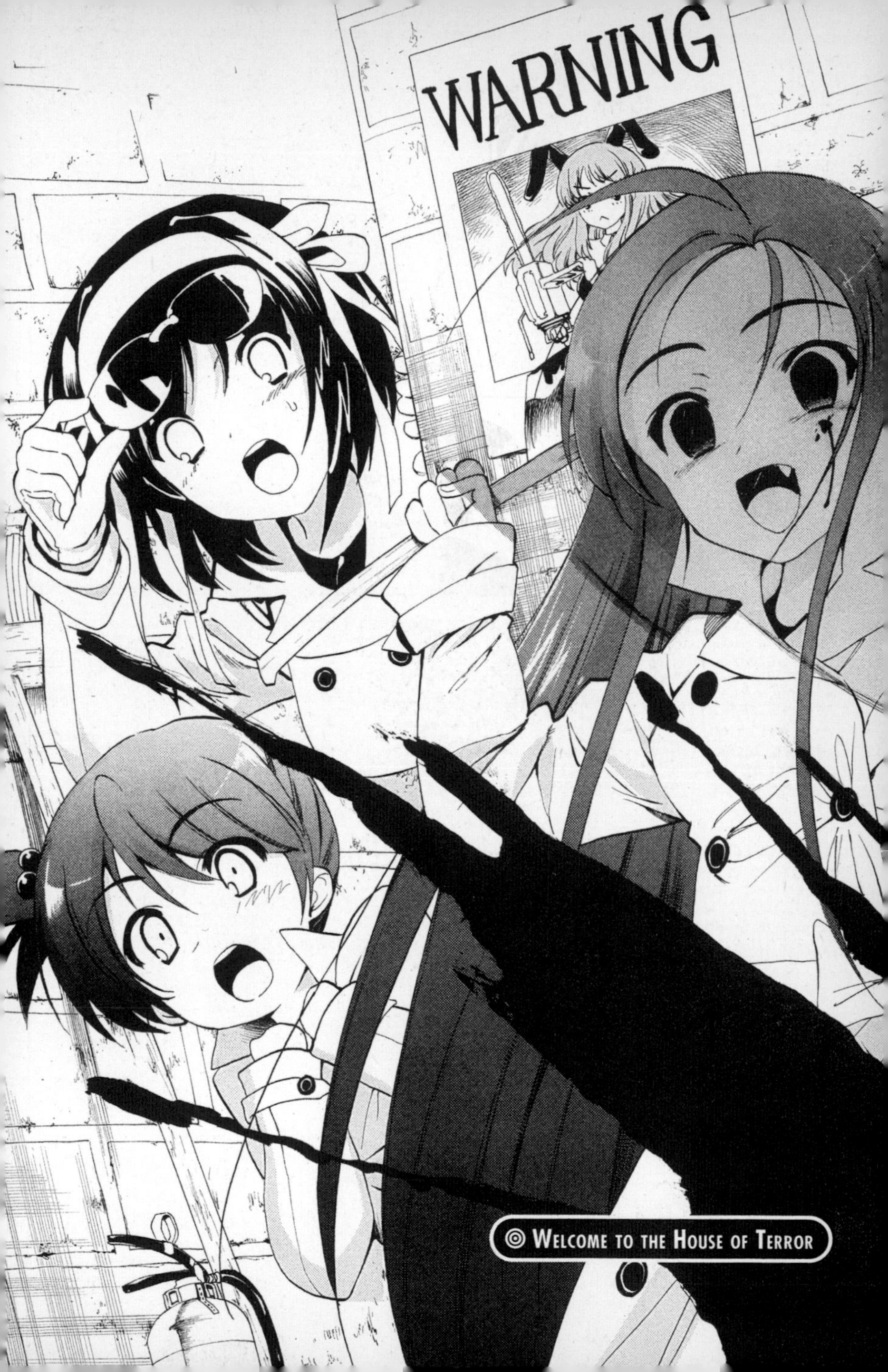
WARNING

◎ Welcome to the House of Terror

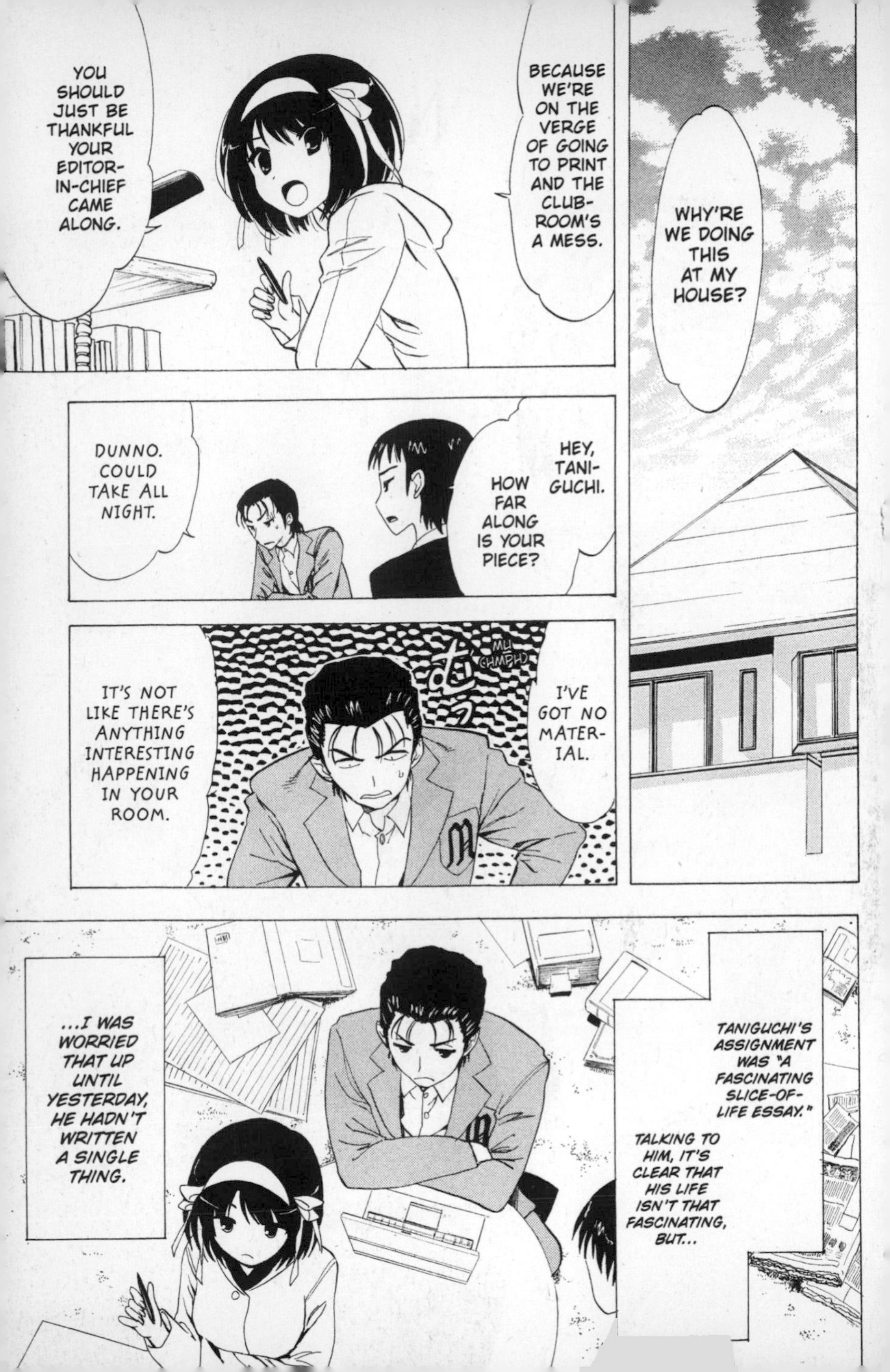
WHY'RE WE DOING THIS AT MY HOUSE?
BECAUSE WE'RE ON THE VERGE OF GOING TO PRINT AND THE CLUB-ROOM'S A MESS.
YOU SHOULD JUST BE THANKFUL YOUR EDITOR-IN-CHIEF CAME ALONG.
HEY, TANI-GUCHI.
HOW FAR ALONG IS YOUR PIECE?
DUNNO. COULD TAKE ALL NIGHT.
MUGHMPH
I'VE GOT NO MATER-IAL.
IT'S NOT LIKE THERE'S ANYTHING INTERESTING HAPPENING IN YOUR ROOM.
TANIGUCHI'S ASSIGNMENT WAS "A FASCINATING SLICE-OF-LIFE ESSAY."
TALKING TO HIM, IT'S CLEAR THAT HIS LIFE ISN'T THAT FASCINATING, BUT...
...I WAS WORRIED THAT UP UNTIL YESTERDAY, HE HADN'T WRITTEN A SINGLE THING.

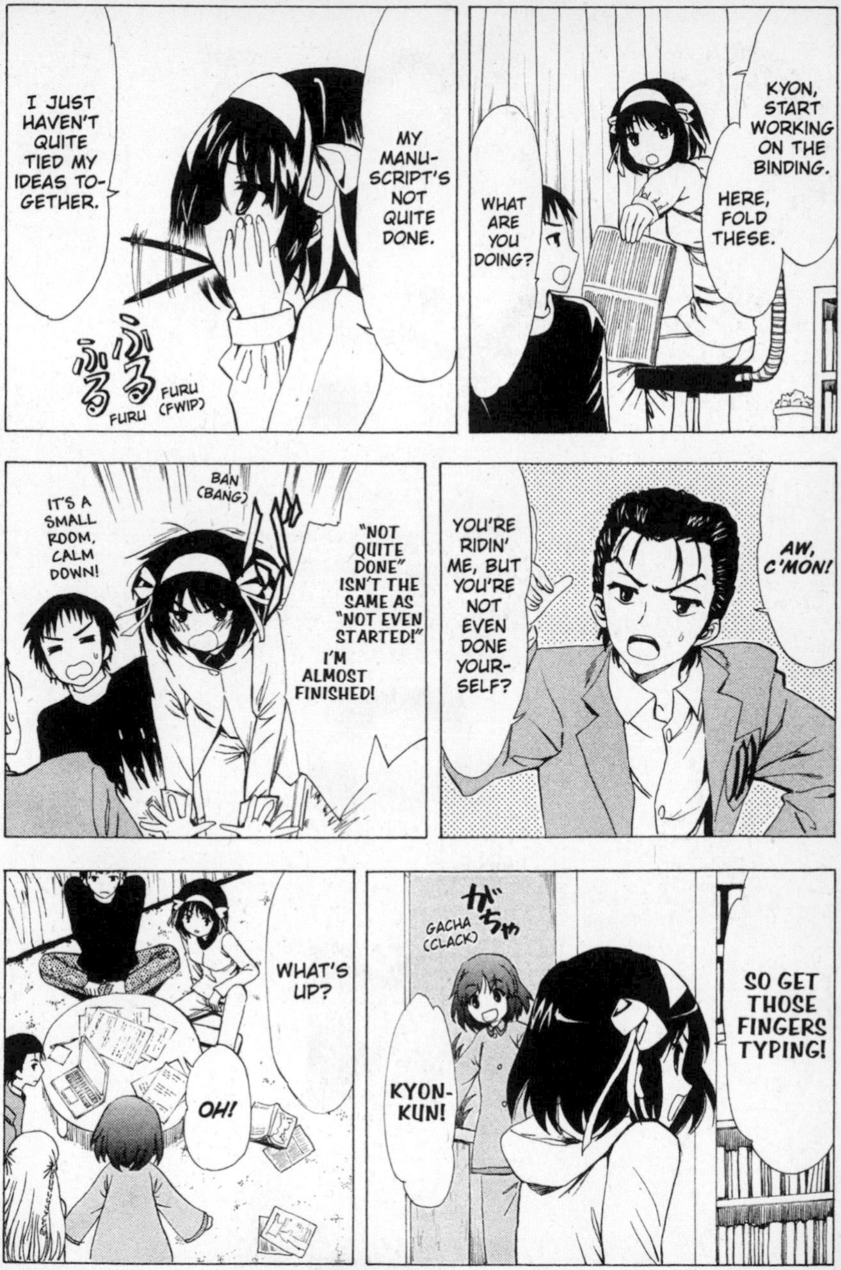
KYON, START WORKING ON THE BINDING.
HERE, FOLD THESE.
WHAT ARE YOU DOING?
MY MANU-SCRIPT'S NOT QUITE DONE.
I JUST HAVEN'T QUITE TIED MY IDEAS TO-GETHER.
ふる
ふる
FURU
FURU (FWIP)
AW, C'MON!
YOU'RE RIDIN' ME, BUT YOU'RE NOT EVEN DONE YOUR-SELF?
BAN (BANG)
"NOT QUITE DONE" ISN'T THE SAME AS "NOT EVEN STARTED!"
I'M ALMOST FINISHED!
IT'S A SMALL ROOM, CALM DOWN!
SO GET THOSE FINGERS TYPING!
がちゃ
GACHA (CLACK)
KYON-KUN!
WHAT'S UP?
OH!

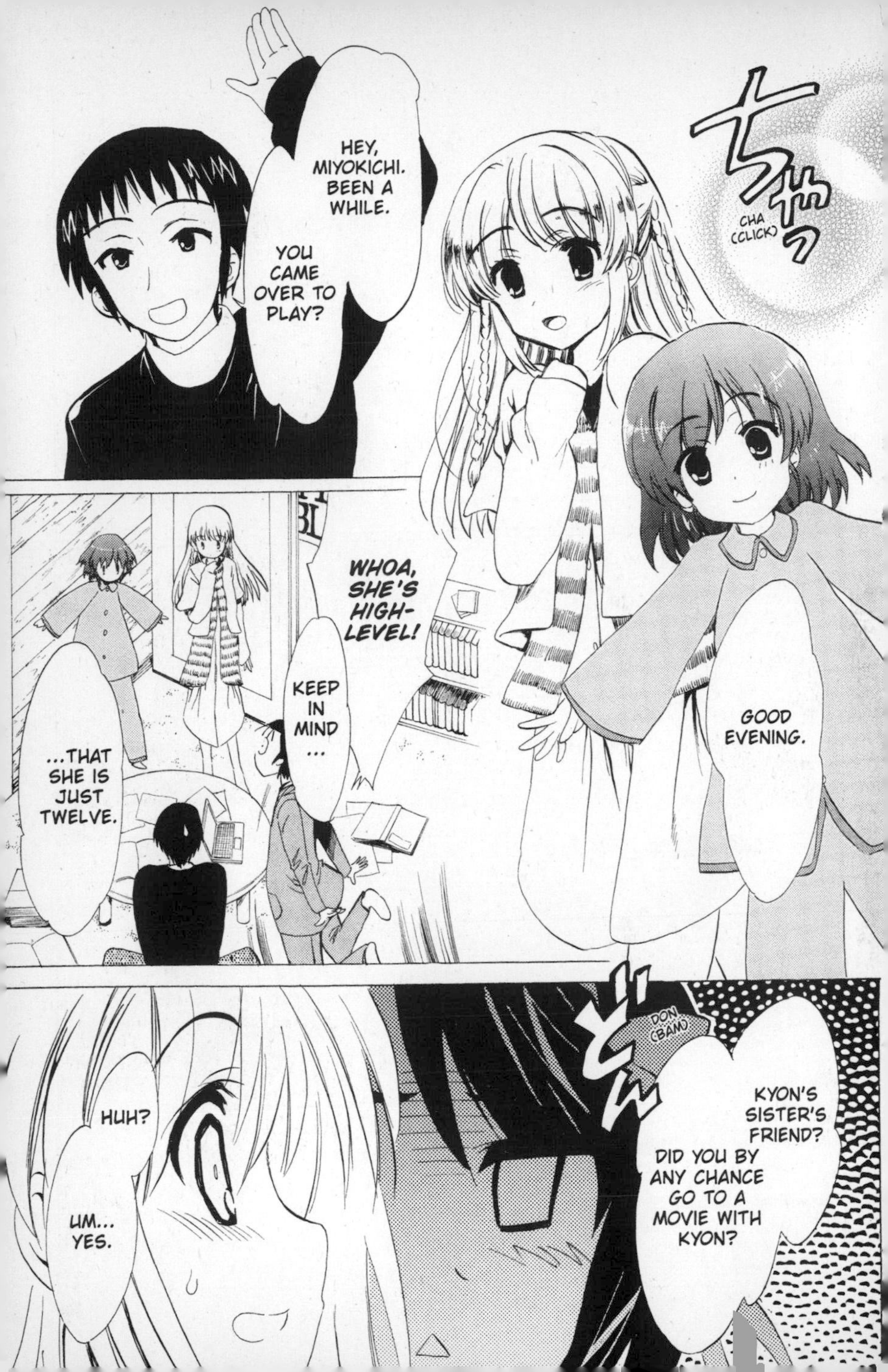
CHA (CLICK)
GOOD EVENING.
HEY, MIYOKICHI. BEEN A WHILE.
YOU CAME OVER TO PLAY?
WHOA, SHE'S HIGH-LEVEL!
KEEP IN MIND...
...THAT SHE IS JUST TWELVE.
DON (BAM)
KYON'S SISTER'S FRIEND?
DID YOU BY ANY CHANCE GO TO A MOVIE WITH KYON?
HUH?
UM... YES.

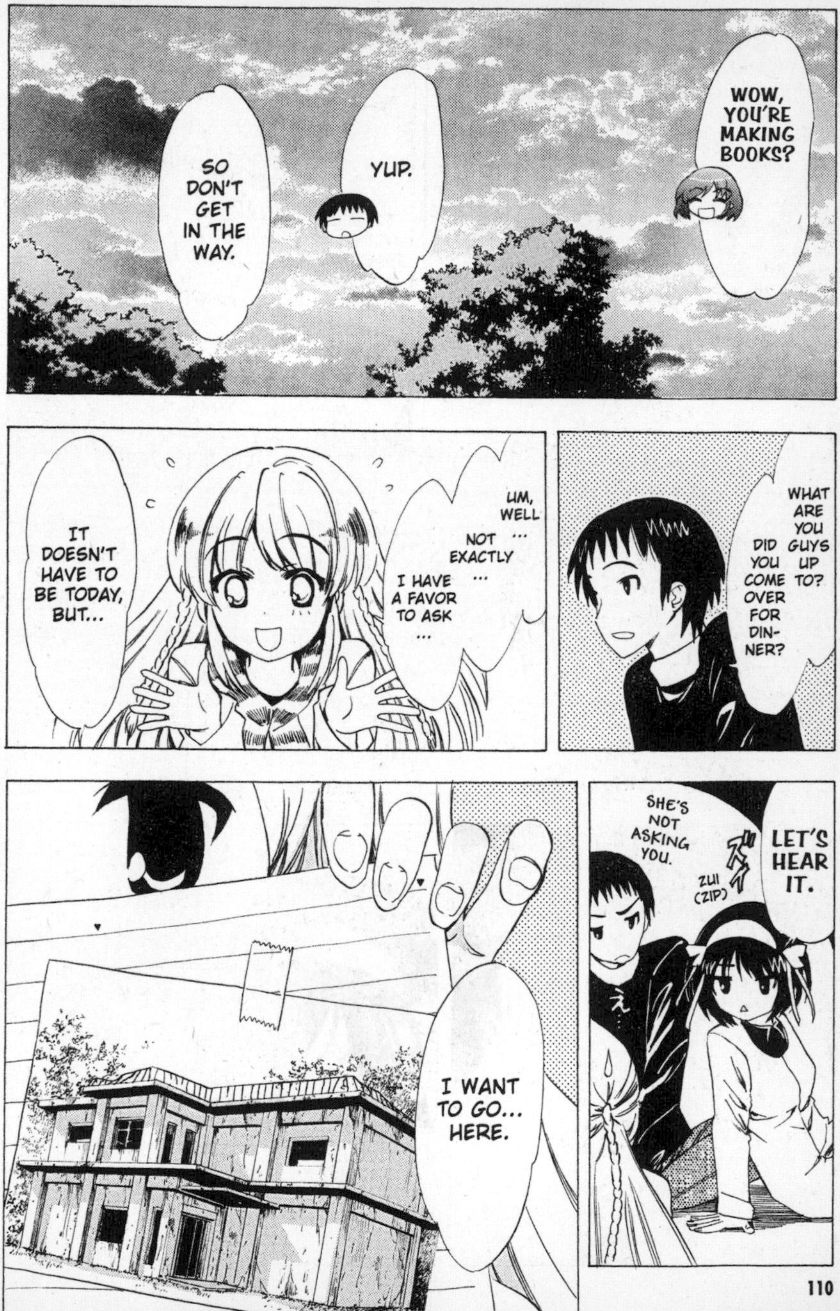
WOW, YOU'RE MAKING BOOKS?
YUP.
SO DON'T GET IN THE WAY.
WHAT ARE YOU GUYS UP TO?
DID YOU COME OVER FOR DIN-NER?
UM, WELL ...
NOT EXACTLY ...
I HAVE A FAVOR TO ASK ...
IT DOESN'T HAVE TO BE TODAY, BUT...
LET'S HEAR IT.
ZUI (ZIP)
SHE'S NOT ASKING YOU.
I WANT TO GO... HERE.

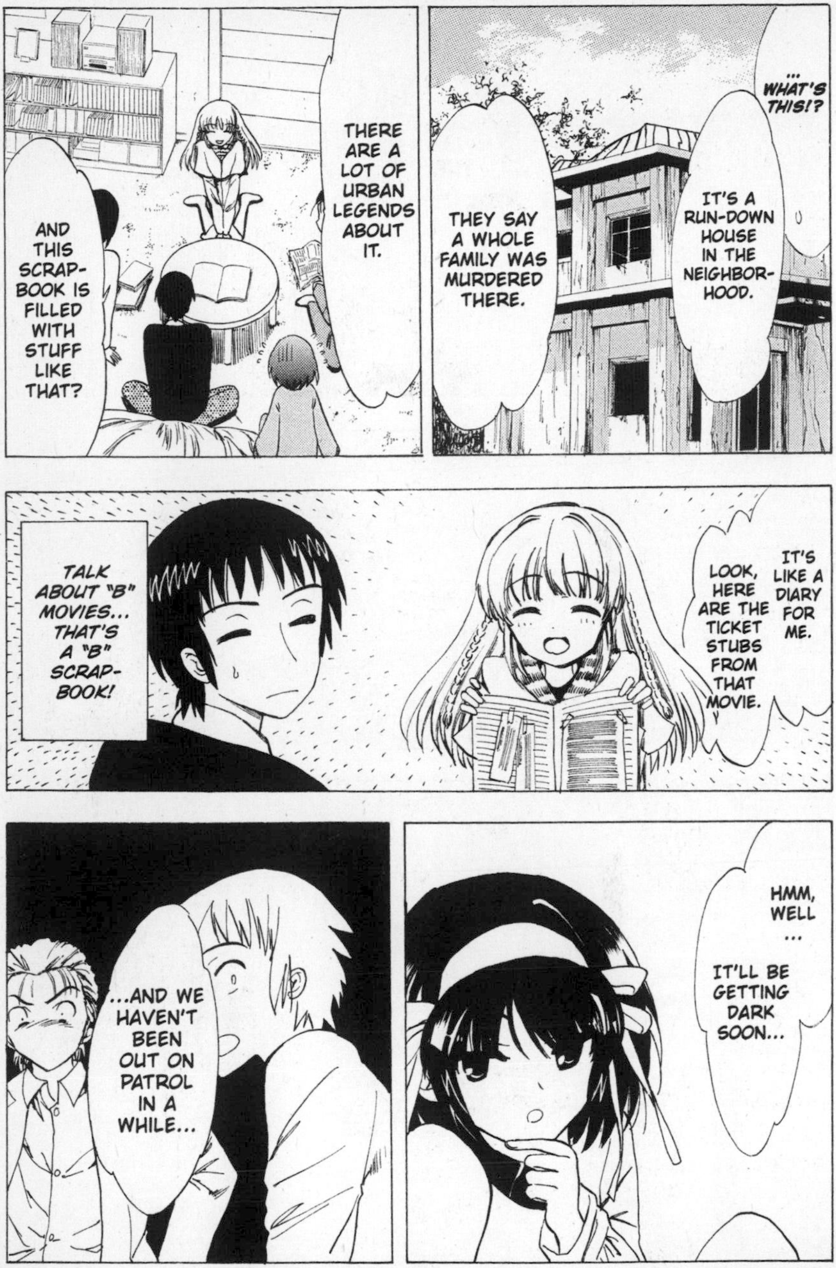
...WHAT'S THIS!?
IT'S A RUN-DOWN HOUSE IN THE NEIGHBORHOOD.
THEY SAY A WHOLE FAMILY WAS MURDERED THERE.
THERE ARE A LOT OF URBAN LEGENDS ABOUT IT.
AND THIS SCRAP-BOOK IS FILLED WITH STUFF LIKE THAT?
IT'S LIKE A DIARY FOR ME.
LOOK, HERE ARE THE TICKET STUBS FROM THAT MOVIE.
TALK ABOUT "B" MOVIES... THAT'S A "B" SCRAP-BOOK!
HMM, WELL ...
IT'LL BE GETTING DARK SOON...
...AND WE HAVEN'T BEEN OUT ON PATROL IN A WHILE...

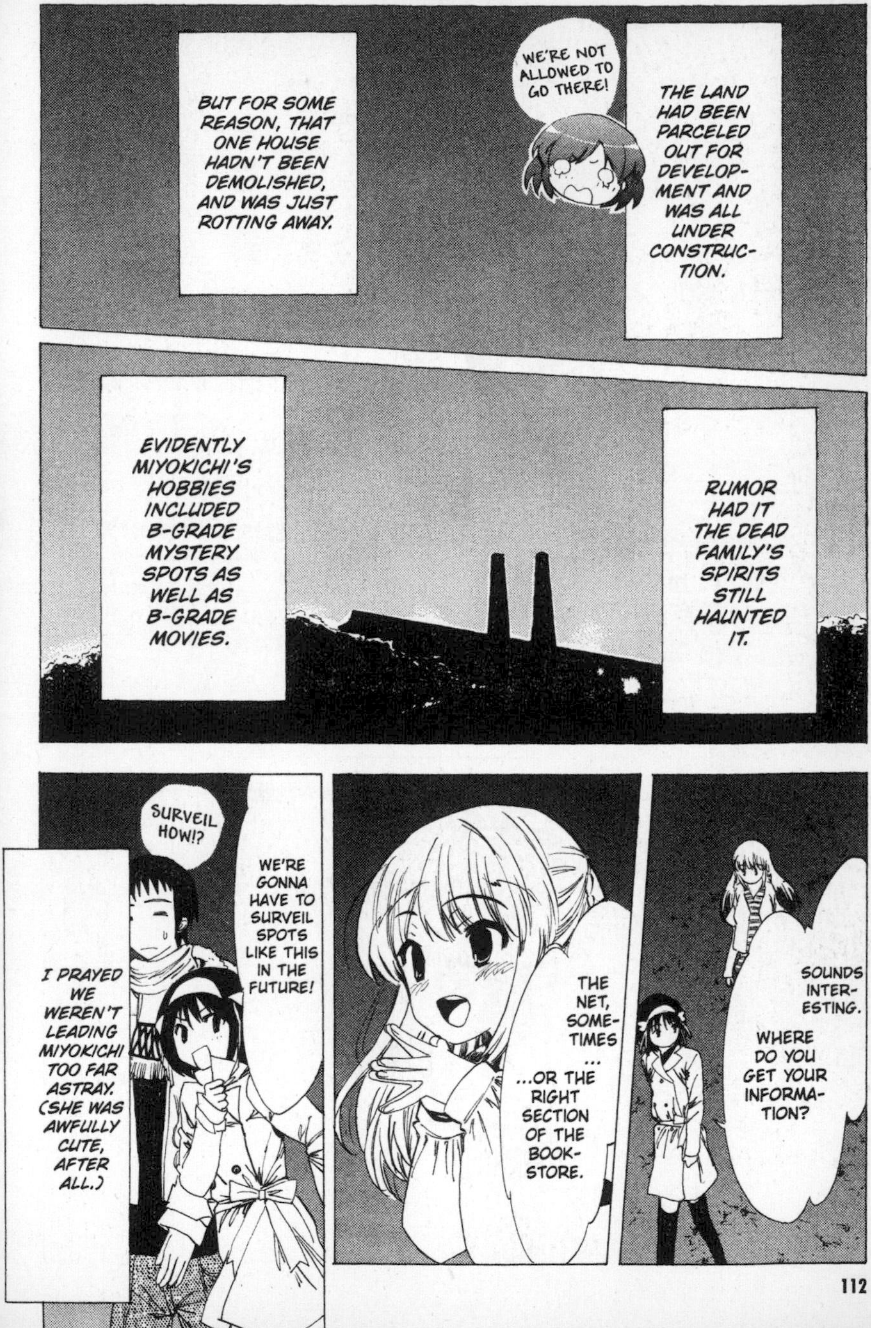
THE LAND HAD BEEN PARCELED OUT FOR DEVELOPMENT AND WAS ALL UNDER CONSTRUCTION.
WE'RE NOT ALLOWED TO GO THERE!
BUT FOR SOME REASON, THAT ONE HOUSE HADN'T BEEN DEMOLISHED, AND WAS JUST ROTTING AWAY.
RUMOR HAD IT THE DEAD FAMILY'S SPIRITS STILL HAUNTED IT.
EVIDENTLY MIYOKICHI'S HOBBIES INCLUDED B-GRADE MYSTERY SPOTS AS WELL AS B-GRADE MOVIES.
SOUNDS INTERESTING.
WHERE DO YOU GET YOUR INFORMATION?
THE NET, SOMETIMES ...
...OR THE RIGHT SECTION OF THE BOOKSTORE.
WE'RE GONNA HAVE TO SURVEIL SPOTS LIKE THIS IN THE FUTURE!
SURVEIL HOW!?
I PRAYED WE WEREN'T LEADING MIYOKICHI TOO FAR ASTRAY. (SHE WAS AWFULLY CUTE, AFTER ALL.)

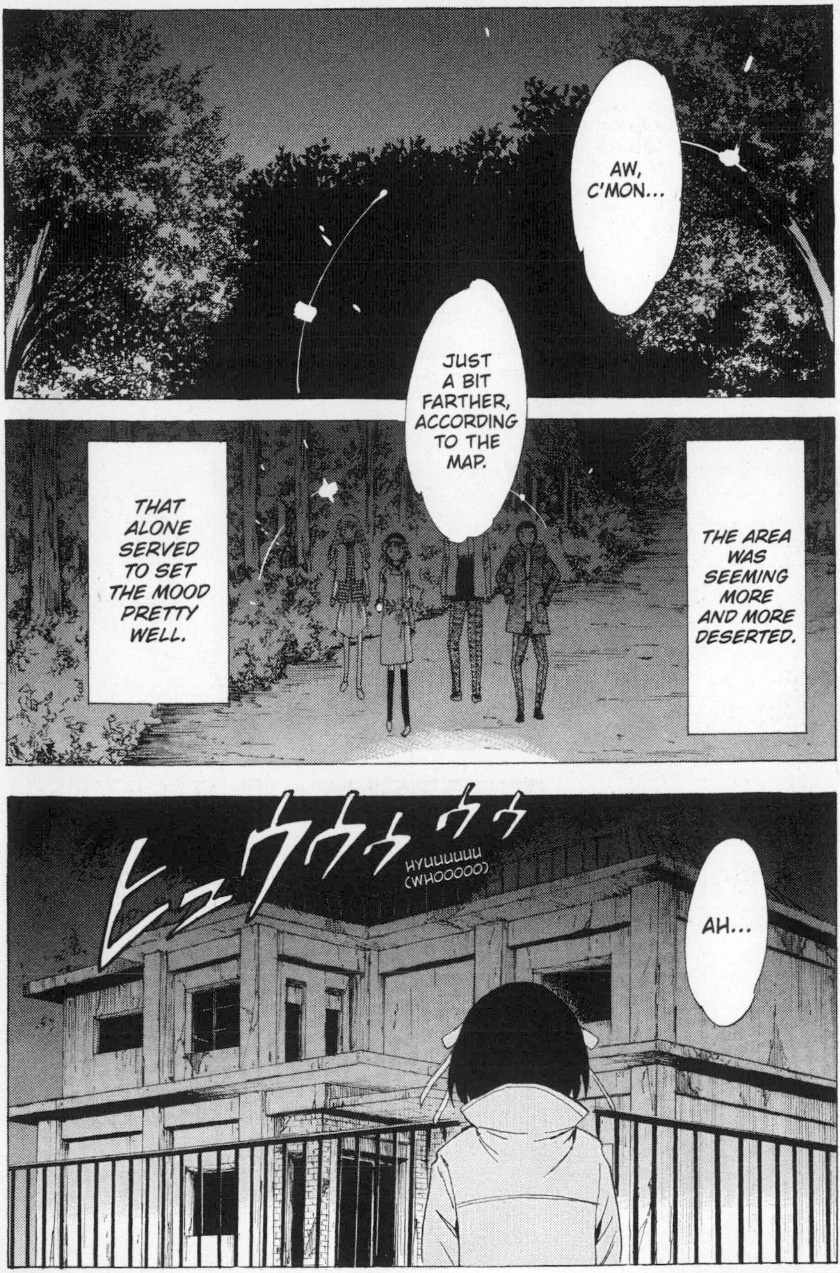
AW, C'MON...
JUST A BIT FARTHER, ACCORDING TO THE MAP.
THE AREA WAS SEEMING MORE AND MORE DESERTED.
THAT ALONE SERVED TO SET THE MOOD PRETTY WELL.
AH...
ヒュウウゥウウ
HYUUUUUUU (WHOOOOO)

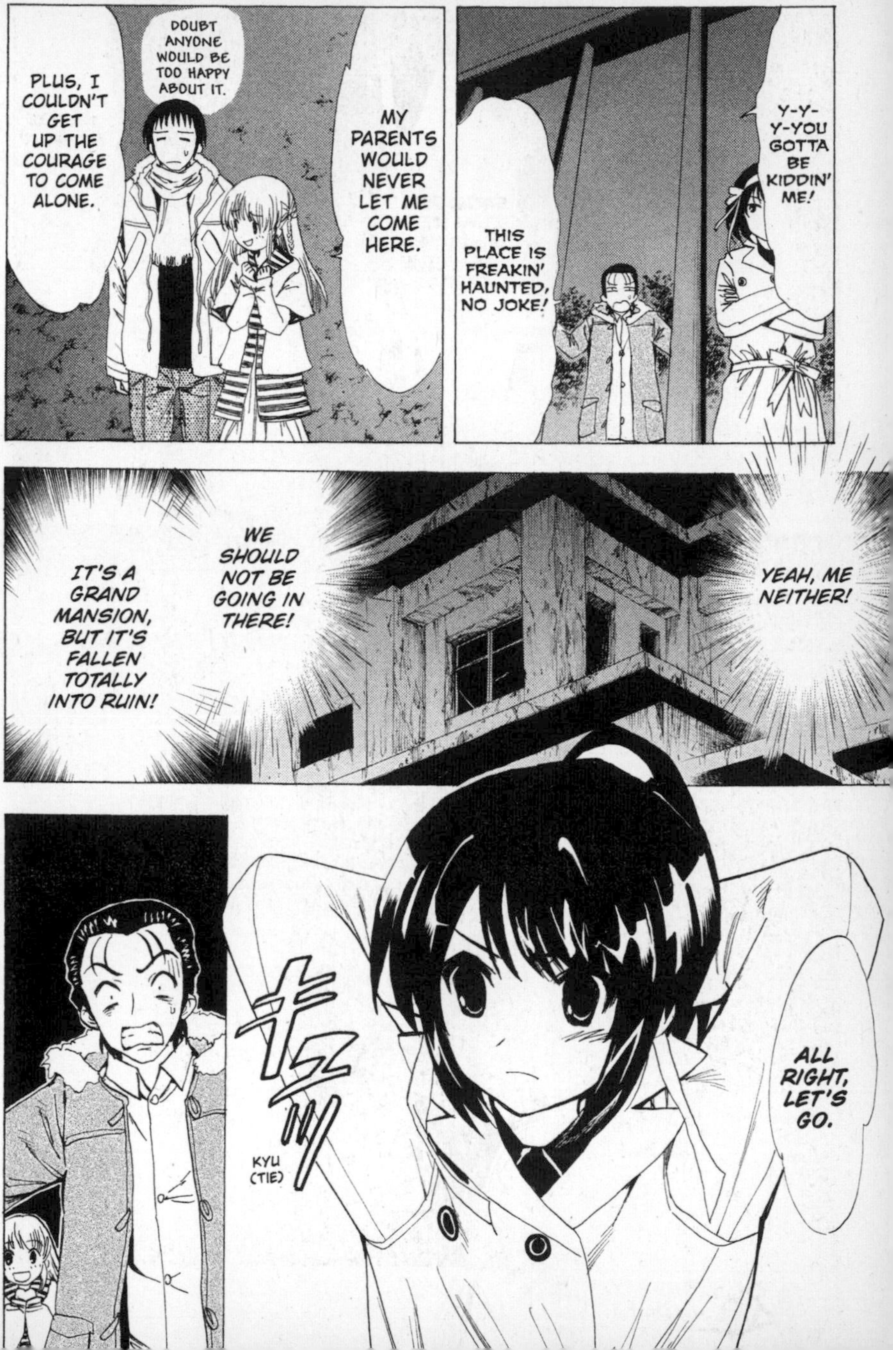
Y-Y-Y-YOU GOTTA BE KIDDIN' ME!
THIS PLACE IS FREAKIN' HAUNTED, NO JOKE!
MY PARENTS WOULD NEVER LET ME COME HERE.
DOUBT ANYONE WOULD BE TOO HAPPY ABOUT IT.
PLUS, I COULDN'T GET UP THE COURAGE TO COME ALONE.
YEAH, ME NEITHER!
WE SHOULD NOT BE GOING IN THERE!
IT'S A GRAND MANSION, BUT IT'S FALLEN TOTALLY INTO RUIN!
ALL RIGHT, LET'S GO.
KYU (TIE)

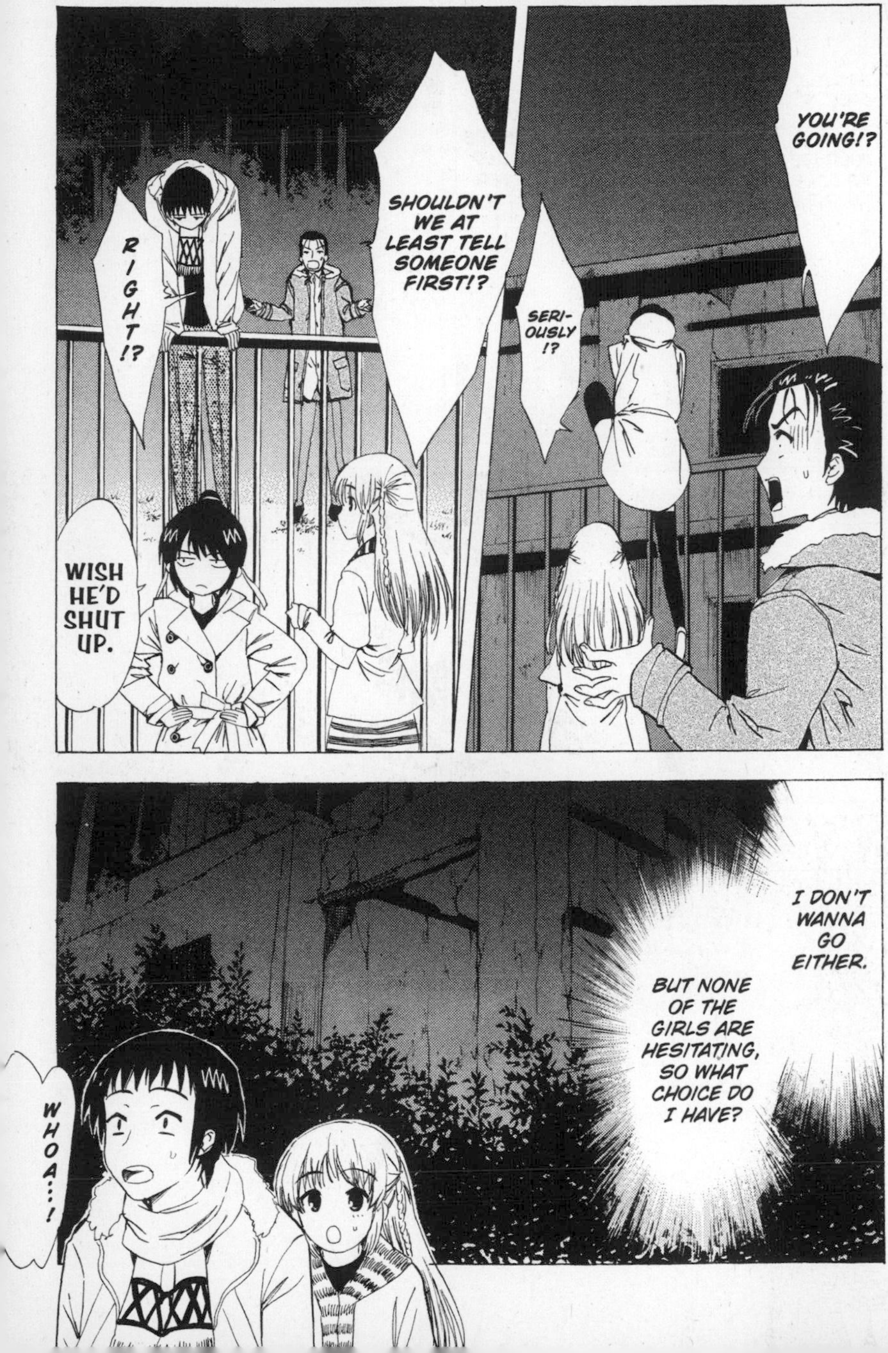
YOU'RE GOING!?
SERIOUSLY!?
SHOULDN'T WE AT LEAST TELL SOMEONE FIRST!?
RIGHT!?
WISH HE'D SHUT UP.
I DON'T WANNA GO EITHER.
BUT NONE OF THE GIRLS ARE HESITATING, SO WHAT CHOICE DO I HAVE?
WHOA...!

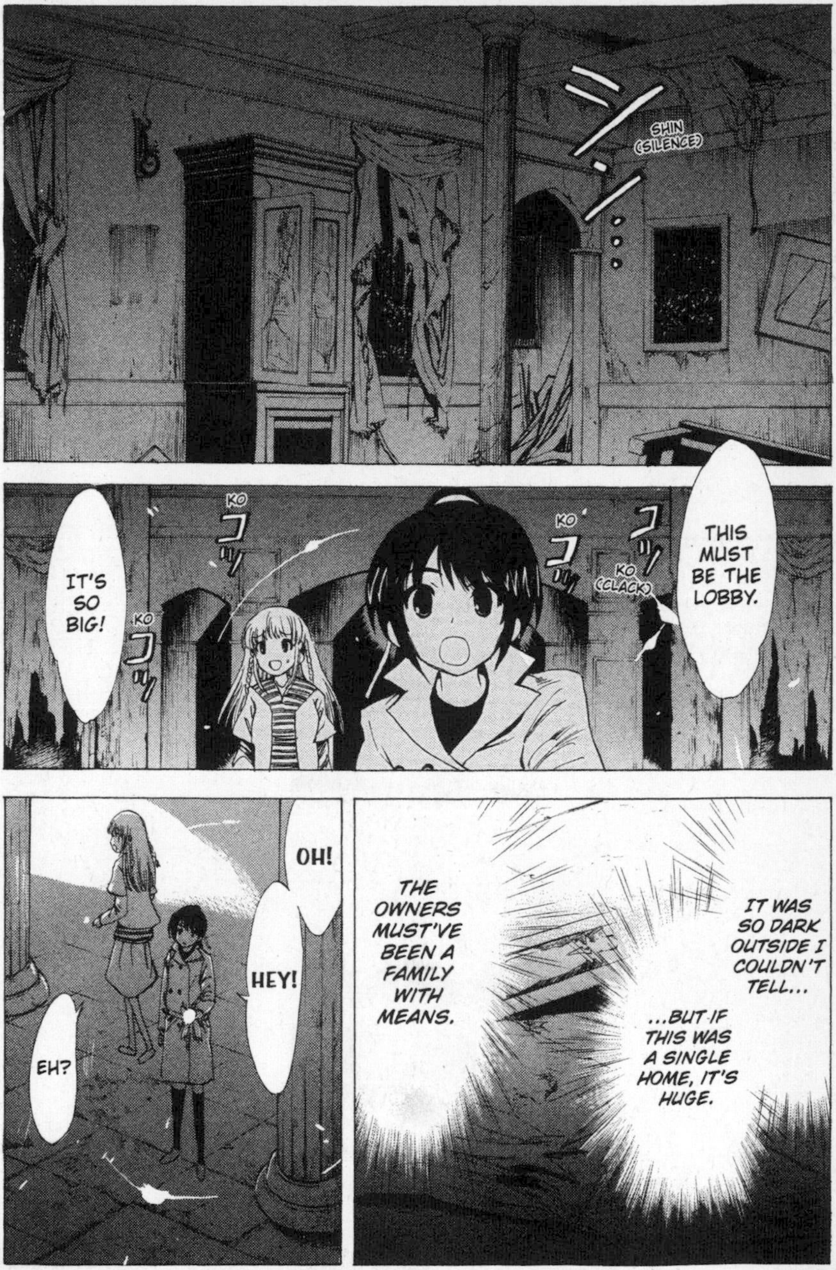

SHIN (SILENCE)
...
THIS MUST BE THE LOBBY.
KO (CLACK)
KO
KO
IT'S SO BIG!
KO
IT WAS SO DARK OUTSIDE I COULDN'T TELL...
...BUT IF THIS WAS A SINGLE HOME, IT'S HUGE.
THE OWNERS MUST'VE BEEN A FAMILY WITH MEANS.
OH!
HEY!
EH?

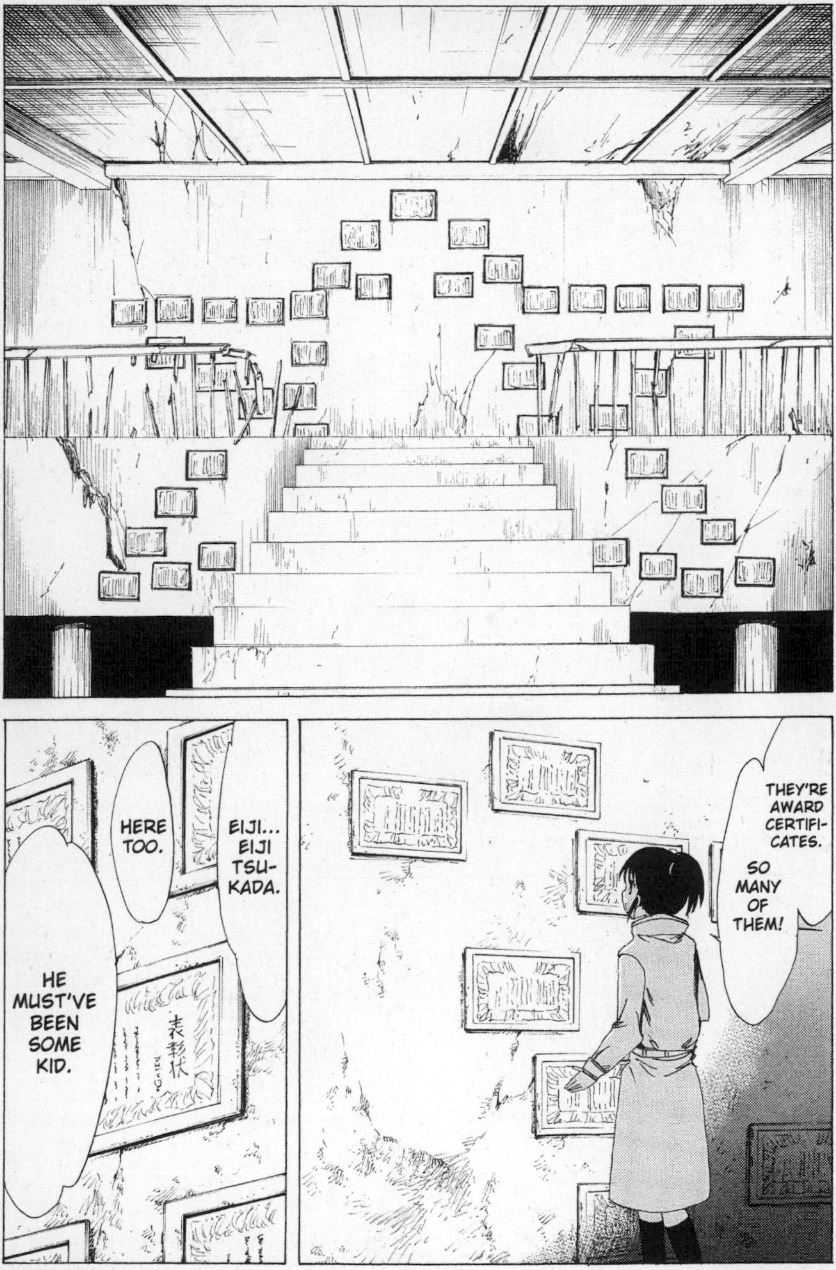
THEY'RE AWARD CERTIFICATES.
SO MANY OF THEM!
EIJI... EIJI TSUKADA.
HERE TOO.
表彰状
HE MUST'VE BEEN SOME KID.

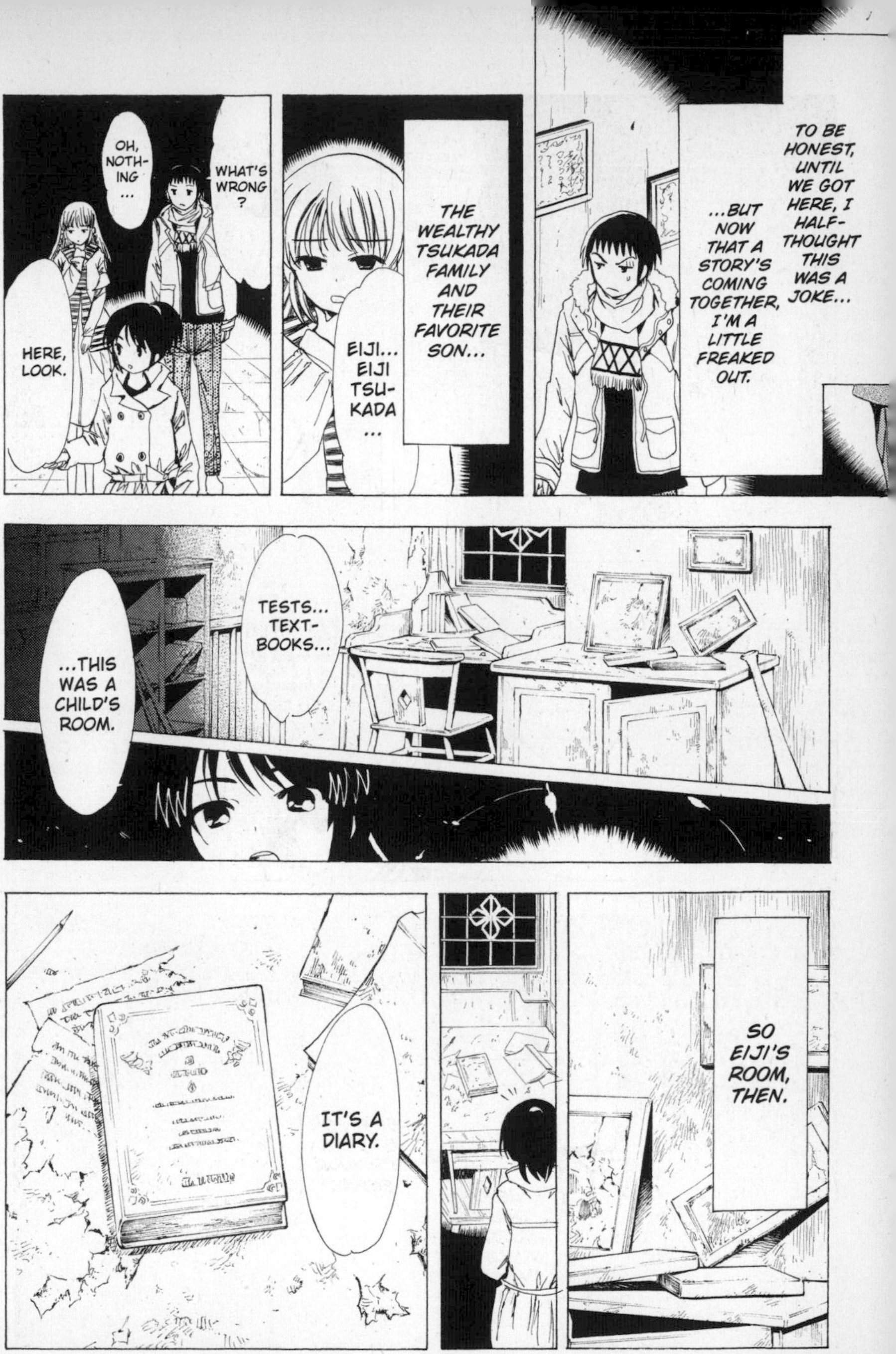
TO BE HONEST, UNTIL WE GOT HERE, I HALF-THOUGHT THIS WAS A JOKE...
...BUT NOW THAT A STORY'S COMING TOGETHER, I'M A LITTLE FREAKED OUT.
THE WEALTHY TSUKADA FAMILY AND THEIR FAVORITE SON...
EIJI... EIJI TSUKADA...
WHAT'S WRONG?
OH, NOTHING...
HERE, LOOK.
TESTS... TEXT-BOOKS...
...THIS WAS A CHILD'S ROOM.
SO EIJI'S ROOM, THEN.
IT'S A DIARY.

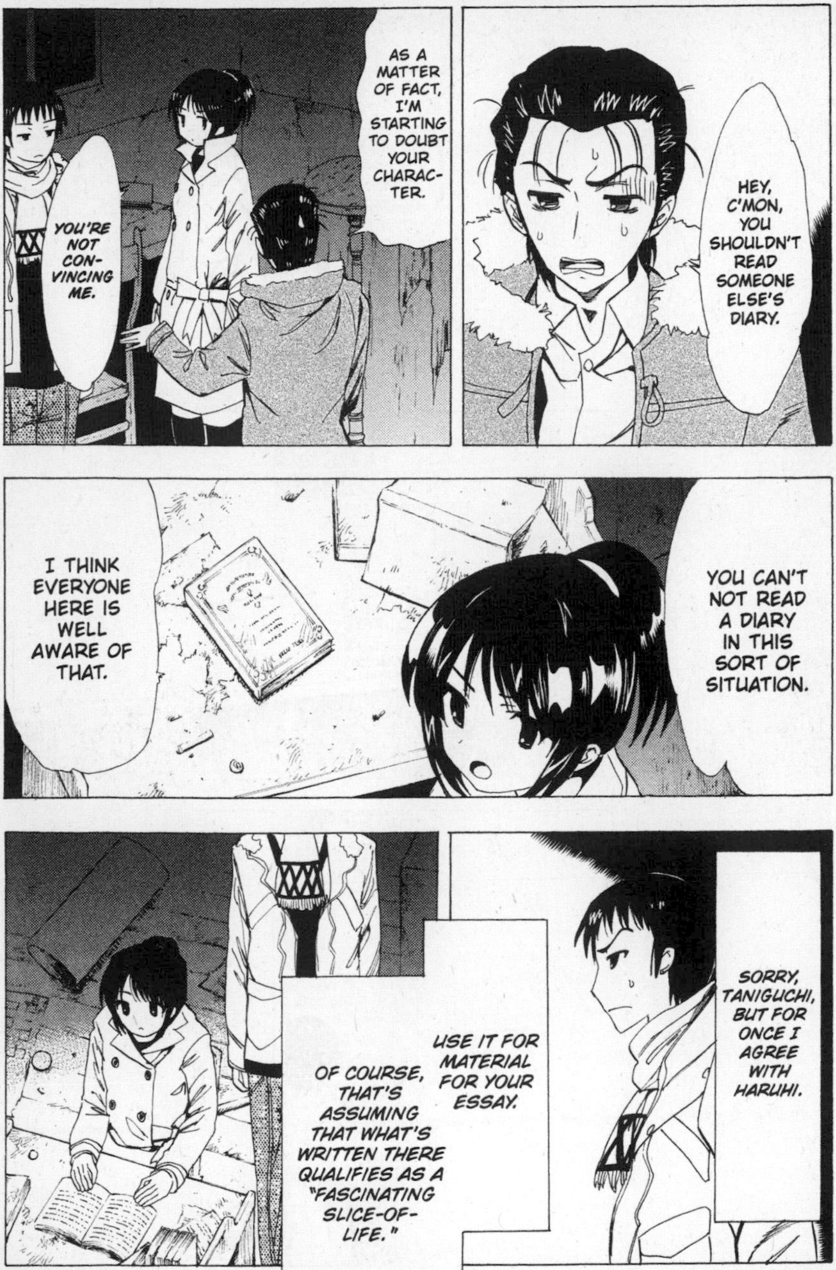
HEY, C'MON, YOU SHOULDN'T READ SOMEONE ELSE'S DIARY.
AS A MATTER OF FACT, I'M STARTING TO DOUBT YOUR CHARACTER.
YOU'RE NOT CONVINCING ME.
YOU CAN'T NOT READ A DIARY IN THIS SORT OF SITUATION.
I THINK EVERYONE HERE IS WELL AWARE OF THAT.
SORRY, TANIGUCHI, BUT FOR ONCE I AGREE WITH HARUHI.
USE IT FOR MATERIAL FOR YOUR ESSAY.
OF COURSE, THAT'S ASSUMING THAT WHAT'S WRITTEN THERE QUALIFIES AS A "FASCINATING SLICE-OF-LIFE."

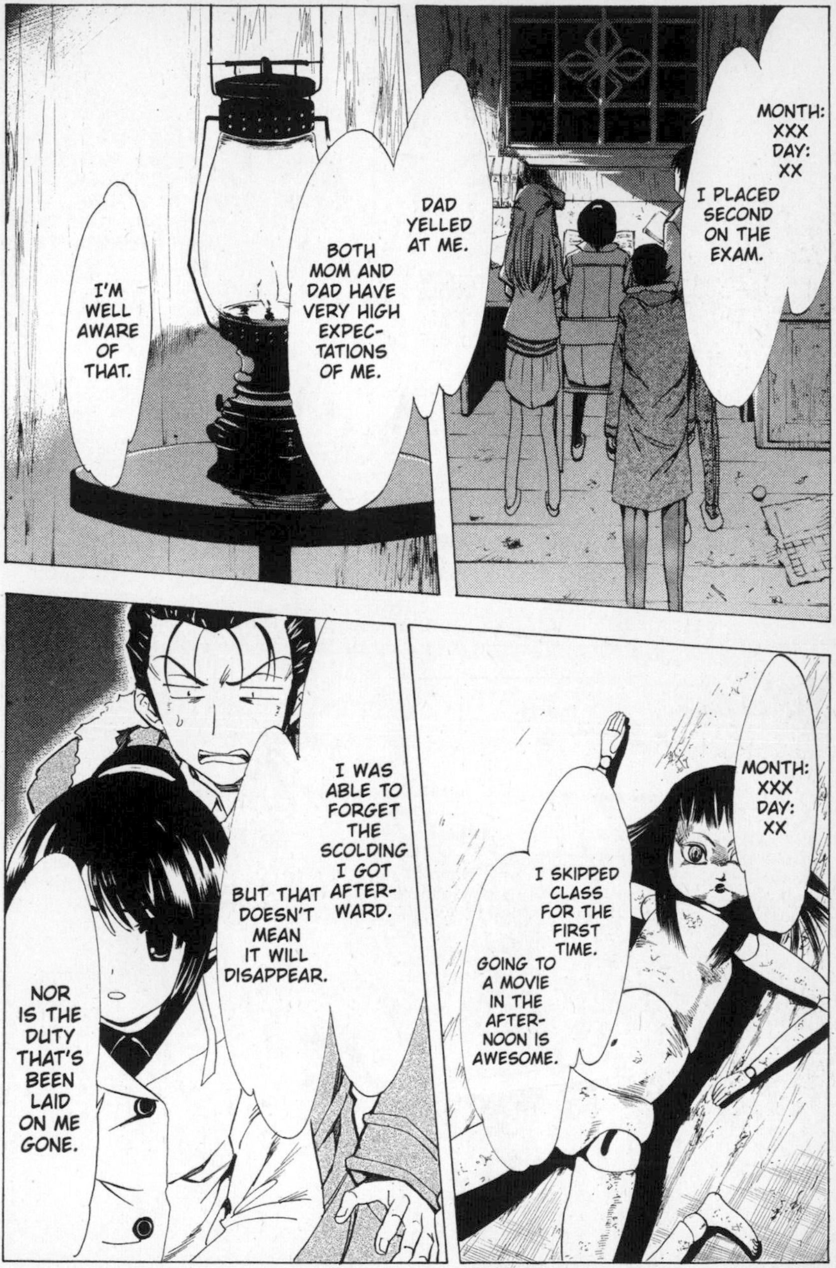
MONTH: XXX DAY: XX
I PLACED SECOND ON THE EXAM.
DAD YELLED AT ME.
BOTH MOM AND DAD HAVE VERY HIGH EXPECTATIONS OF ME.
I'M WELL AWARE OF THAT.
MONTH: XXX DAY: XX
I SKIPPED CLASS FOR THE FIRST TIME.
GOING TO A MOVIE IN THE AFTERNOON IS AWESOME.
I WAS ABLE TO FORGET THE SCOLDING I GOT AFTERWARD.
BUT THAT DOESN'T MEAN IT WILL DISAPPEAR.
NOR IS THE DUTY THAT'S BEEN LAID ON ME GONE.

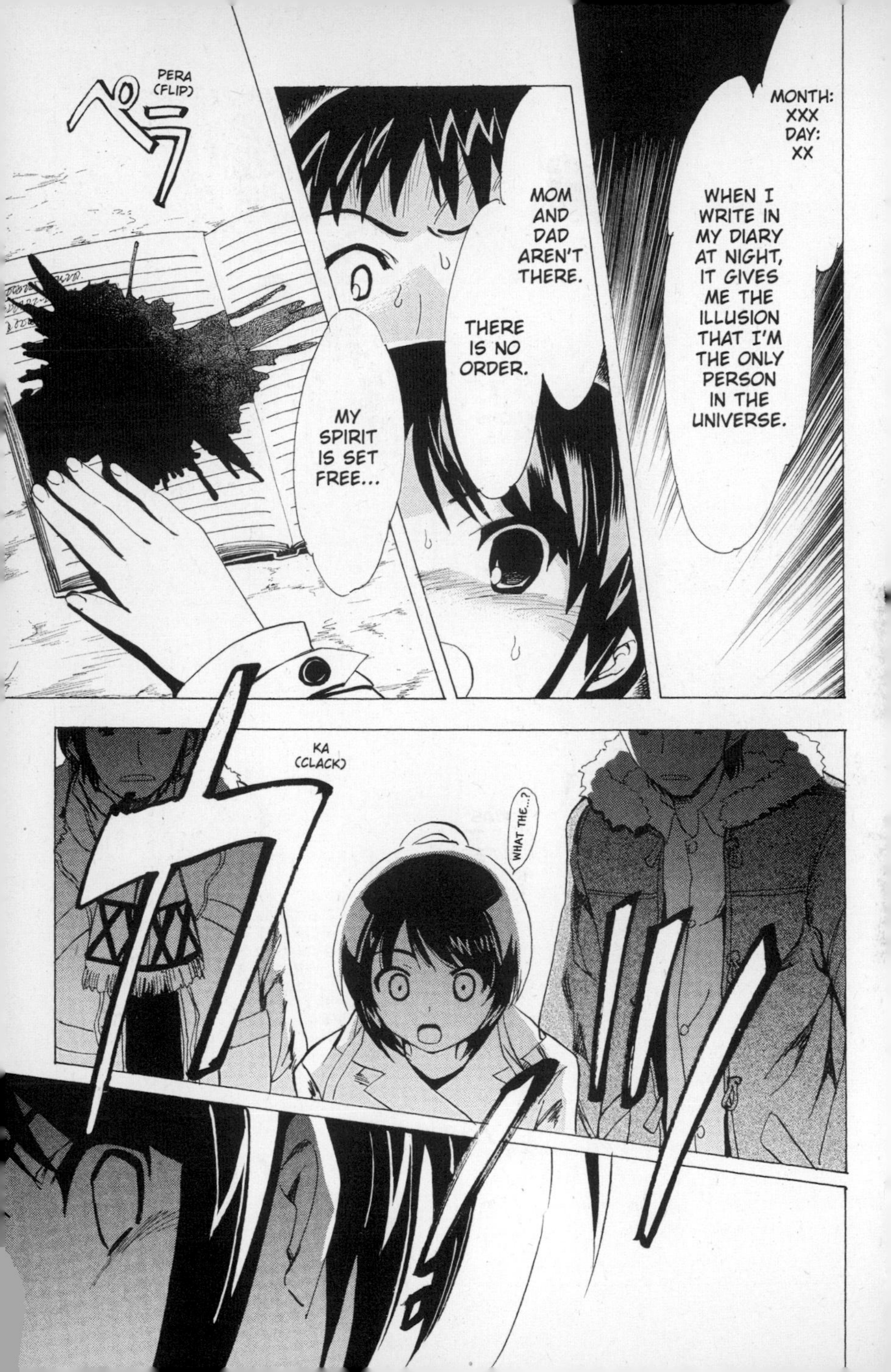
MONTH: XXX DAY: XX
WHEN I WRITE IN MY DIARY AT NIGHT, IT GIVES ME THE ILLUSION THAT I'M THE ONLY PERSON IN THE UNIVERSE.
MOM AND DAD AREN'T THERE.
THERE IS NO ORDER.
MY SPIRIT IS SET FREE...
PERA (FLIP)
KA (CLACK)
WHAT THE...?

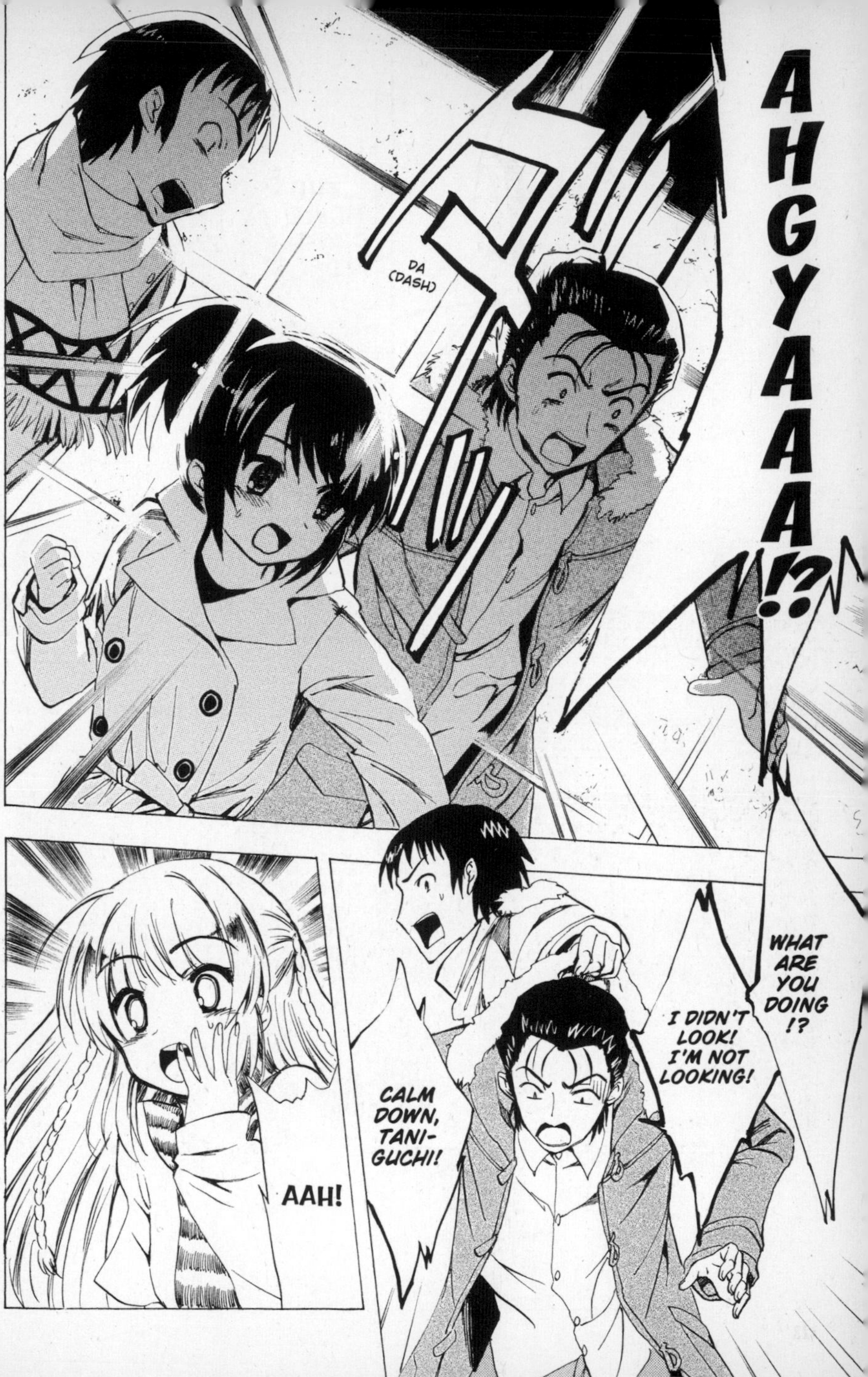
AHGYAAAA!?
DA (DASH)
WHAT ARE YOU DOING!?
I DIDN'T LOOK! I'M NOT LOOKING!
CALM DOWN, TANI-GUCHI!
AAH!

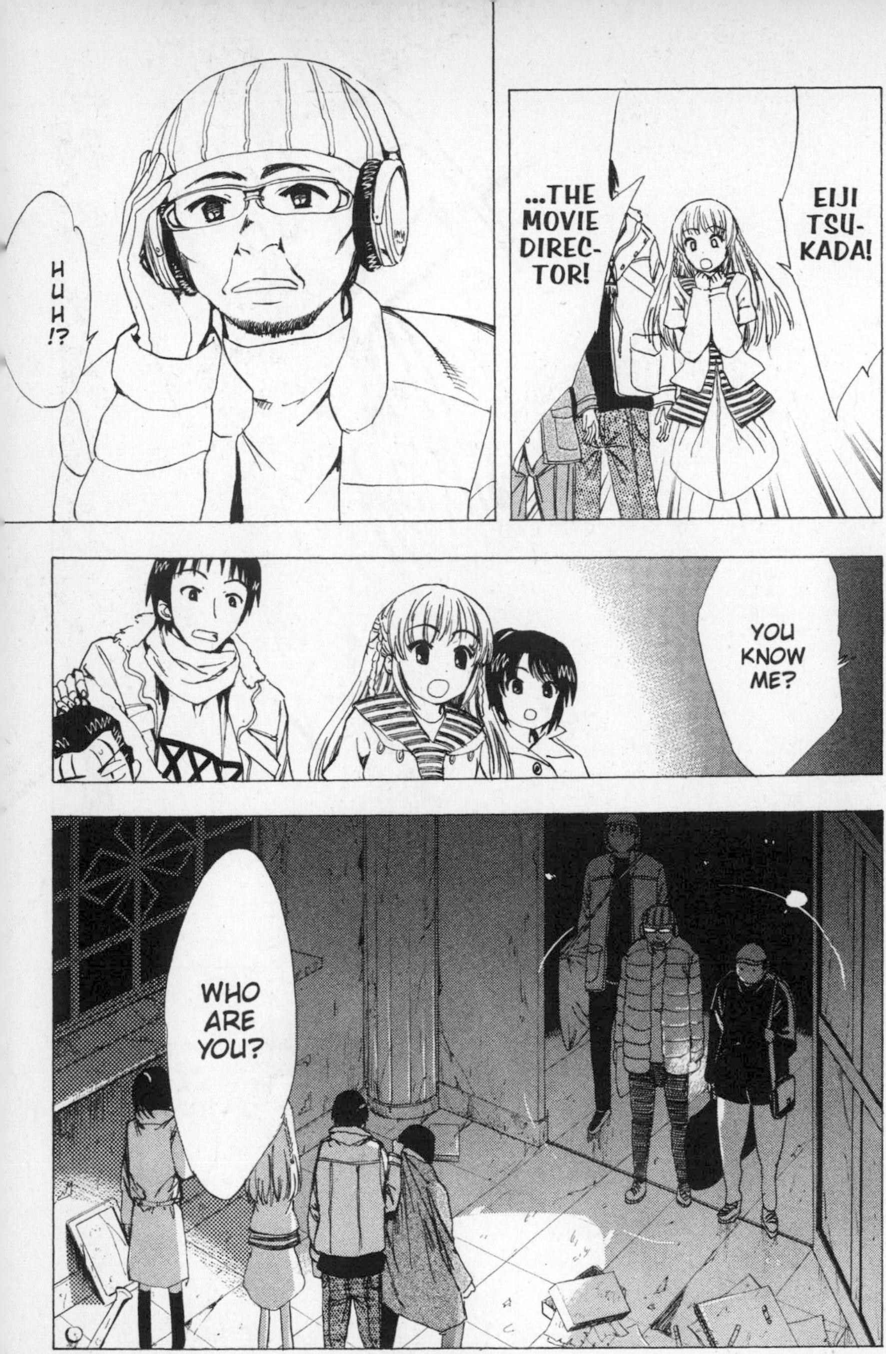
EIJI TSU-KADA!
...THE MOVIE DIREC-TOR!
HUH!?
YOU KNOW ME?
WHO ARE YOU?

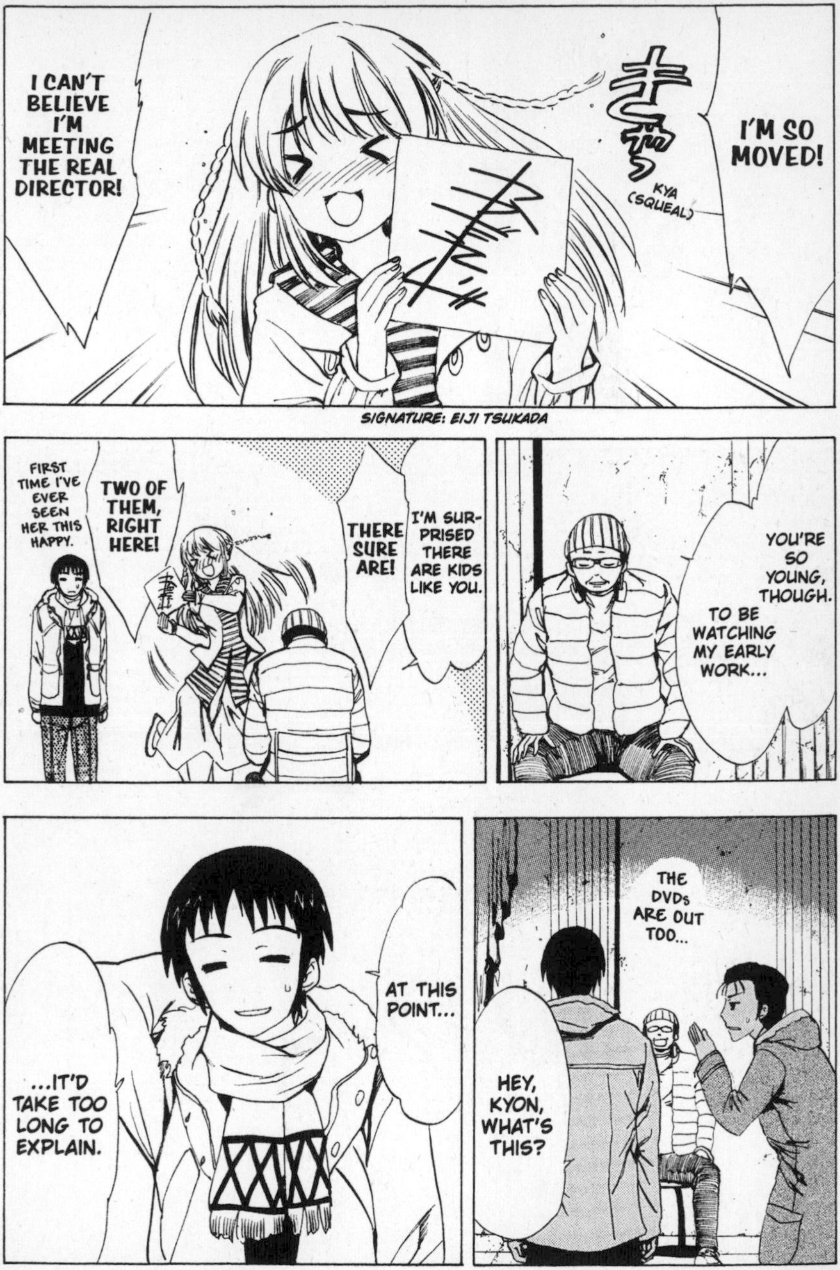
I'M SO MOVED!
KYA (SQUEAL)
I CAN'T BELIEVE I'M MEETING THE REAL DIRECTOR!
SIGNATURE: EIJI TSUKADA
YOU'RE SO YOUNG, THOUGH.
TO BE WATCHING MY EARLY WORK...
I'M SURPRISED THERE ARE KIDS LIKE YOU.
THERE SURE ARE!
TWO OF THEM, RIGHT HERE!
FIRST TIME I'VE EVER SEEN HER THIS HAPPY.
THE DVDs ARE OUT TOO...
HEY, KYON, WHAT'S THIS?
AT THIS POINT...
...IT'D TAKE TOO LONG TO EXPLAIN.

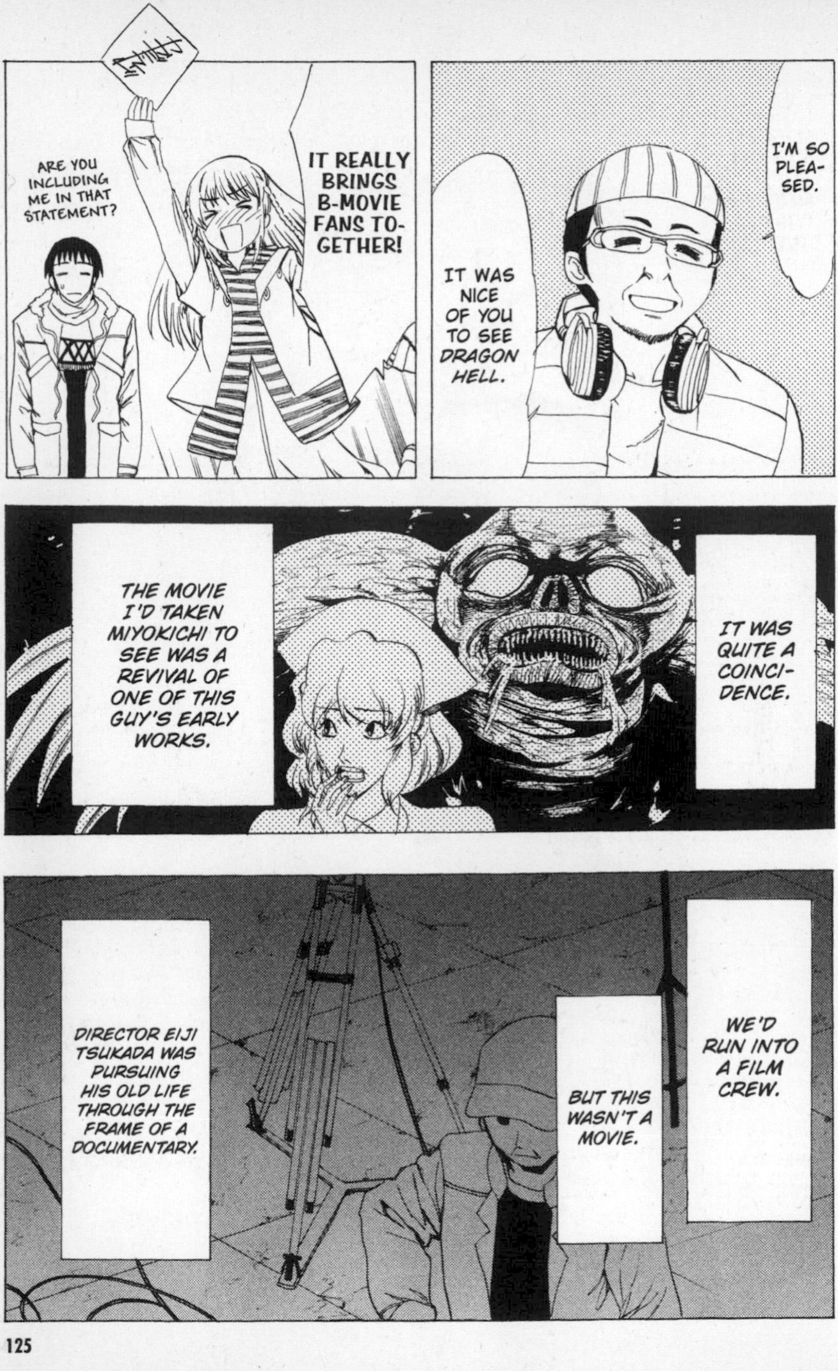
I'M SO PLEA-SED.
IT WAS NICE OF YOU TO SEE DRAGON HELL.
IT REALLY BRINGS B-MOVIE FANS TO-GETHER!
ARE YOU INCLUDING ME IN THAT STATEMENT?
IT WAS QUITE A COINCI-DENCE.
THE MOVIE I'D TAKEN MIYOKICHI TO SEE WAS A REVIVAL OF ONE OF THIS GUY'S EARLY WORKS.
WE'D RUN INTO A FILM CREW.
BUT THIS WASN'T A MOVIE.
DIRECTOR EIJI TSUKADA WAS PURSUING HIS OLD LIFE THROUGH THE FRAME OF A DOCUMENTARY.

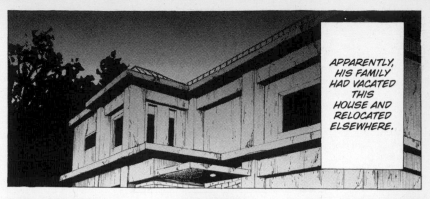

APPARENTLY, HIS FAMILY HAD VACATED THIS HOUSE AND RELOCATED ELSEWHERE.
YET EIJI TSUKADA HADN'T SOLD THE PLACE.
ONE REASON WAS THAT THANKS TO HIS SUCCESS AS A DIRECTOR, HE DIDN'T NEED TO.
THE OTHER REASON WAS...
LOOK, HERE...
NORMAL HOUSES DON'T HAVE PILLARS LIKE THIS.
IT'S FAKE LUXURY.

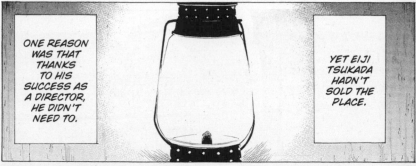

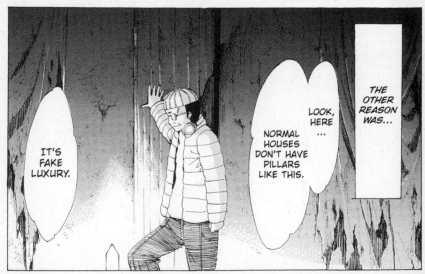

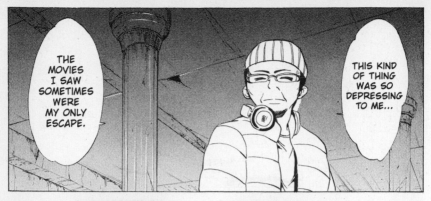

THIS KIND OF THING WAS SO DEPRESSING TO ME...
THE MOVIES I SAW SOMETIMES WERE MY ONLY ESCAPE.
IT WAS FUN...
I REALIZED I ENJOYED THINGS OF A DISORGANIZED NATURE.
THAT'S BECAUSE OF THE LIFE I HAD IN THIS HOUSE.
THAT'S WHY I CAN'T DEMOLISH THIS PLACE.
WHEN I COME HERE, I REMEMBER WHY I FELL IN LOVE WITH MOVIES.
ALTHOUGH I'VE NEGLECTED IT TOO MUCH...

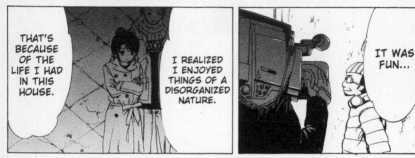

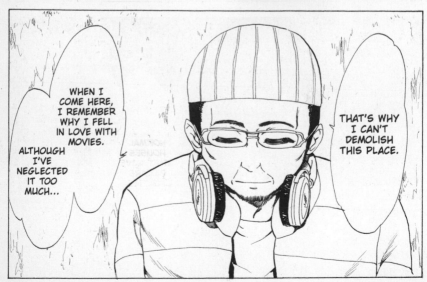

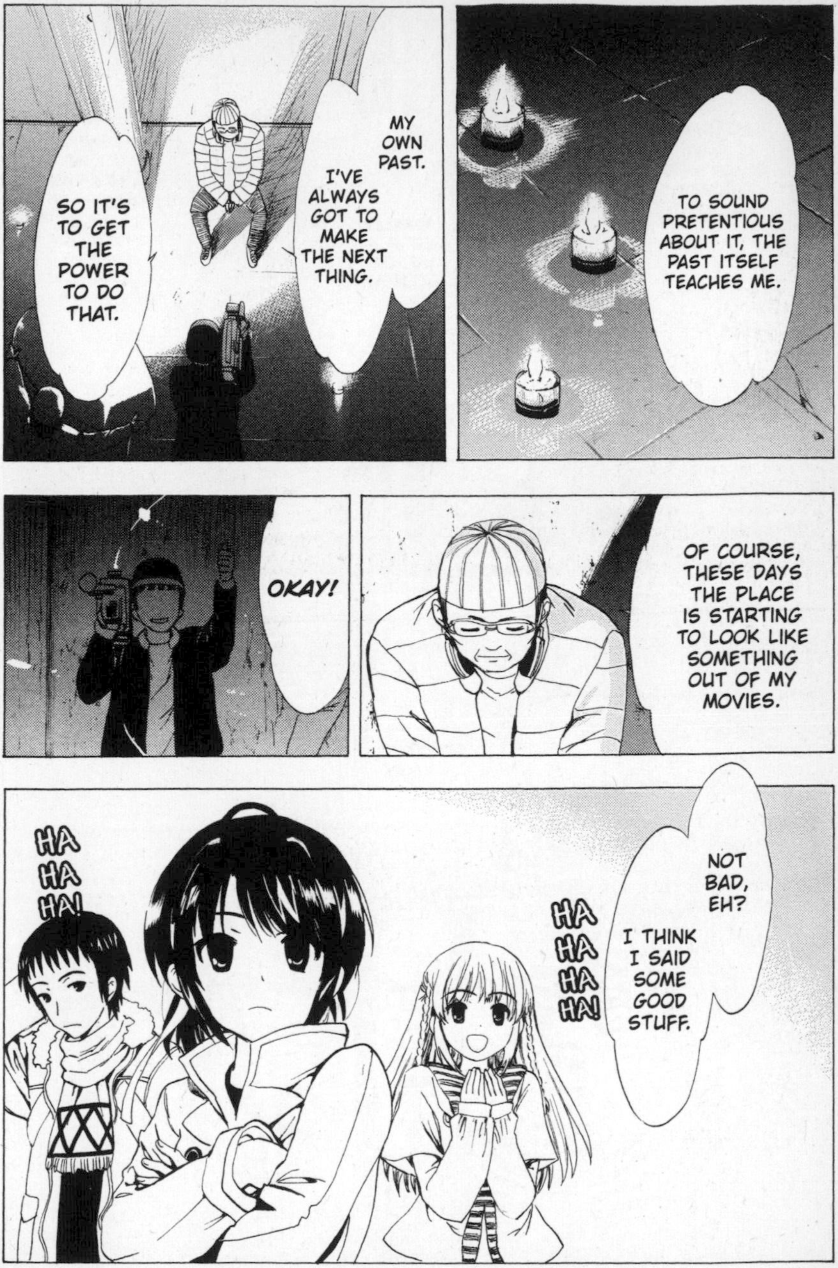
TO SOUND PRETENTIOUS ABOUT IT, THE PAST ITSELF TEACHES ME.
MY OWN PAST.
I'VE ALWAYS GOT TO MAKE THE NEXT THING.
SO IT'S TO GET THE POWER TO DO THAT.
OF COURSE, THESE DAYS THE PLACE IS STARTING TO LOOK LIKE SOMETHING OUT OF MY MOVIES.
OKAY!
NOT BAD, EH?
I THINK I SAID SOME GOOD STUFF.
HA HA HA HA!
HA HA HA!

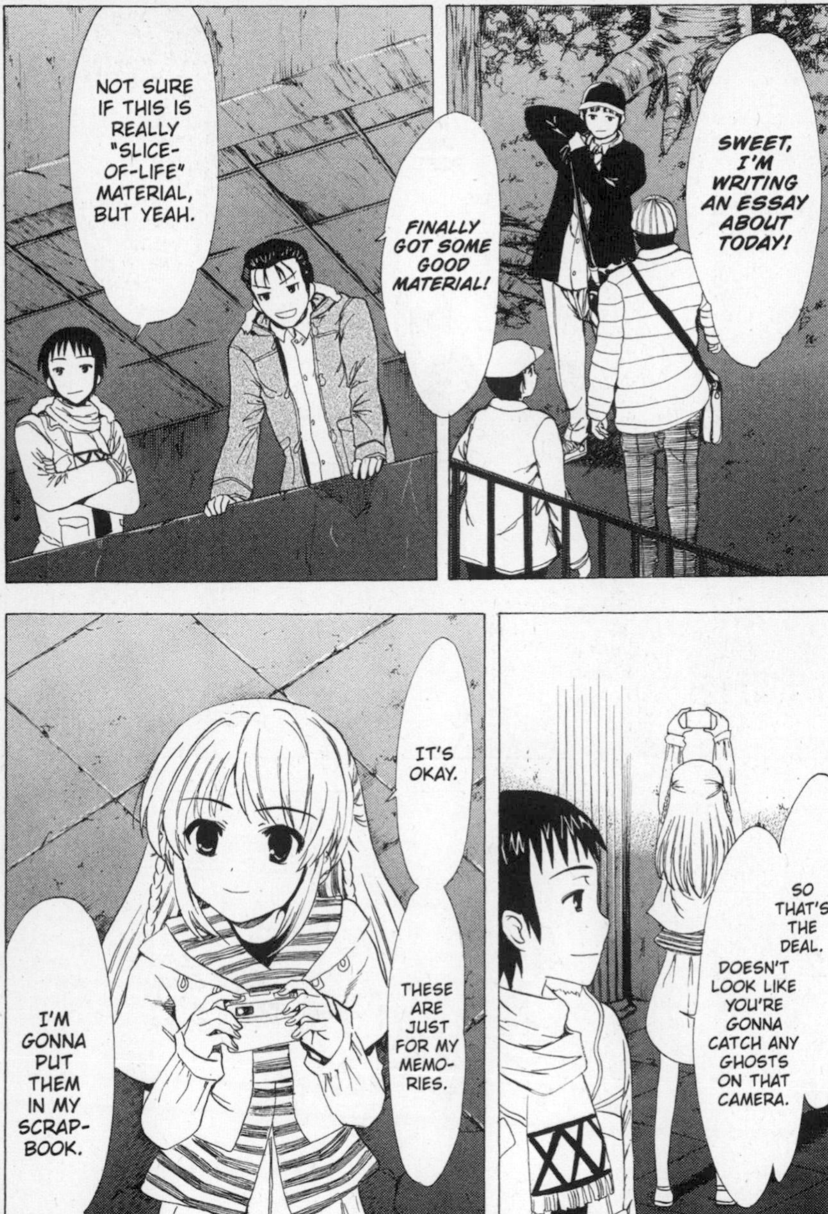
SWEET, I'M WRITING AN ESSAY ABOUT TODAY!
FINALLY GOT SOME GOOD MATERIAL!
NOT SURE IF THIS IS REALLY "SLICE-OF-LIFE" MATERIAL, BUT YEAH.
SO THAT'S THE DEAL.
DOESN'T LOOK LIKE YOU'RE GONNA CATCH ANY GHOSTS ON THAT CAMERA.
IT'S OKAY.
THESE ARE JUST FOR MY MEMO-RIES.
I'M GONNA PUT THEM IN MY SCRAP-BOOK.

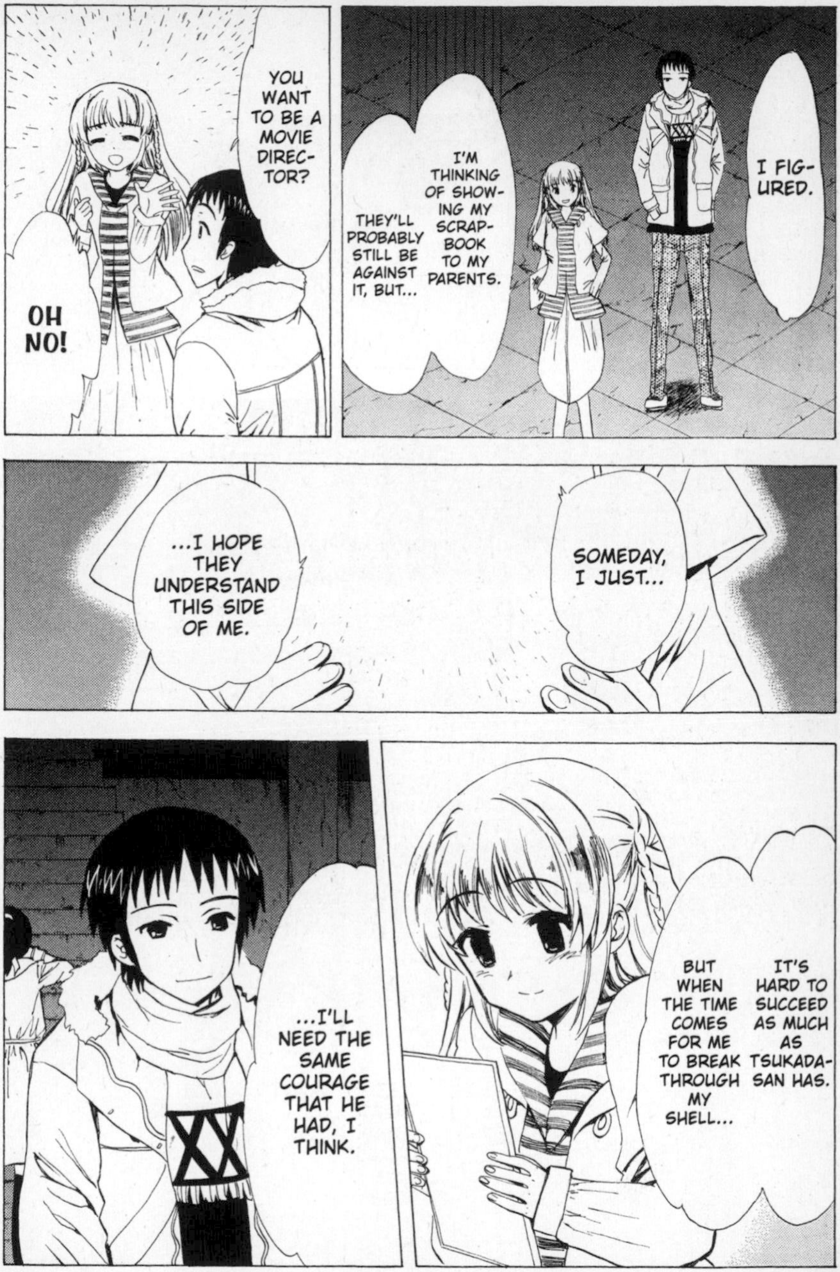
I FIGURED.
I'M THINKING OF SHOWING MY SCRAPBOOK TO MY PARENTS.
THEY'LL PROBABLY STILL BE AGAINST IT, BUT...
YOU WANT TO BE A MOVIE DIRECTOR?
OH NO!
SOMEDAY, I JUST...
...I HOPE THEY UNDERSTAND THIS SIDE OF ME.
IT'S HARD TO SUCCEED AS MUCH AS TSUKADA-SAN HAS.
BUT WHEN THE TIME COMES FOR ME TO BREAK THROUGH MY SHELL...
...I'LL NEED THE SAME COURAGE THAT HE HAD, I THINK.

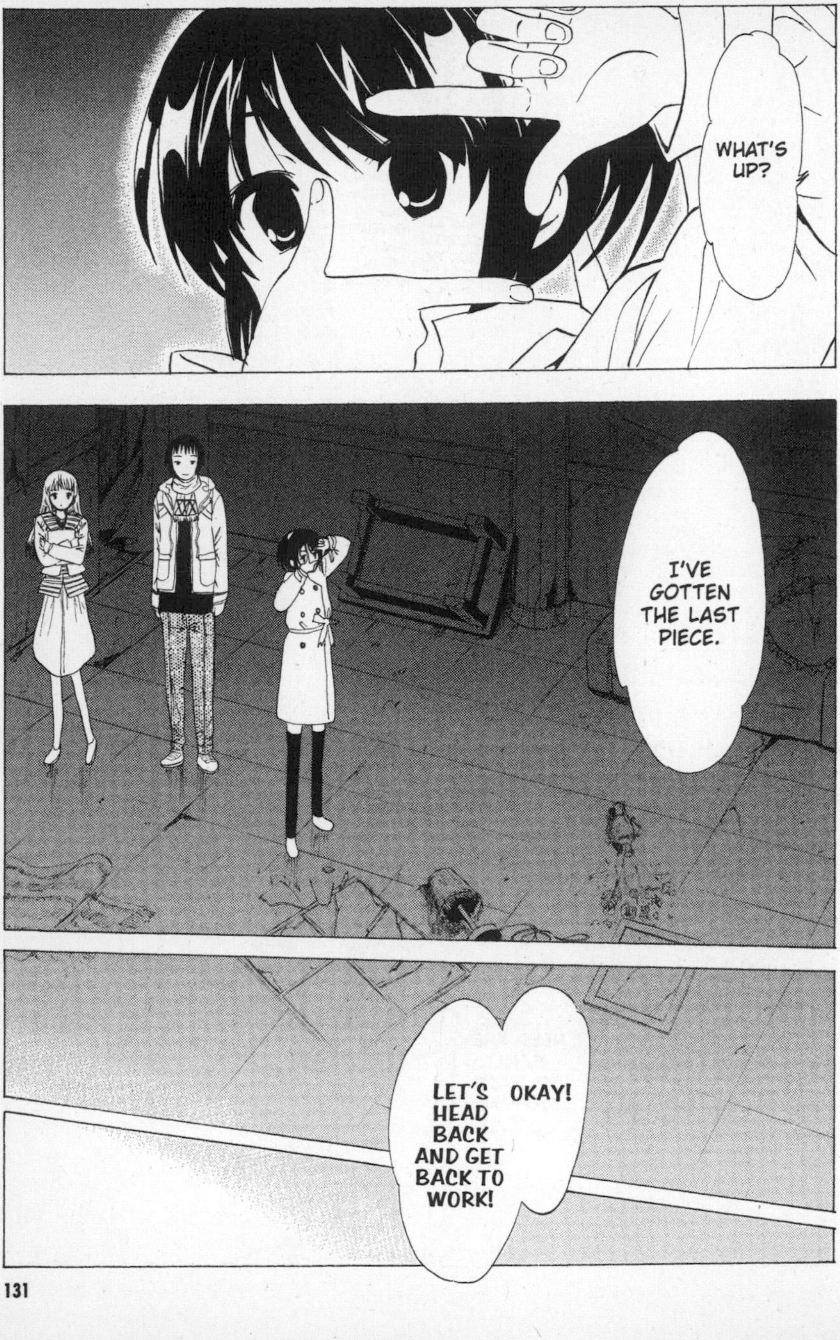
WHAT'S UP?
I'VE GOTTEN THE LAST PIECE.
OKAY!
LET'S HEAD BACK AND GET BACK TO WORK!

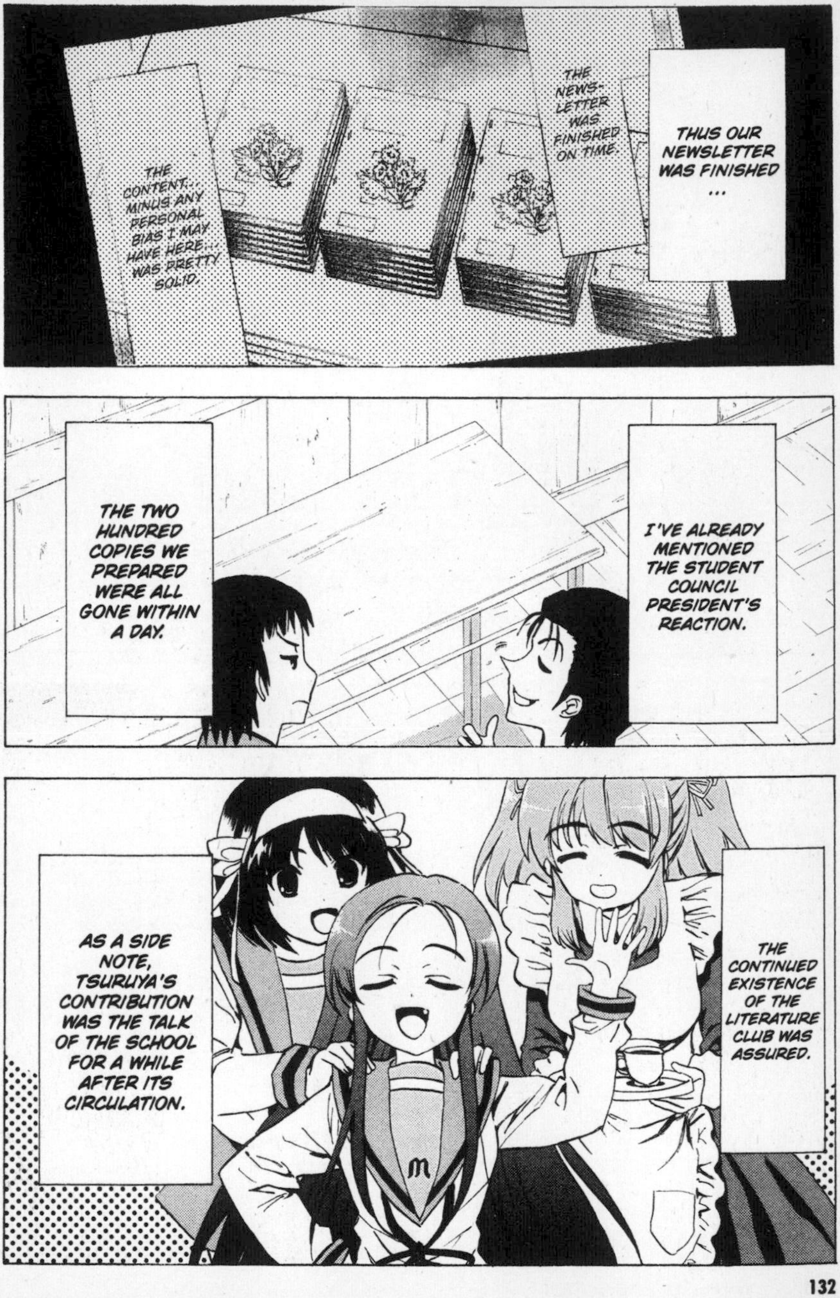
THUS OUR NEWSLETTER WAS FINISHED ...
THE NEWS-LETTER WAS FINISHED ON TIME.
THE CONTENT... MINUS ANY PERSONAL BIAS I MAY HAVE HERE... WAS PRETTY SOLID.
I'VE ALREADY MENTIONED THE STUDENT COUNCIL PRESIDENT'S REACTION.
THE TWO HUNDRED COPIES WE PREPARED WERE ALL GONE WITHIN A DAY.
THE CONTINUED EXISTENCE OF THE LITERATURE CLUB WAS ASSURED.
AS A SIDE NOTE, TSURUYA'S CONTRIBUTION WAS THE TALK OF THE SCHOOL FOR A WHILE AFTER ITS CIRCULATION.

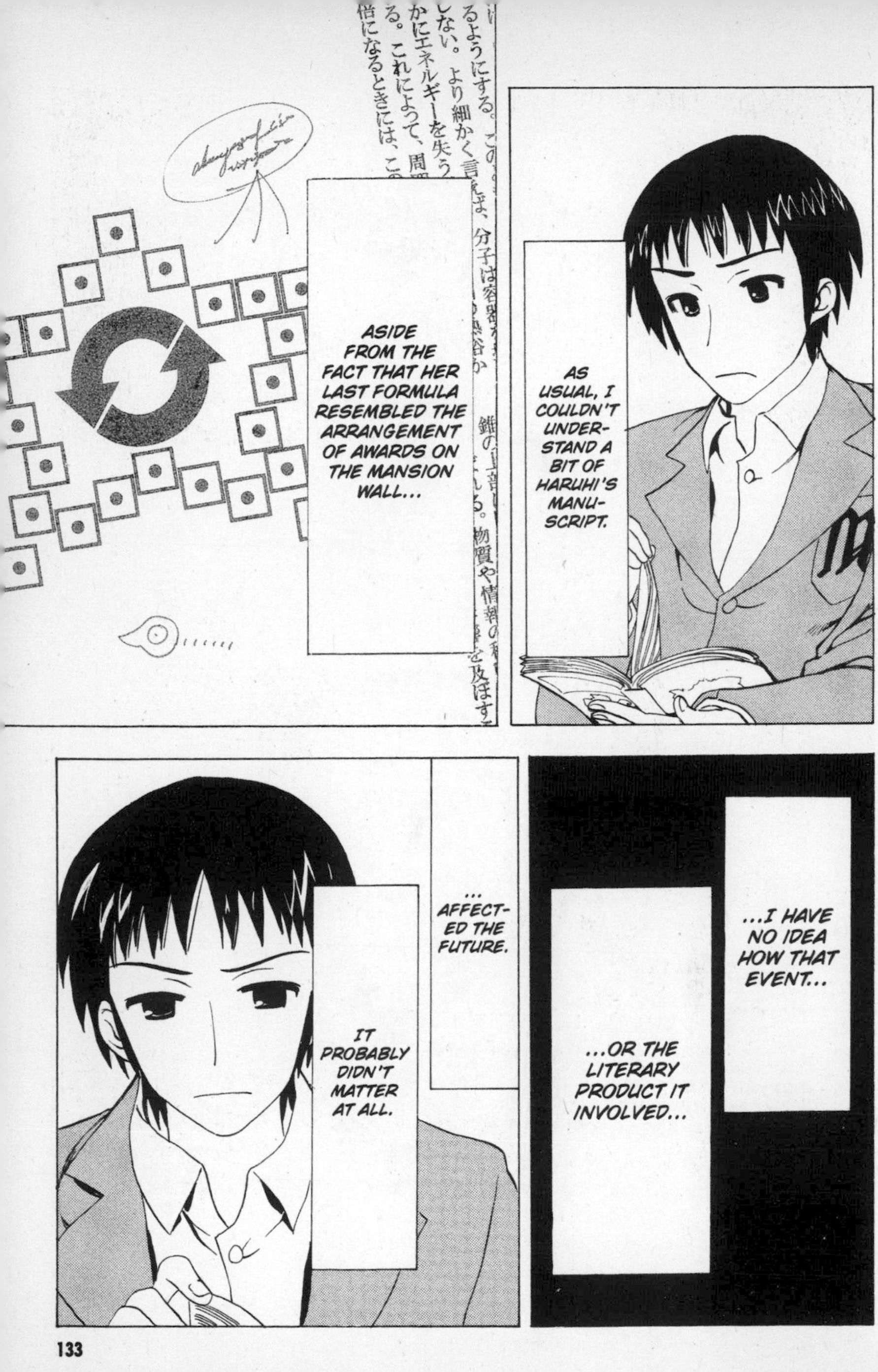
AS USUAL, I COULDN'T UNDER-STAND A BIT OF HARUHI'S MANU-SCRIPT.
ASIDE FROM THE FACT THAT HER LAST FORMULA RESEMBLED THE ARRANGEMENT OF AWARDS ON THE MANSION WALL...
...I HAVE NO IDEA HOW THAT EVENT...
...OR THE LITERARY PRODUCT IT INVOLVED...
...AFFECT-ED THE FUTURE.
IT PROBABLY DIDN'T MATTER AT ALL.

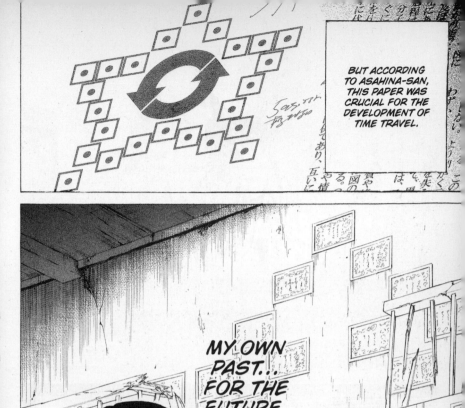

BUT ACCORDING TO ASAHINA-SAN, THIS PAPER WAS CRUCIAL FOR THE DEVELOPMENT OF TIME TRAVEL.

MY OWN PAST... FOR THE FUTURE.

SOMETIMES I THINK BACK ON TSUKADA-SAN'S WORDS...

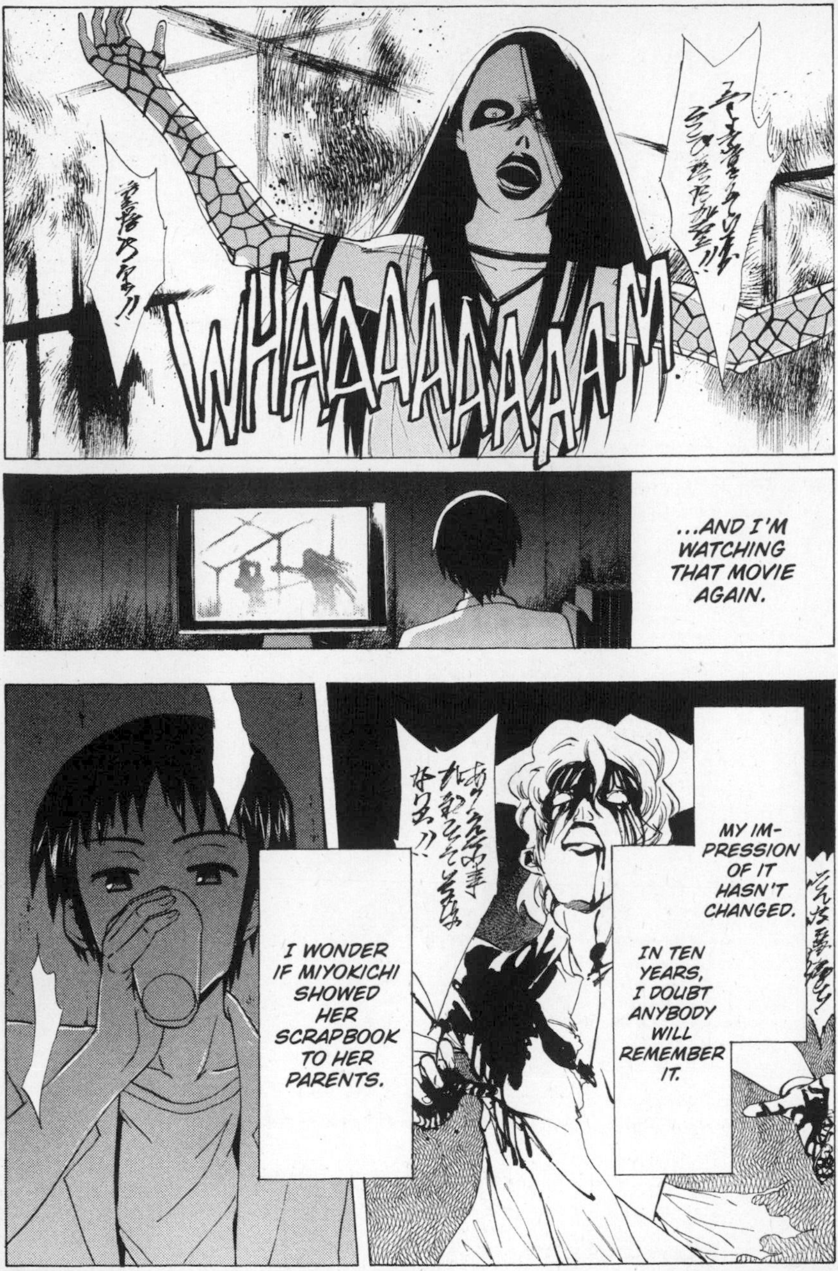

WHAAAAAAAAAM
...AND I'M WATCHING THAT MOVIE AGAIN.
MY IM-PRESSION OF IT HASN'T CHANGED.
IN TEN YEARS, I DOUBT ANYBODY WILL REMEMBER IT.
I WONDER IF MIYOKICHI SHOWED HER SCRAPBOOK TO HER PARENTS.

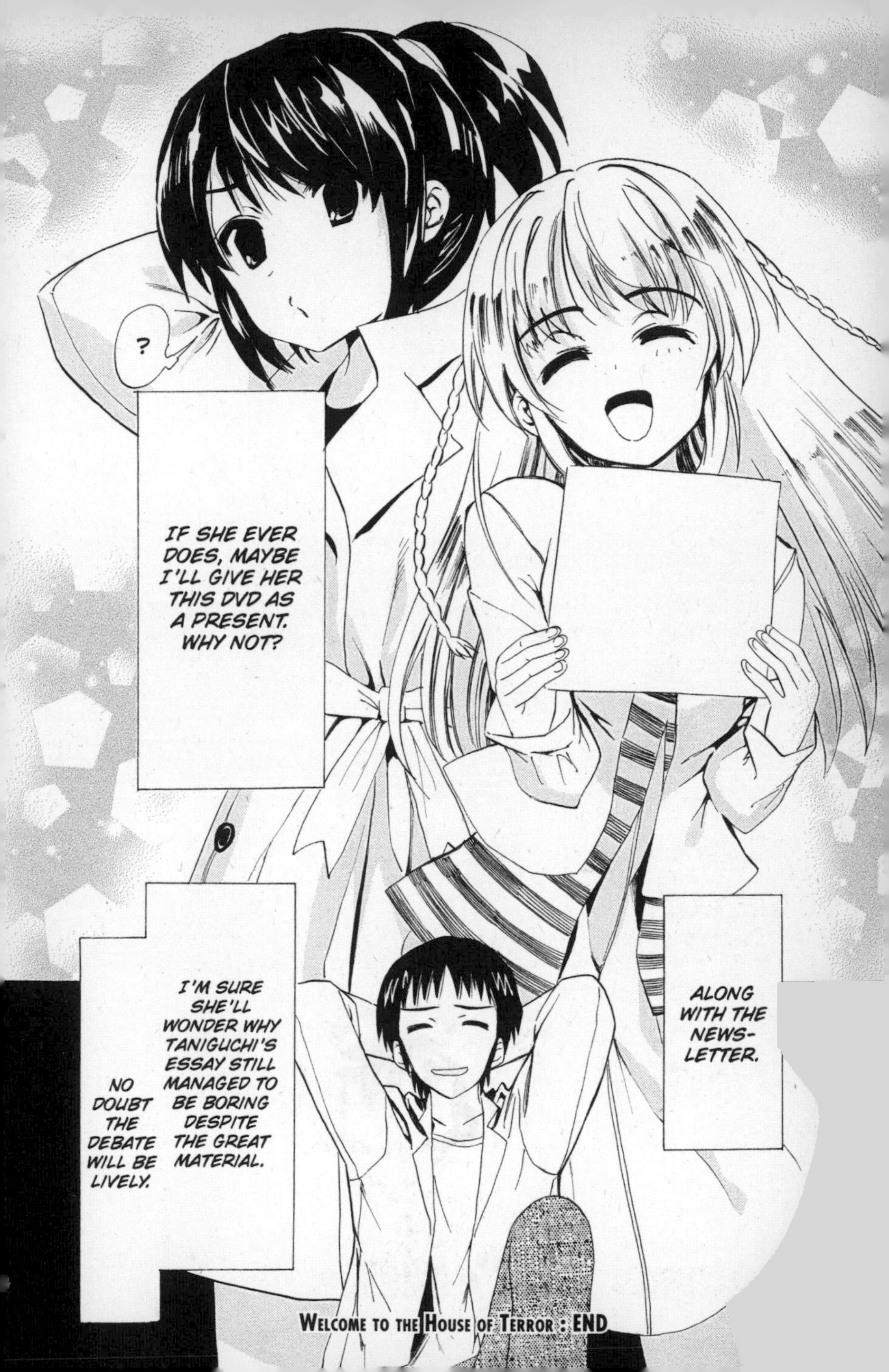
?
IF SHE EVER DOES, MAYBE I'LL GIVE HER THIS DVD AS A PRESENT. WHY NOT?
ALONG WITH THE NEWS-LETTER.
I'M SURE SHE'LL WONDER WHY TANIGUCHI'S ESSAY STILL MANAGED TO BE BORING DESPITE THE GREAT MATERIAL.
NO DOUBT THE DEBATE WILL BE LIVELY.
WELCOME TO THE HOUSE OF TERROR : END

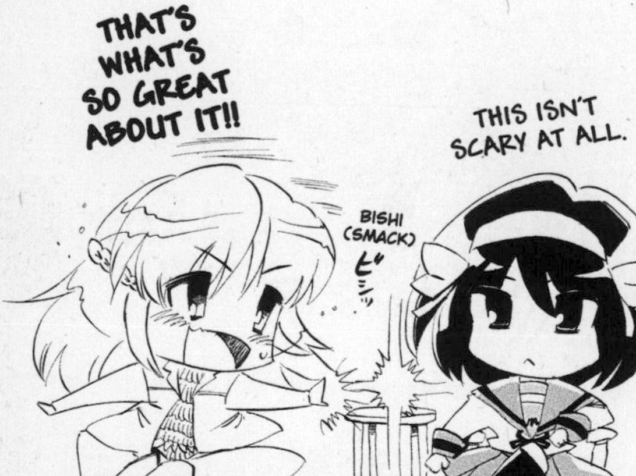
THIS ISN'T SCARY AT ALL.
BISHI (SMACK)
THAT'S WHAT'S SO GREAT ABOUT IT!!

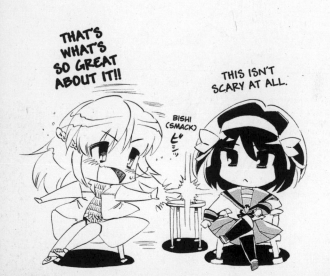

THE MELANCHOLY OF HARUHI SUZUMIYA

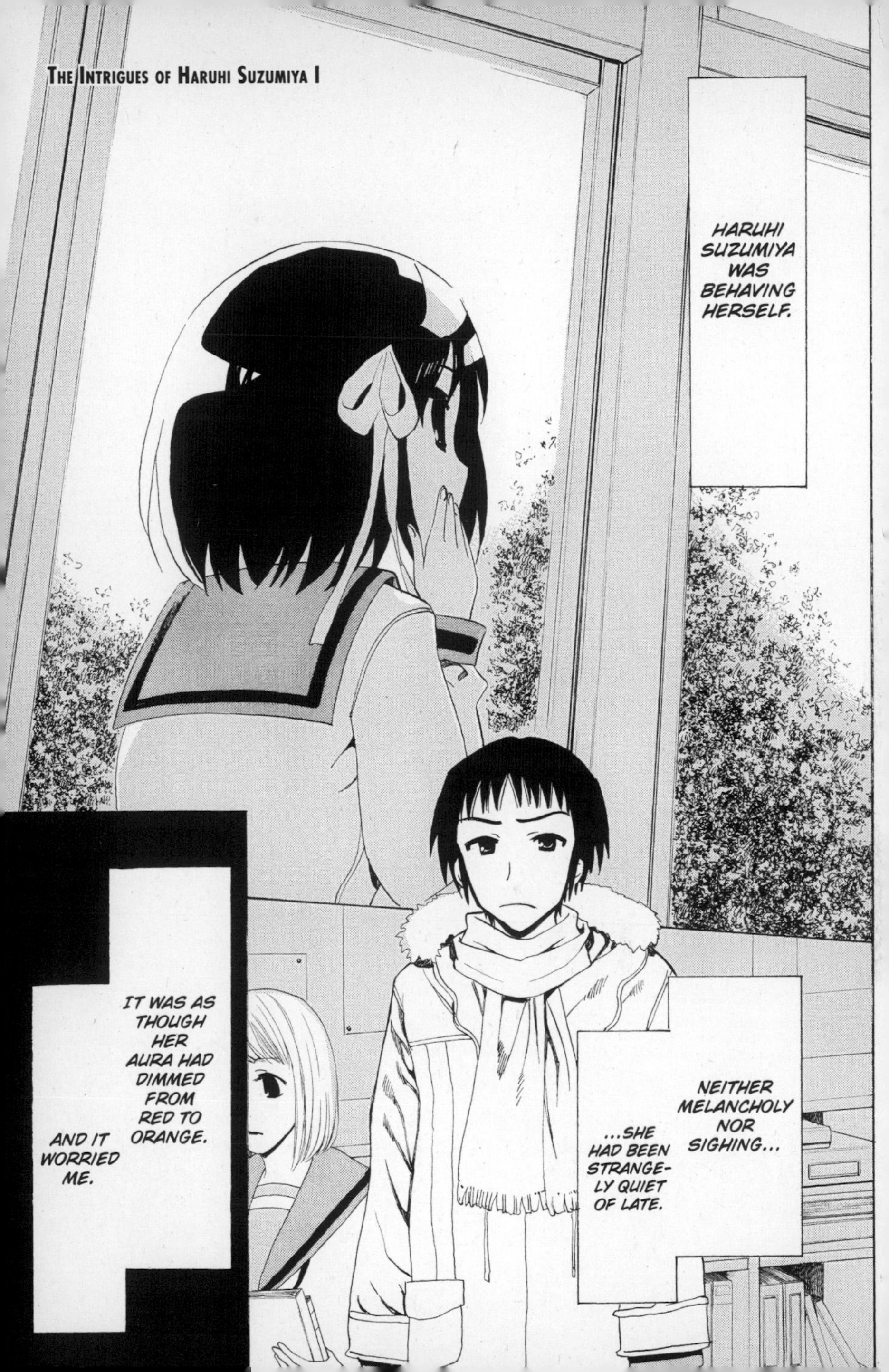
HARUHI SUZUMIYA WAS BEHAVING HERSELF.
NEITHER MELANCHOLY NOR SIGHING...
...SHE HAD BEEN STRANGE-LY QUIET OF LATE.
IT WAS AS THOUGH HER AURA HAD DIMMED FROM RED TO ORANGE.
AND IT WORRIED ME.

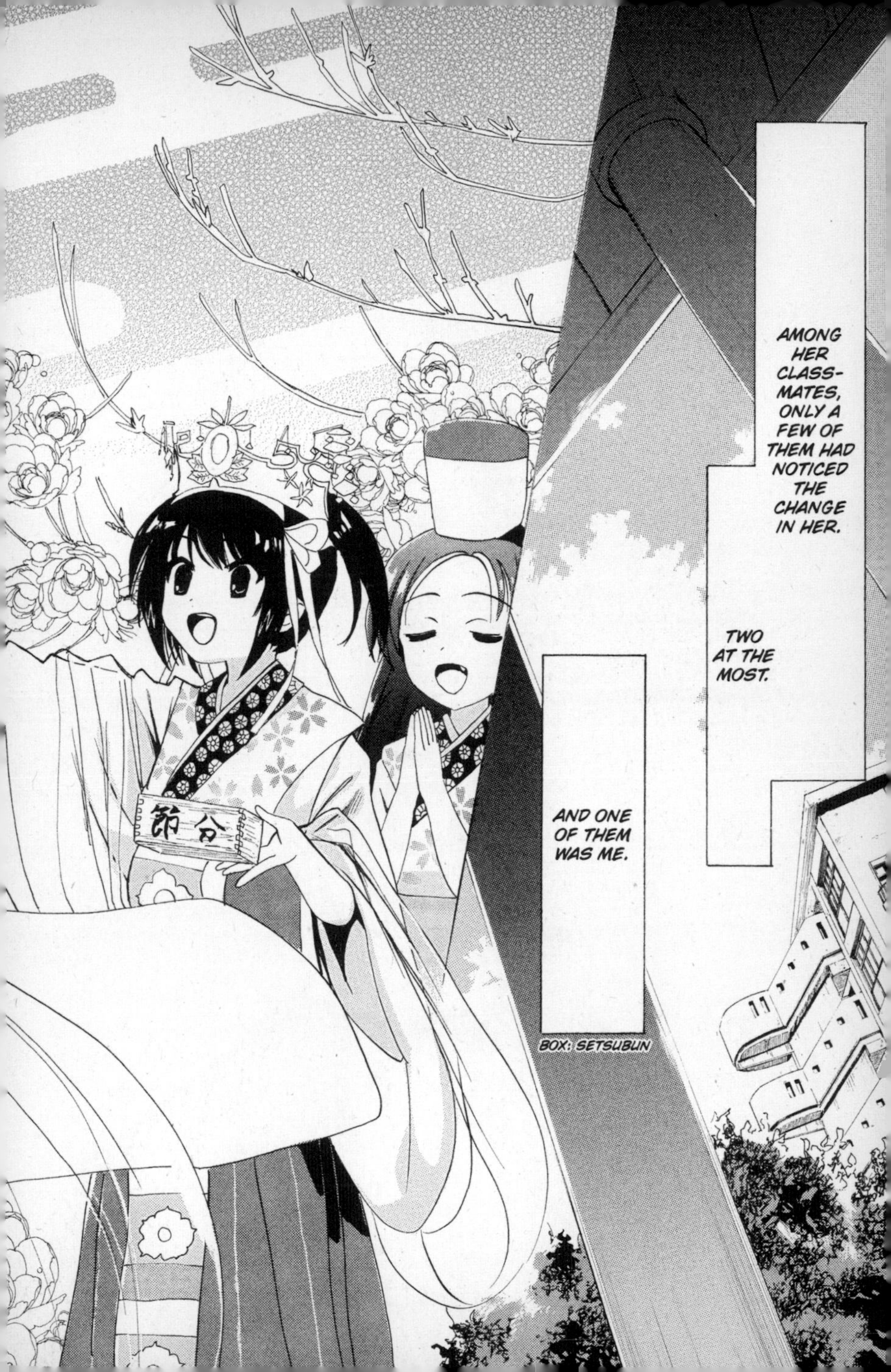
AMONG HER CLASS-MATES, ONLY A FEW OF THEM HAD NOTICED THE CHANGE IN HER.
TWO AT THE MOST.
AND ONE OF THEM WAS ME.
節分
BOX: SETSUBUN

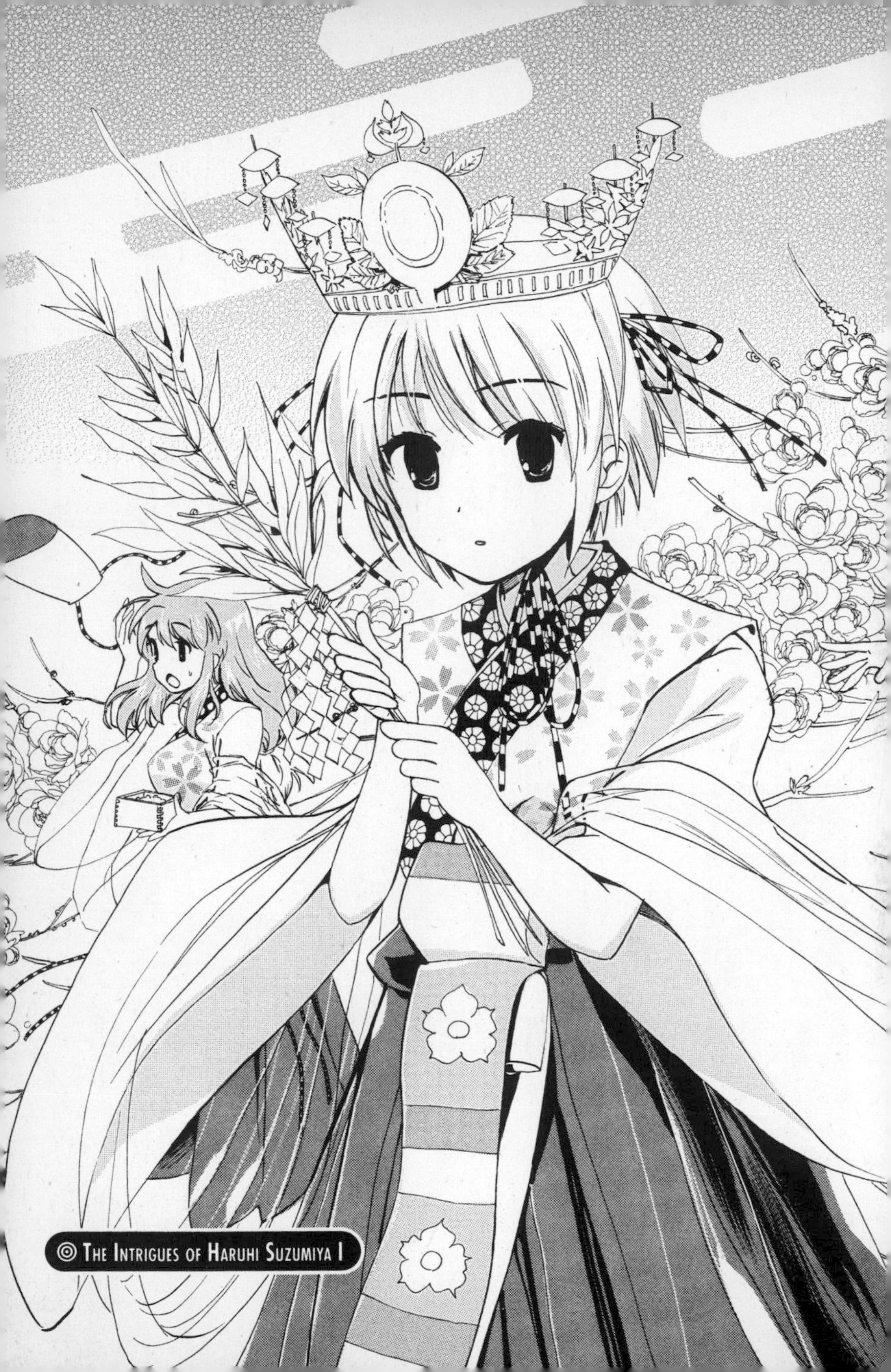
◎ The Intrigues of Haruhi Suzumiya I

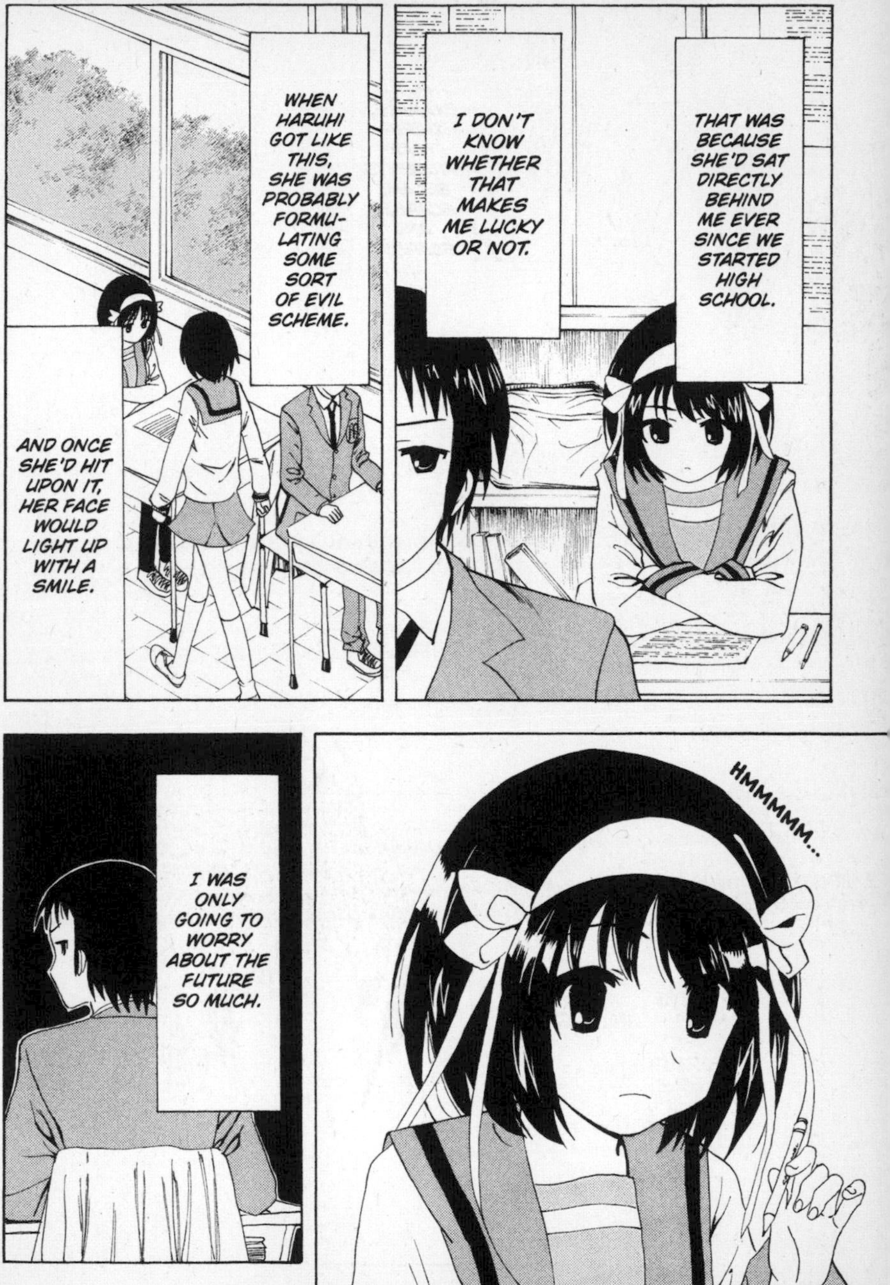
THAT WAS BECAUSE SHE'D SAT DIRECTLY BEHIND ME EVER SINCE WE STARTED HIGH SCHOOL.
I DON'T KNOW WHETHER THAT MAKES ME LUCKY OR NOT.
WHEN HARUHI GOT LIKE THIS, SHE WAS PROBABLY FORMU-LATING SOME SORT OF EVIL SCHEME.
AND ONCE SHE'D HIT UPON IT, HER FACE WOULD LIGHT UP WITH A SMILE.
HMMMMMM...
I WAS ONLY GOING TO WORRY ABOUT THE FUTURE SO MUCH.

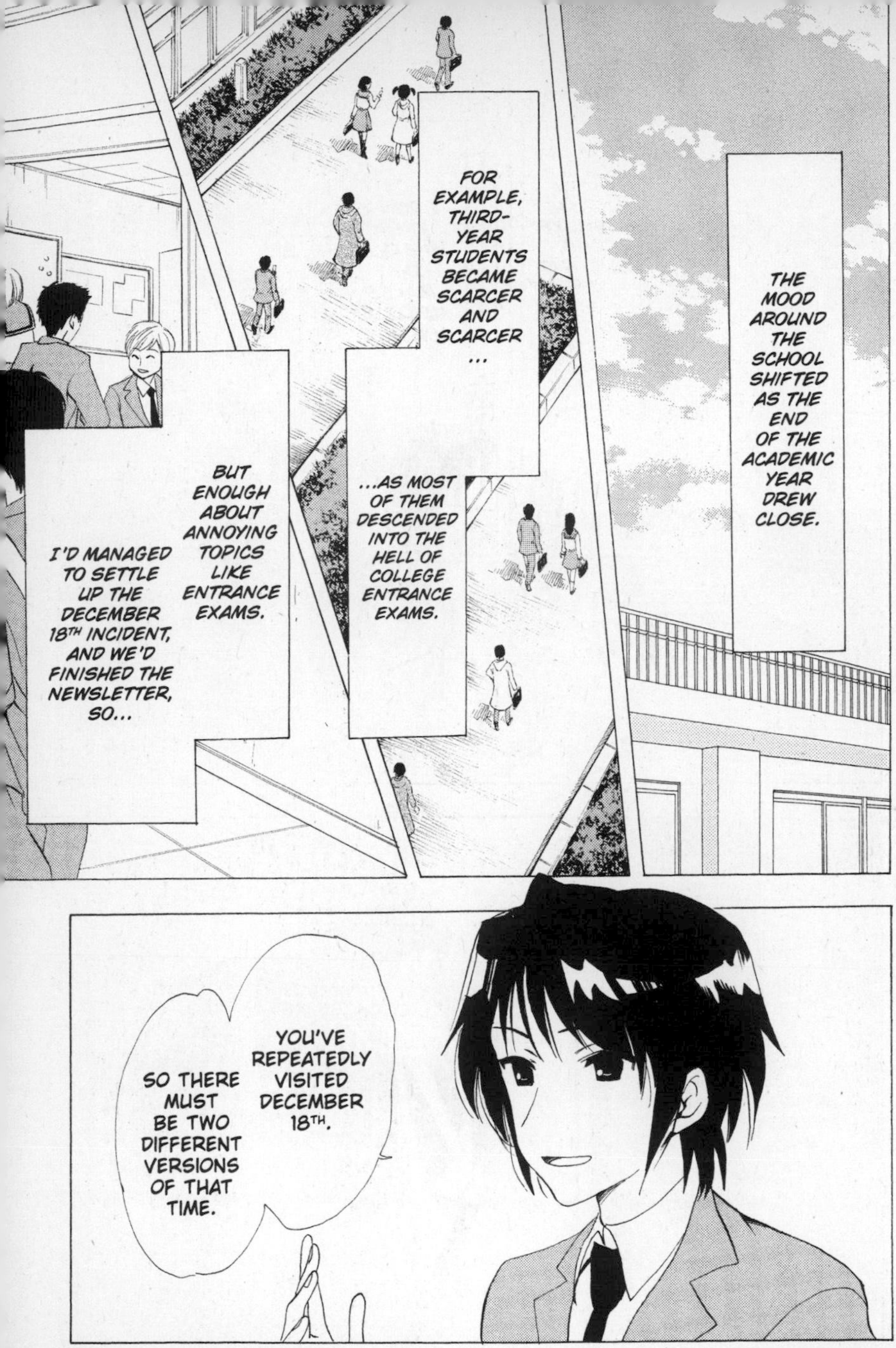
THE MOOD AROUND THE SCHOOL SHIFTED AS THE END OF THE ACADEMIC YEAR DREW CLOSE.
FOR EXAMPLE, THIRD-YEAR STUDENTS BECAME SCARCER AND SCARCER ...
...AS MOST OF THEM DESCENDED INTO THE HELL OF COLLEGE ENTRANCE EXAMS.
BUT ENOUGH ABOUT ANNOYING TOPICS LIKE ENTRANCE EXAMS.
I'D MANAGED TO SETTLE UP THE DECEMBER 18TH INCIDENT, AND WE'D FINISHED THE NEWSLETTER, SO...
YOU'VE REPEATEDLY VISITED DECEMBER 18TH.
SO THERE MUST BE TWO DIFFERENT VERSIONS OF THAT TIME.

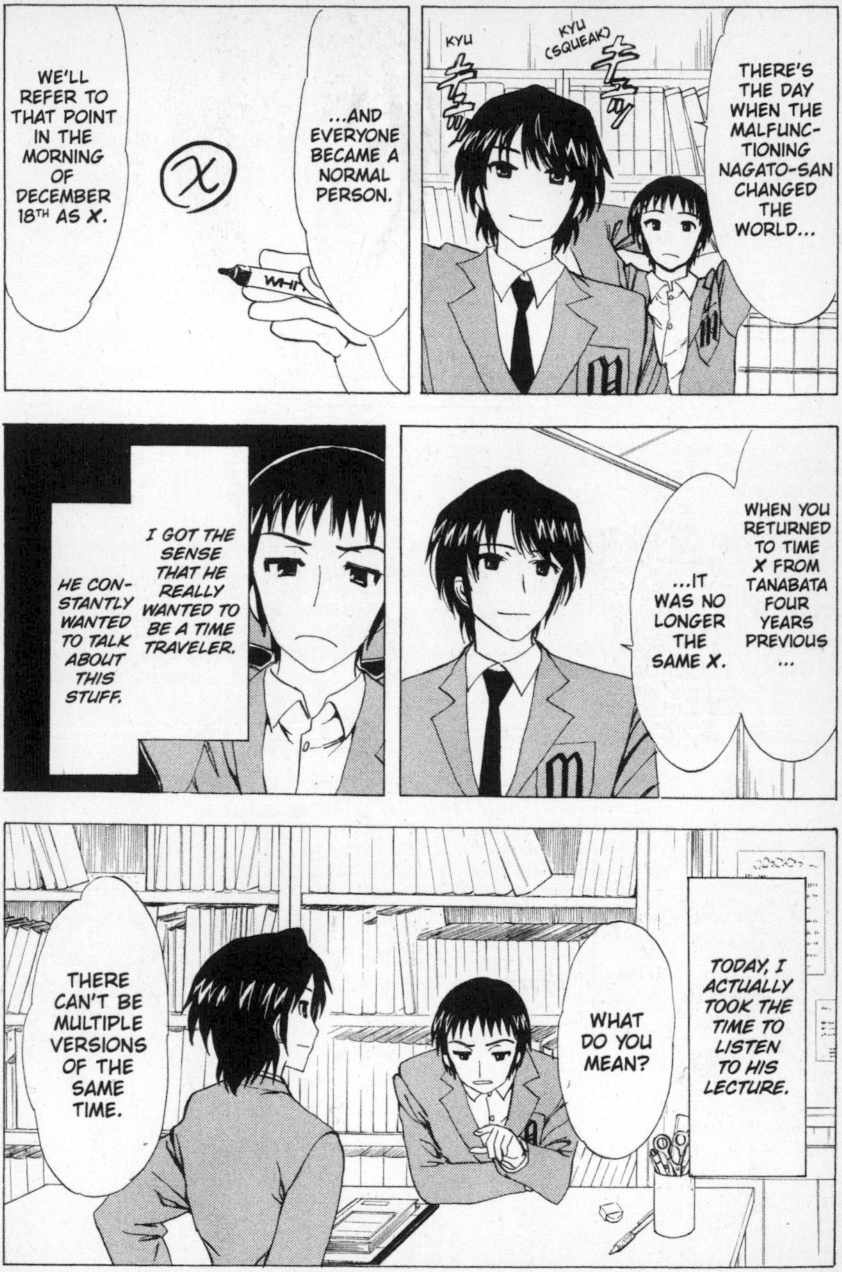
KYU (SQUEAK)
KYU
THERE'S THE DAY WHEN THE MALFUNCTIONING NAGATO-SAN CHANGED THE WORLD...
...AND EVERYONE BECAME A NORMAL PERSON.
WE'LL REFER TO THAT POINT IN THE MORNING OF DECEMBER 18TH AS X.
X
WHEN YOU RETURNED TO TIME X FROM TANABATA FOUR YEARS PREVIOUS...
...IT WAS NO LONGER THE SAME X.
I GOT THE SENSE THAT HE REALLY WANTED TO BE A TIME TRAVELER.
HE CONSTANTLY WANTED TO TALK ABOUT THIS STUFF.
TODAY, I ACTUALLY TOOK THE TIME TO LISTEN TO HIS LECTURE.
WHAT DO YOU MEAN?
THERE CAN'T BE MULTIPLE VERSIONS OF THE SAME TIME.

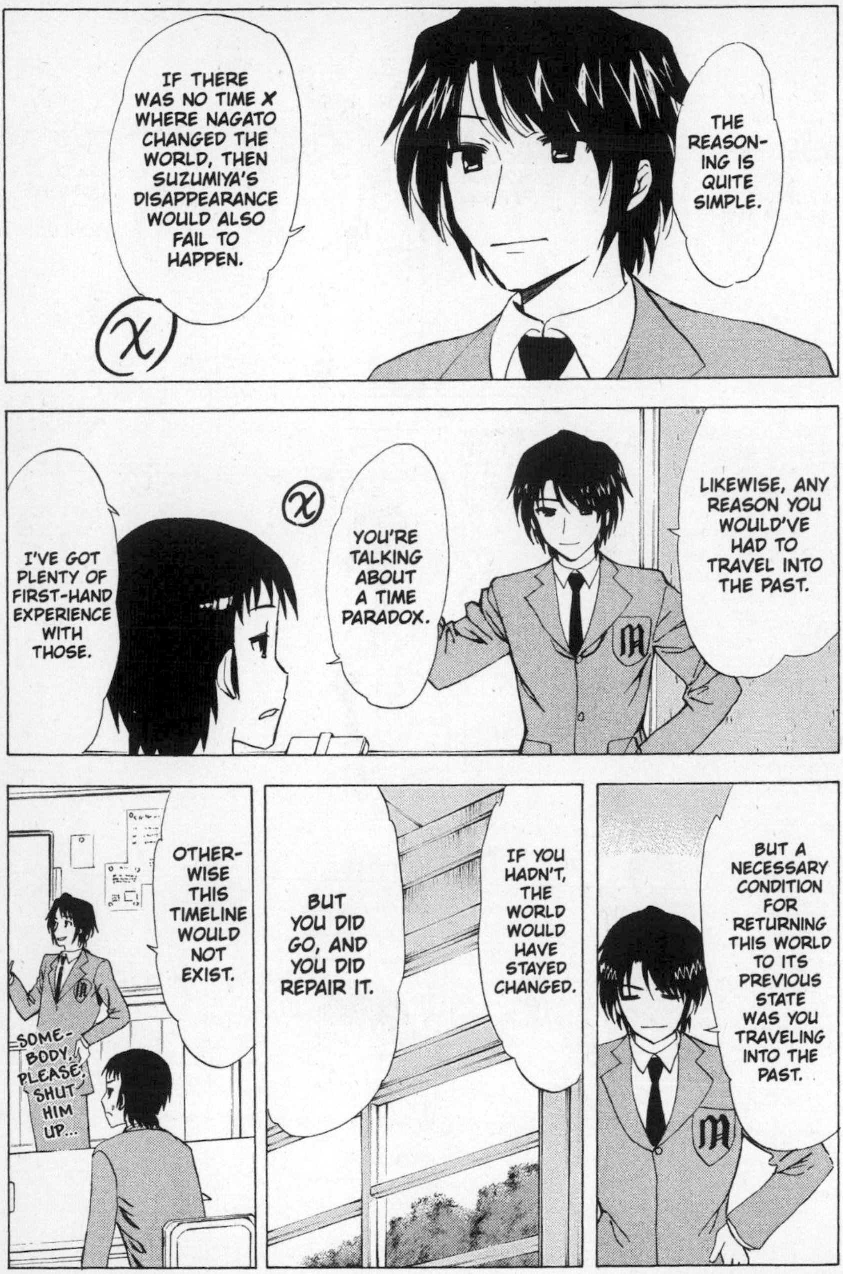
THE REASONING IS QUITE SIMPLE.
IF THERE WAS NO TIME X WHERE NAGATO CHANGED THE WORLD, THEN SUZUMIYA'S DISAPPEARANCE WOULD ALSO FAIL TO HAPPEN.
LIKEWISE, ANY REASON YOU WOULD'VE HAD TO TRAVEL INTO THE PAST.
YOU'RE TALKING ABOUT A TIME PARADOX.
I'VE GOT PLENTY OF FIRST-HAND EXPERIENCE WITH THOSE.
BUT A NECESSARY CONDITION FOR RETURNING THIS WORLD TO ITS PREVIOUS STATE WAS YOU TRAVELING INTO THE PAST.
IF YOU HADN'T, THE WORLD WOULD HAVE STAYED CHANGED.
BUT YOU DID GO, AND YOU DID REPAIR IT.
OTHERWISE THIS TIMELINE WOULD NOT EXIST.
SOMEBODY, PLEASE, SHUT HIM UP...

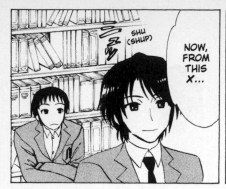

SAY THIS VERTICAL LINE REPRESENTS THE FLOW OF TIME FROM PAST TO FUTURE.
TSUU (SHHT)
NOW, FROM THIS X...
SHU (SHUP)
THE CIRCLE IS THE HISTORY THAT YOU REMEMBER SINCE DECEMBER 18TH.
YOU USED THE ESCAPE PROGRAM TO TRAVEL BACK TO THE TANABATA FOUR YEARS EARLIER, THEN JUMPED BACK TO DECEMBER 18TH.
IF NAGATO HAD BEEN REPAIRED AT THAT MOMENT, IT WOULD'VE BEEN FINE.
EXCEPT RYOUKO ASAKURA WAS THERE.
BUT YOU AND ASAHINA, COMING FROM THE FUTURE...
...MAN-AGED TO PUT THE WORLD RIGHT.
YOU SAVED YOUR-SELVES.

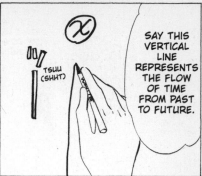

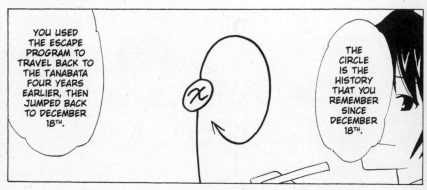

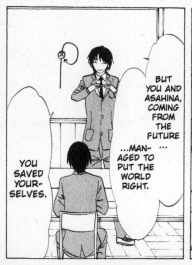

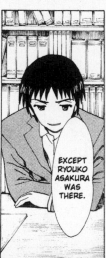

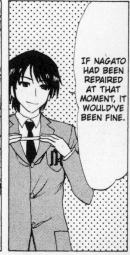

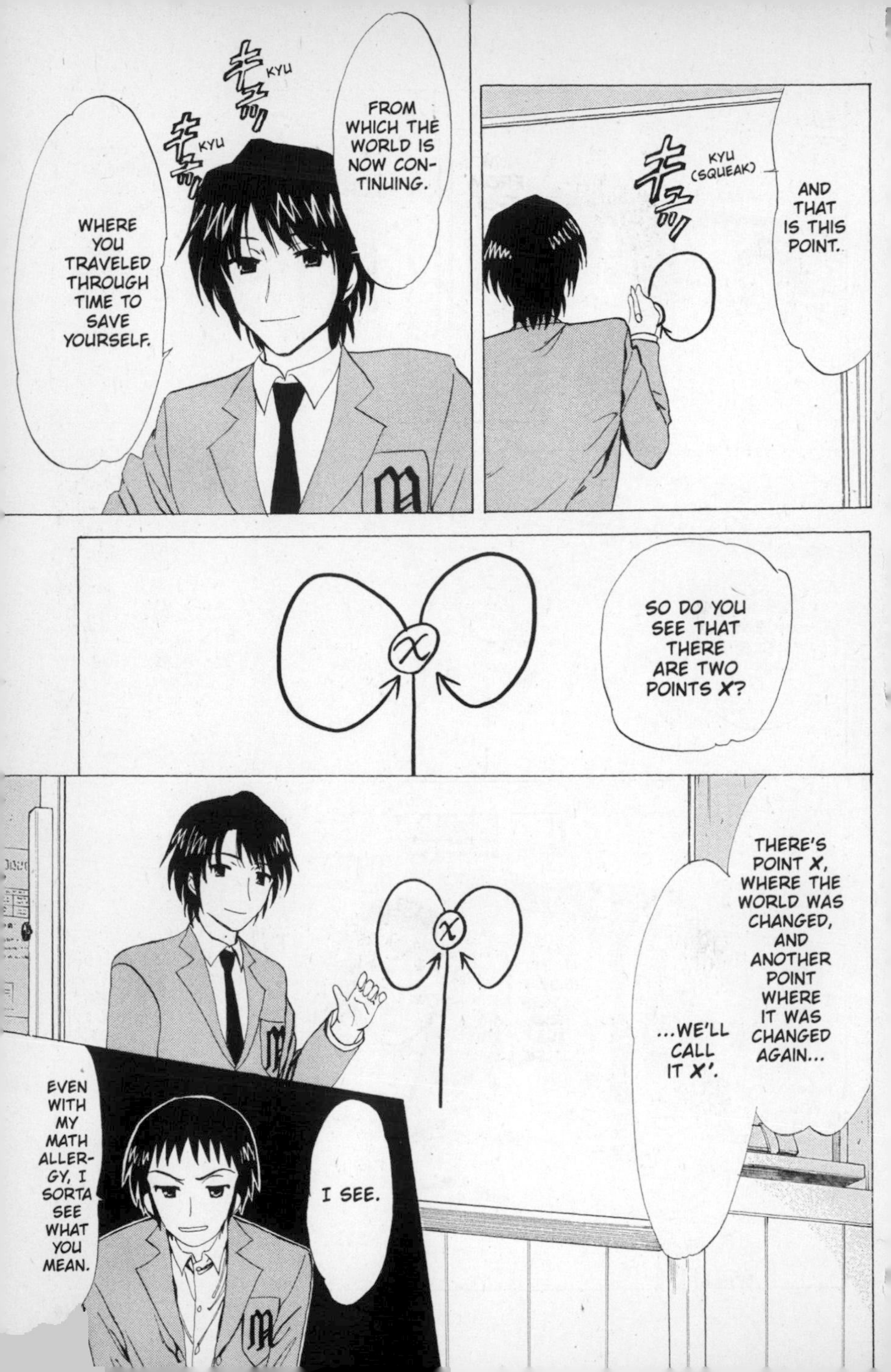
KYU (SQUEAK)
AND THAT IS THIS POINT.
FROM WHICH THE WORLD IS NOW CON-TINUING.
KYU
KYU
WHERE YOU TRAVELED THROUGH TIME TO SAVE YOURSELF.
SO DO YOU SEE THAT THERE ARE TWO POINTS X?
x
THERE'S POINT X, WHERE THE WORLD WAS CHANGED, AND ANOTHER POINT WHERE IT WAS CHANGED AGAIN...
...WE'LL CALL IT X'.
x
I SEE.
EVEN WITH MY MATH ALLER-GY, I SORTA SEE WHAT YOU MEAN.

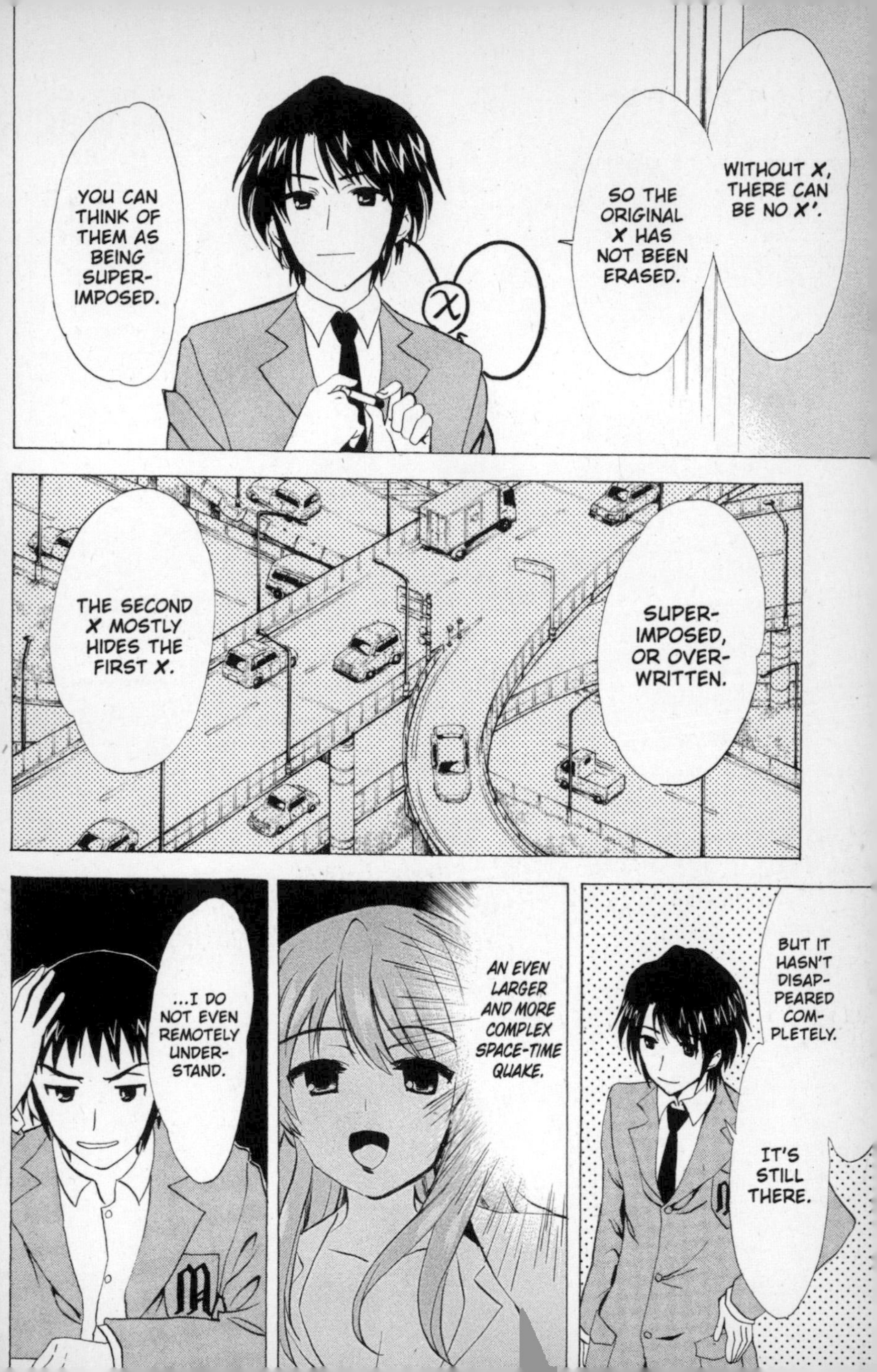
WITHOUT X, THERE CAN BE NO X'.
SO THE ORIGINAL X HAS NOT BEEN ERASED.
YOU CAN THINK OF THEM AS BEING SUPER-IMPOSED.
SUPER-IMPOSED, OR OVER-WRITTEN.
THE SECOND X MOSTLY HIDES THE FIRST X.
BUT IT HASN'T DISAP-PEARED COM-PLETELY.
IT'S STILL THERE.
AN EVEN LARGER AND MORE COMPLEX SPACE-TIME QUAKE.
...I DO NOT EVEN REMOTELY UNDER-STAND.

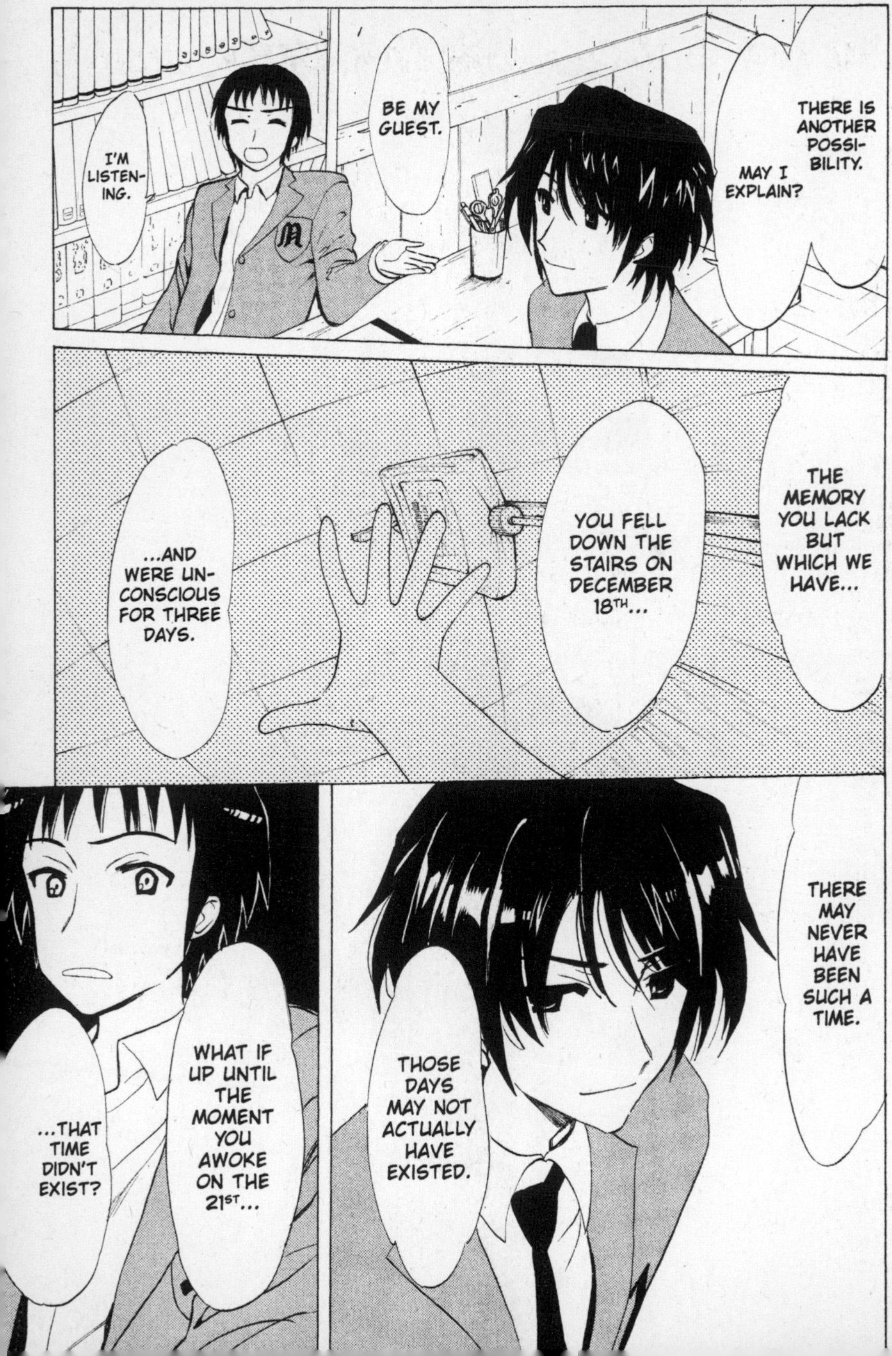
THERE IS ANOTHER POSSI-BILITY.
MAY I EXPLAIN?
BE MY GUEST.
I'M LISTEN-ING.
THE MEMORY YOU LACK BUT WHICH WE HAVE...
YOU FELL DOWN THE STAIRS ON DECEMBER 18TH...
...AND WERE UN-CONSCIOUS FOR THREE DAYS.
THERE MAY NEVER HAVE BEEN SUCH A TIME.
THOSE DAYS MAY NOT ACTUALLY HAVE EXISTED.
WHAT IF UP UNTIL THE MOMENT YOU AWOKE ON THE 21ST...
...THAT TIME DIDN'T EXIST?

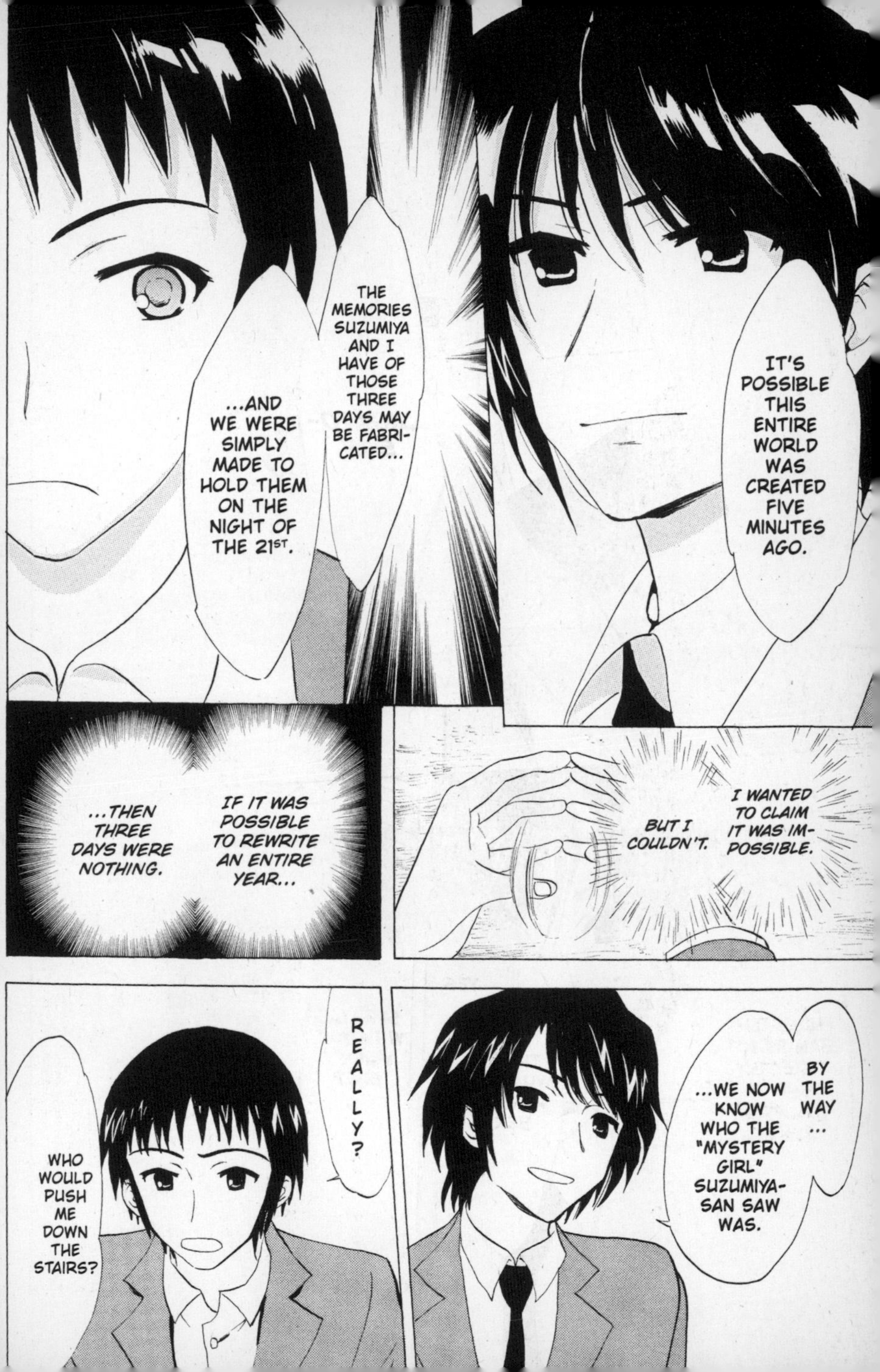
IT'S POSSIBLE THIS ENTIRE WORLD WAS CREATED FIVE MINUTES AGO.
THE MEMORIES SUZUMIYA AND I HAVE OF THOSE THREE DAYS MAY BE FABRICATED...
...AND WE WERE SIMPLY MADE TO HOLD THEM ON THE NIGHT OF THE 21ST.
I WANTED TO CLAIM IT WAS IMPOSSIBLE.
BUT I COULDN'T.
IF IT WAS POSSIBLE TO REWRITE AN ENTIRE YEAR...
...THEN THREE DAYS WERE NOTHING.
BY THE WAY...
...WE NOW KNOW WHO THE "MYSTERY GIRL" SUZUMIYA-SAN SAW WAS.
REALLY?
WHO WOULD PUSH ME DOWN THE STAIRS?

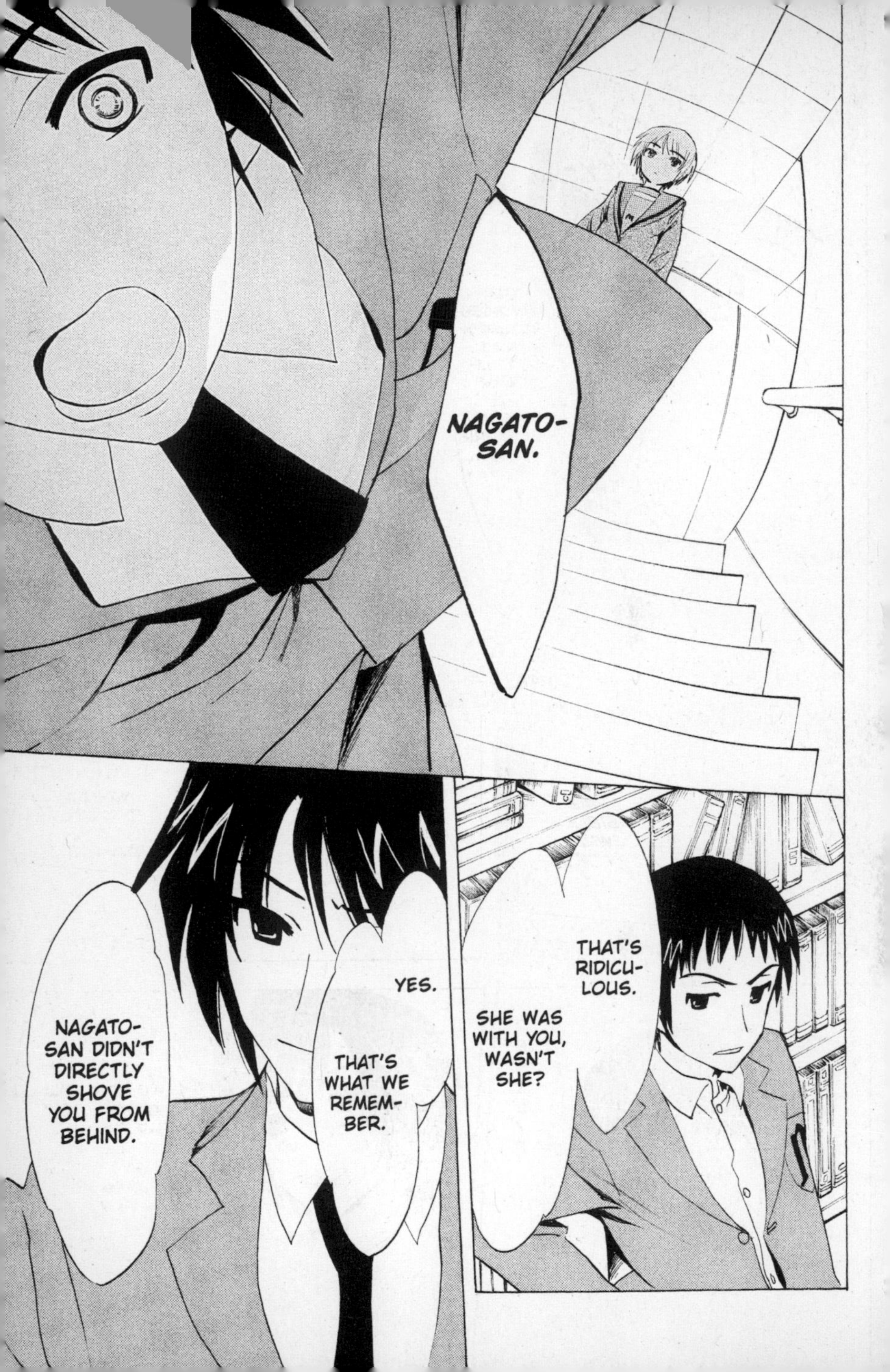
NAGATO-SAN.
THAT'S RIDICULOUS.
SHE WAS WITH YOU, WASN'T SHE?
YES.
THAT'S WHAT WE REMEMBER.
NAGATO-SAN DIDN'T DIRECTLY SHOVE YOU FROM BEHIND.

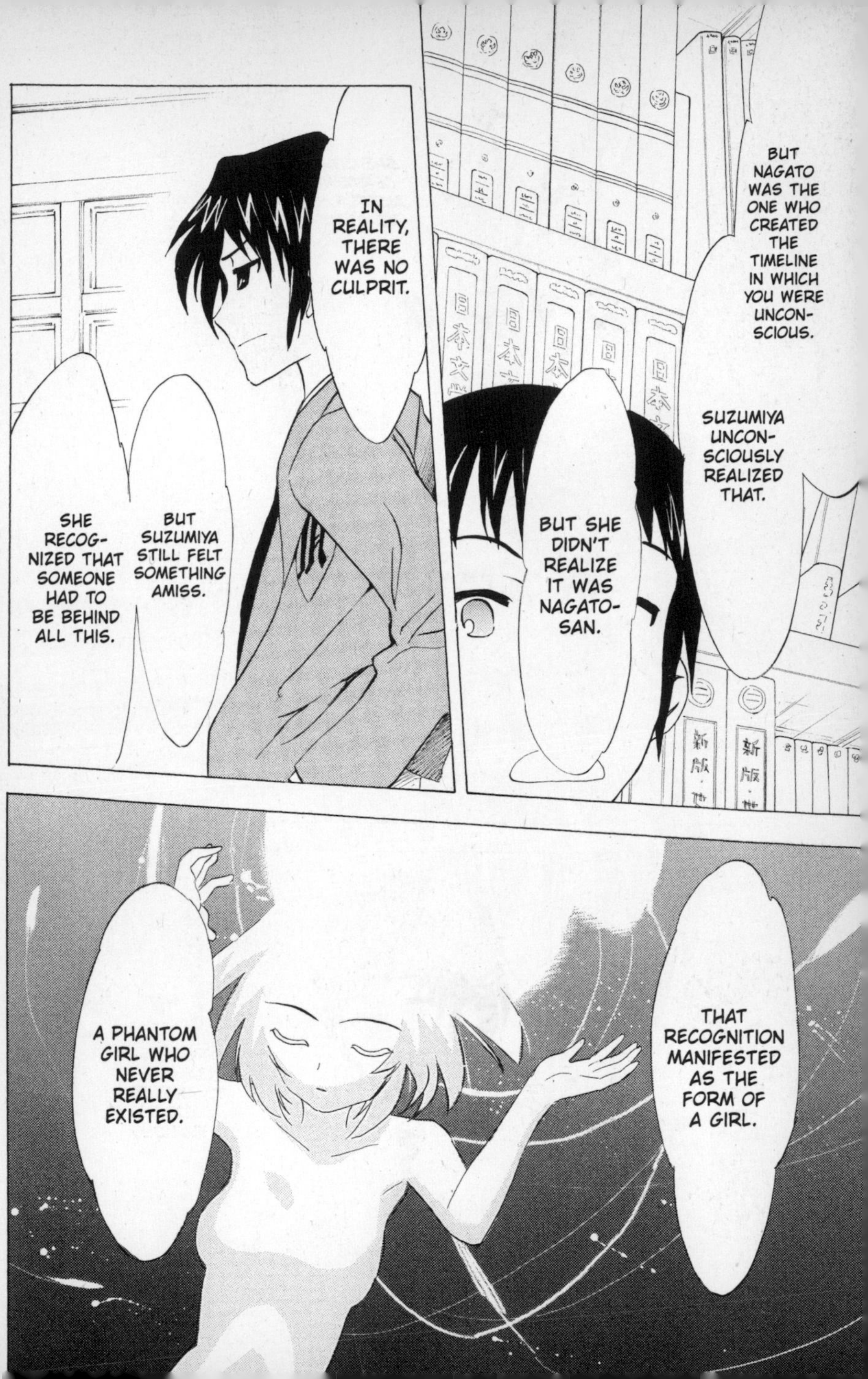
BUT NAGATO WAS THE ONE WHO CREATED THE TIMELINE IN WHICH YOU WERE UNCON-SCIOUS.
SUZUMIYA UNCON-SCIOUSLY REALIZED THAT.
BUT SHE DIDN'T REALIZE IT WAS NAGATO-SAN.
IN REALITY, THERE WAS NO CULPRIT.
BUT SUZUMIYA STILL FELT SOMETHING AMISS.
SHE RECOG-NIZED THAT SOMEONE HAD TO BE BEHIND ALL THIS.
THAT RECOGNITION MANIFESTED AS THE FORM OF A GIRL.
A PHANTOM GIRL WHO NEVER REALLY EXISTED.

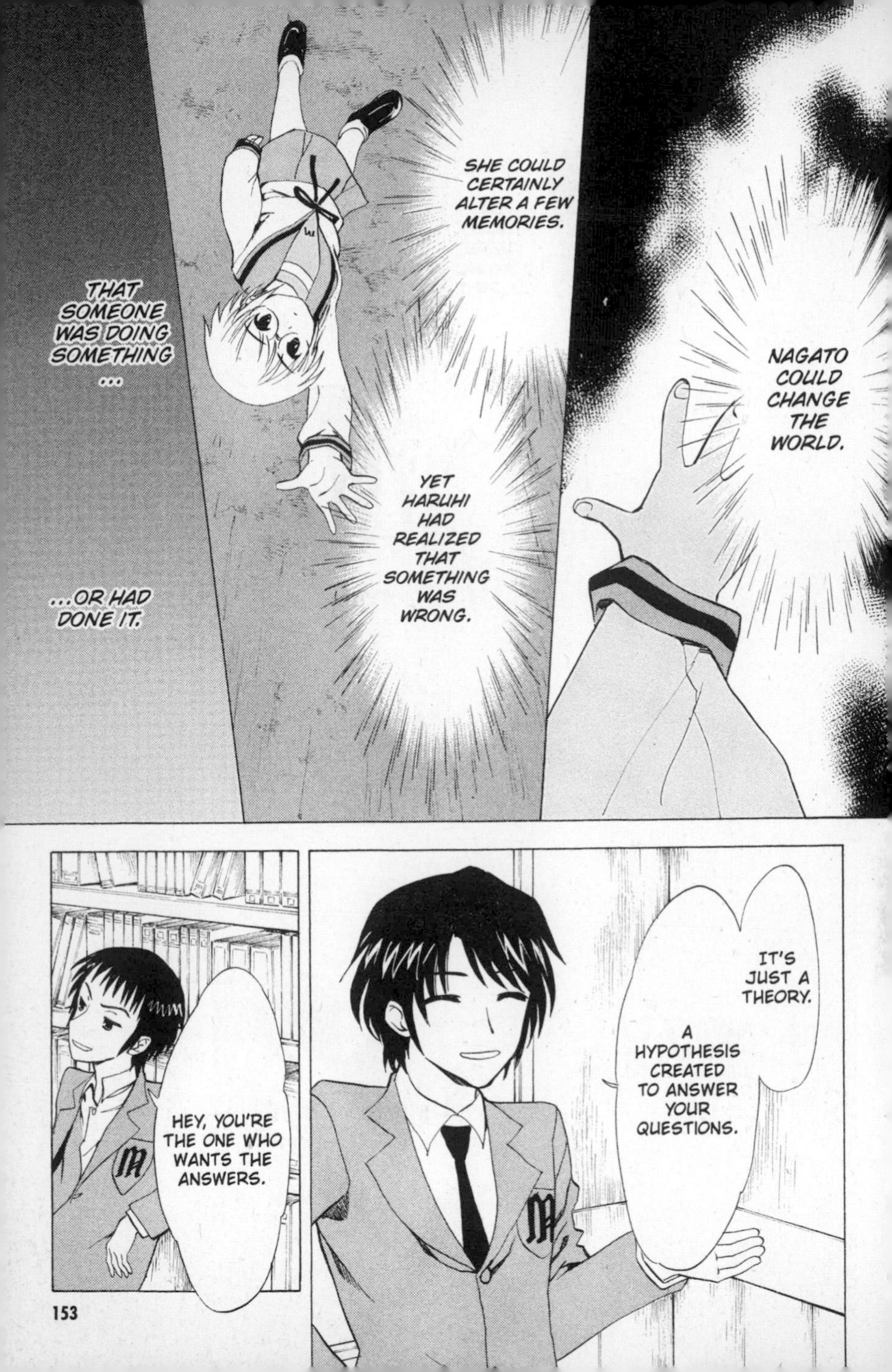
NAGATO COULD CHANGE THE WORLD.
SHE COULD CERTAINLY ALTER A FEW MEMORIES.
YET HARUHI HAD REALIZED THAT SOMETHING WAS WRONG.
THAT SOMEONE WAS DOING SOMETHING ...
...OR HAD DONE IT.
IT'S JUST A THEORY.
A HYPOTHESIS CREATED TO ANSWER YOUR QUESTIONS.
HEY, YOU'RE THE ONE WHO WANTS THE ANSWERS.

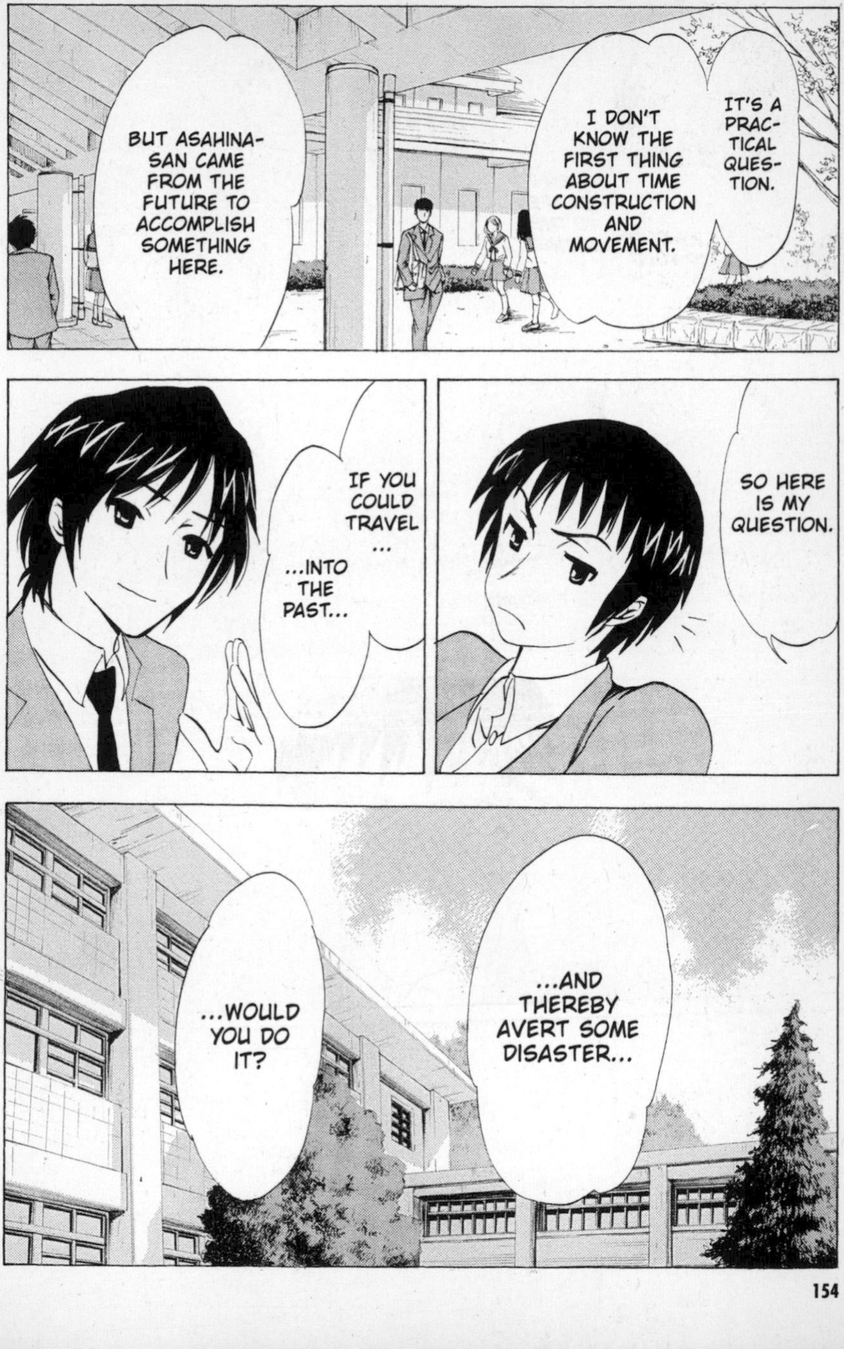
IT'S A PRACTICAL QUESTION.
I DON'T KNOW THE FIRST THING ABOUT TIME CONSTRUCTION AND MOVEMENT.
BUT ASAHINA-SAN CAME FROM THE FUTURE TO ACCOMPLISH SOMETHING HERE.
SO HERE IS MY QUESTION.
IF YOU COULD TRAVEL...
...INTO THE PAST...
...AND THEREBY AVERT SOME DISASTER...
...WOULD YOU DO IT?

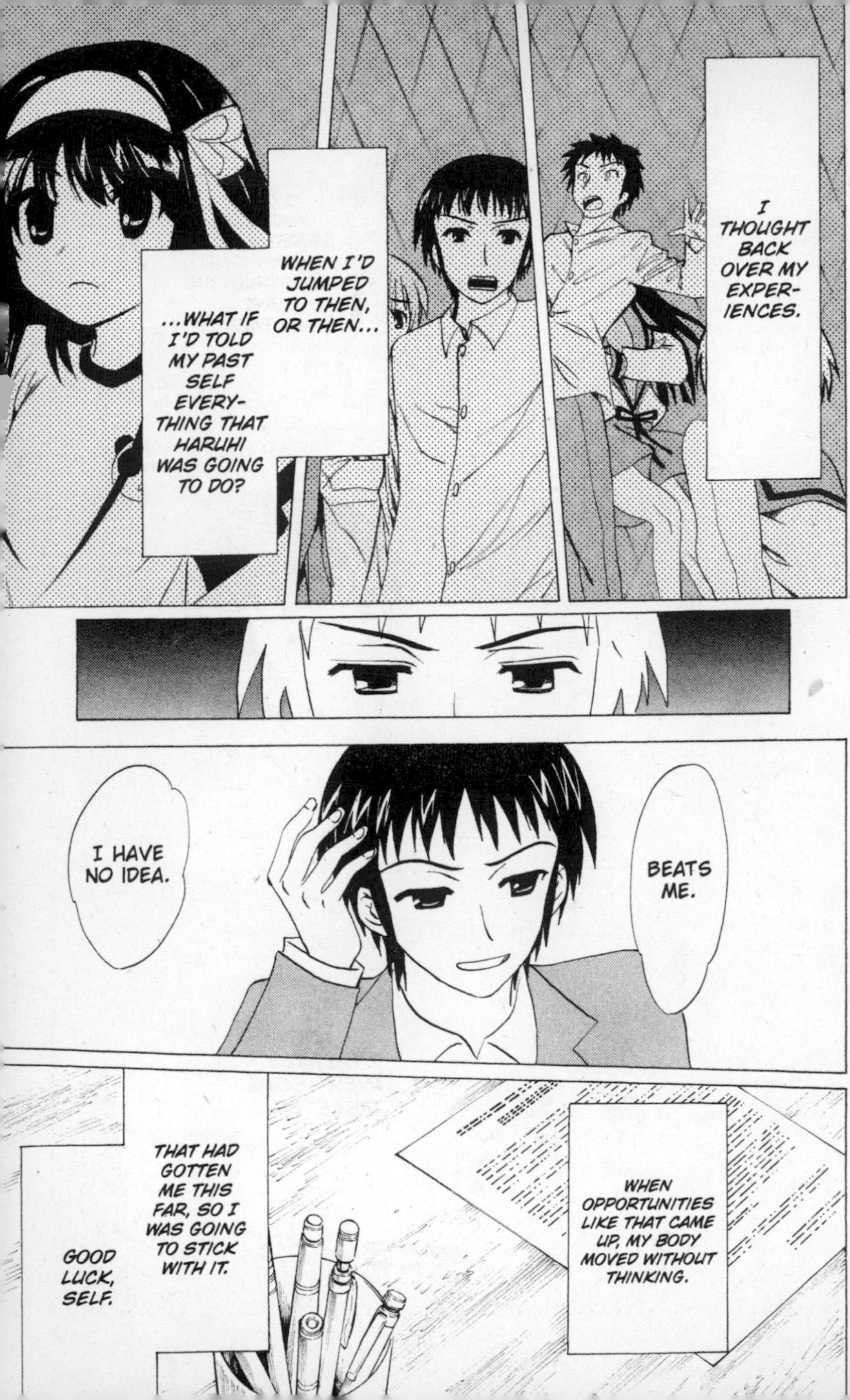
I THOUGHT BACK OVER MY EXPERIENCES.
WHEN I'D JUMPED TO THEN, OR THEN...
...WHAT IF I'D TOLD MY PAST SELF EVERYTHING THAT HARUHI WAS GOING TO DO?
BEATS ME.
I HAVE NO IDEA.
WHEN OPPORTUNITIES LIKE THAT CAME UP, MY BODY MOVED WITHOUT THINKING.
THAT HAD GOTTEN ME THIS FAR, SO I WAS GOING TO STICK WITH IT.
GOOD LUCK, SELF.

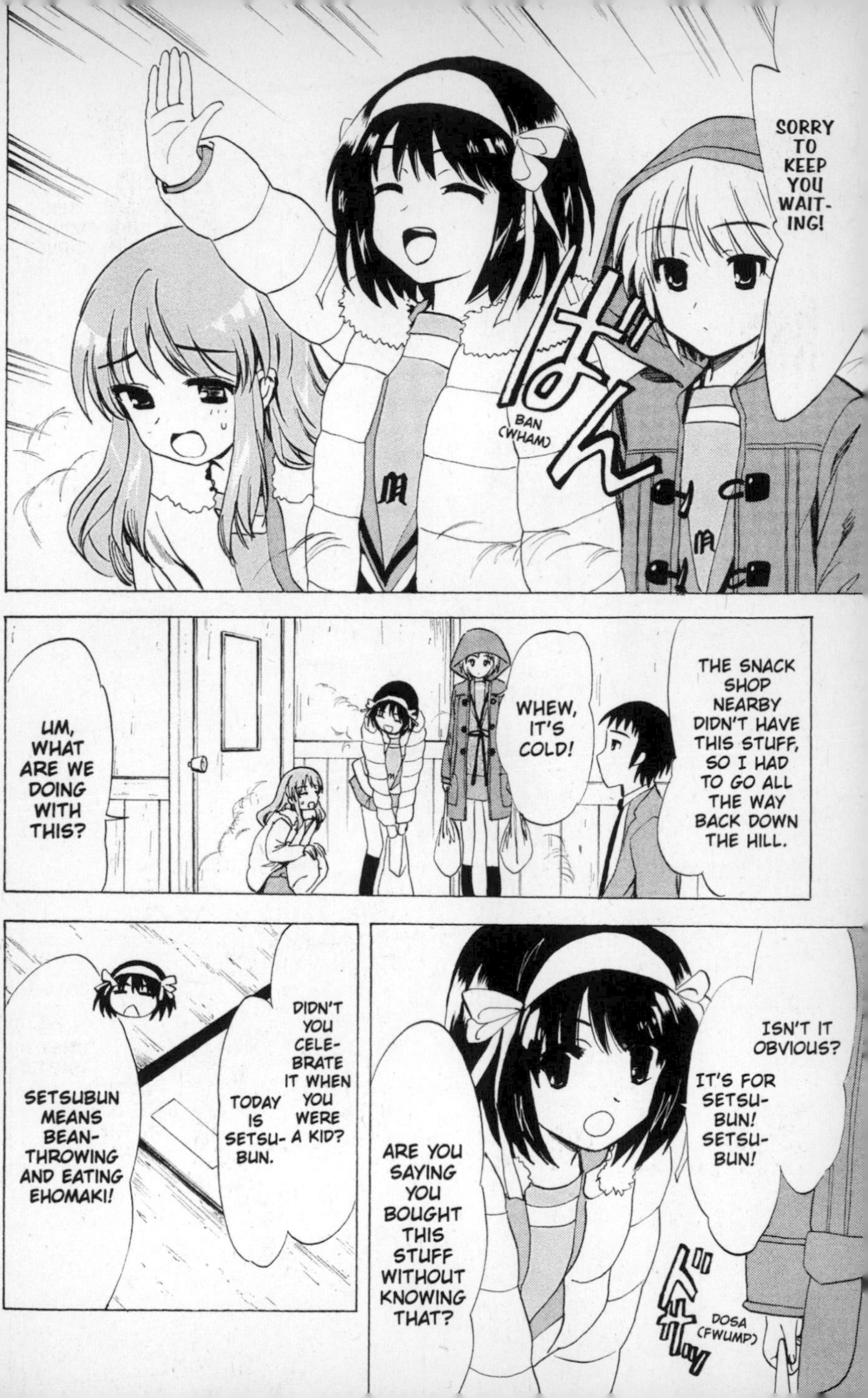
SORRY TO KEEP YOU WAITING!
ばん
BAN (WHAM)
THE SNACK SHOP NEARBY DIDN'T HAVE THIS STUFF, SO I HAD TO GO ALL THE WAY BACK DOWN THE HILL.
WHEW, IT'S COLD!
UM, WHAT ARE WE DOING WITH THIS?
ISN'T IT OBVIOUS?
IT'S FOR SETSUBUN! SETSUBUN!
ARE YOU SAYING YOU BOUGHT THIS STUFF WITHOUT KNOWING THAT?
DOSA (FWUMP)
DIDN'T YOU CELEBRATE IT WHEN YOU WERE A KID?
TODAY IS SETSUBUN.
SETSUBUN MEANS BEAN-THROWING AND EATING EHOMAKI!

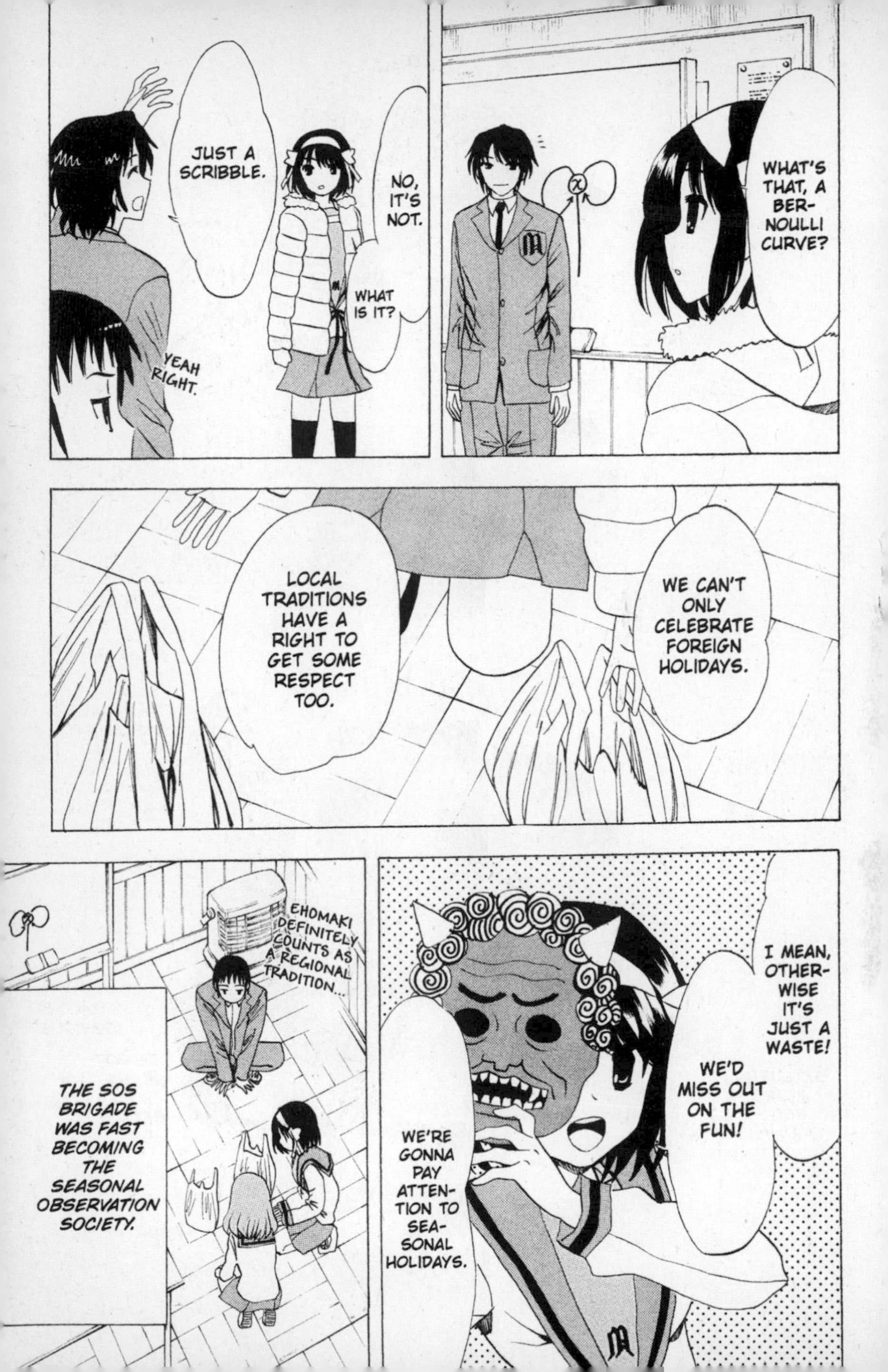
WHAT'S THAT, A BERNOULLI CURVE?
NO, IT'S NOT.
WHAT IS IT?
JUST A SCRIBBLE.
YEAH RIGHT.
WE CAN'T ONLY CELEBRATE FOREIGN HOLIDAYS.
LOCAL TRADITIONS HAVE A RIGHT TO GET SOME RESPECT TOO.
I MEAN, OTHERWISE IT'S JUST A WASTE!
WE'D MISS OUT ON THE FUN!
WE'RE GONNA PAY ATTENTION TO SEASONAL HOLIDAYS.
EHOMAKI DEFINITELY COUNTS AS A REGIONAL TRADITION...
THE SOS BRIGADE WAS FAST BECOMING THE SEASONAL OBSERVATION SOCIETY.

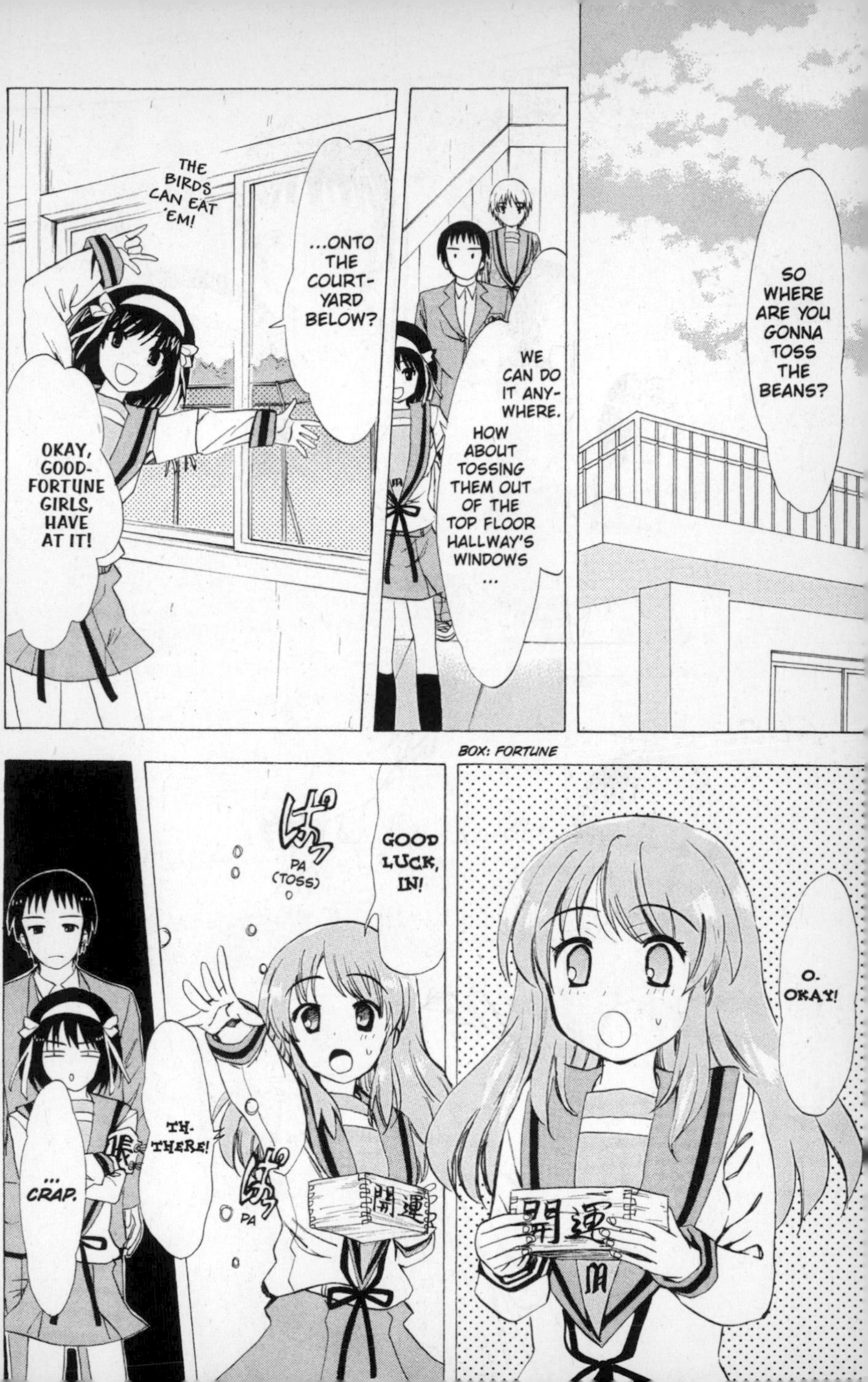
SO WHERE ARE YOU GONNA TOSS THE BEANS?
WE CAN DO IT ANYWHERE. HOW ABOUT TOSSING THEM OUT OF THE TOP FLOOR HALLWAY'S WINDOWS ...
...ONTO THE COURTYARD BELOW?
THE BIRDS CAN EAT 'EM!
OKAY, GOOD-FORTUNE GIRLS, HAVE AT IT!
BOX: FORTUNE
O-OKAY!
開運
GOOD LUCK, IN!
PA (TOSS)
開運
TH-THERE!
PA
... CRAP.

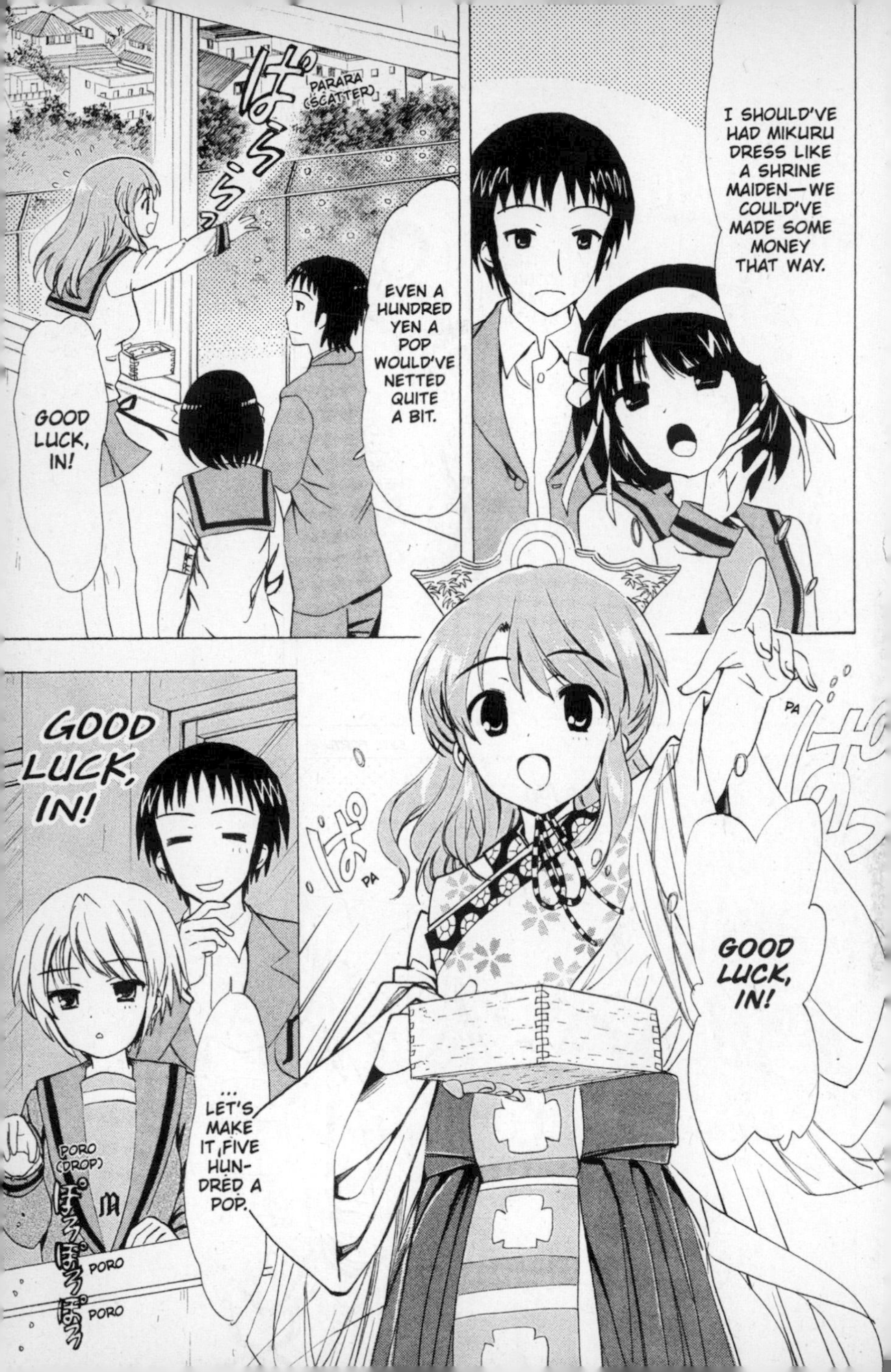
I SHOULD'VE HAD MIKURU DRESS LIKE A SHRINE MAIDEN—WE COULD'VE MADE SOME MONEY THAT WAY.
PARARA (SCATTER)
EVEN A HUNDRED YEN A POP WOULD'VE NETTED QUITE A BIT.
GOOD LUCK, IN!
PA
GOOD LUCK, IN!
PA
GOOD LUCK, IN!
... LET'S MAKE IT FIVE HUNDRED A POP.
PORO (DROP)
PORO
PORO

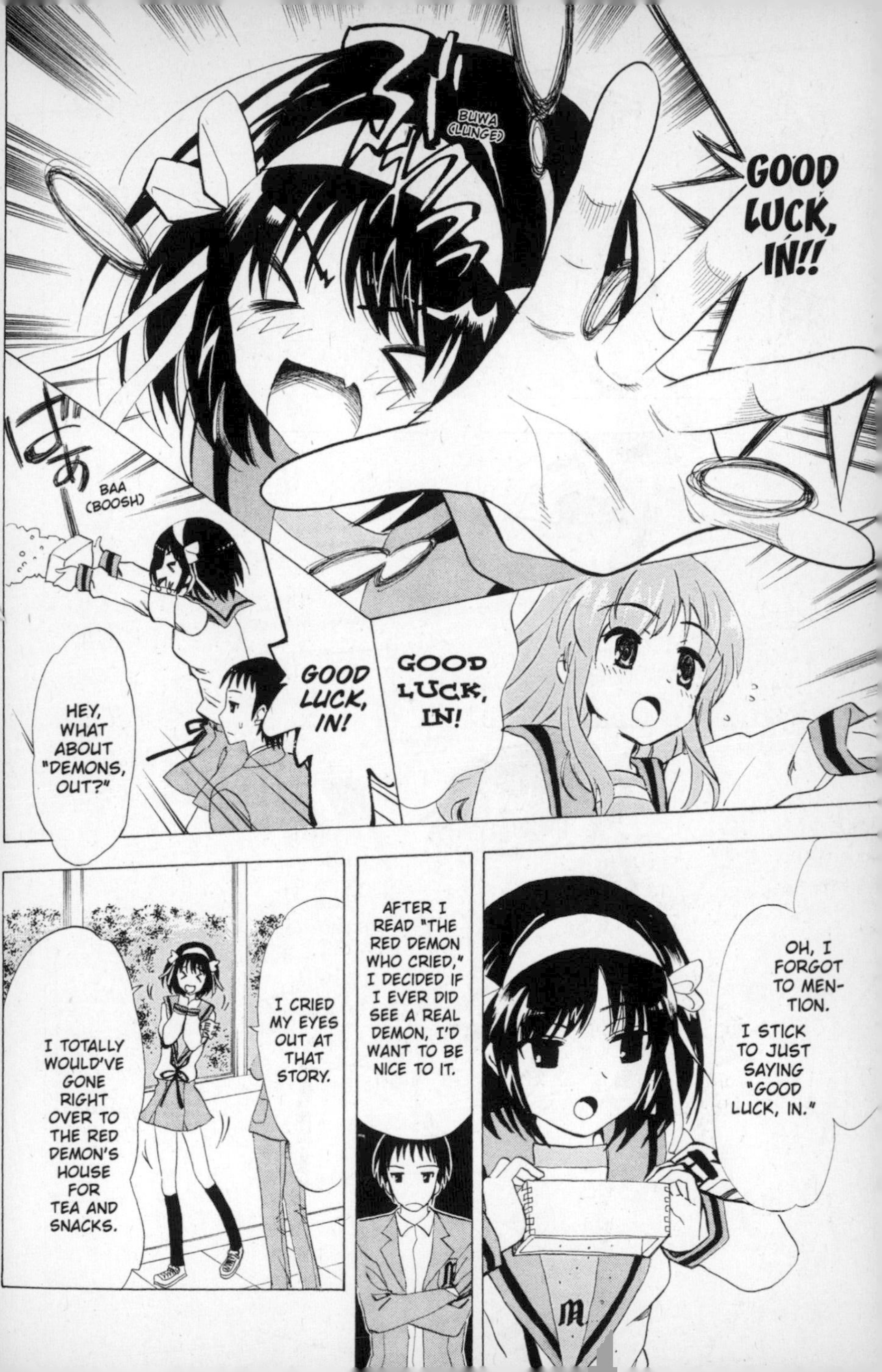
GOOD LUCK, IN!!
BUWA (LUNGE)
GOOD LUCK, IN!
GOOD LUCK, IN!
BAA (BOOSH)
HEY, WHAT ABOUT "DEMONS, OUT?"
OH, I FORGOT TO MEN-TION.
I STICK TO JUST SAYING "GOOD LUCK, IN."
AFTER I READ "THE RED DEMON WHO CRIED," I DECIDED IF I EVER DID SEE A REAL DEMON, I'D WANT TO BE NICE TO IT.
I CRIED MY EYES OUT AT THAT STORY.
I TOTALLY WOULD'VE GONE RIGHT OVER TO THE RED DEMON'S HOUSE FOR TEA AND SNACKS.

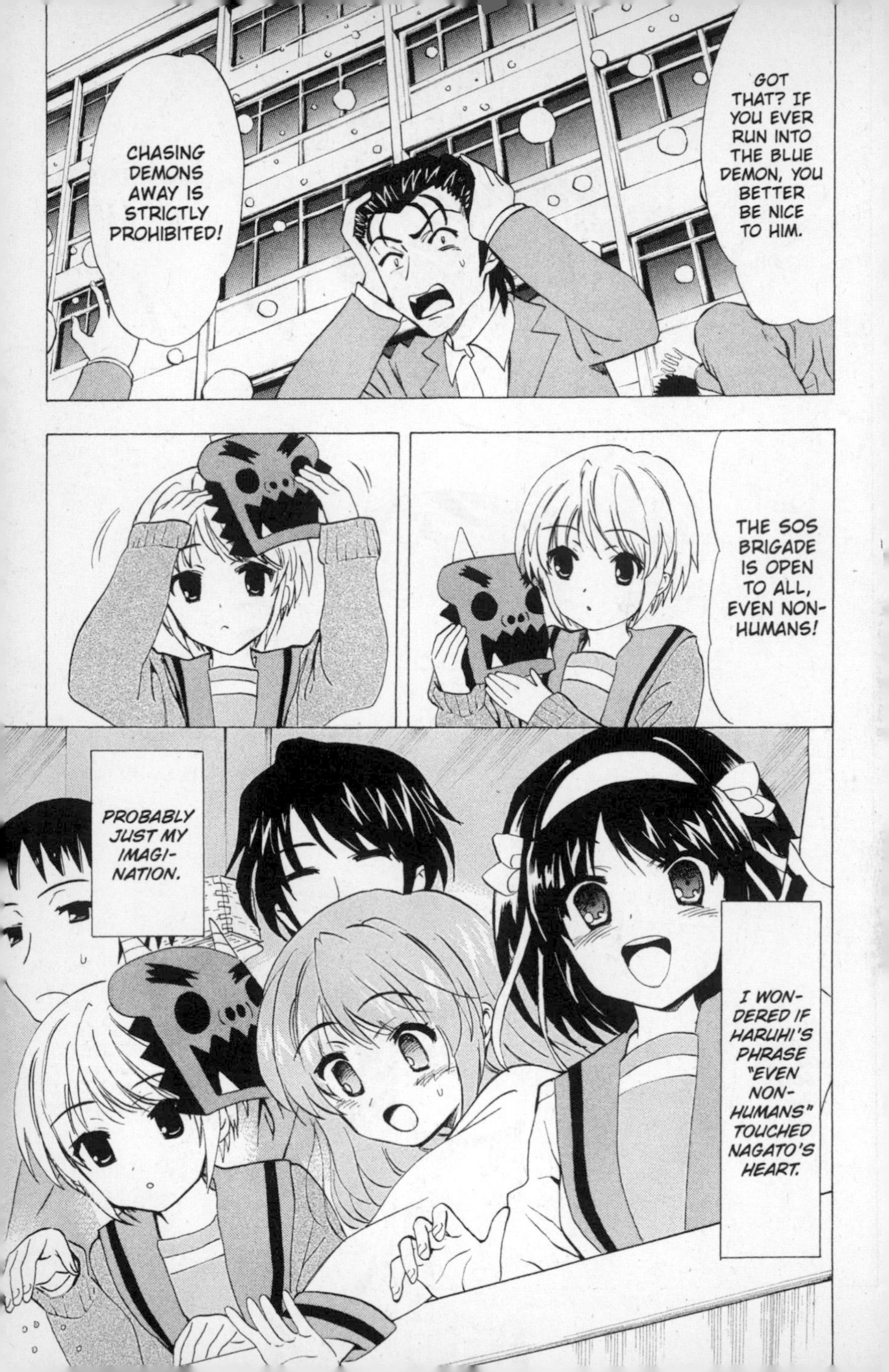
GOT THAT? IF YOU EVER RUN INTO THE BLUE DEMON, YOU BETTER BE NICE TO HIM.
CHASING DEMONS AWAY IS STRICTLY PROHIBITED!
THE SOS BRIGADE IS OPEN TO ALL, EVEN NON-HUMANS!
I WONDERED IF HARUHI'S PHRASE "EVEN NON-HUMANS" TOUCHED NAGATO'S HEART.
PROBABLY JUST MY IMAGINATION.

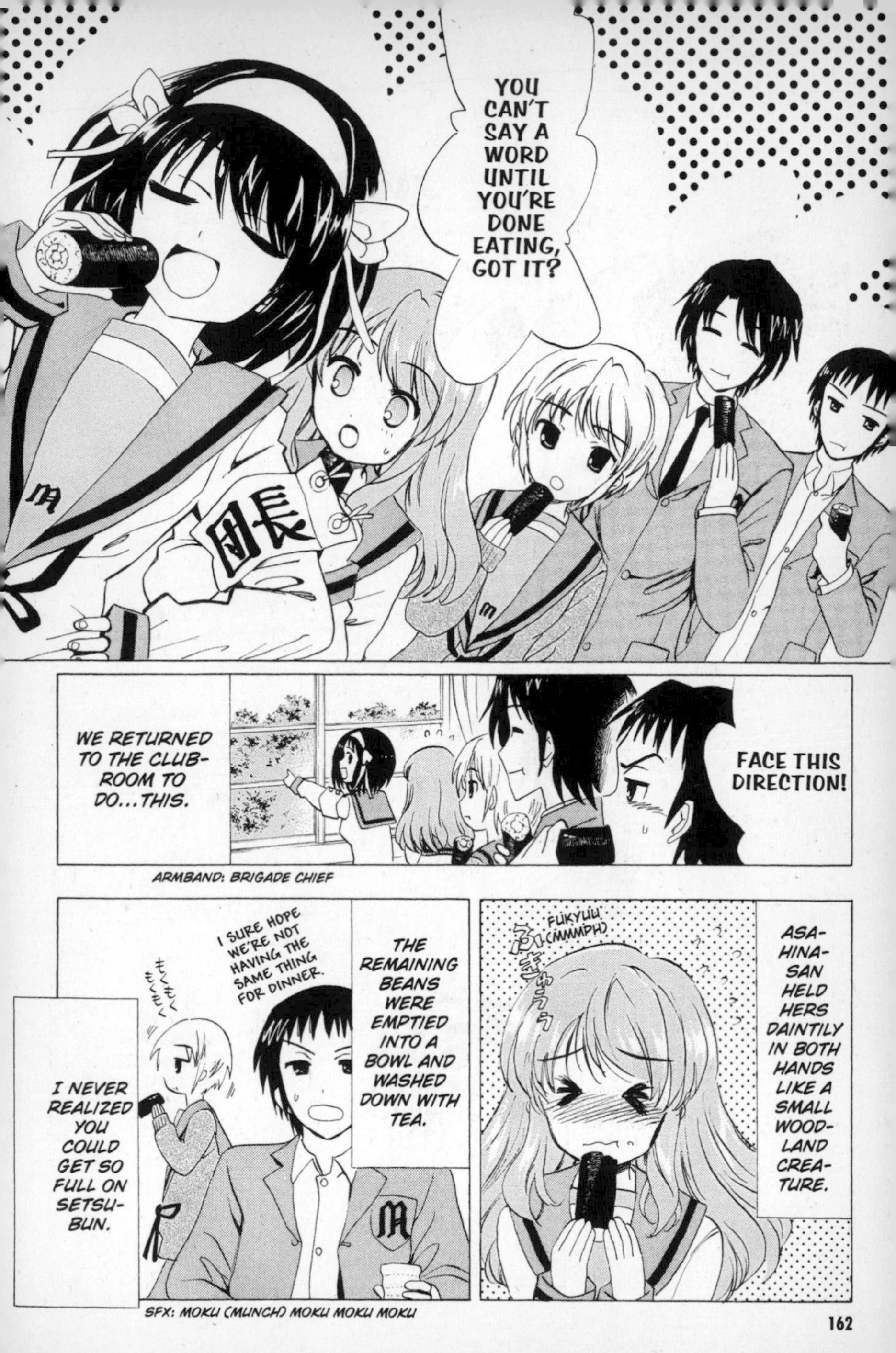
YOU CAN'T SAY A WORD UNTIL YOU'RE DONE EATING, GOT IT?
FACE THIS DIRECTION!
WE RETURNED TO THE CLUB-ROOM TO DO...THIS.
ARMBAND: BRIGADE CHIEF
ASA-HINA-SAN HELD HERS DAINTILY IN BOTH HANDS LIKE A SMALL WOOD-LAND CREA-TURE.
FUKYUU (MMMPH)
THE REMAINING BEANS WERE EMPTIED INTO A BOWL AND WASHED DOWN WITH TEA.
I SURE HOPE WE'RE NOT HAVING THE SAME THING FOR DINNER.
もくもくもくもく
I NEVER REALIZED YOU COULD GET SO FULL ON SETSU-BUN.
SFX: MOKU (MUNCH) MOKU MOKU MOKU

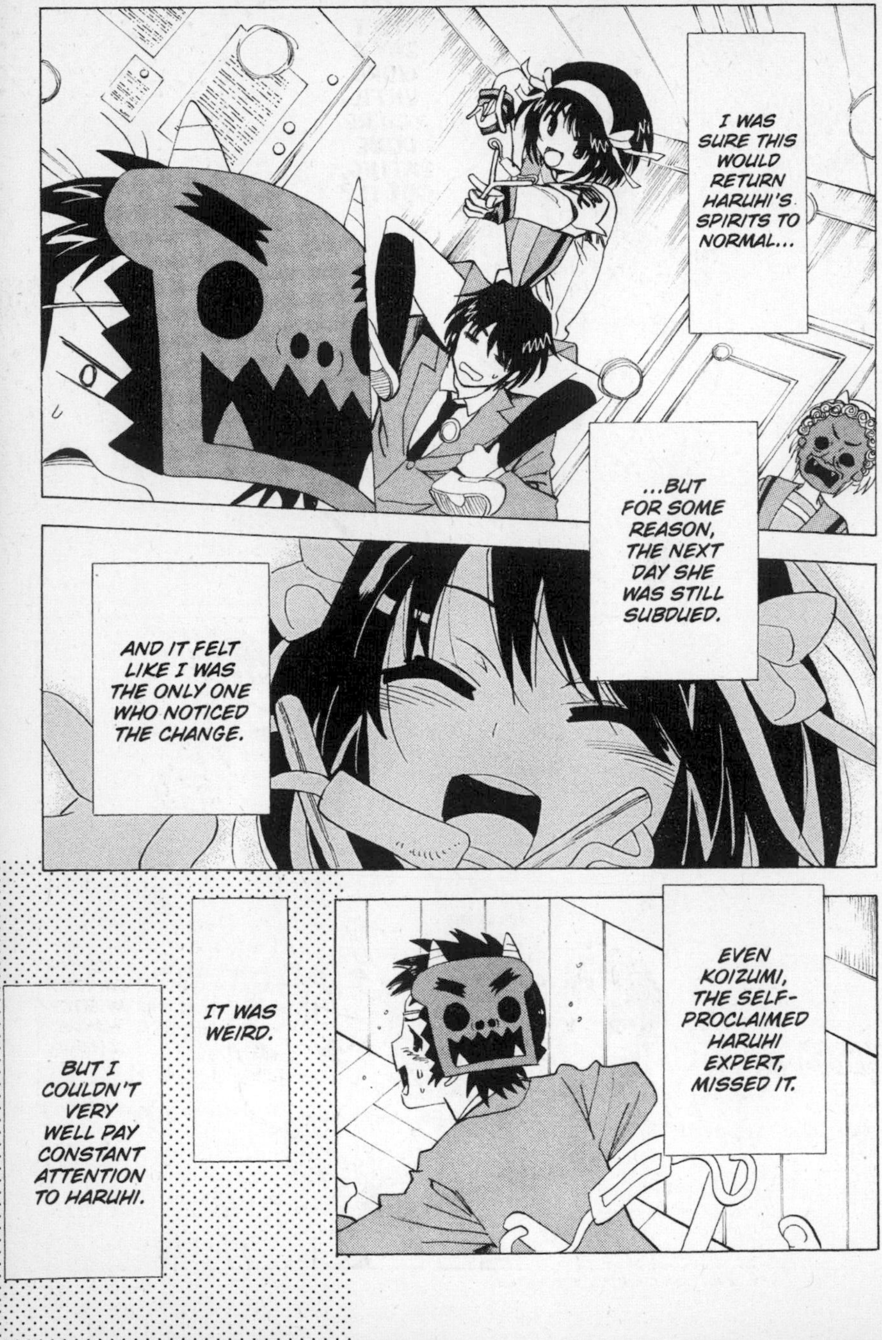
I WAS SURE THIS WOULD RETURN HARUHI'S SPIRITS TO NORMAL...
...BUT FOR SOME REASON, THE NEXT DAY SHE WAS STILL SUBDUED.
AND IT FELT LIKE I WAS THE ONLY ONE WHO NOTICED THE CHANGE.
EVEN KOIZUMI, THE SELF-PROCLAIMED HARUHI EXPERT, MISSED IT.
IT WAS WEIRD.
BUT I COULDN'T VERY WELL PAY CONSTANT ATTENTION TO HARUHI.

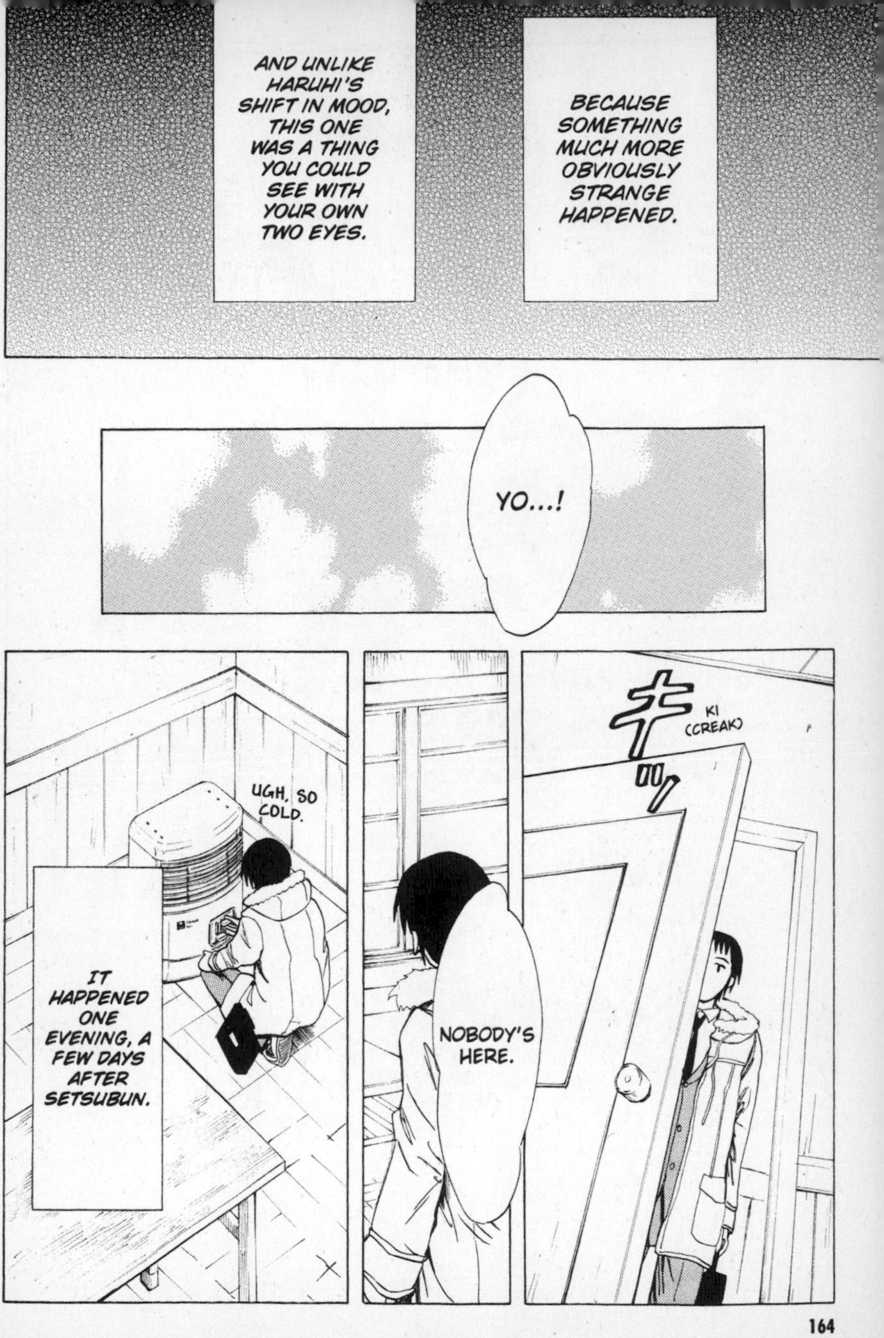
BECAUSE SOMETHING MUCH MORE OBVIOUSLY STRANGE HAPPENED.
AND UNLIKE HARUHI'S SHIFT IN MOOD, THIS ONE WAS A THING YOU COULD SEE WITH YOUR OWN TWO EYES.
YO...!
KI (CREAK)
NOBODY'S HERE.
UGH, SO COLD.
IT HAPPENED ONE EVENING, A FEW DAYS AFTER SETSUBUN.

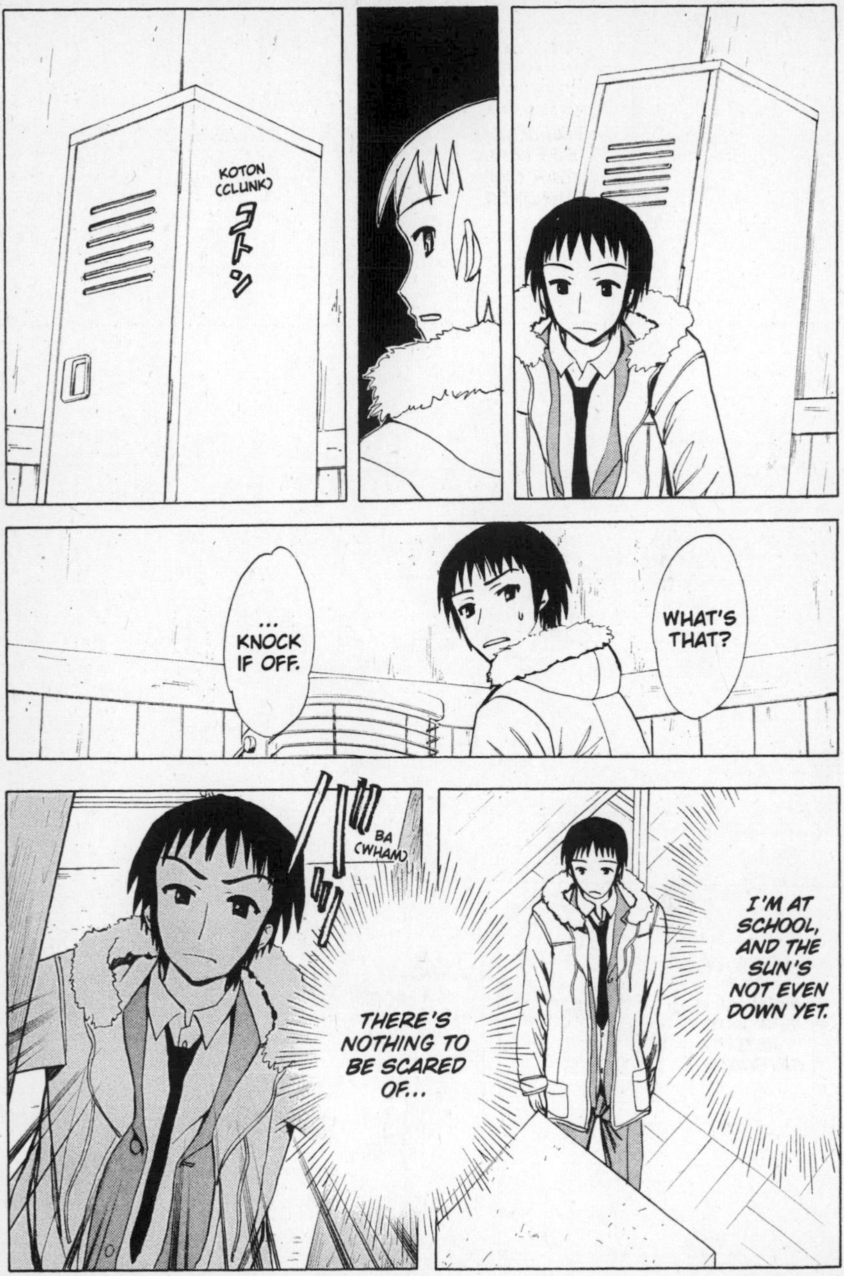
KOTON (CLUNK)
WHAT'S THAT?
... KNOCK IF OFF.
I'M AT SCHOOL, AND THE SUN'S NOT EVEN DOWN YET.
BA (WHAM)
THERE'S NOTHING TO BE SCARED OF...

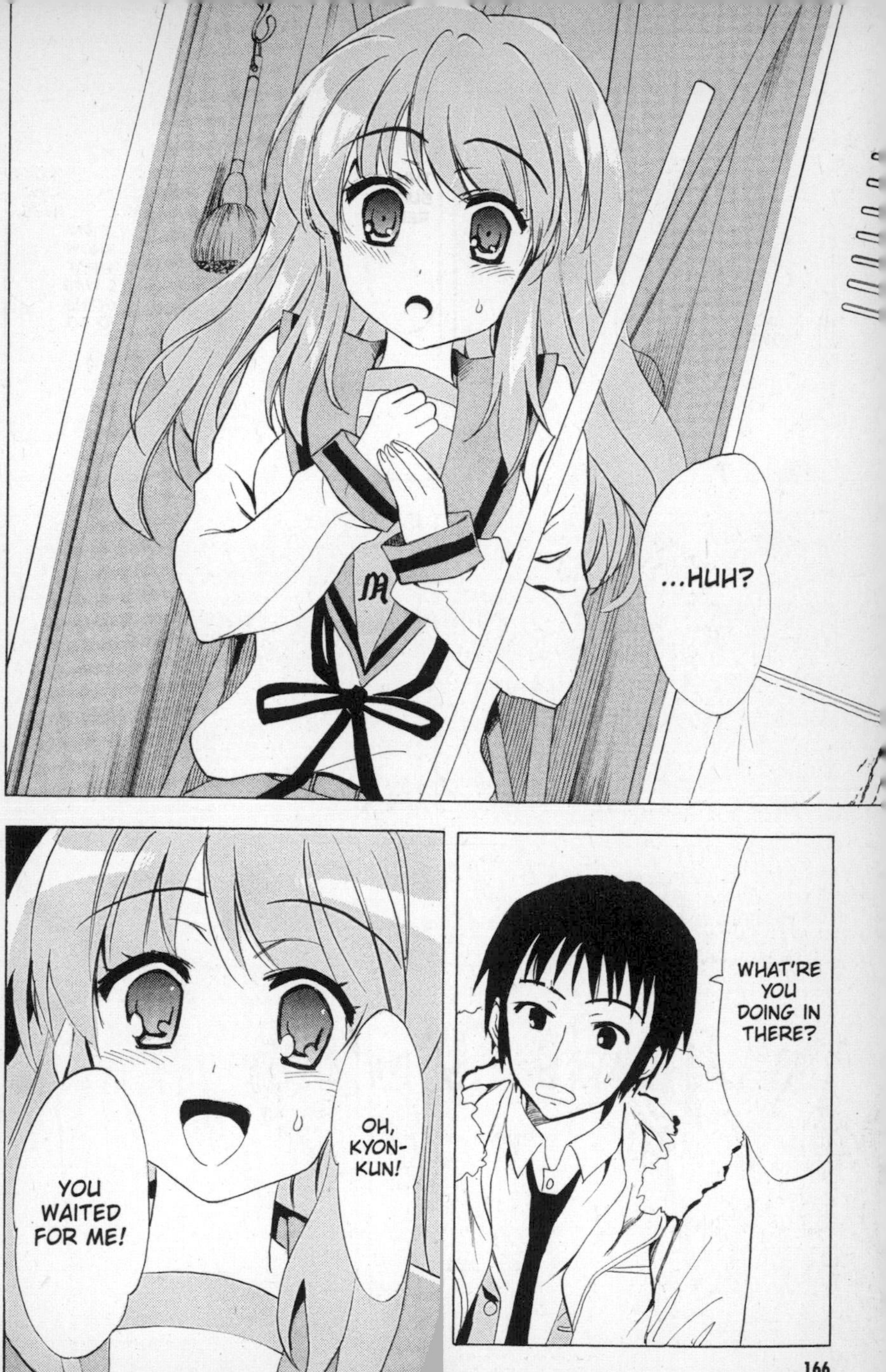
...HUH?
WHAT'RE YOU DOING IN THERE?
OH, KYON-KUN!
YOU WAITED FOR ME!

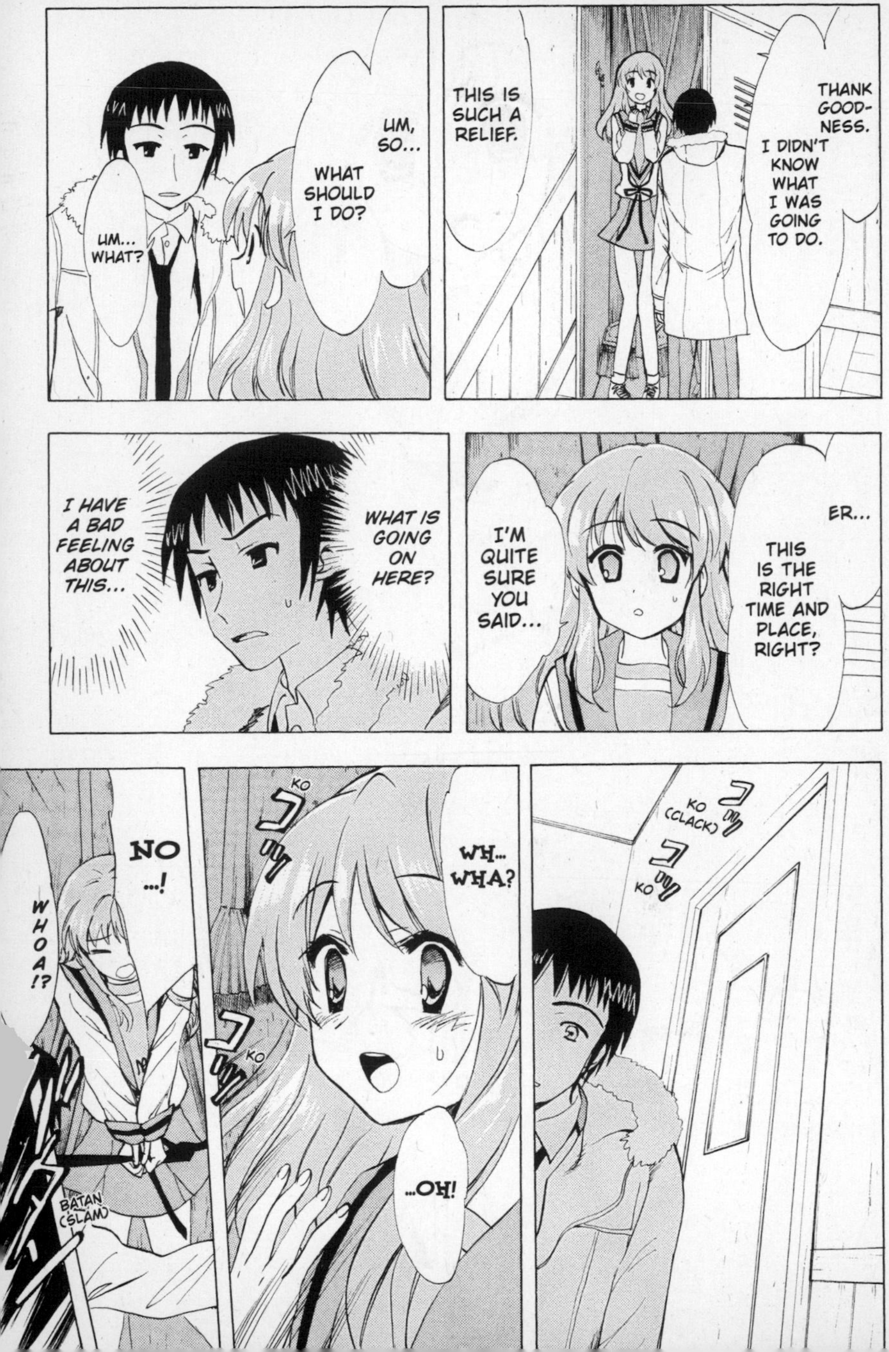
THANK GOOD-NESS. I DIDN'T KNOW WHAT I WAS GOING TO DO.
THIS IS SUCH A RELIEF.
UM, SO...
WHAT SHOULD I DO?
UM... WHAT?
ER...
THIS IS THE RIGHT TIME AND PLACE, RIGHT?
I'M QUITE SURE YOU SAID...
WHAT IS GOING ON HERE?
I HAVE A BAD FEELING ABOUT THIS...
KO (CLACK)
KO
KO
WH... WHA?
KO
...OH!
NO ...!
WHOA!?
BATAN (SLAM)

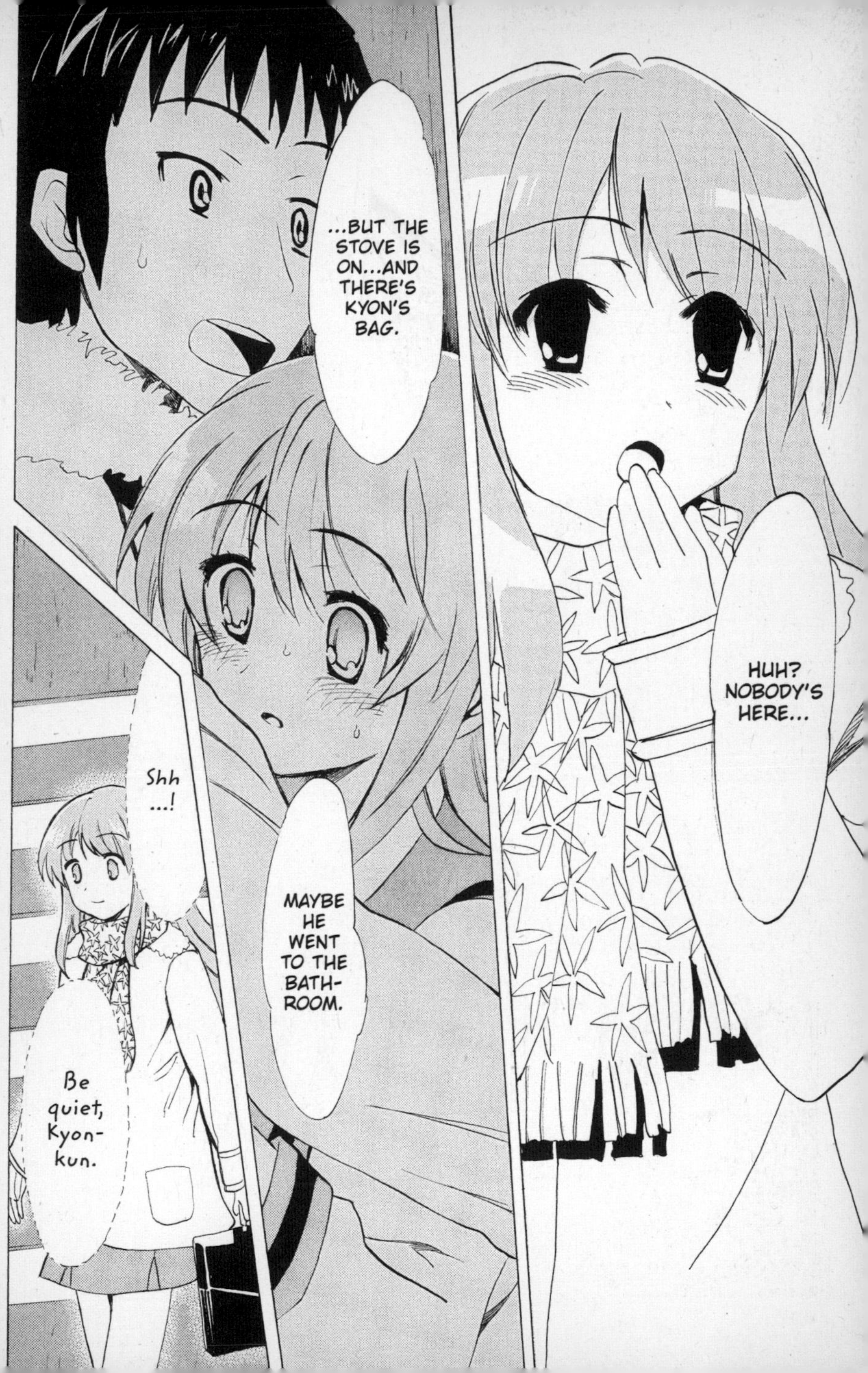
HUH? NOBODY'S HERE...
...BUT THE STOVE IS ON...AND THERE'S KYON'S BAG.
MAYBE HE WENT TO THE BATH-ROOM.
Shh...!
Be quiet, Kyon-kun.

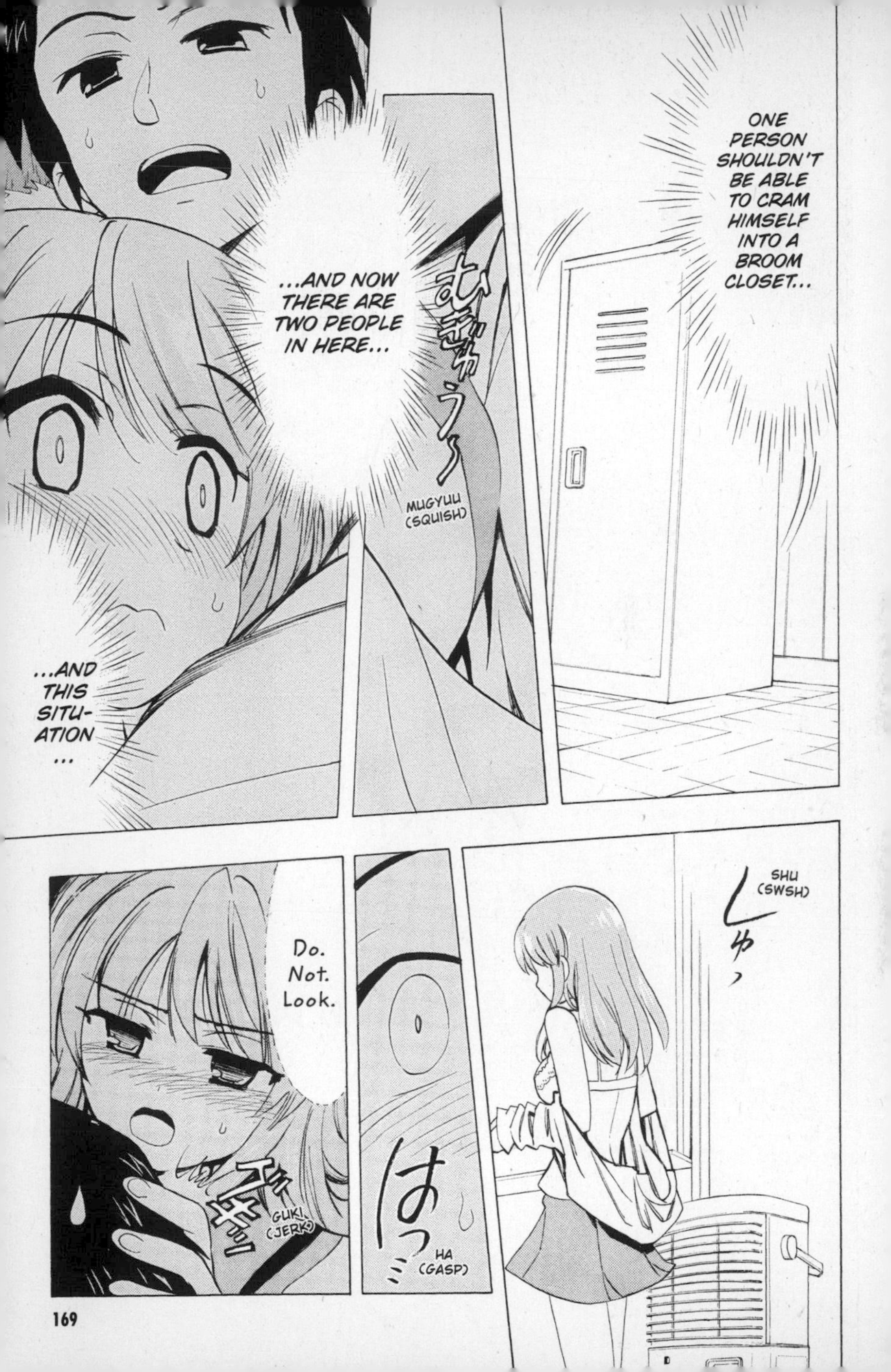
ONE PERSON SHOULDN'T BE ABLE TO CRAM HIMSELF INTO A BROOM CLOSET...
...AND NOW THERE ARE TWO PEOPLE IN HERE...
むぎゅう
MUGYUU (SQUISH)
...AND THIS SITUATION...
しゅっ
SHU (SWSH)
はっ
HA (GASP)
Do. Not. Look.
ギクッ
GUKI (JERK)

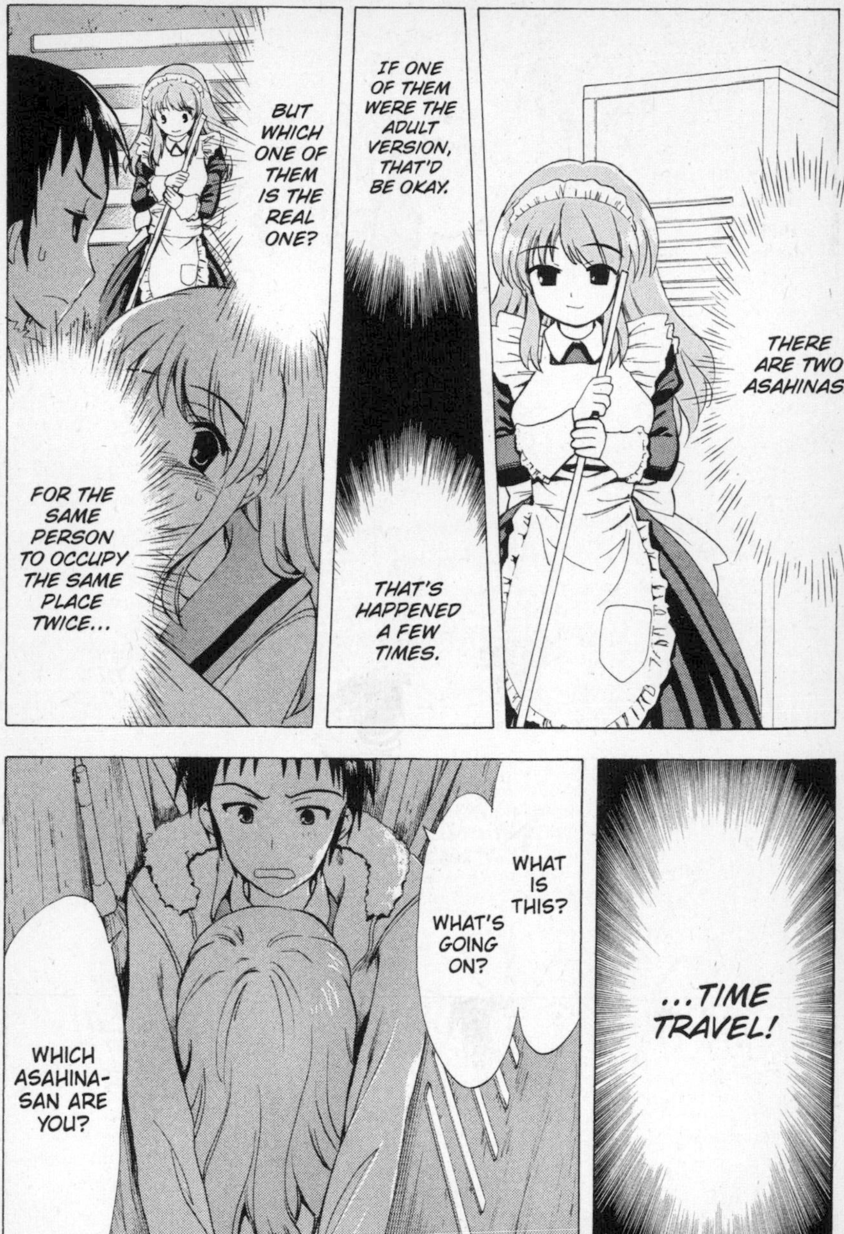
THERE ARE TWO ASAHINAS!
IF ONE OF THEM WERE THE ADULT VERSION, THAT'D BE OKAY.
THAT'S HAPPENED A FEW TIMES.
BUT WHICH ONE OF THEM IS THE REAL ONE?
FOR THE SAME PERSON TO OCCUPY THE SAME PLACE TWICE...
...TIME TRAVEL!
WHAT IS THIS?
WHAT'S GOING ON?
WHICH ASAHINA-SAN ARE YOU?

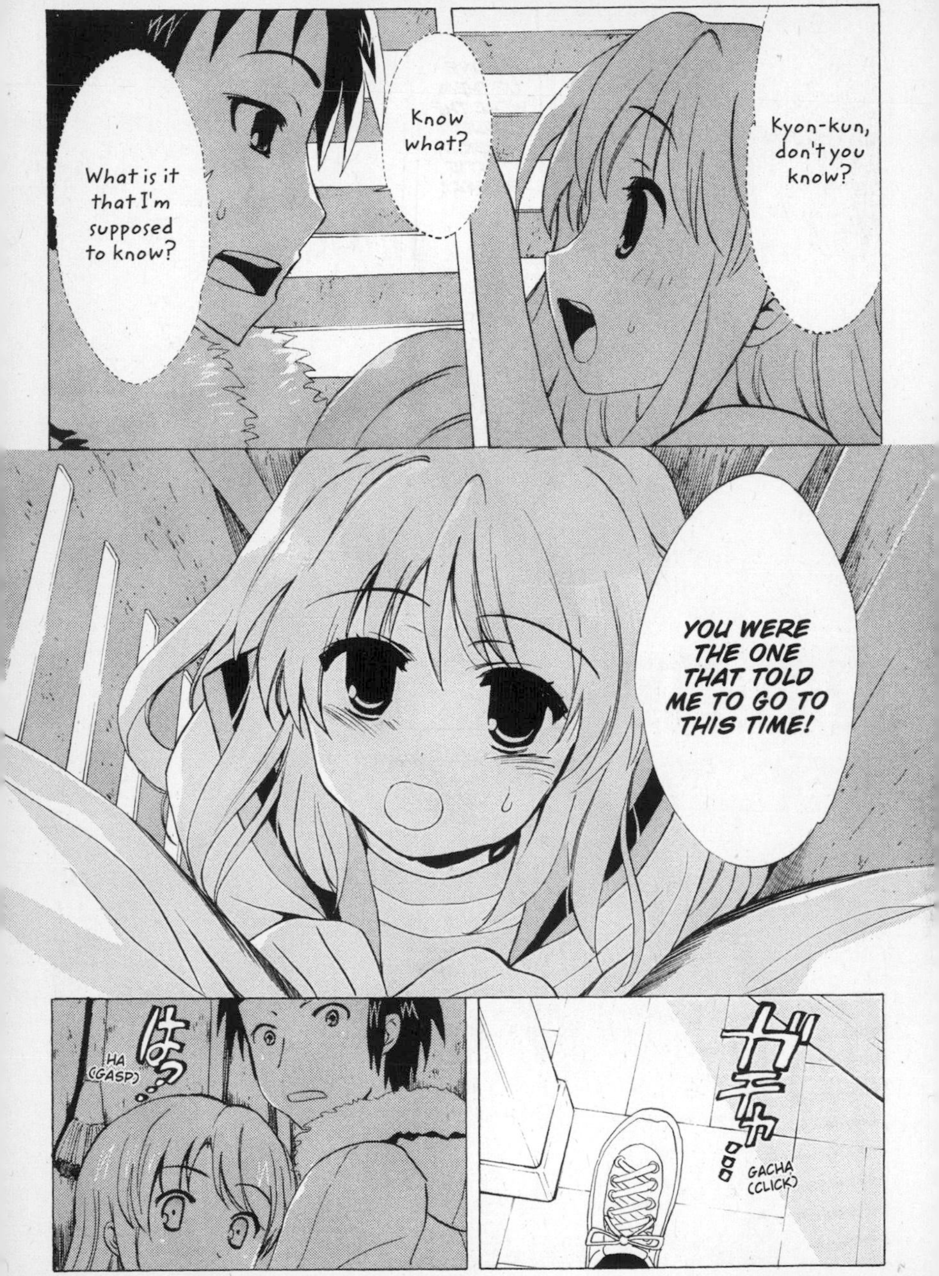
Kyon-kun, don't you know?
Know what?
What is it that I'm supposed to know?
YOU WERE THE ONE THAT TOLD ME TO GO TO THIS TIME!
ガチャ
GACHA (CLICK)
はっ
HA (GASP)

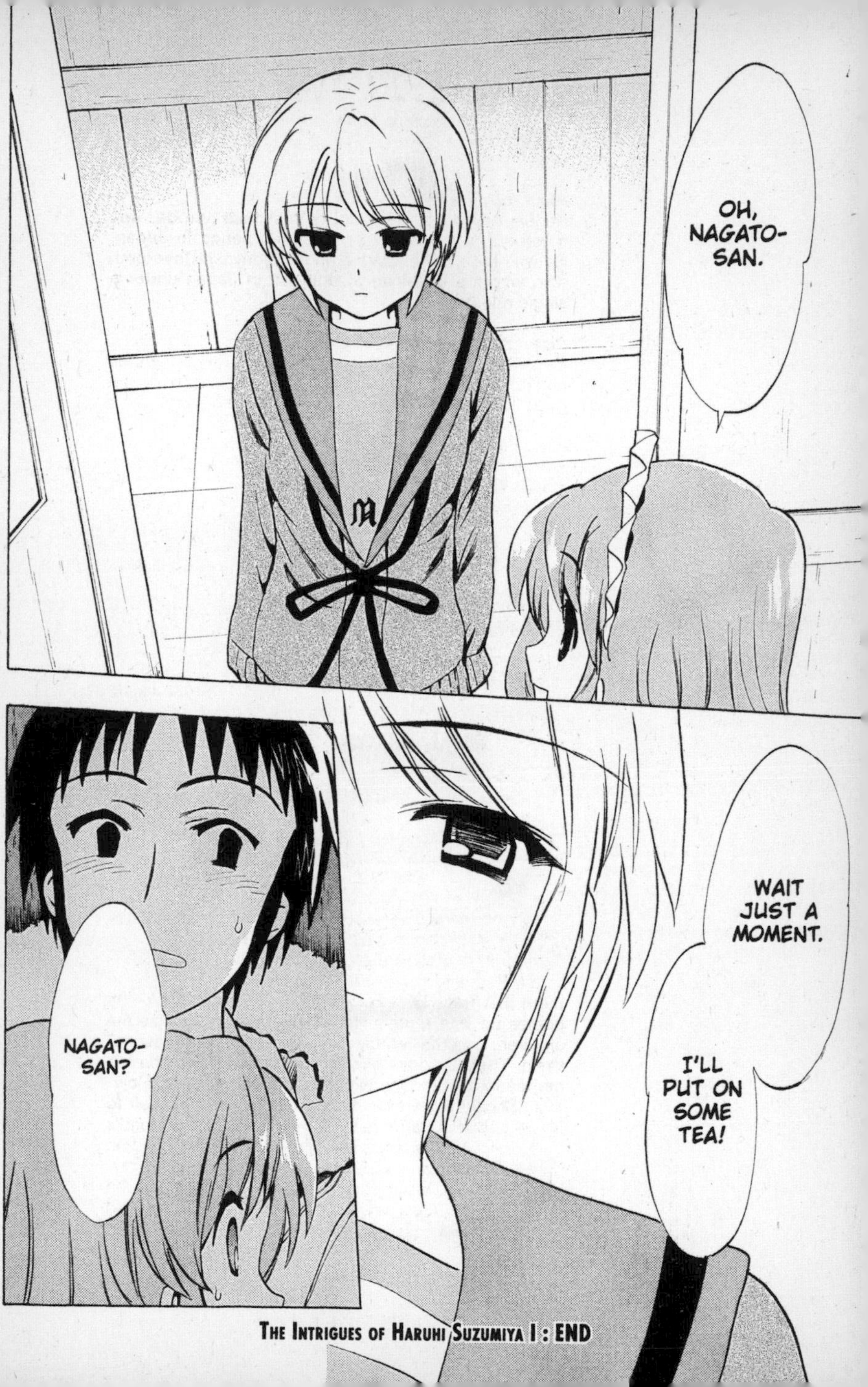
OH, NAGATO-SAN.
WAIT JUST A MOMENT.
I'LL PUT ON SOME TEA!
NAGATO-SAN?
THE INTRIGUES OF HARUHI SUZUMIYA I : END

TRANSLATION NOTES

Page 69
Kanbei Kuroda, also known as Yoshitaka Kuroda, was a warlord in the late warring states period in Japan. He was the head strategist under Hideyoshi Toyotomi, who was the first man to unify all of Japan under a single rule.

Page 156
Setsubun is celebrated in Japan on February 3rd and is considered the first holiday of spring. In order to secure good fortune for the year, families once dressed up a single member in a demon mask, then threw beans at him or her while crying, "Demon, out! Good luck, in!" before closing the door. This ritual is now more commonly done at temples rather than homes.

Ehomaki, literally "auspicious direction rolls," are a type of sushi roll that it is considered good luck to eat on Setsubun. The correct ehomaki-eating procedure involves facing in that year's auspicious direction (as determined by the Taoist reckoning and the zodiac symbol of the year) and eating the entire uncut roll in one bite, eyes closed, while silently contemplating one's hopes and wishes for the upcoming year. Ehomaki is a tradition mostly limited to the Kansai region of Japan, which includes Kobe, the city in which North High School is situated.

Page 158
Fukumusume, or "good-fortune girls," are a part of some Setsubun festivals. Their role primarily involves dressing in shrine maiden-like outfits and handing out (or selling) good-luck charms.

Page 160
Haruhi is referencing a famous children's story, "Naita Akaoni," "The Red Demon Who Cried" or "The Red Ogre Who Cried." In the story, the red demon wishes to befriend the local children but is unable to convince them that he is friendly. So his friend the blue demon comes up with a plan: He will pretend to terrorize the children, and the red demon will step in and "rescue" them. The plan goes exactly as intended, and the red demon is able to play with the grateful children. However, because the blue demon has allowed himself to be perceived as a monster for the sake of his friend's wish, he and the red demon cannot let the children find out that they are friends. And so the blue demon goes far away, leaving only a letter behind for the red demon. Upon discovering his friend's letter, the red demon weeps.

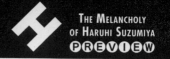

TO HIDE THIS NEW MIKURU, THEY GO TO NAGATO. BUT THIS MIKURU DOES NOT SEEM VERY PLEASED...

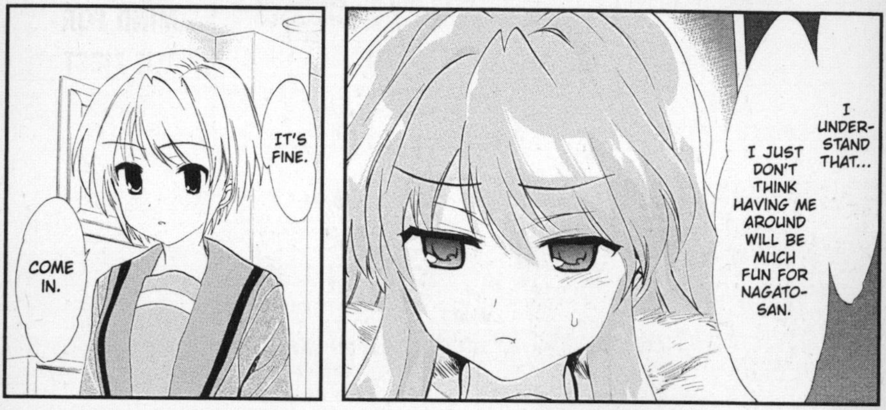
I UNDER-STAND THAT...
I JUST DON'T THINK HAVING ME AROUND WILL BE MUCH FUN FOR NAGATO-SAN.
IT'S FINE.
COME IN.

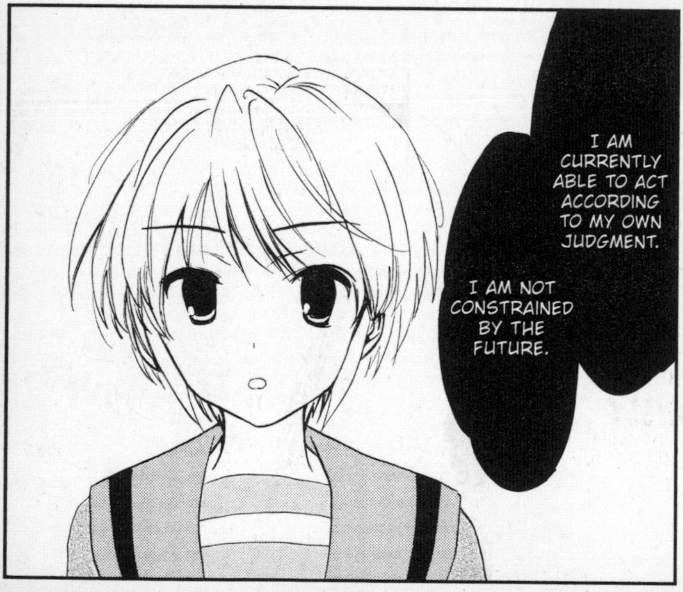
I AM CURRENTLY ABLE TO ACT ACCORDING TO MY OWN JUDGMENT.
I AM NOT CONSTRAINED BY THE FUTURE.

NAGATO IS THE SAME AS ALWAYS... BUT WAIT! SOMETHING HAS CHANGED!?

VOLUME 14, AVAILABLE SOON!

NAGATO SPEAKS HER MIND FOR THE FIRST TIME!

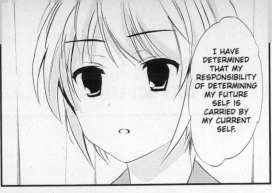

I HAVE DETERMINED THAT MY RESPONSIBILITY OF DETERMINING MY FUTURE SELF IS CARRIED BY MY CURRENT SELF.

AND THE SAME DAY, A MYSTERIOUS MESSAGE COMES FOR KYON!

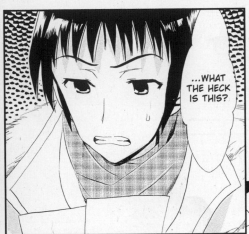

...WHAT THE HECK IS THIS?

NOTE: AT THE INTERSECTION OF XXXX AND YYYY, PROCEED SOUTH UNTIL YOU FIND AN UNPAVED ALLEY. PLEASE LEAVE THE OBJECT AT THAT INTERSECTION AS DIRECTED ON THE MAP, BETWEEN 6:12 AND 6:15 PM.

〇〇町××番△△号にあ
交差点を南に進むと 近
舗装されていない裏道が
今日午後六時十二分か
間、その裏道と市道が
下の図の通りのもの

WHAT HAPPENED DURING THOSE EIGHT DAYS!?

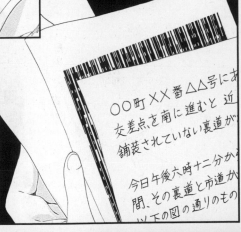

THE RIDDLES ONLY DEEPEN DURING THE "INTRIGUES!"

Can't wait for the next volume?
You don't have to!

Keep up with the latest chapters of some of your favorite manga every month online in the pages of YEN PLUS!

READ IT THE SAME DAY AS JAPAN!

SOUL EATER NOT?

MAXIMUM RIDE

SOULLESS

WITCH & WIZARD

THE INFERNAL DEVICES
CLOCKWORK ANGEL

Visit us at
www.yenplus.com
for details!

WELCOME TO IKEBUKURO, WHERE TOKYO'S WILDEST CHARACTERS GATHER!!

AS THEIR PATHS CROSS, THIS ECCENTRIC CAST WEAVES A TWISTED, CRACKED LOVE STORY...

AVAILABLE NOW!!

THE MELANCHOLY OF HARUHI SUZUMIYA
⑬

Original Story: Nagaru Tanigawa
Manga: Gaku Tsugano
Character Design: Noizi Ito

Translation: Paul Starr
Lettering: Alexis Eckerman

SUZUMIYA HARUHI NO YUUTSU Volume 13 © Nagaru TANIGAWA • Noizi ITO 2011 © Gaku TSUGANO 2011. First published in Japan in 2011 by KADOKAWA SHOTEN CO., LTD., Tokyo. English translation rights arranged with KADOKAWA SHOTEN CO., LTD., Tokyo through TUTTLE-MORI AGENCY, INC., Tokyo.

English translation © 2012 by Hachette Book Group, Inc.

Yen Press
Hachette Book Group
237 Park Avenue, New York, NY 10017

www.HachetteBookGroup.com
www.YenPress.com

Yen Press is an imprint of Hachette Book Group, Inc. The Yen Press name and logo are trademarks of Hachette Book Group, Inc.

First Yen Press Edition: August 2012

ISBN: 978-0-316-20949-6

10 9 8 7 6 5 4 3 2 1

BVG

Printed in the United States of America

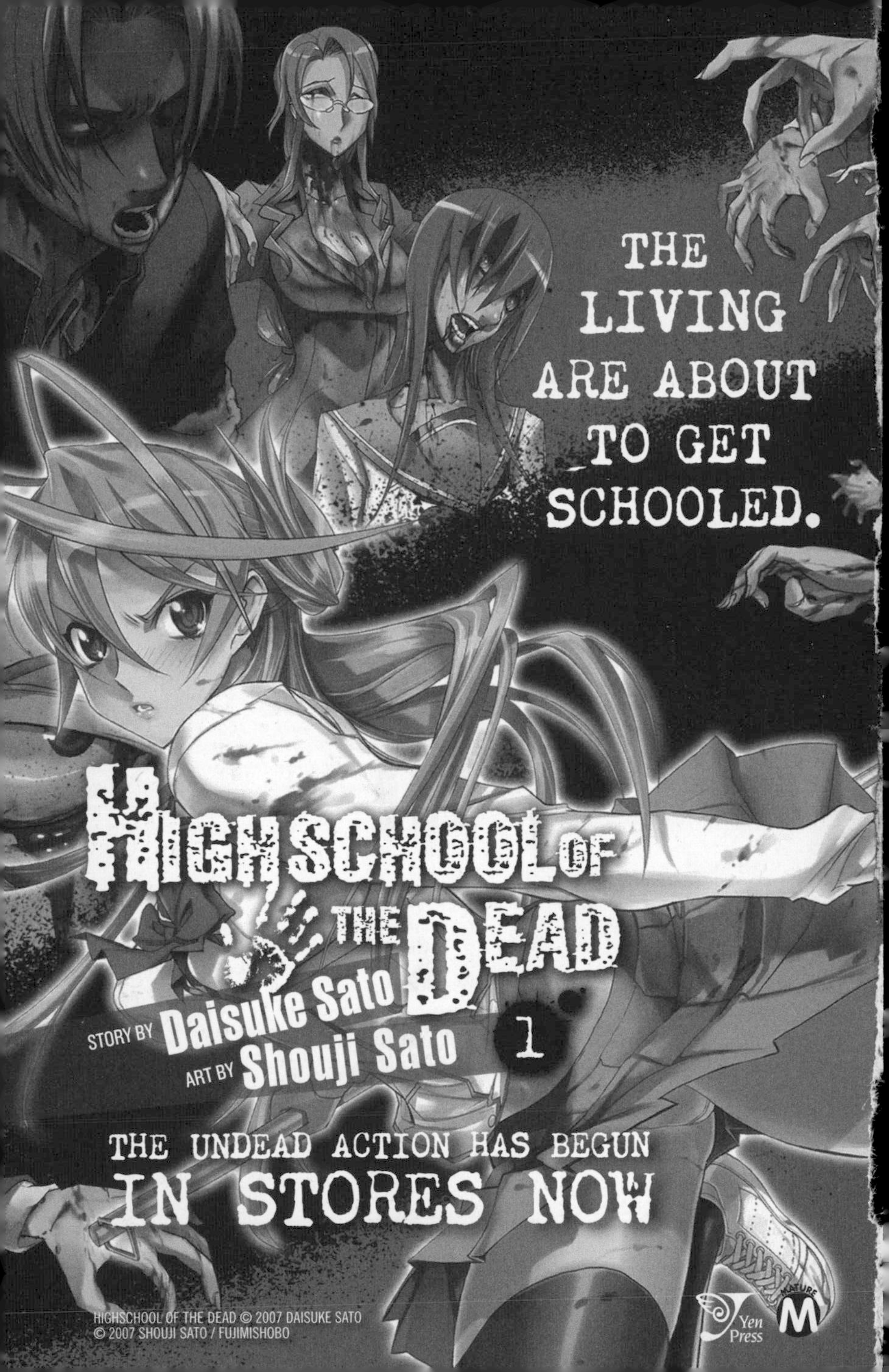
THE LIVING ARE ABOUT TO GET SCHOOLED.
HIGHSCHOOL OF THE DEAD
STORY BY Daisuke Sato
ART BY Shouji Sato
1
THE UNDEAD ACTION HAS BEGUN
IN STORES NOW
HIGHSCHOOL OF THE DEAD © 2007 DAISUKE SATO
© 2007 SHOUJI SATO / FUJIMISHOBO
Yen Press
MATURE
M